Foundations of Decision Support Systems

OPERATIONS RESEARCH
AND INDUSTRIAL ENGINEERING

Consulting Editor: J. William Schmidt

Virginia Polytechnic Institute and State University
Blacksburg, Virginia

Applied Statistical Methods, *I. W. Burr*

Mathematical Foundations of Management Science and Systems Analysis, *J. William Schmidt*

Urban Systems Models, *Walter Helly*

Introduction to Discrete Linear Controls: Theory and Application, *Albert B. Bishop*

Integer Programming: Theory, Applications, and Computations, *Hamdy A. Taha*

Transform Techniques for Probability Modeling, *Walter C. Giffin*

Analysis of Queueing Systems, *J. A. White, J. W. Schmidt, and G. K. Bennett*

Models for Public Systems Analysis, *Edward J. Beltrami*

Computer Methods in Operations Research, *Arne Thesen*

Cost-Benefit Analysis: A Handbook, *Peter G. Sassone and William A. Schaffer*

Modeling of Complex Systems, *V. Vemuri*

Applied Linear Programming: For the Socioeconomic and Environmental Sciences, *Michael R. Greenberg*

Foundations of Analysis in Operations Research, *J. William Schmidt and Robert P. Davis*

Foundations of Decision Support Systems, *Robert H. Bonczek, Clyde W. Holsapple, and Andrew B. Whinston*

Foundations of Decision Support Systems

ROBERT H. BONCZEK

Krannert Graduate School of Management
Purdue University
West Lafayette, Indiana

CLYDE W. HOLSAPPLE

Department of Business Administration
University of Illinois
Urbana, Illinois

ANDREW B. WHINSTON

Krannert Graduate School of Management
*   and Department of Computer Science*
Purdue University
West Lafayette, Indiana

 1981

ACADEMIC PRESS

A Subsidiary of Harcourt Brace Jovanovich, Publishers

New York   London   Toronto   Sydney   San Francisco

ACADEMIC PRESS, INC.
111 Fifth Avenue, New York, New York 10003

United Kingdom Edition published by
ACADEMIC PRESS, INC. (LONDON) LTD.
24/28 Oval Road, London NW1 7DX

Library of Congress Cataloging in Publication Data

Bonczek, R. H.
   Foundations of decision support systems.

   (Operations research and industrial engineering)
   Includes bibliographies and index.
   1. Decision-making. 2. Management information
systems. I. Holsapple, C. W. II. Whinston, Andrew B.
III. Title. IV. Series.
T57.95.B66   658.4'03   80-1779
ISBN 0-12-113050-9

PRINTED IN THE UNITED STATES OF AMERICA

81 82 83 84   9 8 7 6 5 4 3 2 1

CONTENTS

Foreword   xi

Preface   xv

Part I INFORMATION PROCESSING, DECISION MAKING, AND DECISION SUPPORT—SOME PERSPECTIVES

Chapter 1 Introduction to Information Processing, Decision Making, and Decision Support

1.00 The Information Age   3
1.10 Decision Making   11
1.20 Decision Support   17
1.30 Conclusion   23
References   24

Chapter 2 Frameworks for Organizational Information Processing and Decision Making

2.00 Introductory Comments   26
2.10 Division of Information-Processing Labor
      within an Organization   28

v

2.20   Abilities Required for Decision Making   34
References   41

Part II   REPRESENTATIVE SYSTEMS FOR DECISION SUPPORT

Chapter 3   Representative Decision Support Systems

3.00   Systems That Include Models   45
3.10   Classification Scheme for DSS   56
3.20   Conclusion   67
References   68

Chapter 4   New Ideas in Decision Support

4.00   Generic Description for Decision Support Systems   69
4.10   The Shape of Systems to Come   73
4.20   Rationale for the Study of a Generalized
       Problem Processor   83
4.30   Conclusion   85
References   86

Chapter 5   Formalizations of Purposive Systems

5.00   Formalizing Purposive Behavior   87
5.10   The State Space Approach to Decision Support   88
5.20   The Problem Reduction Approach to Decision Support   93
5.30   A Production System Approach to DSS   105
5.40   Conclusion   120
References   121

Part III   DECISION SUPPORT SYSTEMS FROM THE DATA
           BASE ANGLE

Chapter 6   Conceptual and Operational Constructs
            for Building a Data Base Knowledge System

6.00   Introductory Comments   125
6.10   Conceptual Constructs for Representing Knowledge   128
6.20   Simple Files and Tables   131
6.30   Associative Relationship between Aggregate Concepts   142
References   150

Chapter 7 Building a Data Base Knowledge System

7.00   More Complex Data Structures   151
7.10   Indirect Associations among Concepts   153
7.20   The Major Varieties of Logical Data Structures   170
7.30   A Design Procedure   178
References   186

Chapter 8 Language Systems for Data Base Knowledge Systems

8.00   Introduction   188
8.10   Languages for Directing Retrieval   189
8.20   Languages for Directing Computations
       in the Case of Data Base KS   222
8.30   Appendix: Commands Used with MDBS   226
References   228

Chapter 9 Problem-Processing Systems for Data Base Knowledge Systems

9.00   Overview   230
9.10   Problem Processing for Retrieval—Only DSS   230
9.20   Problem Processors for Computationally
       Oriented DSS   242
9.30   Summary   251
9.40   Appendix: A Category L Processing Example   252
References   258

Chapter 10 Extensions

10.00   Introduction   259
10.10   Language Extensions   260
10.20   Data Base Extensions   275
10.30   Conclusion   285
References   285

Part IV FORMAL LOGIC APPROACH TO DECISION SUPPORT

Chapter 11 The Language and Knowledge Systems of a DSS Based on Formal Logic

11.00   Introductory Remarks   289
11.10   Conceptual Framework   290

11.20   Operational Constructs   294
11.30   A Language System for Predicate Expressions   304
References   311

Chapter 12   Problem-Processing Systems for Predicate Calculus

12.00   Introduction   313
12.10   Information Collection   314
12.20   Problem Recognition   319
12.30   Examples of Resolution   323
References   331

Part V   INTEGRATING THE DATA BASE AND FORMAL LOGIC APPROACHES TO DECISION SUPPORT

Chapter 13   Combining the Data Base and Formal Logic Approaches

13.00   Introduction   335
13.10   Viewing Retrieval as Inference   336
13.20   A Mixed System of Knowledge Representation
        and Its Problem Processor   337
13.30   Knowledge Representation via Frames   353
13.40   Conclusion   356
References   357

Chapter 14   Operationalizing Modeling Knowledge in Terms of Predicate Calculus

14.00   Introduction   358
14.10   Conceptual Description of the Dynamic Approach   359
14.20   Operationalization Overview   366
14.30   Conclusion   375
References   376

Chapter 15   Concluding Remarks

15.00   Introduction   377
15.10   Background   377

15.20   The Setting of DSS within an Expanded View
        of Decision Making   379
15.30   An Outline of DSS Implementation Issues   380
15.40   Further Research Topics   385
References   388

Index   389

FOREWORD

Operations research and management science have now reached middle age—about 35 years by some reckonings of the birthdate. Awareness of middle age is, in the conventional wisdom, a signal for self-examination to ward off the approaching dangers of stagnation. I do not think that stagnation is a present danger in operations research and management science; tools continue to be sharpened and new applications are found each year.

At the same time, it is notable that the principal tools for scientific decision making in management are tools that had already been forged a quarter century ago, during the first burst of enthusiasm and energy in this field: linear and integer programming, queuing theory, quadratic decision rules, dynamic programming, simulation. The traveling salesman is still traveling, inventories are still being ordered, oil is being blended, with the help of these tools.

In very recent years, partly as a consequence of the microcomputer revolution, but also partly as a consequence of continuing progress in such domains as artificial intelligence and data base management, new tools have been emerging—not to replace the time-tried ones, but to supplement them. Of course, even the newer tools have their origins in the past. Heuristic programming, christened about 1957, has had continuing application, especially to scheduling problems, ever since. Data base management had its primitive origins in such developments as the COBOL programming language.

The major force that has been driving this gradual enlargement of aids to decision making is the nature of the decision-making task itself. Many important decisions (some would say "most") have important qualitative components that do not lend themselves easily to the calculus of real numbers. In a great deal of executive decision making, natural language inputs are a crucial data source. Much decision making leads to complexities beyond the reach of optimizing techniques, requiring approaches that are more heuristic than algorithmic.

A major testing ground for new ideas about computer-aided and automated decision making has been the discipline of artificial intelligence, a subdiscipline of computer science. While there has been intermittent communication between artificial intelligence, on the one hand, and OR and management science, on the other, the two disciplines have grown up along parallel, but largely independent, paths. The AI path has been characterized by attention to goal-seeking systems (like the original heuristic search systems) and, especially in the past decade, to systems that draw on large knowledge bases. Examples of the former are the General Problem Solver and STRIPS; of the latter, the medical diagnosis systems, MYCIN, and INTERNIST.

The number of real-world applications of AI systems is now growing rapidly—at a rate comparable to the growth of OR applications in the late 1950s and early 1960s. GPS-like systems now design reaction paths for the manufacture of new chemical compounds. Medical diagnosis systems are at or near the clinical testing stage. A PROSPECTOR system analyzes geological data to assess the probabilities of the presence of ore bodies.

Up to the present time, relatively few of these applications—with the possible exception of the use of heuristic search in large combinatorial problems like scheduling problems—have been in the domain of management. The authors of this book have set about to remedy this imbalance and to explore the applicability of techniques drawn from computer science—from artificial intelligence and data base management to decision making in organizations. Because the domain is a vast one, they have had to be selective. They have directed their attention primarily to goal-driven systems and to the organization and management of data bases. In deference to the mathematical tastes of the OR field, they have perhaps emphasized the formal foundations of these topics a little more than I should have been inclined to do. But books cannot be all things to all men, and they have wisely adopted a consistent focus around which to build their descriptions of the new developments.

A few years from now, a single book will be too small to even sketch out the uses of AI techniques in management—just as no single book can any longer do that for OR. But this volume takes an important step in this new direction, and can provide us with a valuable guide to the art in its present state—until the research and development work that it helps to stimulate causes its own obsolescence. That is all we can ask of a pioneering book.

HERBERT A. SIMON

Carnegie-Mellon University

PREFACE

The existence of the modern computer has already had a profound impact on many aspects of society. To a large extent the role of the computer has been to automate routine functions that had previously been carried out less efficiently by humans. Examples abound, but typical applications involve record keeping for business and governmental agencies. The computer has a potential for playing yet a different kind of role in organizations: the support of decision-making activities.

A key element in our effort to improve the productivity of our resources and to raise our level of living is the ability to make better decisions. Thus, individuals in their private lives must constantly make decisions on how to allocate their time and physical resources so as to improve their well-being. In companies, individuals must resolve mundane issues and make decisions on vital corporate policy that may affect the survival of the corporate entity. From the point of view of economic theory a decision may be viewed as the output of a productive activity whose inputs include intellectual efforts of an individual or a group of individuals, computing hardware and software, volumes of data, etc. The general issue of developing and organizing these inputs in a cost-effective way to produce useful decisions is a fundamental area of research. This issue constitutes the focal point of study in the decision support system field.

The material in this book is based on research conducted during the past six years in the area of decision support systems (DSS). A basic objective of the book is to provide the foundations necessary for understanding and developing decision support systems. Against this background we sketch out strategies for DSS development and pursue these strategies by detailing specific techniques of data handling, model handling, language handling, and problem handling.

These frameworks, strategies, and techniques are developed primarily at conceptual and operational levels. Implementation issues are briefly described as they arise. Our approach to DSS considers, in particular, the integration of concepts and tools from various fields, including data base management, linguistics, and artificial intelligence. Apart from the novel *frameworks* that it introduces, this book is unique in its *interdisciplinary* emphasis and in its emphasis on a *generalized* approach to decision support systems. As such, it comprises an initial contribution to the development of a theory of decision support systems.

The book is partitioned into five parts. In Part I we examine connections among information processing, decision making, and decision support. We also introduce frameworks for understanding organizational information processing and decision making. DSS design and development in subsequent parts of the book build on these frameworks. In Part II we descend from the broad perspective of Part I. It opens with a survey of typical systems that have been developed to aid decision makers, and this survey leads to a DSS classification scheme and the generic view of DSS that governs the rest of the book. We show how several experimental systems fit into this generic view. We conclude Part II with an introduction to techniques for formalizing purposive behavior of a DSS.

In Part III we examine DSS construction from the angle of a data base knowledge system. This is developed within the generic view of DSS. In Part IV we also explore DSS construction within the generic view. However, there we adopt a formal logic approach rather than the data base approach. In Part V we demonstrate how the data base and formal logic approaches can be integrated during DSS design. We conclude the book with suggestions for further research issues in the design and development of decision support systems.

At this point, it is appropriate to acknowledge the financial support received during the period of our research and preparation of the manuscript. The National Science Foundation and Special Projects group in the Computer Science Division, then under the direction of Dr. Fred Weingarten, provided support for many years. We especially appreciate their willingness to fund outside the traditional boundaries of computer science. The IBM Corporation has supported the doctoral program of the Krannert Graduate School of Management at Purdue University for many years. This type of financial support has ensured vigorous MIS research activity from which we have all benefited. Mr. Frank G. Rodgers, Vice President of Marketing, and Mr. Charles Bowen, Director of Plans and Program Administration, both at IBM, have supported our MIS program in many ways, and we wish to thank them. More recently, the Army Research Office has provided summer financial support for DSS research. Finally, we wish to thank our co-workers in this exciting new field for their suggestions and criticisms of our work.

Several chapters are based on published papers, which include

R. H. Bonczek, C. W. Holsapple, and A. B. Whinston, Future directions for developing decision support systems, *Decision Sciences,* 616–631 (October 1980).

R. H. Bonczek, C. W. Holsapple, and A. B. Whinston, Aiding decision makers with a generalized data base management system, *Decision Sciences,* 228–245 (April 1978).

R. H. Bonczek, C. W. Holsapple, and A. B. Whinston, Computer based support of organizational decision making, *Decision Sciences,* 268–291 (April 1979).

R. H. Bonczek, C. W. Holsapple, and A. B. Whinston, The integration of data base management and problem resolution, *Information Systems,* 4(2), 143–154 (1979).

R. H. Bonczek, C. W. Holsapple, and A. B. Whinston, Representing modeling knowledge with first order predicate calculus, *Operations Research* (1981).

R. H. Bonczek, C. W. Holsapple, and A. B. Whinston, The evolving roles of models in decision support systems, *Decision Sciences,* 337–356 (April 1980).

We are indebted to the publishers of these journals for allowing us to adapt that material for use here.

Part I

**INFORMATION PROCESSING,
DECISION MAKING, AND DECISION
SUPPORT—SOME PERSPECTIVES**

Chapter 1

INTRODUCTION TO INFORMATION PROCESSING, DECISION MAKING, AND DECISION SUPPORT

1.00 THE INFORMATION AGE

Historians of the future, looking back on our present era, may very well characterize it as the information age. For it is a period in which the volume and complexity of information processed by individuals and organizations have grown dramatically. The interdependence and rapidity of information processing are unprecedented. Simon [38] has observed that we are experiencing the initial stages of an information revolution that began a bit more than a century ago. He terms it the *third information revolution,* indicating that its two predecessors resulted in written language and the printed book. This third information revolution is characterized by

(1)   technological innovations in information processing;

(2)   dramatic growth of groups and organizations in number, size, and complexity; and

(3)   human–machine information-processing systems.

1.01   Technological Innovation

The present revolution in the technology of information processing includes the photograph (and motion picture), phonograph, radio, television, and telephone. These are devices for the storage, transmission, and display of information. There is yet another device that is prominent in this revolution: the computer. The computer differs from the other devices in that one of its major functions is to transform information, as well as to handle its storage and display. This property gives the computer a special significance when it is realized that the human thinking process also involves the transformation of information. The computer is the only means currently available with a potential for modeling human thought processes [13, 38].

The automation of information processing may be likened to the automation of materials processing, which is often referred to as the Industrial Revolution. In each instance manual or mental (i.e., human) processing has been superseded by electromechanical processing (materials in one case and information in the other). Furthermore, the mechanization of processing (be it material or information) has in many cases tended to furnish a capacity for more complex, more precise, and faster processing than is feasible with a manual/mental approach [30].

Just as the Industrial Revolution engendered sweeping social changes, one might reasonably expect the same from the revolution in information processing technology. Many such changes can already be observed. An exhaustive enumeration of these and speculations on future impacts of this ongoing technological development are beyond the scope of this book (see Simon [38]). Nevertheless, in the course of the ensuing chapters we shall touch on the impacts of the computer on organizational decision making. This follows quite readily from our primary emphasis on computer-based *techniques* for furnishing support for decision makers.

Earlier we alluded to the computer's potential for modeling human thought processes involving information retention, presentation, and (especially) transformation. It is precisely this potential that is explored in this book, by means of our emphasis on computer-based techniques for furnishing support for decision makers.

1.02   Growth of Groups and Organizations

The pervasive phenomenon of complex organizations is often taken for granted, but from a historical perspective the proliferation of groups and the accompanying appearance of numerous large-scale, complex, interdependent organizations is a fairly recent development. All of these organizations are information processors, and many are exclusively oriented toward the processing of information. News organizations, governmental organizations, and banks are prime examples of the latter.

Although we will not conjecture about the causes of this organization phenomenon, we do pause to make cogent observations. The organization "explosion" began to emerge in the same time period that witnessed the beginnings of the Industrial and information revolutions. Before the advent of the new information-processing technologies, information processing in organizations was of a manual/mental nature. Organizations were fewer in number, smaller in scale, and less complex; but with the appearance of this technology, organizations were no longer predominantly human systems. The typical present-day organization is best characterized as a human–machine system in both its materials-processing and information-processing aspects. The machines are used for processing that is routine or repetitive, that demands precision and speed, or that is exceedingly complex (yet algorithmic).

It may be going too far to say that technological innovations in information processing caused the present-day prominence of organizations. However, since organizations are information processors, the technological innovations in information processing most certainly have had an enabling influence on the growth of organizations. At any rate, the growth in size and complexity of the information-processing aspect of organizations is an important characteristic of the information revolution, and it furnishes the context within which we shall examine computer-based techniques for supporting decision making.

1.03   Human–Machine Information-Processing Systems

Technological innovations in information processing began as inventions of individual products and spawned the emergence of complex human–machine information-processing systems. Given humans and computers, both of which are information processors, the broad problem is one of how to integrate these effectively into an information-processing system whose outputs are "good" decisions. Kami [24] has pointed out that future treatments of this problem depend mainly on advances in

(1)   computer technology, and
(2)   the methodology of information–decision systems

Whereas technological advances are frequently revolutionary, methodological advances are comparatively evolutionary. Increases in computer speed and memory tend to occur by leaps and bounds. In comparison, methodological progress toward harnessing the potential of computers tends to be ground out in the crucible of experience.

1.03.1   Advances in Computer Technology

We shall approach the issue of advances in computer technology from the angle of present-day limitations. It is well known that the capabilities of computers are constrained principally by elementary processing speeds and by memory sizes (subject to retrieval in a practical amount of time). Simon has argued that all limits on the potential scope of "computer intelligence" are also restrictions on human intelligence and that the "scale of available computer memories is increasing rapidly, to the point where memory size may not be much longer an effective limit on the capacity of computers to match human performance" [38].

The extent to which we accept Simon's arguments will affect our assessment of the computer's potential for assisting human information processing–decision making in a human–machine system. At one extreme are those who would claim that the computer's potential has already been largely realized, because they foresee a lack of significant advances in either technology or methodology. At the other extreme are those who would maintain that the machine may eventually usurp all the human activities in human–machine systems, leaving only machine systems. As will be revealed in the course of this treatise, we adopt a stance between these extremes.

Simon's arguments have a bearing on the practicality of a *general* computerized system for assisting human decision makers. The phrase "computerized system" refers to the machine part of a human–machine system that carries out the information processing required to make decisions. The phrase "general computerized system" as it is applied throughout this book, connotes a computerized system (1) whose design does not restrict it to consideration of problems in a single problem domain and (2) whose design tends to encompass several information-processing abilities. Strictly speaking, the term "general" is a relative one; that is, there are degrees of generality. Some dimensions of generality are depicted in Fig. 1.1, and the notion of generality is progressively sharpened and amplified in the chapters that follow.

Returning now to Simon's arguments and their implication for a general computerized system for assisting decision makers, several observations can be made. If Simon's arguments are rejected, then the practical viability of a *general* computerized system for assisting human decision makers (not to mention a *general* computerized system that makes deci-

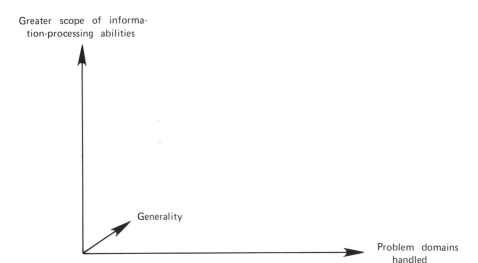

Greater scope of informa-
tion-processing abilities

Generality

Problem domains
handled

Fig. 1.1.   Dimensions of generality.

sions) must be severely limited. On balance, however, general computerized systems for assisting human decision makers can offer insights in
the study of specialized systems. They can also offer conceptual guidelines for the implementation of comparatively specialized decision support systems. For these reasons the orientation of this book is toward
general frameworks for studying human–machine decision systems and
general computer-based techniques for furnishing support to decision
makers. This culminates in Part V with the description of a quite general
computer-based system for aiding decision makers.

As a final point related to technological advance, mention must be
made of certain economic considerations. Advances in computer technology have resulted in computer hardware becoming quite inexpensive.
Computer speed is increasing in such a way that the cost of performing a
given set of operations is steadily decreasing. Furthermore, effective
computer memory sizes have increased, so that the per unit cost of data
storage is being continually reduced. The significance of these trends for
the design of human–machine systems will become apparent later in this
chapter.

1.03.2   Methodology for Information–Decision Systems

Our assessment of the computer's potential for supporting human decision activities is not affected only by technological progress. Equally
important are methodologies (1) for implementing mechanical information

processing and (2) for integrating the mechanical information processing with the human elements in a human–machine system. The former depends on detailed knowledge and development of computer-based techniques for handling information. The latter is predicated on a more or less global perspective of the nature of the information processing involved in organizational decision making. For example, how can one describe information processors and the dynamics of information processing in an organization? What abilities must an organization possess in order to make decisions?

This treatise is organized so that the global enterprise view of information processing is presented first (in Chapter 2). The more detailed and lengthy issues of computer-based techniques for realizing decision support follow in Parts II–V. Part V stresses the use of computer-based techniques from the global enterprise view as a means for designing human–machine decision systems. The remainder of the present section is devoted to an overview of some of the major methodological issues.

Both individual and collective decision makers (i.e., both managers and managerial systems) are essentially information processors. In this respect there is a common bond between decision makers and computers, for the history of computer science has been that of developing increasingly powerful techniques for information processing. On the other hand, there are clearly differences in the nature and capabilities of human versus computerized information processing. Some of these differences are touched on in the ensuing chapters. Our primary focus, however, is on the extent to which the bond between decision makers and computers can be enhanced. Of particular interest is the computerized support of relatively unstructured, nonprogrammed decision activities such as those involved in strategic planning.

The information-processing bond between decision makers and computers is strengthened by increasing the computer's ability to recognize and carry out requests while at the same time decreasing the decision maker's effort in specifying those requests. It must be emphasized that we shall not consider computer-based support of decision making solely in the sense of people writing and/or running computer application programs (e.g., mathematical programming) or in the sense of people writing and running programs to manipulate files of data.

The methodologies for developing information–decision systems must not ignore economic questions. The term "software" refers to methodologies for directing the information-processing capabilities of the hardware (i.e., for actually implementing desired information processing on available hardware). In contrast to per unit hardware costs, which are diminishing, per unit software costs are rising. The cost of software is primarily a labor cost, including the costs of systems analysts, programmers, and keypunchers. The increased expense is due in part to increasing wage scales and in part to efforts at handling more complex problems than have heretofore been tackled. Today's cost of producing 100 lines of computer code is greater than yesterday's cost for the same 100 lines. Moreover, 100 lines of code dealing with a simple problem are less expensive than another 100 lines that treat a relatively complex problem, since the former requires either less time to produce or less skilled (less expensive) personnel.

There is very little evidence to suggest that the trends of rising per unit software costs and declining per unit hardware costs will reverse in the near future. Furthermore, we can observe that software costs have risen not only in absolute per unit terms, but also as a percentage of total (software and hardware) computer costs. By 1965 it had increased to one-half of the total, and in 1970 it accounted for approximately 80% of total computer costs [25].

It is important that methodologies used for the design of information–decision systems take heed of these economic considerations. Kleijnen [25] has classified, in economic terms, ways for grappling with rising software costs. These include (1) labor–capital substitution, (2) mass production of software, (3) division of labor, and (4) increased life expectancy of software.

(1) *Labor–capital substitution* refers to the substitution of capital (i.e., hardware) expenditures for labor (i.e., software) expenditures. This is accomplished via the design and use of increasingly "higher-level" languages for writing software instructions. With a low-level language the software designed by a programmer (in order to specify just what the hardware is to do) is typically in the form of numerical (or mnemonic) codes [12]. Since these are quite cumbersome to work with, higher-level languages (e.g., FORTRAN, COBOL, PL/1) were devised to decrease the programmer's effort in writing software.

A programmer's instructions in a higher-level language are input to a compiler. The compiler is a program that translates statements in the higher-level language into equivalent statements in a lower-level language. Although the compiler is itself a program, the reader must be careful not to confuse it with programs that are written by a programmer who is using the computer system. Such software, which along with hardware makes up a computer system, is termed *system software* or *system programs*.

Given two languages, one has a higher level than the other if it is easier to learn and makes it easier (more succinct, or more English-like) to state instructions. The net result is a decrease in programmer effort involved in devising and debugging (software cost) but an increase in the amount of time required to compile and execute the program (i.e., an increase in hardware costs). Thus capital, as represented by computer speed and size needed for compilation and execution, is substituted for labor, as represented by human programming effort.

The simplification or even elimination of human programming effort is the central concern of present-day research into automatic programming [5]. The activity of a compiler may be viewed as a sort of automatic programming. For instance, given some instructions in the FORTRAN language, a FORTRAN compiler automatically generates a program in a lower-level language. Automatic programming of a more sophisticated nature altogether eliminates the programmer. The user of the computer no longer must be a programmer but merely must state what data are desired. On the basis of this statement, a program is automatically generated that, when executed, provides the desired data. This notion of automatically generating computer programs is developed in later chapters as a crucial element of decision support systems.

(2) *Mass production of software* has enabled nonprogrammers to utilize computer systems. The nonprogrammer purchases a software package from a software vendor. This package consists of one or more programs that the purchaser (or user) can direct the computer system to execute. The precise method for invoking the execution of a particular program in the package differs from package to package. Often the user is permitted to specify a particular program parametrically. Software packages are frequently incorporated into the system software so that a user need not be concerned with handling a package's computer code.

Thus mass production of software involves a single programming effort to produce a package that is then mechanically duplicated and sold to numerous users. This eliminates duplication of programming effort by relieving each of these users from writing his or her own program. For mass production of a software package to be practical, the tasks performed by that package must be of interest to a considerable number of potential users. Examples are mathematical programming packages, project management packages, and packages for statistical analysis.

(3) *Division of labor* involves splitting programming effort so that each programmer works on some independent module of a large-scale program that is his or her specialty. This enables each programmer to work more efficiently by permitting concentrated effort on a limited domain. One problem in this modular approach is the question of how to coordinate the modules in order to form larger-scale programs. For example, several modules may have been programmed, each one modeling some activity in

an organization. The problem of how to formulate these into a more comprehensive model of organizational activity lies with persons experienced in management science or systems analysis. In later chapters we explore this integrative function, particularly with respect to languages for specifying how models can be constructed from modules. Note that there may be many levels of models, so that after a model has been constructed from several modules, that model can be combined with others to form a still more comprehensive model.

(4) *Increased life expectancy* of a program reduces long-run programming effort. Changes in large-scale programs are facilitated by the modular design approach. A program is also more durable if written in a comparatively high-level language although in some cases execution efficiency could be diminished.

The life expectancy of system software is quite important, since it is often the subject of large investment. The generality of this software (see Fig. 1.1) is a critical factor in the life expectancy of system software in those situations where the human—machine system is confronted by a volatile environment.

1.10 DECISION MAKING

To this point we have focused on the importance of the information-processing phenomenon, examining its impact from the angles of technological innovation, organizational growth, and human—machine systems. However, it must be stressed that information processing is not always an end in itself. Rather it is a means to an end, a means to decisions. Decisions, in the guise of information, are the "finished products" of a human—machine information-processing system. We refer to information-processing systems that yield that finished product as *decision-making systems.*

Note that information is a raw material, an intermediate product, and a finished good of a decision-making process. The terms "information processing" and "decision making" as used in this book are closely related. Various information-processing procedures (systems) might deal exclusively with the raw materials or intermediate products of decision making. But when these are combined with other information-processing procedures (systems) that involve the finished goods, the resultant and more global information-processing procedure (system) is a decision-making system. We refer to an information-processing system that is embedded within a decision-making system as a *decision support system.*

A decision support system may be a human information processor, a mechanical information processor, or a human–machine information-processing system embedded within an organizational decision-making system. Furthermore, a decision support system may be more or less general in the sense of Fig. 1.1. That is, it may deal with a variety of problem areas or perhaps only one; it may possess one or several of the kinds of information-processing abilities that are involved in decision making (see Chapter 2), and it may do so in varying degrees. Before delving more deeply into systems for decision support, it is advisable to sharpen our understanding of the notions of decisions and decision making.

1.11   Managers, Management Scientists, Computer Scientists

All managerial activity revolves around decision making. The manager is first and foremost a decision maker. Organizations are filled with decision makers at various levels, so that the decision made by one constrains decisions to be made by others. Each manager is charged with a certain part of an organization's decision-making activities.

In the effort to aid practicing decision makers in dealing with complex problems, the field of management science has developed. The management scientist's principal task is one of discovering valid quantitative and mathematical descriptions and algorithms for generating information that is usable to a manager. The management scientist thereby endeavors to reduce the amount of guesswork in which a manager must engage.

Note that the algorithms are formal information-processing models, i.e., they specify patterns according to which information is transformed (inputs to outputs). They are literally plans for information processing. As such they are readily amenable to conversion into computer programs, enabling the plans for information processing to be executed. Indeed, many of the models developed by management scientists have been made feasible by the computer's information-processing speed.

The term "model" as it is used in the remainder of this text should be taken as meaning a plan for information processing that involves some transformation of information (and not merely the storage, retrieval, or display of information). A model may be specified in any of several ways, including mathematical expressions, English statements, or computer programs. The context should make clear which of these is intended. Furthermore, some models may be unspecified, in the sense that they exist only as mental information-processing plans. In this case the information processing is not mechanical, as with models in the form of computer programs, but it is mental, or human, processing.

The models of management scientists are tools for extending a decision maker's capacity for coping with complex, large-scale problems. However, the decision maker also performs internal information processing, in which the pattern of thought may be considered as a mental model. In attempting to observe this pattern, we find that it is frequently quite elusive. It is difficult to describe or externalize and is usually referred to as being "subjective." It is nonetheless a type of information transformation that is an important, valuable aspect of decision making.

In addition to management science, another source of information-processing aid for managers has come from the field of computer science. This aid not only has come in the guise of rendering certain management science results feasible but has furnished various means for storing and then retrieving data that serve as the "raw materials" of decision making. As a working definition of the term "data," we use (cf. Johnson *et al.* [22]) "facts which can be used as a basis for reasoning." A collection of data will be called a *data base*. As we shall see in a later chapter, the term "data base" can be more rigorously defined not only in terms of the data it contains but also in terms of its structure (i.e., how the data are structured or organized).

The term "information" is often used synonymously with "data." Yet many authors (e.g., Davis [9] and Johnson *et al.* [22]) distinguish between the two. One distinction that is drawn is that data are potentially information. Data *can* be used as a basis for reasoning, but when data actually *are* used (processed), they are called information. Another but related view holds that information is an abstraction. That is, it is not "something" that can be pointed to or seen, but it can be conveyed. A pattern of symbols that conveys information could be considered to be data. For example, the symbols on this printed page are not information, but they are data that can convey information. In view of the inseparable nature of data and information we shall not belabor the dichotomy. Thus it should be understood that a data base can convey information, that information processing goes hand in hand with data handling, and that usage of a data base is a kind of information processing.

To recapitulate, managers are decision makers and, therefore, information processors. Two sources of assistance for managers are management science and computer science. Management scientists build models for processing information. Computer scientists restate the models as computer programs to take advantage of the computer's information-processing speed and its ability to execute complex algorithms. Computer science techniques also provide mechanisms for storage and retrieval of the data (or information), which serve as raw materials in the manager's decision activities.

1.12 Structured and Unstructured Decision Processes

Decision-making processes fall along a continuum that ranges from highly structured to highly unstructured. These two end points are sometimes referred to as programmed and nonprogrammed, respectively [17]. The former refers to decision making that is routine and repetitive. The latter is descriptive of situations where there is not a "cut-and-dried method for handling the problem because it hasn't arisen before, or because its precise nature and structure are elusive or complex, or because it is so important that it deserves custom-tailored treatment" [37].

As noted in Section 1.11, a model is a strategy (e.g., a program) for processing information. The psychological perspective [10] taken here is that human memory contains "programs" or strategies for processing information, even though the person may be unable to articulate (or may be unconscious of) the strategy employed in a given decision-making situation. A discussion of this view and the contrasting behavioral position appear in Forehand [11].

To the extent that an information-processing strategy can be precisely stated as an algorithm, it can be incorporated into a computer program. Thus part of the information processing needed to solve a particular decision problem can be automated. If all information processing required to produce a particular decision has been automated (or is capable of automation), then that decision process is completely structured or programmed. The degree of structuredness diminishes as the mental strategies employed become fuzzy and incapable of externalization. Nevertheless, there are still specialized strategies or mental programs that are invoked to solve a particular decision problem.

A question arises concerning what governs a decision process in the even more unstructured, nonprogrammed situation of infrequently encountered or novel decision problems. Simon [37] maintains that the governing agent is a set of general rules of procedure that exists to augment those strategies that are not peculiar to a particular decision problem. Figure 1.2 depicts the spectrum of decision processes.

If a routine, well-known type of decision problem is encountered, the pertinent specialized information-processing strategies are invoked. If the problem is new, such that no habitual pattern of specialized strategies is applicable, then the more general strategies are applied. The precise na-

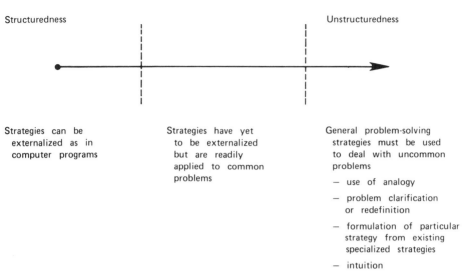

Structuredness   Unstructuredness

Strategies can be   Strategies have yet   General problem-solving
  externalized as in   to be externalized   strategies must be used
  computer programs   but are readily   to deal with uncommon
                             applied to common   problems
                             problems
                                                         — use of analogy

                                                         — problem clarification
                                                           or redefinition

                                                         — formulation of particular
                                                           strategy from existing
                                                           specialized strategies

                                                         — intuition

Fig. 1.2.   Decision process.

ture of these strategies has yet to be explored. Possibilities include (1) the use of analogy to find analogous, well-known problems whose known solution strategies can be used to construct an analogue strategy for the new problem; (2) the collection of further information in order to redefine or more clearly define the decision problem; (3) attempts to combine existing solution strategies to form a new strategy; and (4) the utilization of intuitive faculties. Much later (Part V) we shall return to these general strategies, examining the extent to which some of them may be incorporated into computer system software.

One of the effects of work in the field of management science has been to push the boundary between structured and unstructured decision problems to the right in Fig. 1.2. Problems that were considered unstructured 30 years ago have been squeezed into the structured realm. Decision makers were thereby allowed to devote greater attention to those problems still considered unstructured. In commenting on future directions for management science in dealing with complex and otherwise messy problems, Zeleny [44] has stated that the "decision maker's mind becomes an integral part of an analytical algorithm, its most interactive subroutine. This symbiotic, intricate and elegant cooperation of manager and management scientist leads to a stagewise, adaptive procedure where mutual learning helps to understand what the solutions should be and why. Men and machines cooperate rather than compete."

In effect, the management scientist's algorithm calls on human experts to execute their relatively subjective problem-solving strategies. The information resulting from such executions is then delivered to the calling algorithm so that its execution can proceed. This is the recursive extension of the customary procedure of a decision maker calling for the execution of a management scientist's algorithm. Combinations of both directions of inquiry, human to machine and machine to human, form an important topic in the study of human–machine information-processing systems. Computer-based techniques, which must necessarily underlie this approach to decision making, will become apparent in later chapters.

1.13   The Anthony Taxonomy

We have seen that organizational decision processes can be loosely classified as structured or unstructured, with many gradations between those two extremes. Another important way of classifying decision-making processes is the Anthony taxonomy of strategic planning–management control–operational control [2]. In Anthony's conceptual scheme strategic planning refers to the "process of deciding on the objectives of an organization, on changes in these objectives, and on the policies used to govern the acquisition, use and disposition of these resources." Management control is described as a combination of planning and control functions whereby managers assure that resources are acquired and utilized in an effective, efficient manner. Management control is constrained by the objectives and policies that result from strategic planning. Whereas management control requires judgment, operational control (as defined by Anthony) does not since it is entirely governed by precisely specified decision rules. These rules are used to decide efficiently and effectively about which specific tasks should be undertaken.

Anthony and others [8, 26] have observed that it is, in practice, difficult to separate planning and control. There is, in effect, a continuum with operational control at one end, strategic planning at the other, and management control in the center. As one proceeds along the continuum from operational control, through management control, to strategic planning, the associated decision activity becomes less and less structured; it can be described as partaking less of control and more of planning. This is not to imply that planners do not make use of formal models, but rather that planning (especially strategic planning) is relatively difficult to formalize. It involves qualitative judgments, intuition, and creativity.

The planning decisions of management control are different in character from those of strategic planning. This difference is analogous to the difference between the planning decisions of a builder versus those of an architect. Strategic planning problems, like architectural problems, tend to be complex, ill structured, and irregular, requiring a creative and guiding intelligence. Planning problems in management control tend to be less complex and more rhythmic in their occurrence, i.e., using common tools according to a given pattern. The information needed for strategic planning is of a more varied nature, is used less frequently, is less precise, and has more of an external origin than that used in management control planning. In the remaining chapters of this book use of the term "planning" should be understood to encompass both types. That is, our discussion of supporting decision activities is applicable to both types of planning decisions.

Even though planning is a relatively unstructured activity, there is continuing research involving formal planning systems. This research is predicated on the premises that (1) decision making in complex organizations can be facilitated by the use of formal planning systems, (2) there may be an ability to tailor a formal planning system to fit the peculiarities of a given situation, and (3) the study of formal planning can offer practical insights and suggestions to aid decision makers [40]. A formal planning system may be defined as an integrated set of "policies and procedures consciously designed to improve management's decisions," where these policies and procedures are intended as guides and constraints for the activities of subordinates [40]. In short, this line of research aspires to formalize a traditionally "informal" activity. The same could be said of research pertaining to decision support systems, for in the process of computerization there is necessarily a formalization that culminates in computer code.

1.20 DECISION SUPPORT

The preceding sections of this chapter, in dealing with information processing and decision making, furnish the context within which decision support will be examined. The remainder of this chapter amplifies the notion of decision support, as introduced in Section 1.10, by commenting on

(1) the emerging discipline of computerized decision support systems, and

(2) sources of techniques for providing decision support, including data base management, linguistics, and logic.

The remainder of the book is a further unfolding of the decision support notion, uncovering a variety of techniques and presenting frameworks within which the techniques may be studied, integrated, and applied.

1.21   The Computerized Decision Support Discipline

The broad outlines of this emerging discipline have only recently begun to take shape. The term "decision support" first began appearing in the titles of conferences and research papers in the early 1970s. It appears to be an outgrowth of the management information systems (MIS) area, which in turn stems from data base management, which has its roots in file management. There is no clear breaking point between any two adjacent areas in this fourfold progression, where it can be said that one ends and the other begins. However, the progression does involve a broadening of scope and a shifting of emphasis.

The decision support system area includes the other three areas. It differs from the management information systems area in its emphasis on the three following issues: (1) incorporating models into the information system software, (2) providing useful information to higher-level management so as to support comparatively unstructured decision activities, and (3) furnishing the system's users with powerful yet simple to use languages for problem solving. These three issues certainly were not ignored in the MIS area, but neither were they emphasized. Decision support systems may be considered to be a renaming of MIS in order to call attention to this new emphasis.

It has been estimated [38] that, to date, 95% of all computer power has been consumed in record keeping and in performing large-scale scientific and engineering computations. However, as we shall see, computerized decision support entails considerably more than this. A survey of the small, but rapidly growing, literature concerned with decision support reveals an absence of fundamental theory about decision making and decision support. It is largely concerned with describing particular systems and with attempts at short definitions of the term "decision support systems." The literature further reveals that the primary impetus for interest in this area comes from advances in the field of data base management, rather than from any advance in our understanding of the mechanisms of decision making.

The various definitions that have been suggested for decision support (e.g., Benbasat [3], Berger and Edelman [4], Grace [14], Hackathorn [16], Joyce and Oliver [23], and McLean and Riesing [29]) will not be listed here. It suffices to observe that these definitions agree that the system must aid a decision maker in solving unprogrammed, unstructured (or "semistructured") problems. A review of the definitions also shows a widespread agreement that the system must possess an interactive query facility, with a query language that resembles English or is at least easy to learn and use. A query language is a language with which a system's user can interrogate the system or state the problem that the system is to solve.

An examination of existing systems that have been called decision support systems (e.g., Berger and Edelman [4], Joyce and Oliver [23], Mantey and Sutton [27], and McLean and Riesing [29]) shows that each is composed of software for managing a data base plus some sort of software for accepting and interpreting a user's queries. The query facility typically permits *ad hoc* (i.e., nonroutine, nonstandard) queries for retrieval and in some cases handles *ad hoc* analyses (i.e., the execution of some model with some data). Alter [1] has discussed six types of decision support systems, including examples of each. This typology is based on uses of the system and consists of (1) retrieval of isolated data values, (2) performance of *ad hoc* analysis, (3) production of standard reports, (4) estimation of consequences of proposed decisions, (5) proposal of decisions, and (6) decision making. With few exceptions (e.g., Haseman [18]), systems that have been termed decision support systems are specific to a particular problem domain.

1.22 A Decision Support Perspective

The approach to computerized decision support systems adopted here is one of utilizing ideas and techniques from the areas of management science, data base management, formal logic, and linguistics, all within the global frameworks of organizational information processing and decision making. These frameworks, to be presented in Chapter 2, draw on work in the areas of psychology and organizational behavior. The result of this multifaceted approach leaves the unmistakable impression that the emerging decision support "discipline" can (or should) eventually be quite interdisciplinary in nature.

Having already introduced the management science area in Section 1.11, brief introductions to data base management, logic, and linguistics follow.

1.22.1 Data Base Management

In Section 1.11 we loosely defined a data base as a collection of data. Data base management involves the organization and manipulation of data in a data base. In file management, the forerunner of data base management, data are organized in a particular way, namely, into files. For the present a file may be thought of as a sequence of related or similar "parcels" of data. For example, we might have several parcels of data about employees, where each parcel is composed of data about a different employee (such as the employee's name, age, skills, title, pay rate, etc.). A sequence of these employee data parcels constitutes an employee file. File management is concerned with the organization of this file (e.g., how it is sequenced, which employees are included in the file, what data about each employee are included, etc.). It is also concerned with ways of manipulating data in the file, such as how particular pieces of data can be extracted from the file to produce a report or create a new file, how data in one file can be merged with data in another file, how the file can be updated by adding or deleting pieces of data, etc.

An organization's human–machine information-processing system typically needs many files of data. Each of these files is customarily designed for use in solving a particular problem. For instance, several files might be designed for use in solving problems in a manufacturing department and several other files might be designed for use in an engineering department. In the extreme, files of data might be developed and maintained exclusively as input for a single program. Thus in file management the emphasis is on a fragmented treatment of data, involving many separate files.

Data base management grew out of a shift in emphasis toward a more integrated treatment of data. Creation and maintenance of a common data base is the spirit of data base management. The data base is common in the sense that it is accessible to all, e.g., to the manufacturing department, to the engineering department, and to every program.

With many separate files developed for different uses (or users), there was often an overlap in the data stored within an organization. That is, some data in one file appeared in other files also. This redundancy not only was costly from a storage viewpoint but led to difficulties in maintaining the consistency of a large organization's data. Data base management grew out of a recognized need to overcome these shortcomings, and its development was aided by technological advances in computer hardware involved in secondary storage.

The study of data base management, therefore, emphasizes techniques for organizing data into a common data base, for collapsing separate files into a single memory mechanism in which redundancy is eliminated (or at least reduced). A discussion of such "memory mechanisms" appears in Part III. A study of data base management must also address the various languages that can be used to manipulate data in a common data base. These are referred to as *data manipulation languages* and are also described in Part III.

1.22.2 Logic, Linguistics, and Artificial Intelligence

Our interest in logic and linguistics derives principally from the potential of their incorporation into computer system software. Organizational decision-making processes involve both data storage and retrieval (be it human or machine) and thus data base management. They also involve (1) the use of logic, to determine information-processing strategies that are appropriate for a given problem; (2) the use of linguistics, to communicate about a given problem and recognize the meaning of a statement in a particular language.

To the extent that logic and linguistics can be incorporated into the machine portion of a human–machine decision-making system, the common bond between human and mechanical information processing is enhanced and the machine begins to appear intelligent (at least in some artificial sense). That is, the machine's externally observable behavior begins to give the impression that it has some intelligence. If a blind is constructed in front of the computer, it becomes difficult to ascertain whether the response to a problem came from a computer or from a human information processor.

The automation of logic and linguistics forms the core of a field of study called artificial intelligence. Hereafter we shall use this term to refer to the incorporation of logic and linguistics into a computerized decision support system.

Marr [28] has described artificial intelligence as the ''study of complex information processing problems that often have their roots in some aspect of biological information processing. The goal of the subject is to identify interesting and solvable information processing problems, and solve them.'' In view of this stated aim, it is clearly important to investigate the concepts and techniques developed in the artificial intelligence field and their potential applicability to the development of computerized, *intelligent* decision support systems. We shall do so in the ensuing chapters.

1.23 Comparison of Data Base Management and Artificial Intelligence Objectives

The perspective on computerized decision support systems held throughout the remainder of this book is that they can (and should) be approached as a synthesis of both data base management techniques and artificial intelligence techniques. That is, the data base and query facilities can use artificial intelligence techniques. In a rather exhaustive survey, Wong and Mylopoulos [42] have exhibited that there is a strong relationship between recent research in artificial intelligence and topical issues in the data base management area. These two can be compared and contrasted with respect to three questions: How is knowledge represented? What is the nature of the system–user interface? What applications are dealt with? Thus they share the same broad objectives, although their approaches to meeting these objectives have different starting points.

1.23.1 Representation of Knowledge

Regarding the representation of knowledge, artificial intelligence has concentrated on the modeling of abstract, rather than concrete, knowledge. The way in which these models have been implemented is "often haphazard and rarely formalized to the point where they could be duplicated with any degree of success" [42]. In contrast, data base management has been primarily concerned with representing large volumes of concrete knowledge, and its treatment of abstract knowledge has been comparatively meager. However, as one traces the evolution of data base management, there is a discernible trend in the direction of representing more and more complex types of abstract knowledge. A final point about the data base management approaches to knowledge representation is that they are considerably more formal with respect to implementation [19] than those of artificial intelligence.

1.23.2 System–User Interface

The trend in data base management has been a progression from procedural, programming languages toward nonprocedural, English-like interface languages [19]. These are based on the myriad parsing and compiling techniques developed by computer scientists. It must be emphasized that "procedurality" is a relative term; there are degrees of procedurality. A procedural language is one in which statements are made about how to perform some task. In a relatively nonprocedural language statements are made about *what* task to perform but not how to perform it.

The emphasis in artificial intelligence has been on nonprocedurality and on natural language processing. This nonprocedurality can be accomplished by evaluating queries with theorem-proving methods of logic [33]. These methods have been used for special-purpose systems (e.g., Raphael [35]) by inserting rules for performing logical deductions into the system's programs. A more general procedure for performing logical deduction, called the resolution principle [36], has been used to build more general systems (e.g., Green and Raphael [15]) that are independent of rules of logic that they employ. Others [6, 32] have suggested interaction with the system's user in order to select the rules needed to execute a logical proof.

Artificial intelligence research also involves natural language processing. This may be viewed as a type of automatic code generation (recall Section 1.03.2). Existing studies in this area (e.g., Bobrow [7], Woods [43], and Zeleny[44]) are concerned with allowing human–computer interaction via some subset of the English language. The desirability and utility of strictly natural language discourse is a point of controversy [21, 31]. From one viewpoint, marginal utility diminishes as we approach a strict natural language capability, and marginal cost increases sharply.

1.23.3   Applications

With respect to the third question raised previously, data base systems have been extensively used in practical applications. Most natural language systems (and other question-answering systems devised via artificial intelligence) deal only with toy problems and are application specific. There are exceptions. The NLP system [20] is used for constructing and executing simulation models. More general systems, in terms of application areas supported, are REL [39] and REQUEST [34]; but these systems are primarily for retrieval of data from a data base; they are not concerned with building or executing computational models such as those involved in management science.

The applicability of data base management in supporting organizational decision making is well known. Some major objectives of this book are to present certain artificial intelligence techniques involving linguistics and logic, to show that those techniques are complementary with those of data base management, and to suggest their applicability in supporting organizational decision making.

1.30   CONCLUSION

This chapter has dealt with three major topics: information processing, decision making, and decision support. Information processing by humans and machines pervades organizational decision-making processes. The aim of this book is to present computer-based techniques that can be used in the development of systems for supporting decision makers. The presentation of these techniques is founded on an "enterprise" view of information processing and decision making. This view is described in Chapter 2 as a dual framework, one part of which involves the division of information-processing labor in an organization and the other part of which involves the abilities required for decision making.

REFERENCES

1. S. L. Alter, How effective managers use information systems, *Harvard Business Review* (December 1976).
2. R. N. Anthony, Planning and Control Systems, pp. 13–43. Harvard Business School of Business Administration, Boston, Massachusetts, 1965.
3. I. Benbasat, Cognitive style considerations in DSS design, *Data Base* **8**, No. 3 (1977).
4. P. Berger and F. Edelman, IRIS: A transactions-Based DSS for human resources management, *Data Base* **8**, No. 3 (1977).
5. A. W. Biermann, Approaches to automatic programming, *in* "Advances in Computers" (M. Rubinoff and M. C. Yovits eds.). Academic Press, New York, 1976.
6. W. W. Bledsoe and P. Bruell, A man-machine theorem proving system, *Artificial Intelligence* **5**, Spring (1974).
7. D. G. Bobrow, Natural language input for a computer problem solving system, *in* "Semantic Information Processing" (M. Minsky, ed.). MIT Press, Boston, Massachusetts, 1968.
8. R. O. Boyce, "Integrated Managerial Controls," p. 71. Longmans, London, 1968.
9. G. B. Davis, "Management Information Systems: Conceptual Foundations, Structure and Development." McGraw-Hill, New York, 1974.
10. R. J. Ebert and T. R. Mitchell, "Organizational Decision Processes," pp. 15–17. Crane, Russak & Co., New York, 1975.
11. G. A. Forehand, Constructs and strategies for problem solving research, *in* "Problem Solving" (B. Keleinmuntz, ed.). Wiley, New York, 1966.
12. C. W. Gear, "Computer Organization and Programming." McGraw-Hill, New York, 1969.
13. F. H. George, "The Anatomy of Business," pp. 139–149. Wiley, New York, 1974.
14. B. F. Grace, Training users of a prototype DSS, *Data Base* **8**, No. 3 (1977).
15. C. C. Green and B. Raphael, Research on intelligent question answering systems, *Proc. Nat. Comput. Conf., Princeton, New Jersey* (1968).
16. R. D. Hackathorn, Modeling unstructured decision making, *Data Base* **8**, No. 3 (1977).
17. E. F. Harrison, "The Managerial Decision Making Process," pp. 11–15. Houghton Mifflin Co., Boston, 1975.
18. W. D. Haseman, GPLAN: An operational DSS, *Data Base* **8**, No. 3 (1977).
19. W. D. Haseman and A. B. Whinston, "Introduction to Data Management." Irwin, Homewood, Illinois, 1977.
20. G. E. Heidorn, English as a very high level language for simulation programming, *Proc. Symp. Very High Level Languages, SIGPLAN Notices* **9** (1974).
21. I. D. Hill, Wouldn't it be nice if we could write computer programs in English or would it? *Compt. Bull.* **16** (1972).
22. R. A. Johnson, F. E. Kast, and J. E. Rosenzweig, "The Theory and Management of Systems," 2nd. ed., pp. 235–236. McGraw-Hill, New York, 1967.
23. J. D. Joyce and N. N. Oliver, Impacts of a relational information system on industrial decision, *Data Base* **8**, No. 3 (1977).

24. M. J. Kami, Electronic data processing: Primise and problems, *California Management Rev.* Fall, 77 (1978).
25. J. P. C. Kleijnen, Computers and operations research: A survey, *Comput. Operations Res.* **3** (1976).
26. H. Koontz and C. O'Donnell, "Principles of Management." McGraw-Hill, New York, 1968.
27. P. E. Mantey and J. A. Sutton, Computer Support for Management Decision Making, IBM Research Report, RJ 1893 (1976).
28. D. Marr, Artificial intelligence—A personal view, *Artificial Intelligence* **9** (1977).
29. E. R. McLean and T. F. Riesing, MAPP: A DSS for financial planning, *Data Base* **8**, No. 3 (1977).
30. H. D. Mills, Software development, *IEEE Trans. Software Eng.* **SE-2**, No. 4 (1976).
31. C. A. Montgomery, Is natural language an unnatural query language? *Proc. ACM Annu. Conf., New York* (1972).
32. A. J. Nevins, A human oriented logic for automatic theorem proving, *J. ACM* **21**, October (1974).
33. N. Nilsson, "Problem Solving Methods in Artificial Intelligence." McGraw-Hill, New York, 1971.
34. W. J. Plath, Transformational Grammar and Transformation Parsing in the REQUEST System, IBM Res. Report 4396 (1973).
35. B. Raphael, SIR: A Computer Program for Semantic Information Retrieval. Doctoral Dissertation, Mathematics Department, Massachusetts Institute of Technology (1964).
36. J. A. Robinson, A machine-oriented logic based on the resolution principle, *J. ACM* **12**, January (1965).
37. H. A. Simon, "The New Science of Management Decision," pp. 1–8. Harper, New York, 1960.
38. H. A. Simon, What computers mean to man and society, *Science* **195**, March (1977).
39. F. B. Thompson *et al.*, REL: A rapidly extensible language system, *Proc. Nat. Comput. Conf.* (1969).
40. R. F. Vancil (ed.), Formal Planning Systems—1971 (preface), pp. 1–3. Harvard Business School (1971).
41. T. Winograd, "Understanding Natural Language," pp. 23–27. Academic Press, New York, 1972.
42. H. K. T. Wong and J. Mylopoulos, Two Views of Data Semantics. Department of Computer Science, Univ. of Toronto (December 1976).
43. W. A. Woods, Transition network grammars for natural language analysis, *Commun. ACM* **13** (1970).
44. M. Zeleny, Notes, ideas, and techniques: New vistas of management science, *Comput. Operat. Res.* **2** (1975).

Chapter 2

FRAMEWORKS FOR ORGANIZATIONAL INFORMATION PROCESSING AND DECISION MAKING

2.00 INTRODUCTORY COMMENTS

The preceding chapter contained general remarks about information processing and decision making. In this chapter we give each of these a more formal treatment in terms of two conceptual frameworks. These frameworks may be characterized as follows:

(1) division of information-processing labor within an organization, and

(2) abilities required of a decision maker.

We repeatedly refer to these frameworks in the course of our study of decision support systems, beginning with Part II.

Frameworks such as these are important as devices for establishing an environment within which the decision support systems (DSS) discipline can develop and flourish. Without conceptual frameworks of information processing and decision making, expositions on decision support will probably remain in the realms of chatty discourses on the importance or existence of DSS, enumerations of computer science techniques, or citations of case studies about systems that purport to be DSS. All of these are valuable, but they are also incomplete.

The chatty discourses are not practical aids to the design of decision support systems. Enumerations of techniques give little indication of how to integrate these techniques into a human–machine system, since they furnish no enterprise view of just what a human–machine system entails. Without stated frameworks of organizational decision making and information processing, citing case studies does not provide an organized way for comparing and contrasting the salient features of various systems, that is, it is the framework that identifies the salient features.

The objective of the frameworks presented here is to provide a common thread with which the various aspects of decision support may be joined, thereby offering a more complete picture of this field. The frameworks allow us to weave various computer-based techniques into a human–machine information-processing view. Without the perspective that the frameworks afford, the techniques look like the backside of a tapestry. That is, they are analogous to many strands that appear to be related in some way, but the nature of that relationship and the pattern it produces are not discernible. The frameworks permit us to view the front as well, to see not only behind-the-scenes mechanics but also the nature of relationships among the mechanics and the patterns produced.

It must be stressed that the two frameworks presented here are not peculiar to any given information-processing–decision-making organization. They do, nevertheless, furnish concepts and terminology that can be used in describing a given information-processing–decision-making organization. It must also be emphasized that the concepts and terminology are independent of implementation. That is, they can describe various aspects of information processing and decision making within an organization, but they do not bind one aspect to machines and another to humans. Thus the frameworks furnish a basis for comparative study of various human–machine systems, which differ according to which aspects are accomplished by humans and which are accomplished by machines. In later chapters we discuss methods for operationalizing the concepts involved in these frameworks.

Finally, the reader certainly must not take these frameworks as being complete. They are clearly capable of elaboration, and it may be that other conceptual frameworks can be developed that are equally as flexible and that provide greater descriptive powers. At any rate, the present frameworks call attention to the need for more research into conceptual frameworks of information processing and decision making in human–machine systems. The two frameworks introduced suffice for the purposes of this book.

2.10   DIVISION OF INFORMATION-PROCESSING LABOR WITHIN AN ORGANIZATION

Study of information processing in an organization must begin with consideration of what an organization is. Organizations are processors of materials and information [12]. Our principal concern here is with their information-processing aspects. The nature of organizational information processing depends on organizational structure and style, but what are the components in an organizational structure and how can we characterize their interrelationships? It has been remarked [5] that an organization is a structure of roles tied together with lines of communication.

This view holds that the essential units of an organization are roles, not persons. That is, there may be several persons, each of whom could fill a certain role or carry out a certain information-processing function. On the other hand, a person may be capable of filling several roles and of performing several distinct information-processing functions. Furthermore, the person actually filling a role may change from time to time. Notice that roles may also be filled by machines.

Whereas organizational structure is given by the information channels among roles, organizational style refers both to the *way* in which roles are filled (e.g., by what persons, groups, or machines). Style also refers to the *selection* of particular lines of communication, in the face of a given problem.

As the organization encounters increasingly complex problems, it tends to exhibit division of labor, greater specialization of roles, and a hierarchic structure of communication and authority. There is a proliferation of roles, lines of communication, and structural complexity. Another phenomenon that can be observed is that some roles are created that are filled by other roles. For instance, role A may be played by B or C or D, where each of these three is itself a role that could be filled by yet other roles. "Divisional Planner" is a broad role, which may be played by "Division 1 Planner," "Division 2 Planner," or "Division 3 Planner." "Division 1 Planner" may in turn be filled by "Planner 1" or "Planner 2," where these describe two different kinds of planning that can be done in Division 1.

2.11   Conventions and Constructs

Several conventions are adopted in the discussion of roles and their interrelationships. First, our attention is confined to those roles that are information processors or, in other words, problem solvers. Thus each role can be described in terms of the nature of information processing that it performs or in terms of the problem that it solves. Second, roles that do not fill any other roles are said to be the most abstract roles in the organization (e.g., "Divisional Planner" in the preceding example). Symmetrically, roles that are not filled by any other roles are said to make up the most concrete level of organizational structure.

There is a range between the most abstract level and the most concrete. A *concrete* role, then, is either a person or an information-processing mechanism (e.g., a computer program). Persons or programs are not abstract roles, capable of being filled by anything that is more concrete. It could be argued that persons and programs are not roles at all. However, for simplicity of exposition they will be treated as roles of the most concrete sort. Finally, if two roles are not identical in terms of the information processing they perform, they are referred to as distinct.

The framework for representing division of labor in organizational decision making utilizes three constructs: *the role, definitional relationships* among roles, and *associative relationships* among roles. The reader may find it helpful to think of roles and their interrelationships in a theatrical sense. A *definitional relationship* between roles A and B indicates that role B is capable of playing role A. Suppose that C (where C is distinct from B) is also capable of filling role A. Then we say that role A may be defined in terms of either of the more concrete roles B or C. An *associative relationship* between roles D and E indicates that role D must "associate" with (receive information from) role E in order to carry out its information-processing task.

2.12 Pictorial Formalisms

An example is used to illustrate these constructs in more detail. In addition, a pictorial formalism is used to depict each construct.

Consider a system whose most abstract role is Divisional Planning (DP). This role can be filled (i.e., defined) in any one of several ways. That is, a request to perform Divisional Planning could be a reference to planning performed by Division 1 (DP1), or planning performed by Division 2 (DP2), . . . , or planning performed by Division K (DPK). With respect to a particular context, one of these must play the role of Divisional Planning.

2.12.1 Definitional Relationships

In Fig. 2.1, roles are denoted by nodes. The K definition relationships just described are denoted by the K directed arcs emanating from DP. The arc from DP to DP1 indicates that DP1 can define (play the role of) DP;

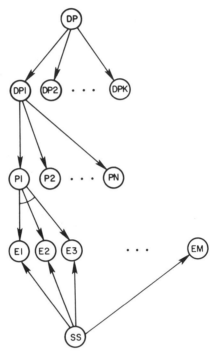

Fig. 2.1.   Structure of roles in a hypothetical planning situation.

planning performed by Division 1 is a particular instance of Divisional Planning. This arc does *not* indicate a flow of information between DP and DP1. The entire group of definitional arcs departing from DP describes the various ways in which Divisional Planning can be performed. Recognition of a divisional planning problem confronting the organization results in DP being played by DP1, DP2, . . . , or DPK.

As the foregoing example suggests, a role can be defined (filled) in no more than one way with respect to a particular context. Taking a theatrical analogue, a role cannot be cast in more than one way for a particular performance, although the casting may change from one performance (context) to the next. Definitional relationships by themselves are clearly inadequate for representing the nature of organizational decision making. They do not account for the passage of information between roles involved in a particular decision process. Such relationships, therefore, do not address the issue of interaction among roles, as in the case of group activities. This nondefinitional type of relationship between roles is represented by the aforementioned associative construct.

2.12.2   Associative Relationships

It must be emphasized that, unlike a definitional relationship, an associative relationship involves a passage of information between two roles. One role, in order to execute its information-processing task, may need the assistance of other roles. The relationship between the assisted role and a role that provides assistance (an assisting role) is termed *associative*. The association consists of a transferral of information from an assisting role to an assisted role.

Assistance is given according to the needs of the assisted role. That is, the assisted role controls the initiation and sequencing of information transferrals. Furthermore, the assisted role gives the assumptions under which an assisting role is to operate in its attempt to provide the needed information. The role being assisted also has control over how to use the information it receives from other roles. The particular character of the information received may affect subsequent initiation and sequencing of information transferrals, as well as the set of assumptions under which assisting roles must operate.

Roles differ not only according to their specific information-processing tasks but also according to the structuredness of control that they exhibit. Where control is highly structured, an algorithm can be written depicting all sequencing of requests for assistance and depicting the assumptions that accompany each request. When control is highly unstructured such algorithms cannot be written. We can only indicate which roles are available to provide assistance. The manner in which these assisting roles are controlled in order to solve the problem of the assisted role is unknown *a priori* (recall the discussion in Section 1.12).

Some assisted roles may be interpreted as being persons (or programs) that request information from other roles in order to solve their problems. Programs are examples of highly structured roles, whereas the information processing performed by a person may or may not be highly structured. To the extent that unstructuredness enters, the information processing is called creative or intuitive. Other assisted roles may be interpreted as "group" processes, where the "group" process may involve persons and/or mechanisms.

The group is not a mere sum of individual problem solvers, but in the course of solving its problem, the group utilizes individual problem solvers in its own particular way. It is this particular method of utilization (specifying the nature of the group's information processing), along with the problem being attacked, that defines the group. A group may be viewed as a multiargument function with individual (or other group) processors as its arguments. Participation in a group problem-solving process is akin to the associative connections between an assisted role (group) and assisting roles (other groups, persons, or mechanisms).

The group process may be highly structured or relatively unstructured. In the former case the group process consists of rigid, well-defined, formal procedures that control the participation of assisting roles. In the latter case, procedures are informal, are not well defined, and may be spontaneous; the assisted role's control over assisting roles manifests through the use of associative connections to solve the assisted role's problem. In other words, the nature of interaction among assisting roles is not known (a priori), but the interaction is governed by the problem to be solved.

Associative connections are pictorially represented by arcs emanating from the node of the assisted role to the nodes of the assisting roles; associative arcs are joined by a semicircle. In Fig. 2.1, for instance, the role Planner 1 (P1) receives assistance from Expert 1 (E1), Expert 2 (E2), and Expert 3 (E3) in the course of solving its problem. Observe that Planner 1 (P1), Planner 2 (P2), . . . , Planner N (PN) are capable of filling the role of Division 1 Planning (DP1). Similarly, E1, E2, . . . , EM are experts capable of filling the role of Staff Support (SS).

The only flows of information shown here are between the first three experts and the first planner. More complex communication patterns may exist among the roles. One planner, for instance, may make requests on other planners. Specialist E6 may need assistance from E8. There may also be recursion such as E8 assisting E6 and being assisted by E9, where E9 needs the assistance of E6. Each of the experts could, of course, be a role that is capable of being filled by other roles.

2.13   Representation of Human—Machine
Information-Processing Systems

A conceptual framework, consisting of the simple constructs, furnishes quite a flexible tool for describing the patterns of information processing in an organization. A given pattern may be implemented in a variety of ways, depending on the desired human–machine mix at the most concrete role levels. Notice that an organizational pattern indicates not only the passage of messages between roles, but also the structure of control *among* roles (i.e., which role controls which other roles). However, this descriptive technique says nothing about the previously noted control mechanisms *within* a role that govern the sequencing and conditioning of message passing.

In the passage of messages it is necessary to have a means for translating the information that one role is attempting to convey into a form that is comprehensible to the other role. Otherwise there is misunderstanding or nonunderstanding. This translation issue is not incorporated into the modeling technique shown in Fig. 2.1. If both roles have the same "world view" and the same terminology, then the translation problem is trivial. If their views and terminology differ (e.g., a local view versus a more global view), then the issue of mapping information from one to the other becomes important. The study of languages for passing messages between human roles and machine roles is very important from the standpoint of designing computerized decision support systems.

Thus far we have a framework for representing the patterns of control and information flow among roles (e.g., experts) in an organization. Suppose that we have a means for automating the information processing performed by the various experts. Remember that this information processing includes the sequencing of requests for information, the specification of assumptions within each request, and the transformation or manipulation of available information. If this processing is automated for each of a sizable number of roles, a question arises concerning how to coordinate (manage) these automated roles. In particular, can we computerize this coordination activity such that, in response to a problem statement, the problem is automatically solved?

If the answer is affirmative then we have a joint human–computer decision-making (e.g., planning) system in which the human instigates the decision-making process and in which the computer supports the process by furnishing pertinent information. Since the computer manages a network of "experts" or "specialists," it may be viewed as a sort of collective expert with which the human user can interact in the effort to make a decision. The user would have no need to interact directly with the more specialized experts (i.e., with specific computer programs); this is handled by the collective expert which is a decision support system.

Unstructuredness is accommodated (1) in the nature of and sequencing of requests made on the decision support system; (2) in the manner in which decision support system responses are utilized; and (3) in the decision support system's recognition of alternative methods for satisfying a given request. Note that it is conceivable (recall Section 1.12) to have a mixed system of programmed experts and experts who are not programs but who must be consulted by the system in the course of problem solving.

Thus there are two varieties of unstructuredness in the joint human–computer decision-making system. One variety is addressed by the system's user (see items 1 and 2 above). The other is treated by the decision support system. This second variety of unstructuredness derives from the existence of alternative methods for solving a problem (as suggested by definitional relationships among information-processing roles). In completely structured problems there is only a single alternative way for finding a solution.

Structured problems are routine and repetitive precisely because they are unambiguous (because each such problem has a single solution method). A less structured problem has more alternative solution methods, and the solutions given by these methods may not be equivalent. A "completely" unstructured problem has unknown solution methods or too many solution methods to evaluate effectively.

Our discussion of this framework for representing the division of information-processing labor in organizations closes with indications of a few of the ways in which it impinges on the upcoming investigation of decision support systems. In later chapters it will become apparent that there is a direct correspondence between this framework for representing the division of labor in organizations and a problem-solving method in classical artificial intelligence. There is also a correspondence between the framework's definitional and associative constructs, on the one hand, and data base management techniques for data organization, on the other.

2.20 ABILITIES REQUIRED FOR DECISION MAKING

The second major conceptual framework introduced in this chapter identifies the basic abilities needed in order to make a decision. A human–machine system that can be said to make decisions possesses these abilities. It is of interest to notice which of these abilities are exercised by the human elements of a system and which are left with the machine part. A more detailed examination of these abilities appears in Holsapple and Moskowitz [9].

Decision support systems may be compared and contrasted in terms of those abilities that they possess. The decision support system can be viewed as emulating (in some degree) human cognitive abilities. Those abilities that it does not possess must lie with the system's user (i.e., the decision maker). Taken together, the decision support system and its user constitute a decision-making system.

It cannot be emphasized too strongly that we are *not* proposing a paradigm for how decisions are made, but rather a framework that can be used to construct or describe models about how decisions are made.

Although this distinction may seem subtle, it must be kept in mind if the ensuing discussion is to be fully understood.

It has been argued [2] that frameworks of decision making may be classified as taking either a process approach or a content approach. The former is concerned with phases or stages of decision making and the latter deals with characteristics of resultant decisions or the nature of the decision maker. Although the framework introduced in this chapter falls into the second category, it may be used to study or construct paradigms of decision processes. That is, it offers a different, but complementary, perspective to process frameworks. A discussion of the many proposed process frameworks is beyond the present scope; some representatives are found in March and Simon [10], Miller *et al.* [11], Simon [13], and Soelberg [14].

2.21 First Postulate

The central postulate is that decision making has three basic aspects: *power, perception,* and *design*. These three are basic in the sense that none of them can be expressed in terms of the other two. Power refers to directive force, the ability to govern and to eliminate that which is unresponsive. Perception includes vision and insight; it is the ability to observe, to gather information. Design refers to the ability to formulate (e.g., to formulate models).

In order to preserve the generality of the framework, these facets are not more tightly defined. The definitions may, of course, be narrowed with respect to a particular decision maker. With regard to power, for instance, this narrowing could specify which organizational components (e.g., persons, machines) hold power, the kinds of power held [6], etc. Examples of ways for narrowing the definition of perception to a specific context are given in Bergen [3], and Zalind and Costello [16]. One way to narrow the design facet is to consider models to be algorithms. Depending on the way in which it is used, an algorithm is one of two types. Some algorithms are used primarily to guide the processing of gathered information, resulting in some new information or facts. Models of this sort were discussed in Sections 1.11 and 1.12. Other algorithms are primarily guides for action, indicating how to use available powers, and resulting in some new state of nature. Another approach for tying the design facet to a particular context is to view design as the building of an "image," in the sense of Boulding [5].

2.22   Second Postulate

A second postulate maintains that the existence of the three basic facets implies the existence of four additional facets, each of which may be described by a unique subset of the original three. These four additional facets will be called *analysis, idealism, implementation,* and *adaptation.*

Analysis.   Consider the subset (of the original three) consisting of perception and design. The existence of these abilities of information collection and design suggests the potential for another ability which mediates them. We shall refer to this ability as analysis and define it as the continuing adjustment between perceptions and formulations, between gathered information and models for processing information. This adjustment (or interfacing) results in beliefs, knowledge, or expectations.

An example of narrowing this definition of analysis will be seen in Chapter 3, where analysis consists of the automated interfacing of computer programs (models) with computer-collected information in order to produce some "facts" or expectations.

Idealism.   Idealism is devotion to (or promotion of) an ideal, the ability to hold a vision in sight during the application of power, such that that vision may be forced into reality; it is therefore a continuing adjustment between power and perception. Idealism, as it is used here, may also be considered as the ability to evaluate. For given some set of values (standards, utilities, preferences, attitudes, etc.), evaluation is essentially the act of promoting that set of values.

Observe that the notion of evaluation or idealism may be narrowed by considering the set of values or ideals to be hierarchic [4], by establishing a specific interpretation of values or ideals that is appropriate to the context at hand, or by using interpretations such as those found in Alexis and Wilson [1], England [7], and Guth and Tagiuri [8].

In general, the existence of the power and perception facets (exclusive of the design facet) implies the existence of the idealism–evaluation facet. As such, values (ideals) are based on available information and available powers. That is, if there is no information about X, it is meaningless to speak of the value of X; similarly, if there is no power with respect to X, then it is irrelevant to speak of the value of X.

Implementation.   The term "implementation" means the execution of a plan (a model or algorithm for action) via issuance of directives. It involves the imposition of some rhythm or coordination on activity and the imposition of certain patterns on structure, all according to a plan. It is a continuing adjustment between the two basic facets of design and power. That is, the existence of these two facets (exclusive of the perception facet) suggests the potential for another facet that mediates them; given powers and a plan, there is the potential for implementation. This general notion of implementation is subject to being narrowed to fit a particular context; for example, it could be narrowed according to variables suggested in Trull [15].

Adaptation.   Finally, the ability termed adaptation may be described as a continuing adjustment among all three of the basic facets. Given conflicts in or alterations in the available powers, perceptions, and designs, adaptation refers to the struggle within the decision maker to create a viable equilibrium. Since this facet involves the mediation of the three basic facets, it also involves adjustments among the three facets that are pairwise derivatives of the three basic facets; in other words, the adaptation facet is the adjustment process among the other six facets.

With this in mind, the adaptation facet may be considered to constitute the core or kernel or essence of a decision-making system. It is the ability to recognize problems (disequilibriums) and resolve them. (Problem recognition should not be confused with the facet of perception, which is information collection.) This general notion of adaptation can be more narrowly defined only within specific contexts. Such definitions should identify the ways in which this facet utilizes (and is constrained by) the other six facets.

The Seven Abilities.   The relationships among these seven postulated facets of the decision maker may be visualized as illustrated in Fig. 2.2.

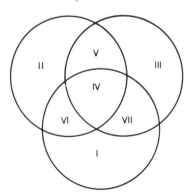

Fig. 2.2.   The seven facets of decision making. Three aspects of decision making (I, power; directive force. II, perception; information collection. III, design; formulation of models) and four attributes (IV, adaptation; continuing adjustment among the six other facets. V, analysis; continuing adjustment between perception and design. VI, idealism; continuing adjustment between power and perception. VII, implementation; continuing adjustment between plan and power).

The diagram is not to be taken as a Venn diagram. Each of the three circles may be considered to represent the sphere of expression of one of the three basic aspects. Each area of intersection is indicative of an attribute whose existence is implied by an interaction of (and hence an adjustment between) elements of a particular subset of the three basic aspects. For instance, analysis (V) is the adjustment between perceptions (II) and designs (III), e.g., the fitting of data to models and vice versa.

It is imperative to note that, with respect to a particular participant in a decision process (e.g., some human or machine), a prominent display of analysis does not necessarily imply prominence of the perception and design aspects, nor does a preponderance of the perception and design aspects necessarily imply outstanding analytical tendencies. A similar argument holds for the other three derived facets.

Another way of conceptualizing the relationships among the seven facets is that each of the three basic aspects fulfills a dual function. Power (I) provides the forces needed as a basis for the realization of ideals, values, or preferences (VI) and the forces needed as a basis for implementation (VII). Perception provides empirical information needed as a basis of valuation (VI) and as a basis of knowledge, beliefs, and expectations (V). Design (III) formulates models that provide a basis for implementation (VII) and a basis for analysis (V).

The adaptive factor (IV) involves the maintenance of an equilibrium among the other six factors and is effectively constrained by them. Adaptation may be considered to be a sequence of problem recognitions that, as a result of the activity of the other facets, tends toward a problem that is minimal; that is, the minimal problem consists of a single alternative.

2.23 Relationship to Decision Support Systems

If these postulates are accepted as portraying the important abilities used in decision making, then they furnish a framework for studying and designing computer-based systems for providing decision support. That is, which of these human abilities are performed by a given DSS, to what degree is it performed, and what computer-based techniques are used to emulate each of these human abilities? Another primary question is how do a given DSS's abilities interact with each other? For instance, does model formulation precede, accompany, or follow problem recognition? Depending on the answers to such questions, we can distinguish among decision support systems. The number of abilities incorporated into the machine part of a human–machine system, along with the degree of each, may be taken as a rough measure of the decision support system's (artificial) intelligence.

We say that the computer-based system supports (rather than makes) decisions because some of the facets are not accounted for within it. For instance, the system may have no intrinsic power or authority; it has authority only in proportion to the weight that the decision maker attaches to its activities. For each of the abilities, the machine participates in the joint human–computer decision activity only to the extent that the ability can be formally expressed. For example, the facet of evaluation may involve some nonformalizable subjective processes.

In Fig. 2.3 the human decision maker is an information-processing role that requests and receives aid from another role, a computerized information processor. Recall from Section 2.13 the importance of languages for passing messages between two roles. The possible behaviors of the assisting (computer) role are determined by (1) the language, (2) the degree and mix of abilities possessed as software and, (3) the available information about the decision maker's problem domain. We shall refer to the system software of (2) as the problem processor.

A problem processor's information-collecting ability can potentially utilize two sources: a user (decision maker) via the language and/or stored knowledge (e.g., a data base). With respect to the first source, the perception ability involves accepting strings of symbols and converting them into a form that can be used in conjunction with the other abilities (e.g., problem recognition) of the processor. With respect to the other source of information, the perception ability consists largely of data base manage-

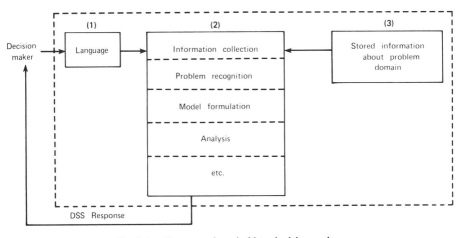

Fig. 2.3. Computer-based aid to decision maker.

ment techniques (i.e., the use of a data manipulation language as mentioned in Section 1.11).

In cases where the user's language is identical to a data manipulation language, the only ability possessed by the decision support system is that of information collection. Such a DSS is nothing more than a data base management system and all other abilities involved in decision making reside with the system's users. In such cases the degree of a DSS's information-collecting ability from a data base source is less than that of decision support systems whose users do not need to be as explicit in telling how to extract information from a data base. Systems of the latter type are able to do more on their own with respect to collecting information.

Whereas information collecting of some sort is essential to all decision support systems, the other abilities are not. Since the processing of information pervades all abilities involved in decision making, it is essential that in the very least a decision support system be able to collect information. Many different decision support systems can be devised by varying the abilities included and the degree of each. These are examined in more detail in subsequent chapters. For the moment we shall consider only a brief discussion of the inclusion of model formulation (III), and then problem recognition (IV), as DSS abilities.

Decision support systems may have the ability to construct models that can transform information. Remembering the discussion of Section 1.11, we can see that this ability is closely related to the task of management scientists. Just as in the case of the perception ability, the degree of a DSS's formulation ability is reflected in the nature of the language available to the system's user.

At one extreme the information collected by a DSS is an explicit statement of a model. The system's user performs a very large share of the model design, if not the entire formulation. At the other extreme one can imagine decision support systems whose model formulation abilities are developed to a point where the user's language conveys only the limits within which model building is to occur (e.g., desired kinds of outputs, what kinds of inputs the model should have, etc.). The DSS itself builds an algorithm on its own, without being explicitly told how to do so.

Note that in systems with highly developed formulation abilities and/or highly developed information collection abilities, where the user's language is less explicit, there is the possibility of ambiguity in a statement made by the user. That is, on converting the statement to an internally comprehensible form, the system may recognize that there are alternative ways (e.g., alternative models, alternative retrievals of information from a data base, etc.) to satisfy the user's request. These alternative ways may not give equivalent responses to the user.

If the DSS has some ability to recognize and deal with such problems, then we say that it has some problem recognition (IV) ability. The lowest degree of problem recognition involves a simple rejection of a user's statement with, perhaps, an explanation of the ambiguity it contains. A decision support system with more highly developed problem recognition abilities might attempt to remove the ambiguity on its own, based on its knowledge of the user and its knowledge of the problem domain.

Techniques for incorporating the various abilities into a decision support system are dealt with in Parts III through V. Until then the reader should remain aware of these abilities as we survey some representative decision support systems in Part II.

REFERENCES

1. M. Alexis and C. Z. Wilson, "Organizational Decision Making," p. 155. Prentice-Hall, Englewood Cliffs, New Jersey, 1967.
2. O. Behling and C. Shriesheim, "Organizational Behavior," p. 15. Allyn and Bacon, Boston, Massachusetts, 1976.
3. J. R. Bergen, The structure of perception, *J. Assoc. Study of Percept.* Spring (1969).
4. W. F. Bernthal, Value perspectives in management decisions, *Acad. Management J.* **5,** December (1962).
5. K. E. Boulding, "The Image," pp. 1–30. Univ. of Michigan Press, Ann Arbor, Michigan, 1956.
6. D. Emmet, The concept of power, *in* "Power" (J. R. Champlin, ed.), pp. 78–102. Atherton Press, New York, 1971.
7. G. W. England, Personal value systems of American managers, *Acad. Management J.* **10,** March (1967).
8. W. D. Guth and Tagiuri, Personal values and corporate strategy, *Harvard Business Review* October (1965).
9. C. W. Holsapple and H. Moskowitz, A conceptual framework for studying complex decision processes, *Policy Sci.* **12,** No. 1, June 1980.
10. J. G. March and H. A. Simon, "Organizations," p. 49. Wiley, New York, 1958.
11. G. A. Miller, E. Galanter, and K. H. Pribram, "Plans and the Structure of Behavior." Holt, New York, 1960.
12. J. Miller, Living systems: The organization, *Behavioral Sci.* **17,** January (1972).
13. H. A. Simon, "The New Science of Management Decision," Harper, pp. 1–8. New York, 1960.
14. P. O. Soelberg, Unprogrammed decision making, *Ind. Management Rev.* **8** (1967).
15. S. G. Trull, Some factors involved in determining total decision success, *Management Sci.* February, 270–280 (1966).
16. S. A. Zalind and T. W. Costello, Perception: Some recent research and implications for administration, *Administrative Sci. Q.* September (1962).

Part II

REPRESENTATIVE SYSTEMS FOR
DECISION SUPPORT

In this part of the book we descend from the global, enterprise perspectives of Part I and more closely scrutinize several representative computerized decision support systems. Part II consists of three chapters. The first of these surveys some typical systems that have been developed in or for businesses and these lead into a classification scheme for decision support systems. Chapter 4 commences with a generic view of decision support systems which will guide our study in the remainder of the book. This view is based upon concepts introduced in Chapter 2 and it may be thought of as a frame of reference for the study of decision support systems. Chapter 4 concludes with a survey of several systems which appear on the horizon of the decision support field, even though they do not all have a business orientation. All of these systems exhibit some degree of purposive behavior. Three approaches to formalizing purposive behavior are presented in Chapter 5. Current managerial decision support systems, such as those described in Chapter 3, are not designed on the basis of formal models of purposive behavior. In subsequent chapters we examine how to utilize aspects of these formal approaches in the design of generalized decision support systems, oriented toward managerial problem solving.

Chapter 3

REPRESENTATIVE DECISION SUPPORT SYSTEMS

3.00 SYSTEMS THAT INCLUDE MODELS

Two major areas of study in management or business schools are accounting and management science. The purpose of each is to provide a particular form of decision support. In accounting, emphasis is placed on supplying accurate, useful information to decision makers. As such, accounting is an important part (dealing mainly with financial information) of the information collection ability involved in organizational decision making.

As noted earlier, management science is an important part (dealing with formal algorithms) of the formulation ability involved in organizational decision making. A quick survey of the *Operations Research* and *Management Science* journals reveals an emphasis on this model-building aspect of decision support. Although these are the emphases, it should be clear that accounting is not uninterested in models, nor is management science unconcerned with data.

Having identified these two main sources of decision support, it is of interest to comment on their correspondence with the two primary uses of computers [7]:

(1) data storage and retrieval, and
(2) numerical computations.

The first is a means for implementing the accounting functions, although these functions were successfully applied long before the advent of the computer. On the other hand, dramatic increases in the computer's number crunching power have been a prerequisite to the successful practical utilization of many management science models requiring very large amounts of numerical computation.

Recent surveys [4, 8] have documented a marked growth in the use of corporate modeling in the past decade, and there is no reason to suspect that this trend is peculiar to the private sector. These models, which are used to aid planning activities, range from limited modeling to comprehensive modeling [8]. The development of computer-based modeling can be traced from an early stage characterized by a long communication chain between the decision maker and the computer, a concentration on operational control problems, and primitive data-handling methods.

Developments in the management science and information systems fields have led to the present recognition of the importance and feasibility of incorporating extensive data-handling capabilities and models into a single system with which decision makers can directly communicate. Thus the trend has been away from fragmented views of decision support (the accounting view versus the management science view) toward a workable integration of the two decision support functions of data handling and modeling. The system to be described in Section 3.05, for instance, involves both the supplying of financial information (directly to the user or to models) and the use of models within a single system.

With this background, we can proceed to summarize the salient aspects of several representative computer-based systems that have been developed to aid decision makers. An element that is common to the systems considered here is that all incorporate modeling capabilities in addition to more mundane data handling. For most the degree of model formulation is not particularly high. That is, the systems do not themselves formulate models, but they do make models available. Nevertheless, the inclusion of models into a system is but a step away from systems that formulate models on their own. Descriptions of the systems are ordered to reflect, roughly, increasing sophistication and flexibility.

3.01 Computer Support of Project Management

Computer support of project management is particularly applicable in cases where the project's actions and events are large in number and where there is simultaneous management of several projects. The decisions supported are those that must be made in the course of project management. The multitude of computer-based systems (see, for example

Archibald [1]) for supporting project management have as common elements (1) a data storage and handling system and (2) a model based on some PERT (Project Evaluation and Review Technique) method.

The data storage and handling is specifically oriented toward the treatment of the action–event networks that make up a project. The action–event planning model (e.g., Critical Path Method [1]) is tied to the data storage and handling mechanisms so that the latest project status may be input to it for analysis. (Recall the notion of analysis introduced in Section 2.22 as an interfacing of data and models.) Thus computer systems to assist project management are customarily highly specialized, addressing a very narrow aspect of corporate decision activities.

Because of the interdependent treatment of their data-handling elements and modeling elements these systems are often referred to as software packages. The packages fall into three categories [1], depending on the types of modeling they furnish. One category involves the scheduling and forecasting of resources. Another category aids in cost and resource control by contrasting estimated versus actual project progress and costs. A third category consists of models that use both scheduling information and cost information in performing analyses.

An enumeration of the capabilities of the more advanced software packages for supporting project management appears in Archibald [1]. Depending on a package's category, it can produce any of a predefined set of reports; that is, each category is characterized by a different set of report types. Many packages allow the user to specify a particular format in which one of the predefined reports is to appear. There are, for instance, different ways of presenting (e.g., sorting) an activity time status report. The user is also permitted to call for the conditional execution of a PERT model. For example, the user could indicate that a model is to be executed using only a certain part of an overall action–event network.

For the purposes of this book, the most important points concerning project management systems are the following:

(1)   the successful utilization of management science and computer science to implement a decision support system;

(2)   the very specialized nature of the resultant decision support system (i.e., the data and the model are used to support only one functional area of management); and

(3)   lack of a design aimed at sharing of its data with other models or at using its model as a module in tandem with other modules to give a model that is broader in scope.

The same three characteristics hold for other specialized decision support systems, such as material requirements planning systems (e.g., IBM [6]).

The model and data of these other specialized decision support systems differ, depending on the functional area being supported. The models of many such systems are the result of simulation logic developed by management scientists. For example, numerous simulation models have been devised to support decision making in the inventory control area.

The practicality and utility of specialized decision support systems within their own narrow domains cannot be argued. It must be realized, however, that higher-level (e.g., strategic) decision making often cuts across (or encompasses) various functional levels. Development of decision support systems for higher-level management could reasonably be expected to model across functional lines and to require data from various functional areas. This is precisely the trend that can be observed in the evolution of decision support systems, as is illustrated in the Potlatch and Banking systems to be described shortly.

The evolution of systems for information storage and retrieval has witnessed a progression from situations where information was stored in bits and pieces, in many places, and in many forms to increasingly unified, coordinated treatment of data. This trend from fragmentation to intergration in the treatment of factual knowledge has paralleled the rise of systems theory. The same can be said of the treatment of model knowledge (i.e., procedural knowledge).

Rather than myriad models, each dealing with a narrow functional area, there is a trend in management science and normative economics toward models that cut across functional areas and that encompass and coordinate model fragments. This is particularly apparent in the field of corporate planning [8].

Finally, the trend from fragmentation to integration can be noted in decision support systems. Instead of several independent, narrowly oriented decision support systems within an organization, the emerging pattern is one of decision support systems that can deal with a much broader domain of problems. Although these systems can cope with a much wider and more global class of problems, they are still specialized to the peculiarities of the type of organization within which they are used.

3.02 SPSS

Before examining representative decision support systems of the type intended for higher-level management, there is yet one more kind of system to be investigated. This is exemplified by the SPSS (Statistical Package for the Social Sciences) system [9].

The user of SPSS has at his or her disposal a collection of strictly independent models, any one of which may be invoked by the user stating its name. Each of these models, on execution, performs a particular type of statistical or econometric analysis. Data inputs to the invoked model are supplied from a file(s) of data that is maintained by the user. SPSS has no "built-in" data files. When stating which model is to be executed, the user must also indicate which data should be extracted from a file for use as input.

SPSS, as a system for decision support, differs in character from the project management, inventory management, or accounting systems in that it may be used to support decision making in many functional areas. Since it is not tied to a particular functional area, it may be viewed as a sort of "utility" decision support system. This support of many kinds of decision makers is directly attributable to the nature of and widespread applicability of statistical and econometric models.

3.03   The Case of Potlatch Forests, Inc.

The Potlatch system as it is described here is of 1970 vintage. A more extensive description may be found in Boulden and Buffa [3]. This interactive system was used to support planning activities of Potlatch. Architecturally, the system consists of a collection of data files and a large program that we shall refer to as the system program. Data files are categorized as being either application specific or nonspecific. Application-specific data files contain data that are pertinent to (and available to) this company only. More general types of information that could be used by other companies are entered in nonspecific data files. For instance, cost information is specific to the company, whereas data on national economic trends are not.

The system program serves as an interface between a corporate planner and the data files. A set of assumptions, stated by the corporate planner, serves as input to the system program, which proceeds to access data files in the process of generating some projections. These system program outputs or projections are returned to the planner so they can be factored into the planner's decision process.

A large portion of the system program consists of models (in the form of computer programs) of the Potlatch operations. On the basis of stated assumptions and stored data, the models can be executed to generate projections of the company's future position. Just as operations within the company are interrelated, so are the models. The entire set of interrelated models embedded within the system program results in the system's ability to generate many types of projection reports. (Recall the information-processing role structures of Chapter 2.) The types of reports that can be generated are determined by, and limited by, the models incorporated into the system program. Finally, the system program has facilities for the maintenance of data files.

The main value of this system is its capacity to support "What if?" types of questions posed by a planner. The precise nature or important elements of the language for posing these questions to the system program have not appeared in the literature [3]. The important points that this system illustrates are the following:

(1) the incorporation of models and data handling into a unified system;

(2) the interrelated nature of models mirroring the interrelated information-processing roles in an organization; and

(3) the importance of integrating the functions of management science and of computer science into a system to support decision making.

Other systems developed along the lines of the one described here are surveyed in Boulden and Buffa [2, 3].

3.04 A Decision Support System for Banks

A decision support system for banks is described [11] as having three primary subsystems: a data base, decision models, and a decision maker. The type of data base organization used is not described, but it must be designed to accommodate the bank's transactions as well as other internal and external data. The models available in this system may be categorized as supporting strategic planning, managerial control, or operational control. Modules of code called "model building blocks" are used by the system designers in constructing these models. Note that the models are constructed when the system is designed. They are not constructed by the DSS. The decision maker directs the system's operations with a "command language." This language plays a dual role of allowing the decision maker to retrieve data from the data base and to request that some model be executed.

The emphasis in this decision support system for banks is on the decision models. These models are integrated into a subsystem in which some models utilize other models. For instance, a strategic model could encompass the code of tactical models, but each tactical model can also be used on a stand-alone basis. Designers of this integrated decision model subsystem draw on a pool of "model building blocks" in the process of specifying and coding those decision models to be invoked by a decision maker. Examples of these building blocks include regression and linear programmning modules.

Each model available to the decision maker requires certain types of data files (i.e., reports) as inputs. These are extracted from the decision support data base. The description of this system does not have sufficient detail to determine precisely how a model directs the retrieval (i.e., information collection) process. The needed retrieval procedure may be explicitly specified within a model or the model might invoke reports (i.e., execute predefined special report generators) without specifying how they are to be generated. In the former case, the model code would depend on the data base organization. In the latter case, the model code would be independent of and invariant to the data base organization. All dependencies would be embedded in the special report generators. Yet another way of directing retrieval would be through retrieval statements to a general report generator that is independent of the particular data organization for a problem domain, depending only on the constructs used to define data organizations.

As stated earlier, the mechanism for integrating the various models is a philosophy of system design that realizes the plans for model interactions. The model linkages are specified in the guise of data flows, which indicate that an output report of one model serves as an input report to other models. As pointed out in Sprague and Watson [11], the process of actually coding the integrated system of models is no mean task. A model is viewed as a sequence of equations (assignments), each of which consists of a functional form, variables, and coefficients (determined during the model building stage). This sequence is easily represented in a computer programming language such as FORTRAN.

Values of some variables are supplied by the reports that are input to the model, whereas others are developed as functions of previously defined variables. Prior to coding, models are specified in terms of a "model definition language" that has a hierarchical format similar in appearance to a COBOL data division. Specification of a model in this language is intended as an aid to model documentation and modification.

This decision support system for banking was designed to encompass the various functional areas of management and to support decisions at all three levels of management. It is indicated [11] that the command language is simple enough to permit managers to direct the system's activities without reliance on intermediate staff. It is also stated that although the development and use of decision support systems is rapidly spreading, most are not as comprehensive as this decision support system for banking.

3.05   Decision Support Systems for Corporate Planning

We have noted the increasing development of formal models to assist corporate planning. Most of these models involve a financial simulation that allows the exploration of impacts of alternative plans. Development of a corporate model is, however, only one prerequisite to the effective usage of models in the planning process. Also important is the software support of the various interfaces involved. These include the user–model interface, the model–data interface, and the user–data interface (see Fig. 3.1). Furthermore, a modular approach to model development facilitates later extensions and modifications to the model.

For the purposes of this book, a module is a model that is capable of being used in some configuration with other modules in order to form a larger or more comprehensive model. That is, a module is always a model and a model may or may not be used as a module. The "model building blocks" alluded to in the banking case are examples of modules.

As a specific example, we shall now examine a computer-based decision system developed for Xerox corporate planning [10]. This system was founded on a philosophy that it is possible formally and theoretically to describe the management process, that the resultant models can be programmed, and that a combined "man–model–machine" system can be used to make better decisions than could be made without the support of management science and computer science.

The model design phase of system development involved the identifi-

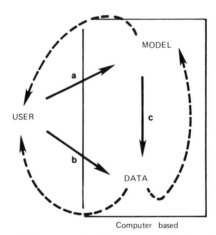

Computer based

Fig. 3.1.   Interfaces. (a) Language for directing computations, (b) language for directing retrieval, (c) language for directing retrieval.

cation and replication of existing decision processes as well as alternative processes specified by a manager. Just as in the Banking system, human elements (not the computer) are in charge of model formulation. The major results of this model design phase were (1) the new insights into their own operations acquired by those managers participating in the design process; (2) a variety of models, including both detailed models and aggregate models; (3) a preponderance of simulation models that more closely reflected managerial decision processes and that were more easily understood by managers than optimization models.

A modular approach to model development was used. A module is a small model that can be used on a stand-alone basis, or it can be used in conjunction with other modules, all of which are linked together in various ways to give more comprehensive models. Thus there is not a single planning model, but a collection of models that can be invoked to assist planning activities and that can change over time. Descriptions of specific models developed at Xerox appear in Seaberg and Seaberg [10].

The programmed models, along with an on-line data base, are the two major components of this computer-based decision support system. The data base contains data describing actual operations and financial performance. It also contains data concerning plans and forecasts that are generated by the execution of models. The precise nature of software for handling the model–data interface is not described in Seaberg and Seaberg [10]. However, it is indicated that data are "made accessible" to models in either of two ways. The first involves establishing the linkage between modules. That is, the output of one module (e.g., a forecast) is organized in a fashion that allows it to be directly read into "decision tables" (i.e., data files) that have been defined in another module (e.g., a simulation). Second, a user's invocation of a model can include assumptions under which that model is to be executed. These assumptions are either inserted into the model's decision tables prior to execution or entered into those tables during execution (presumably as the result of the model prompting the user for further data).

With respect to the user–data interface the user can retrieve data by either invoking a standard report generator or by using another method (the particulars of which are not specified in Seaberg and Seaberg [10]). As for the user–model interface, the decision maker directs the computational process by requesting that a particular model be executed. Information produced by that execution is stored such that it is immediately available to any other model that must use this information in order to execute. The user is required to specify the sequence of model executions desired. In effect, each model in the sequence is a module in the overall model specified by the user.

The observed advantages of this "man–model–machine" system vis-à-vis its predecessor (a manual system) are summarized as follows:

(1) drastic decrease in analyst time required for manipulating data (less than 10% versus 80% in the manual system) and a greater accuracy than was afforded by the more error-prone manual system;

(2) better-defined forecasting logic, eliminating nonstandardized forecasts that had resulted from an absence of universally accepted logic in the manual system;

(3) drastic reduction in the amount of time required to generate plans;

(4) internally consistent forecasts as opposed to the sometimes inconsistent forecasts that resulted from last-minute adjustments to a forecast in the face of severe time constraints imposed by the manual system; and

(5) an increase in the time available for more diligent, elaborate analyses.

A final word of caution regarding the "man–model–machine" system is in order. The models must be devised to support the particular managers who will be using them. That is, it is important that the managers have both motivation and some expertise in using models that are devised. Not only must there be the right "man" and the right "models" but there must be the right "machine" as well; that is, the interfacing software must be effective, flexible, and user oriented. The Xerox experience with this decision support system has suggested that the previously alluded to philosophy is sound, that the scientific method can be usefully applied to a business situation, and that the decision maker can play an integral role in the design, implementation, and execution of on-line corporate planning models.

3.06 Model Usage

Until recently the predominant style of using models developed by the management scientist has been *ad hoc* and fragmented. Sprague and Watson [12] have noted that models developed by the management scientist all too frequently fall into disuse. This is due not to a lack of mathematical validity but to insufficient attention given to data sources and to the utilization of a model's outputs. The focus has been on the model rather than on the overall decision processes that (potentially, at least) use it.

In particular, Sprague and Watson have observed that the principal problems are threefold. First, models are not easily combined; they are not developed as modules that could be combined to form other models as the need arises. Thus there is a lack of flexibility in dealing with new, unanticipated problems. Second, there is not an established data base that a model can use. Data must be repeatedly recollected and reorganized for each run of the model. A third problem is the difficulty in updating a model and in modifying the ways in which it can be used.

Sprague and Watson describe a new approach to handling data models, an approach that is beginning to be realized in practice (e.g., the Banking system, the Xerox system). This approach is characterized by easily accessible models, mechanisms that permit modules to be linked to form larger models, and the ability of models to draw the majority of their data needs from a data base. Given these broad objectives, an important research issue for workers in the decision support field involves the discovery of systematic, general, and conceptually sound methods for integrating models into information systems.

This issue is further developed in the ensuing chapters. For the moment we shall only list the design criteria for a decision support system, as proposed in Sprague and Watson [13]:

1. There must be a set of models (modules) to support decisions in a variety of functional areas and at a variety of managerial levels.

2. Models must be devised as modules that can either be used on a stand-alone basis or in conjunction with one another to form other, more expansive, models.

3. There must exist a mechanism whereby models can extract data from a data base. Thus a model is a "user" of the data base, which suggests that a model must have available to it some language with which it can direct information retrieval.

4. There must be a command language that allows convenient, direct access to the data base and that allows execution of available models.

5. The system must be flexible in terms of modifying the procedural knowledge inherent in the available models and in modifying the ways in which modules can be used. This facility permits the system's modeling capabilities to evolve.

Whereas it is frequently customary to view the model(s) as the focal point of decision support, the emerging perspective shifts the focus to the data base as the foundation for a decision support system. In this view the models may be considered to be users of a common data base where a given parcel of information may be used by several models. The decision maker is a user of both the models and the data base.

3.10   CLASSIFICATION SCHEME FOR DSS

The two major uses of computers are data handling and computation. An extremely important consideration in connection with these is the nature of the user's interface with the computer. In other words, how does a user govern the data handling (Fig. 3.1b) and how is computation (Fig. 3.1a) directed? As the foregoing cases suggest, examination of a decision support system should at least address the three topics of data management, computation management (modeling), and user's interface (i.e., user's language). In many systems these three are intertwined and interdependent. We can, however, speak of these topics independently in order to indicate the way in which each has evolved in the past quarter of a century.

The management of data has been greatly affected by developments in computer hardware. These include the development of secondary storage devices with increasing capacities and decreasing costs. It is thus practical to maintain large volumes of data that can be readily accessed. A consequent area of development has centered more on the content of data than on that of data volumes. This involves methods of data structuring that have capabilities of representing more complex interrelationships among various data items. Thus we have a progression from simple data structures, such as those used in lists, tables, and files, to the network structuring techniques that have arisen in the artificial intelligence and data base management fields. Until very recently, generalized data base management systems were available only on main frame computers (and some minicomputers). Such a system (MDBS by Micro Data Base Systems, Inc.) is now available on microcomputers for a small fraction of the cost of earlier data base management systems.

With respect to the topic of modeling we can observe a trend toward the development of increasingly complex or comprehensive models. Whereas early efforts dealt with modeling one or another particular problem area within an organization, present-day emphasis is on a coordinated modeling of several problem areas. This integration of models is necessary if support of high-level decision making is to be enhanced, since high-level decision making (e.g., planning activities) involves many problem areas. A current research trend in the management field aims at the discovery of formal techniques to aid planners [14].

It is useful to remember at this juncture that model development (and the trend toward integrated model development) lies within the province of the management scientist and operations researcher. In contrast, the topics of data management and user interface have developed largely within the broad domain of computer science. The model logic devised by the management scientist is then translated into computer code by programmers to yield operational models. From both fields there has been a recognition of the importance of modularity for integrated modeling.

We can speculate about the potential impacts of computer science on the development and use of integrated models. From the hardware angle, the advent of "computers on a chip" or "miniaturized computers" may foreshadow the creation of libraries of inexpensive, more efficient modules that can be logically organized or indexed in a variety of ways in order to specify a variety of models (each model being logically specified in terms of chips). From the software angle, the design of integrated models from a pool of modules may benefit from the development of languages particularly suited to such an activity.

Turning to the third topic, that of user interfaces with the computer, we can again observe the influence of hardware advances. In the early days, a manager's communication with the computer was typically indirect, being mediated by a staff that in turn submitted instructions in batch mode to the computer. With the appearance of user terminals and on-line computing, turn-around times were shortened. But it was the development in the software area that brought the computer closer to the manager. Specifically, methods for instructing the computer evolved from machine and assembly languages to the myriad programming languages and then onward to more user-oriented, higher-level languages.

Thus there appeared successively more powerful methods of automatic code generation (some of which are interactive), culminating in languages with which a nonprogrammer can communicate with the computer, software having taken the place of staff. The area of increasingly natural and facile interface languages is one of intense investigation. Some of these languages are highly structured to address a specific application. Others are less structured and more flexible with respect to the applications that can be addressed.

Recall that a person using a language to direct (or interact with) a computer does so with the objective of performing some computation and/or some data management. It is instructive to examine these two major uses of user languages. Initially, each is discussed separately. They can then be combined to provide a rough classification scheme that will guide our study of various types of decision support systems.

3.11   Languages to Direct Retrieval

First, consider languages used to direct data retrieval. These may be characterized as covering a range between the following two extremes. At one extreme are languages in which the user explicitly states how the data is to be retrieved. Languages at this extreme vary from those in which a knowledge of physical data organization is assumed to those that deal with logical data organization. At the other extreme are languages in which the user merely states the data desired; the user is not forced to know how the data is organized in the data base. Systems that process such languages must determine the logic of how to perform the retrieval. This may not always be straightforward, for the user's statement might be ambiguous with respect to the data available. Thus the system may exhibit some problem recognition ability. Determination of logic is followed by generation and execution of retrieval code. Languages at this end of the spectrum may be of an imperative or interrogative form.

Somewhere between the two extremes of data retrieval languages are those languages in which the user invokes one of a number of report generators. That is, the logic of how to produce each report has been worked out during the design of the language processor (information collection ability). The code to generate each report is an integral part of the language processor. Such languages may be flexible enough to allow conditional retrieval in the filling of a given report form, but the types of report forms producible are predefined to meet the anticipated needs of the users.

3.12 Languages to Direct Computation

We now shift attention to languages used to direct numerical computations. These too may be characterized as covering a range between two extremes. At one extreme are languages with which the user explicitly specifies all computations. That is, the user builds the programmed model. These languages vary from low-level (e.g., assembly) to higher-level (e.g., FORTRAN) programming languages. At the other extreme of computational languages are those wherein the user merely states the problem to be solved in terms of the data desired. Here the language-processing system must determine the model logic to be used. This may entail the formulation of model logic from more primitive modular logic. Once the model logic has been formulated the corresponding model code must be generated and executed.

Between these two extremes is a variety of languages that enable the user to invoke a model by name. Such languages allow the user to execute any one of some (possibly integrated) groups of already formulated, already programmed models. Certain options within some model may be selected by the user through parameters associated with the model name.

However, the models available are predefined to meet the anticipated needs of the users.

3.13   Retrieval and Computational Languages in a Single System

A remaining question concerns the ways in which data handling and modeling can be combined into a single system. One approach commences by noticing that one extreme of the range of data retrieval languages is beginning to look very much like the languages at one extreme of the range of computational languages. In languages of the former type the user "states the data desired." In languages of the latter type the user also states the problem to be solved in terms of "the data desired."

There is little, if any, difference in statements in these two types of the languages themselves. What is different is that a computational model is evoked by statements in one type of language, whereas a data retrieval procedure is evoked by statements in the other type of language. Thus there are several distinct ways in which systems could respond to a user's request for some data (i.e., some report):

1. The system could be designed to contain, in an explicit form, all reports that could be requested. Response time would be very fast, but storage requirements are potentially quite vast.

2. The system could be designed to extract a desired report from a data base that explicitly contains all data to be used in that report (although not in the report format). This might be termed a virtual report. Here redundancy is reduced via data base techniques but response time is increased.

3. The system could be designed to generate a desired report from a data base that may explicitly contain some data to be used in that report and set of axioms (rules) that indicates how to infer other items that must appear in the report. The inclusion of axioms in the more traditional data base effectively gives a virtual data base from which reports may be extracted. Thus the system can determine what is implied by the data base, in addition to what it contains.

4. The system could be designed to produce the desired data by executing (and perhaps building) an appropriate model that utilizes data extracted or generated from a data base (as in the preceding items through 3).

A rough indication of possible approaches to the design of systems with embedded models is presented pictorially in Fig. 3.2. The horizontal

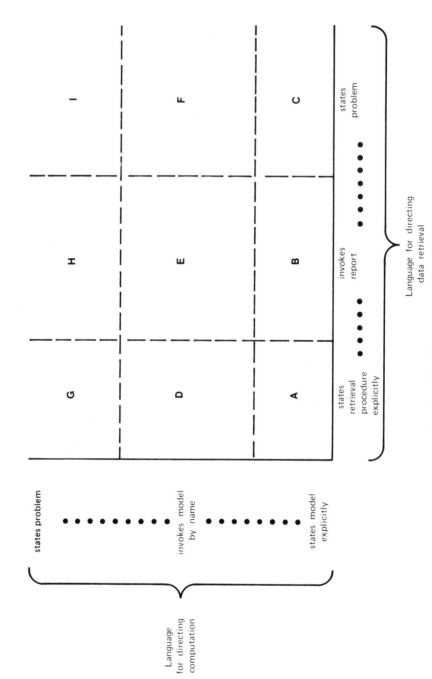

Fig. 3.2. Classification scheme.

axis represents the range of data retrieval languages. The range of languages for directing computations is represented by the vertical axis.

For purposes of explanation the quadrant of Fig. 3.2 has been partitioned into nine sections. We will describe the nature of systems in each of these nine categories. The reader must be careful to realize that the lines separating these categories are somewhat fuzzy. Also there can be fairly large differences among systems within a category.

This categorization is not a comprehensive indicator of all differences among all systems that incorporate models, nor is it a normative categorization. It is descriptive in nature, suggesting various ways in which the two primary uses of computers (data handling and computations) can be incorporated into a single system for the purpose of supporting decision activities. Some systems discussed in the literature are not described in sufficient detail to allow any more than a rough plot on the diagram of Fig. 3.2. Most of the systems described earlier in this chapter fall around the fringes of the central category.

As we examine the archetypal attributes of each category it is important to remember that we are considering only systems that execute models in addition to data retrieval (be it strict retrieval or the result of inference). Systems that do not involve the execution of application models but that deal with retrieval only are briefly discussed later.

Systems falling in category A require the user to specify explicitly the computational algorithm. The procedure for retrieving data required in the model must also be explicitly stated. A typical sort of system that falls into this category consists of a programming language, its associated compiler, and a data base. The system's user directs both the computations and data retrieval via the programming language. Depending on the nature of the data base some portion of the data retrieval procedure may need to be stated in a job control language.

As an example consider the FORTRAN programming language. The user directs the desired computation by specifying the needed algorithmic steps. If a library of modules (e.g., functions, subroutines) is available for this model construction process, then the system tends to appear higher in category A than systems without such libraries. The availability of such modules means that there are submodels that the user can invoke by name. However, the user is still required to indicate steps that constitute the overall model being built.

As for data retrieval methods, these depend on the nature of the data base being accessed. In order to obtain data required in the computational processes it may be necessary to read, sort, merge, and extract from files. Where these are available as utility procedures in the language, the system is farther to the right in category A than those systems where the user must program the sort, merge, or extraction. If an integrated data base is accessed rather than a collection of files, the user typically has available a group of commands for the manipulation of data in this data base. A system of this sort effectively extends the data-handling portion of the FORTRAN language, so that a user can specify a procedure for retrieval from an integrated data base.

Languages in category A run the gamut from the machine and assembly levels to high-level procedural languages. The most common in business applications are FORTRAN, COBOL, and PL/1. The workings of

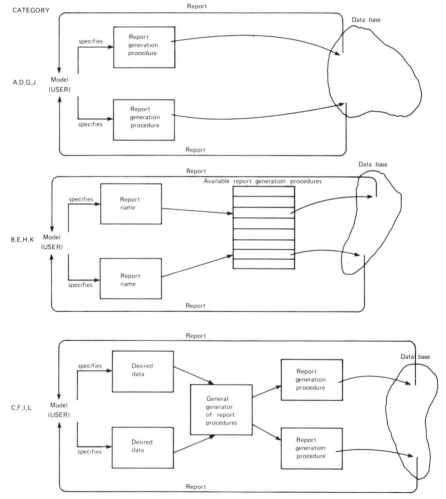

Fig. 3.3. Approaches to directing retrieval.

systems in category A may be visualized by joining the top of Fig. 3.3 onto
the right of the top of Fig. 3.4. For category A, the model at the top of Fig.
3.3 is identical to the model at the top of Fig. 3.4.

Systems in category B differ from those in A in that data are accessed
by invoking a report (middle of Fig. 3.3 with top of Fig. 3.4). Rather than
specifying how a particular set of data is to be retrieved for use by the
model, the report is automatically generated. Consider, for example, the
extended FORTRAN language that allows integrated data base access.
The systems with this language could be moved from category A to B if all
pertinent procedures for retrieval are preprogrammed and made available
via subroutine calls. This approach is useful in cases where types of
reports that are needed are small in number and fairly stable. The number
of models that need the data of one or more of these reports may be
relatively large. The approach is limited since the need for a report that

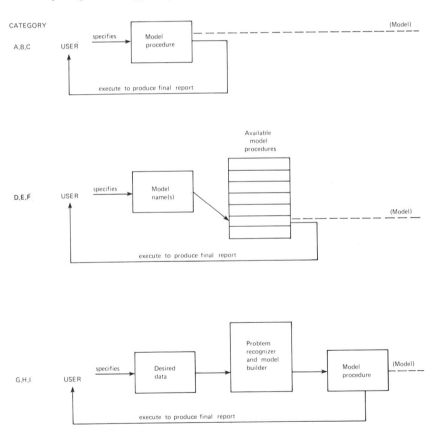

Fig. 3.4. Approaches to directing computations.

differs from those producible by the predefined retrieval subroutine necessitates a return to category A (if possible).

Systems in category C eliminate the need for reliance on a predefined group of report generators. At the same time they maintain the flexibility of report generation offered in category A, but without resorting to procedural specification of retrieval processes. Such systems are able automatically to generate code needed for retrieval, in response to a statement of what data are desired. Thus when the model requires some report, a statement of the data that should appear in that report suffices. There is no invocation of a special predefined report generating code, nor is there an explicit statement of how to produce the report. Such systems are especially useful where the types of reports needed by the various models being constructed are unstable, large in number, or unknown in advance of modeling. Rather than a group of special report generators, there is a single general report generation mechanism.

Note that the distinctions among categories A through C are in terms of the methods available for directing data retrieval (top, middle, and bottom of Fig. 3.3) when the model is explicitly stated (top of Fig. 3.4). The same kind of distinctions hold for categories D, E, and F. In these categories, however, computation is not directed by explicitly stating procedures (see middle of Fig. 3.4). Systems in category D enable the user to direct computations by stating a model's name, and this model obtains needed data by explicitly specifying retrieval procedures. For instance, the user may invoke a simulation model by name, where the model code contains a procedural description of how to retrieve the data it requires.

In category E the invoked model acquires needed data by naming reports. Compared to that of category D, the data retrieval language for E is less complex. This is useful in situations where reports needed by the various models are static and few in number. Unlike category D, the retrieval procedures are not intertwined with computational procedures. A predefined group of report types can be produced and each of these specialized report generators has been preprogrammed. Notice that several models may invoke the same report generator and that each model might call for several specialized reports.

In the crack between categories D and E are those systems where specialized report generators are invoked but where a resultant report contains more data than a given model needs. In such systems the model explicitly specifies how to strip out data it needs from the reports presented to it. Although the specialized report generators produce excess data, they do reduce the data-handling problem. Thus the problem becomes one of how to pluck needed data from a few reports, rather than how to extract it from the entire body of available data.

An invoked model in systems of category F retrieves data via a language that merely states what data are desired. The processor of such a language may be viewed as a generalized report generator. Given a statement (possibly conditional) of data types, it determines the logic for producing that report and proceeds to generate the code required to execute that retrieval logic.

In each of categories D–F the model may be thought of as the "user" of a language for directing data retrieval. These languages range from the procedural and flexible (D) to the nonprocedural and inflexible (E) to the nonprocedural and flexible (F). Notice that the languages available to the user for model management in these three categories are less procedural and comparatively specialized or inflexible *vis-à-vis* those of categories A–C.

This inflexibility of model management is reduced in systems of categories G–I. Here the user states a problem in terms of the data desired. On the basis of this statement the system must determine a model (and generate its code) that can produce the desired data. The distinguishing characteristic among categories G, H, and I is the nature of the language used by an inferred model to accomplish data retrieval. If the model code is punctuated with procedural specifications for data retrieval, then the system falls into category G. If the model collects data by invoking one or more of a predefined group of specialized report generators, then the system is in category H. A system in which inferred models access the data base via statements of data types required would be in category I.

Figure 3.5 gives a rough plot, showing where systems of the sorts discussed earlier fall in the classification scheme. Note that the state of the art in decision support has tended to move diagonally toward the "northeast." Present-day systems are in or around the fringes of category E, whereas the earlier use of models was centered in category A.

3.14   A Special Case

A related but special case of the system types depicted in Fig. 3.2 involves those systems that deal exclusively with retrieval. Since these systems are not concerned with analytical models, they involve no notion of a language for directing computation; they are not represented on the vertical axis in Fig. 3.2. We can, however, classify these systems as shown in Fig. 3.6.

Unless otherwise indicated, the term "retrieval" is used in a broad sense, meaning the extraction of data from some body of knowledge without intervening numerical computation. It involves the ability to collect

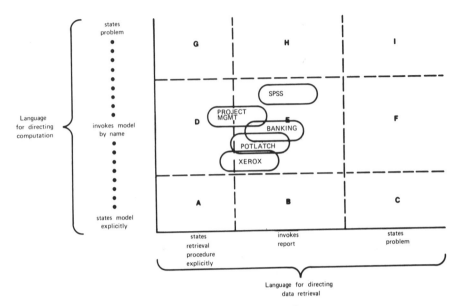

Fig. 3.5.　Decision support system placements.

information needed by a system's user or by the system itself. The extraction may be a withdrawal of data explicitly represented in the body of knowledge or it may be a determination of data that is logically implicit in the body of knowledge. The nature of retrieval is closely related to the method chosen to represent a body of knowledge. Knowledge representation methods are discussed in Part III.

In systems of category J the user must state how the retrieval is to be

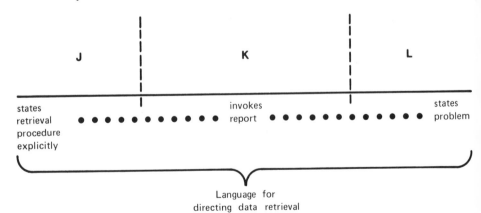

Fig. 3.6.　Classification scheme for retrieval only.

accomplished. If the user is able to acquire any of a group of predefined report types by simply giving its name, then the system falls into category K. Category L consists of systems that enable a user merely to state the data desired; the system then automatically generates the code required to produce the report. In category J the user writes the report generator. In category K the report generator has already been written and is executed when invoked by a user. In category L the system automatically writes a report generator to retrieve data of the types specified by a user.

We have thus considered the horizontal axis of Fig. 3.2 in isolation. Possible systems that involve modeling but that possess no data-handling capabilities are of no interest here. Practical application of a model demands data-handling facilities. Remember that in Section 2.23 we considered an information collection ability as essential to all decision support systems. Even though we shall not consider the vertical axis of Fig. 3.2 in isolation, there is an interesting correspondence between the three rows of categories in Fig. 3.2 and the three categories of strictly retrieval systems described in the preceding paragraph. In categories A, B, and C the user writes out the model in coded form. In categories D, E, and F the model(s) has already been built and is executed when invoked by a user. In the last category row of Fig. 3.2 the system automatically builds a model to retrieve data of the types specified by a user. Compare these descriptions of the preceding paragraph. Also compare Fig. 3.3 with Fig. 3.4.

3.20 CONCLUSION

This chapter began with overviews of some representative decision support systems developed in or used by the business community. An important trait common to all of these is their integration of models with information-handling capabilities. The significance of the user's interface with these systems has become increasingly apparent. With the exception of SPSS, the user's language allows a user to direct retrieval activities and computational activities. Moreover, we saw that models themselves access the data bases of these systems, implying that the model is a user of the system's information-collecting abilities.

This led to a classification scheme for decision support systems in which humans used some sort of language to direct computations and the computational model, in turn, used a language to obtain needed data from the system's data base. The old usage of models (familiar to all who have taken a programming language course) described at the beginning of Section 3.06 falls primarily into category A. The newer usage of models, often in conjunction with integrated data bases and exemplified by the representative systems discussed earlier, falls mainly into category E. If the reader refers to the original literature on these systems, it will be found that there is insufficient detail to determine the precise placement of these systems with respect to each other in Fig. 3.2. However, we can say that they fall largely into category E, and possibly into category D.

In Chapter 4 we consider systems that lie in other categories. Although most of them do not stem from business contexts, they are useful in pointing out directions for future development of business-related decision support systems. Furthermore, presently the empty categories of the classification scheme suggest directions in which the prevalent notions of decision support systems (category E) can be expanded. Such expansions are addressed in Part V of this book.

REFERENCES

1. R. D. Archibald, "Managing High-Technology Programs and Projects," pp. 204–215. Wiley, New York, 1976.
2. J. B. Boulden and E. S. Buffa, A systems approach to corporate modeling, *J. Syst. Management* **24,** No. 6 (1973).
3. J. B. Boulden and E. S. Buffa, Corporate Models: On-line, Realtime systems, *Harvard Business Review* July–August (1970).
4. G. W. Gershefski, Corporate models—The state of the art, *Management Sci.* **16,** No. 6 (1970).
5. B. J. Hansen, Practical PERT, pp. 142–149. America House, Washington, D.C. (1965).
6. IBM, Wholesale IMPACT—Advanced Principles and Implementation Reference Manual, GE 20-0174-1, IBM, White Plains, New York (April 1971).
7. J. P. C. Kleijnen, Computers and operations research: A survey, *Comput. Operat. Res.* **3** (1976).
8. T. H. Naylor and H. Schauland, A survey of users of corporate planning models, *Management Sci.* **22,** No. 9 (1976).
9. N. H. Nie *et al.,* "Statistical Package for the Social Sciences," 2nd ed. McGraw Hill, New York, 1975.
10. R. A. Seaberg and C. Seaberg, Computer based decision systems in Xerox corporate planning, *Management Sci.* **20,** No. 4 (1973).
11. R. H. Sprague, Jr. and H. J. Watson, A decision support system for banks, *OMEGA,* **4,** No. 6 (1976).
12. R. H. Sprague, Jr. and H. J. Watson, MIS Concepts—Part I, *J. Syst. Management* **26,** No. 1 (1975).
13. R. H. Sprague, Jr. and H. J. Watson, MIS Concepts—Part II, *J. Syst. Management* **26,** No. 2 (1975).
14. R. F. Vancil (ed.), Formal Planning Systems, Harvard Business School (1971).

Chapter 4

NEW IDEAS IN DECISION SUPPORT

4.00 GENERIC DESCRIPTIONS FOR DECISION SUPPORT SYSTEMS

This chapter commences with a formal, generic description of decision support systems that will guide the remainder of our study. This description stems from the earlier decision-making framework of Chapter 2 and from the classification scheme of Chapter 3. The generic description views a DSS as having three principal components: a language system (LS), a knowledge system (KS), and a problem-processing system (PPS). Chapter 4 closes with an examination of several computer-based systems that adhere to the generic DSS description. However, most of these systems are not business oriented and some do not lie within the prevalent category E.

4.01 Language System

The previous chapter surveyed systems that have models incorporated into them. Even though the descriptions of such systems in the literature typically pay but scant attention to the languages used to direct retrieval and computation, such languages were emphasized in the Xerox case

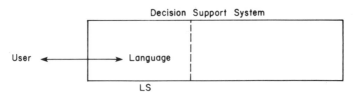

Fig. 4.1.   User interface with decision support system.

(review Fig. 3.1). This served as the basis for a classification scheme that stressed the distinction between languages for retrieval and languages for directing computation. We saw that languages for retrieval could be utilized by either the human user (see Figs. 3.1b and 3.5) or a model (see Figs. 3.1c and 3.2). Languages for directing computation were presented from the standpoint of being used by the human elements of a decision-making system (see Figs. 3.1a and 3.2). However, it is certainly imaginable that one mechanical DSS could direct another mechanical DSS; for the present we shall ignore this possibility.

We shall refer to the language system (LS) as the total of all linguistic facilities made available to the decision maker by a decision support system (see Fig. 4.1). A language system may encompass either or both retrieval languages (categories J, K, or L) and computational languages (the three rows of Fig. 3.2). A language system is not concerned with the interfacing of models and data. That is, it is not concerned with the columns of Fig. 3.2 or with the interface (c) in Fig. 3.1. It deals only with interfaces (a) and (b) in Fig. 3.1. Remember that a user's interface language can be so designed that the user is unaware of whether he or she is directing a retrieval or a modeling process (e.g., categories G, H, I, or L).

A language system is characterized by the syntax that it furnishes to the decision maker, by the statements, commands, or expressions that it allows the user to make. Thus a language system is a vehicle that allows the decision maker to express himself, but at the same time it limits the permissible expressions. We say that an LS is a vehicle in that it is a mode of conveyance not of material, but of information.

4.02   Knowledge System

Unless it contains some knowledge about the decision maker's problem domain, a decision support system is likely to be of little practical value. Indeed, a good deal of the power of a decision support system derives from its knowledgeability about a problem domain (e.g., banking). This knowledge typically includes large volumes of facts that the decision

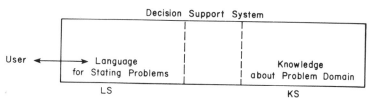

Fig. 4.2. Language and knowledge aspects of decision support system.

maker has neither the time, nor the inclination, nor the opportunity to absorb into his own memory. However, certain subsets of this volume of facts are important to a reasonable or good decision in the face of a particular problem from the problem domain.

We shall refer to a decision support system's body of knowledge about a problem domain as its knowledge system (KS) (see Fig. 4.2). In the systems described in the preceding chapter, the KS consisted of what were termed data files or data bases. In the original descriptions of such systems in the literature the precise nature of their knowledge systems typically is left unexplained. That they possess some sort of KS is unmistakable, and sometimes the kinds of data held in the KS are detailed. But the crucial issue of how these data are organized is left unaddressed, perhaps because of space limits.

Knowledge represented in a KS must be retained in an organized, systematic manner. There are a variety of knowledge representation methods, the most prominent of which are examined in later chapters. The knowledge representation method utilized by a particular knowledge system may be thought of as a set of rules according to which knowledge is expressed for purposes of retention within the decision support system.

4.03 Problem-Processing System

The main function of a decision support system is to take strings of symbols organized according to LS syntax (problems) and to take strings of symbols organized according to KS representation rules (problem domain knowledge) and to produce information that supports (enhances or makes possible) a decision process. To do so there must be an interfacing mechanism between expressions of knowledge in the KS and expressions of problems in the LS. We refer to this interfacing mechanism as the problem processor or the problem-processing system (PPS).

Figure 4.3 provides a bird's-eye view of the generic description of decision support systems. It is the PPS that has one or more of the seven abilities required for decision making. Thus Fig. 4.3 is actually a simplified version of Fig. 2.3.

Examinations of the KS and PPS are considerably more lengthy than that of the LS. This reflects the previously noted trends toward providing simple, easy-to-use high-level languages for the decision maker (Section 1.23.2) and toward integrated representation of increasingly complex kinds of knowledge (Section 1.22.1). The simplicity of language typically belies a relatively more complex translation procedure on the part of the PPS, which must "understand" the decision maker's statements. Moreover, increases in the complexity and kinds of knowledge that can be represented in KS can be accompanied by increases in the scope of abilities the PPS possesses.

4.04   Decision Support Systems: Human and Computer

Referring to Fig. 4.3, a close analogy may be drawn between a computer-based decision support system and a human-based decision support system. The former is implemented with a computer, whereas the latter is implemented with staff personnel or human consultants. In each instance, however, the decision support system must contain an LS, KS, and PPS.

In the computer-based case the PPS is computer software. The PPS in the human-based case consists of the mental skills of staff ("human software"). If decision support is to be provided, the software must be able to understand the decision maker's requests as stated in some language and it must be able to extract pertinent information from some available pool of knowledge about the problem domain. The function of the software (be it human or computer) is to interface these two to produce an answer to the problem posed by a decision maker.

In some systems, interfacing software may be simple, whereas it may be quite complex in others. On another dimension some software may be able to accept statements of problems in many languages; other PPS may be more specialized, accepting statements in one language only. On yet

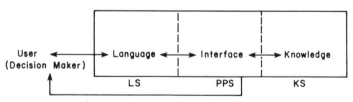

Fig. 4.3.   Structure of a decision support system.

another dimension, some software interfaces are specially constructed to access knowledge of one problem domain only. Other PPS have knowledge of many problem domains (i.e., they can interface with many knowledge systems). On still another dimension, some problem-processing systems may have models embedded within them (e.g., Potlatch, Banking system). Other PPS may be separated from modules that are stored in the KS, but the PPS "knows" how to use these to formulate models. This latter kind of PPS is along the lines of Simon's "general strategies" discussed in Section 1.12.

In both computer-based and human-based decision support systems there is wide variation in the nature of the language used to direct the decision support system. In some decision support systems of each type there is the possibility of the PPS misunderstanding the intention the decision maker is endeavoring to convey through the available language system. There are decision support systems of each genre that have interactive language systems. That is, the decision support system's PPS is permitted to query the decision maker for further information in order to clarify what it recognizes as ambiguity in the decision maker's initial statements. Thus in a decision support system of this type communication via the LS is not a one-way avenue; rather the LS is a two-way avenue through which the decision maker and the PPS can interact.

4.10   THE SHAPE OF SYSTEMS TO COME

Although most were not developed with business applications in mind, the systems described in the remainder of this chapter do fit the generic pattern of a DSS displayed in Fig. 4.3. The systems presented here have certain novel features that are not encountered in typical business-oriented systems. The descriptions given here are intended to provide overviews. Computer-based techniques employed in these systems are identified in subsequent chapters.

The first system discussed was specifically devised to aid managers in the model formulation activity. The next three systems have been drawn from the artificial intelligence literature. Some fairly general ideas on problem solving have been developed in the field of artificial intelligence. Since the ideas of this discipline are oriented toward solving semistructured or unstructured problems, it is useful to explore the basic concepts, with an eye to their possible applications in the decision support field.

The artificial intelligence systems are often characterized as being theorem-proving systems. Use of the term "theorem proving" does not necessarily connote proving theorems in mathematics. It is used in a broad sense, which may be interpreted in various ways, not only as a theorem to be proved but also as a goal to be achieved, a problem to be solved, or a query to be answered.

The chapter closes with the description of a decision support system that is more general (recall Fig. 1.1) than the systems presented in Chapter 3. That is, the system can be tailored to treat different problem domains, such as banking, project management, corporate planning, and so on.

4.11   The IBM Business Definition Language

Here we examine a system for supporting business decisions that is approached from the angle of a language [6]. The language has been designed to provide business people with a means for stating their problems and stating how they are to be solved. This Business Definition Language (BDL) deals with four kinds of elements: documents, steps, paths, and files.

A *document* is a colletion of data values organized according to some *form*. An example of a form is an invoice form (with no data values filled in). A particular group of data values properly written into the invoice form is an invoice document.

A *step* is a procedure that converts some input documents into some output documents. An *irreducible step* may be viewed as an operator that is directly available to the user of BDL. *Paths* connect steps by indicating that output documents of one step are input documents to another step.

The BDL user commences by stating the types of output documents that must be produced from a particular collection of input documents. The user must eventually specify an algorithm (program) for accomplishing this, in terms of paths connecting irreducible steps. The resultant program is a *composite step* in that it is composed of more primitive steps. See Hammer *et al.* [6] for a description of how the program construction process is interactively guided by a series of reductions that break composite steps into more primitive steps, until all primitive steps are irreducible.

Notice that the BDL approach to directing computations differs from that of systems in the last chapter. In those systems the user either called for a model (Potlatch) or specified a sequence of models (Xerox). The BDL language system is more procedural but more flexible than the language systems of Potlatch or Xerox. It falls nearer to the bottom of Fig. 3.2 than do these others. As in these other systems the BDL PPS contains models (i.e., irreducible steps or modules). The BDL knowledge system consists of *files*.

Input documents to a BDL program may be directly provided by the BDL user or they may be extracted from files. A file is composed of documents of a single form that are more or less permanently maintained.

BDL has been described [6] as having three major "components." These are the form definition component (FDC), the document flow component (DFC), and the document transformation component (DTC). The FDC specifies the forms of documents that can be used in the BDL program. The DFC is used to specify the BDL program in terms of paths and steps. Irreducible steps are programmed using a language contained in the DTC component.

BDL is being developed in order to reduce the cost of labor-intensive application software. The user of BDL is interactively guided through a process of program (model) construction, beginning with a composite step and eventuating in a sequence of irreducible steps. (The issues of branching and iteration in a resultant program are not dealt with in Hammer *et al.* [6]. However, branching and iteration do occur within irreducible steps. It is important to observe that the irreducible steps are possibly complex programs.) The thrust of the BDL development is directed toward easing the tasks of writing programs in a business problem domain.

4.12   PLANNER

One of the most prominent theorem-proving systems is PLANNER, which is under continuing development at MIT [13]. In general, a theorem-proving system consists of (1) some language for stating the theorem to be proved (LS); (2) some collection of axioms, assertions, or formulas embodying knowledge about a problem domain the system is concerned with (KS); and (3) a theorem prover (PPS) that utilizes principles of logic to endeavor to deduce a stated theorem from problem domain knowledge.

A major point of variation among theorem-proving systems is the method for handling knowledge about how to perform the deduction involved in a particular proof, i.e., knowledge beyond those general principles of logic that are applicable to any proof. This "reasoning" knowledge is not to be confused with the problem domain knowledge mentioned in the preceding paragraph, since the former is knowledge about how to use the latter.

As the problem domain knowledge becomes large, the exclusive use of general deduction principles to prove a theorem tends to bog down, because of blind examination of the possibly large number of plausible proof procedures for a given theorem; many false starts are involved. Indeed this was the source of some discouragement with the practicality of the theorem-proving field around 1970 [12]. One remedy is to incorporate into a theorem-proving system more specialized reasoning knowledge, i.e., special deductive principles that are applicable to a certain problem domain, to a certain type of theorem, or even to particular theorems themselves.

This specialized reasoning knowledge could be embedded directly into the theorem prover (PPS) as a set of heuristics. Another conceivable approach would involve the storage of this knowledge in the form of rules (in the KS) that would be accessible to the theorem prover for use in governing the deduction process. The PLANNER approach is to have the system's user state this specialized reasoning knowledge (in the LS) at the same time as (actually, as a part of) the theorem to be proved. The philosophy underlying the PLANNER approach is that at the time of stating a theorem to be proved, the user also has some notion about how to carry out the deduction. Thus in the PLANNER language a theorem is really a program for guiding the deduction process, giving the user control over how to prove the theorem (i.e., how to use the problem domain knowledge *vis-à-vis* the theorem).

The primary problem domain in which PLANNER has been applied consists of a world of blocks of various colors, sizes, shapes, and locations that is inhabited by a robot that can act on those blocks. Questions or "theorems" posed by a user can request information about the blocks world; this either is obtained directly from the problem domain knowledge or is deduced (inferred) from that knowledge (category J of Fig. 3.5). A second type of question, problem, or "theorem" can request a change in the state of the blocks world. This entails a deduction of whether the requested change is possible, given the current state of the blocks world and given the actions the robot can carry out; these two "givens" are included in the system's problem domain knowledge. A proof of this second type of theorem results in the execution of robot actions.

Although this PLANNER application is not oriented toward the direction or execution of computations of interest to managers, the execution of robot actions in response to a user's problem is along a similar vein. That is, each involves a plan, but the plans are of different natures. One is a plan of computational analysis (i.e., a model) that, when executed, results in some data (recall abilities III and V from Chapter 2). The other is a plan of implementation that, when carried out, results in some change

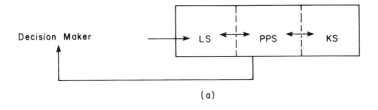

(a)

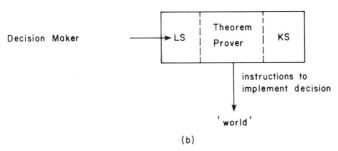

instructions to
implement decision

'world'

(b)

Fig. 4.4.   Decision support versus decision implementation. (a) System oriented toward analysis to support a decision. (b) System oriented toward implementation of a decision.

in a "world" that can be manipulated by the theorem-proving system (recall abilities III and VII from Chapter 2). This contrast is depicted in Fig. 4.4. (Recall that PLANNER can also supply data to the user via inferential retrieval, as discussed earlier.) As a final comment, note that the architecture in Fig. 4.4 could be altered, to allow the decision maker either to approve or to disapprove of the implementation plan devised by the theorem prover, prior to its execution.

4.13   The GPS Approach and STRIPS

A fairly general and abstract approach to problem solving has been developed by Simon [11]. This approach appears in the guise of the General Problem Solver (GPS). The GPS concepts can be easily outlined, although applying them to give an operational system can be quite complicated.

GPS is concerned with three basic elements: states, operators, and goals. A state is simply a situation. Operators permit us to move from one state to another, to transform one situation into another situation. A goal is a desired state. A problem is described in terms of an existing, initial state and a goal. (Recall the discussion of disequilibrium and problem recognition in Section 2.22.)

The GPS concept of problem solving is characterized as selecting a series of operators that will successively move the problem from its initial state, through intermediate states, to the goal state. Given any state it is assumed that a difference can be determined between that state and the goal state. Operators are selected to reduce the difference between the current state and the goal state. However, not any operator can be selected, since for a given state the set of applicable operators is a subset of the set of all operators. If, for example, the current state has a salesman in Chicago, then the operator to fly from New York to Albany is not applicable.

One interesting aspect of the GPS approach is that it can be used recursively. To explain this, suppose that we are in a particular state (e.g., in Chicago) and when calculating the difference with the goal state (e.g., in Albany) we notice that a particular operator (e.g., fly from New York to Albany), if applied, would substantially reduce or eliminate the difference. However, to use this particular operator we need to be in a certain state (e.g., in New York) that we presently are not in. Thus we could set up a new goal (e.g., in New York) that would be to achieve a particular state that would allow the application of the selected operator (e.g., fly from New York to Albany). For the solution of this new problem (e.g., initial state: in Chicago; goal state: in New York) we can reapply the GPS approach. If a solution is found (e.g., fly from Chicago to New York), then we can return to solving our original problem. During the course of solving our new problem we may again have recourse to using GPS in such a recursive fashion (e.g., fly from Chicago to Cleveland and then fly from Cleveland to New York).

A description of an implementation of the GPS approach and its use in solving a number of problems ranging from the cannibal–missionary problem to symbolic integration appears in Ernst and Newell [3]; for comments on the relationship of the GPS approach to human problem solving see Newell and Simon [9]. Notice that the GPS approach involves several of the decision-making abilities described in Chapter 2. These include the collection of information about states and the formulation of models (sequences of operators) as a result of recursively recognizing problems.

The emphasis in GPS is therefore on the use of the means–end (operators–goal) approach and recursive problem solving to determine automatically a *method* of solution. The principal outputs of systems like those described in Chapter 3 are reports such as income statements or sales forecasts. The principal outputs of systems developed in the spirit of GPS are solution methods, in terms of operator sequences.

Now suppose that we use the term "state" in the sense of a state of information (e.g., economic assumptions) and we take operators to be modules (e.g., regression, simulations, etc.). Note that a module enables us to move from one information state (input) to another state (output). If our goal state is one of having a sales forecast, then a GPS approach would yield a sequence of operators (a model) that enables us to arrive at that goal. Incorporation of the GPS approach into a DSS would therefore go a step beyond the BDL system in which the user sequences the operators. Techniques for incorporating the GPS approach into a system that also executes the sequence of operators are examined in ensuing chapters.

One implementation of a problem-solving system based on GPS ideas was developed at Stanford Research Institute [4] and named STRIPS (Stanford Research Institute Problem Solver). Since the implementation was based on using the predicate calculus and theorem proving, we will defer discussion of STRIPS details until after our presentation of these techniques. However, we can sketch some of the ideas here, in the context of our GPS discussion.

The STRIPS problem domain consists of a robot that must rearrange objects, navigate through rooms, and so on. A state for the robot problem solver consists of a large number of facts about positions of the robot and objects, about the characteristics of the objects, and about walls and openings in the rooms the robot can inhabit. Each STRIPS operator has a corresponding "action routine" that, when executed, causes the robot to take a certain action. Problem solving consists of finding a sequence of operators that will transform an initial state into a goal state.

In STRIPS, associated with any operator, there are three lists of information. A prerequisite list specifies what must be true about a state before the operator can be applied. The delete and add lists specify what changes to make in the current state if the operator is applied, i.e., what facts should be added and which should be deleted.

The language system (LS) in STRIPS allows for the specification of goal states. Although the language used is predicate calculus, its statements can be paraphrased into English. An example is "Get boxes B and C to location A." The STRIPS knowledge system (KS) consists of a description of the current state of the robot world. These facts are also represented in terms of the predicate calculus.

The problem-processing system (PPS) in STRIPS finds (if possible) a sequence of operators that permit the goal to be met. The PPS uses theorem-proving techniques to determine whether a goal is met by the current state. If it is, then no operator sequence needs to be determined. If it is not, then the GPS notion of "differences" is used, along with the previously mentioned operator lists, to select an operator giving a new current state that is "closer" to the goal. The PPS then uses theorem-proving techniques again to determine whether the goal is met by the new current state. This process continues until a sequence of operators has been found that gives a state that can be proved to meet the goal.

Heuristic intricacies involved in the selection of operators appear in Fikes and Nilsson [4]. This can be contrasted with PLANNER, where determination of a sequence of robot actions is guided by the user via the PLANNER LS. It can be further contrasted with the BDL approach of the user being guided by the system in eventually specifying a sequence of irreducible steps.

4.14 MYCIN

A very specific and apparently successful consultation system called MYCIN [2] is intended to help physicians diagnose and decide on treat-ments for infectious diseases. Given an initial set of symptoms and basic information on the patient, the system acts as a consultant by requesting what it considers to be pertinent data about the patient such as results of certain laboratory tests. The acquisition of each new bit of data about a patient serves to influence the next piece of data the "consultant" re-quests from the physician. In this way a selective "data base" is gradually built.

The patient-specific "data base," along with some knowledge about infections, allows the MYCIN system to suggest certain possible diag-noses and therapies, each with a likelihood factor. The physician is aided in the search for a diagnosis by the system's suggestions and by the ability on the physician's part to request reasons for the proposed diagnosis. User interaction with MYCIN is via an English-like interface that signifi-cantly enhances its usability.

Although the features of MYCIN differ somewhat from those of the previously discussed systems, it too fits the generic description of a DSS. A consultation session is initiated by the user, but it is perpetuated and guided by MYCIN. Thus MYCIN's information collection from a user via the LS is instigated by the MYCIN PPS (see Davis *et al.* [2] for examples of this). In contrast to the three previously described systems, the MYCIN LS is quite English-like in appearance. However, the user is largely restricted to asking only one kind of question, namely, "What is the diagnosis and therapy?"

The PPS endeavors to condition this query by building a patient-specific "data base" as described earlier, so that the query begins to look like "What is the diagnosis and therapy *for* patient A having history B, symptoms C, D, and E, lab test results F and G, etc.?" This interactive conditioning process may be characterized as the MYCIN PPS's problem recognition ability.

The exercise of this ability depends on facts about infections that are maintained in MYCIN's knowledge system (KS). During the interactive conditioning of a user's query, the next bit of data to be collected from a user (to define or condition the problem further) depends on information already collected from the user (LS) and from the KS. The patient-specific "data base" that results from interactive problem recognition may be considered either as information internally held within the PPS or as a short-term part of the KS that is filled in as data are collected from a user.

The KS holds long-term (yet modifiable) knowledge concerning infections that exists across many consultation sessions. The patient-specific information, which the MYCIN authors call a "data base," exists only for the consultation session involving that specific patient. A new patient demands a new patient-specific "data base." In this sense, a MYCIN "data base" is analogous to the internal representation of a particular query in systems such as those discussed in Chapter 3. Both are comparatively ephemeral.

It is instructive to contrast the MYCIN handling of patient information with another conceivable approach that would store all patient information in the KS on a long-term basis. Where the potential patient population is large, the MYCIN approach is clearly superior, since there would be too much data used too infrequently (and too volatile) to permit feasible long-term storage. The MYCIN approach is entirely consistent with the way in which Chapter 3 systems handle very short-term information. Examples of such short-term information include the assumptions under which some sales-forecasting model should be executed. We may want to execute the model assuming a 5% economic growth factor and a moment later we may want to try a 7% factor. Just as it is not practical to store all patient data on a long-term basis, it is not practical to store all potentially interesting growth factors on a long-term basis. On the contrary, they are supplied by the user as needed through the system's LS.

Even though MYCIN cannot quite be characterized as permitting computational management (recall Fig. 3.2), its approach to decision support has much to offer in terms of ideas for DSS development in business settings. MYCIN lies in category L and its inferential retrieval is based on Post's production system, which is discussed later (Chapter 5). The notion of diagnosis and treatment of human patients can be extended to business firms. This expanded perspective would see corporate planners as "physicians" endeavoring to diagnose and recommend therapies for a firm's "ills." An interesting issue for research is the extent to which the MYCIN principles can be applied to situations where the patient is a business firm. This would necessitate a KS that deals not with medical knowledge but with knowledge about the anatomy, testing procedures, afflictions, and treatments for a business firm.

4.15   GPLAN

The Generalized Planning System (GPLAN), developed at Purdue University [7], is more general than the systems of Chapter 3 in terms of the problem domains it can handle. GPLAN can be tailored to support decision makers in any of a variety of areas (e.g., inventory management [1], water quality planning [8]). The intent was to achieve not only generality but also an easy-to-use user language, a flexible knowledge system, and a problem processor that could automatically interface a model with some data in the KS to perform a desired analysis.

The language system (LS) was designed for use by persons who are not programmers. It is English-like in appearance and with it a user can direct both data retrieval and computation nonprocedurally. When used for data retrieval GPLAN falls into category L. When used for directing computations the system, as currently implemented, falls into category E. That is, models are invoked by name and they obtain needed data from the KS by invoking special report generators.

Part of the system's generality derives from the fact that the LS syntax remains the same, regardless of the problem domain. The syntax is as follows:

⟨Command⟩ ⟨FIND CLAUSE⟩   ⟨CONDITIONAL CLAUSE⟩

The vocabulary does change from one problem domain to another (see Bonczek *et al.* [1] and Holsapple and Whinston [8], for example). But since the GPLAN problem processor handles user statements using syntax-directed compilation techniques, vocabulary changes do not drastically affect the PPS.

On the other hand, changes in the models to be used do affect the PPS in several ways. First of all the models are treated as part of the PPS. So a change in problem domain from inventory management to water quality planning would cause the deletion of inventory management algorithms and the inclusion of water quality simulation models. There are other models that remain in the PPS regardless of the problem domain. These are statistical models, of the sort found in SPSS, which have wide applicability.

The incorporation of a new model into the system affects the LS vocabulary by adding a new command (e.g., RUN WATER SIMULA- TION) and it necessitates other changes in the PPS such as the possible inclusion of additional report generators and checks to assure that the user's CONDITIONAL CLAUSE fully specifies the assumptions (if any) under which the model is to be executed. Thus the modeling aspect of GPLAN is its least general ability. In Chapter 9 we shall see how this can be overcome.

A final aspect of the system that is quite general is its ability to gather information from the KS (which is a type of data base). The PPS is unaffected by the problem domain or the way in which problem domain knowledge is organized in the KS, having the ability to produce practically any subset of the data contained in the KS. In Chapters 10 and 13 we shall see how to extend the power of data bases for representing knowledge.

4.20 RATIONALE FOR THE STUDY OF A GENERALIZED PROBLEM PROCESSOR

The systems surveyed in this and the preceding chapter serve to portray many of the major features and issues pertaining to decision support systems. Rather than continuing to enumerate particular systems, we turn our attention in upcoming chapters to computer-based techniques that can be used to develop decision support systems such as those already described. However, the presentation of techniques is geared to culminate, in Part V, in the design of a general PPS. This general PPS is a single, invariant mechanism, whose code does not change with the problem domains it supports. This implies that such a processor, while possessing various abilities involved in decision making, must be separated from anything that is domain specific.

It is appropriate at this juncture to pause for a consideration of the advantages of such a generalized problem processor *vis-à-vis* domain-specific processors. Perhaps the most significant attribute of the generalized approach is the conceptual framework it affords. This is particularly important from the pedagogical standpoint. Given a knowledge of the general system, the student is in a much better position to comprehend and derive specialized systems than would be the case in the absence of such knowledge. Observe that possession of this knowledge furnishes a basis for systematic comparison, contrast, and discourse regarding special cases.

Of course, we do not mean to suggest that specialists be deterred from their lines of investigation and development. Indeed, the specialist is quick to point out that with respect to execution and storage, a specialized system is almost invariably more efficient than a general system. It must be remembered, however, that the price of greater operational efficiency is the forfeit of some degree of flexibility. Where efficiency is paramount it may be simpler or less costly (more efficient?) to constrain an existing general system to conform with some standard of operational efficiency than to devise a special system from scratch. In this connection, recall the discussion in Section 1.03.2 of labor–capital substitution, mass production of software, and increased life expectancy.

As a topic for research (and as a managerial strategy) there is a good deal to be said for concentrating on how to improve responses to needs over time, under changing conditions. In the long run this may very well be more fruitful than devotion to augmenting one's capabilities for finding solutions that are optimal at a given moment. This would imply a need for flexible systems that can easily adapt to what has been learned and to current needs. One is faced with two distinct causes of action: (1) investment of resources in a system that is optimal until conditions change, causing deterioration or incapacity; or (2) investment in a system that is not optimal (that can be mass produced and that is probably less expensive) but that can be readily modified (and perhaps improved) when conditions change.

Furthermore, in an environment where numerous, diverse specialized systems are derived from the general, there is an advantage of relative ease in understanding each since all have been based on the same general principles. This is contrasted with situations where one must learn several entirely distinct systems that are not derived from a common root. A further asset acquired from the study of a general system is its potential for engendering insights that allow what is known in one system to be translated to others.

In an earlier section (4.04) the notions of machine software and "human software" were compared. Interestingly, this comparison can be continued with respect to the question of generalization versus specialization. So-called idiot savants [5] studied by psychologists are persons who are capable of performing particular mental feats far beyond the capacity of normal humans but are unable to carry on simple conversations or perform ordinary jobs. The unusual mental feats performed by these persons, whose IQs fall in the range of 40 to 80, involve memory and prodigious calculations that surpass the abilities of the most brilliant people [10]. The savant's "software" appears to be extremely specialized, capable of such extreme concentration on a particular problem domain that the mental "software" is not available for the wide range of problem domains addressed by more normal persons [10]. It is left to the reader to elaborate on the interesting parallel between human and machine software with regard to the specialization versus generalization issue.

4.30 CONCLUSION

The chapter began with a generic description of decision support systems that was based on the frameworks, surveys, and classification schemes of earlier chapters. The generic description holds that a DSS has knowledge about a problem domain (a KS) and can accept stated problems (a LS). To solve a stated problem using problem domain knowledge, there must be a PPS that possesses some of the seven abilities involved in decision making.

Several systems were described that fit the generic DSS idea but that were not the customary kinds of systems encountered in business applications. The distinguishing features of each were noted. It is of interest to speculate why systems such as MYCIN are not found in business settings. The ideas and features of such systems certainly look attractive, but in viewing management systems (Chapter 3) there is nothing at this level.

This is in part due to the newness of the systems described in this chapter. It is also due to the origins of such systems. PLANNER, STRIPS, and MYCIN were developed by workers in the artificial intelligence field, which until recently has dealt mainly with toy problems. Furthermore, workers in the field typically do not have business backgrounds. On the other hand, designers of systems such as those of Chapter 3 come predominantly from a data base management–management information systems (DBM–MIS) background. The potential application of artificial intelligence techniques in conjunction with DBM–MIS techniques has yet to be widely recognized or investigated in the DBM–MIS field.

The following chapters are an initial effort at remedying this situation. The effort culminates in the design of a DSS that is built on features and techniques from both traditions. Moreover, the aim of this DSS design is toward a degree of generality that goes beyond such systems as GPLAN. The quest for generality is intended as a pedagogical aid, but it can also have some practical implications in terms of the economic considerations examined in Section 1.03.2.

For implementers or buyers of decision support systems, the question of precisely what level of generality is appropriate is neither a trivial problem nor a problem that has been solved. Nevertheless, an understanding of a quite general system should alert the reader to the various levels of generality that are possible (given continued technological advances referred to in Section 1.03.1) and it should furnish a repertoire of features and techniques that can be used to attain the desired degree of generality.

REFERENCES

1. R. H. Bonczek, C. W. Holsapple, and A. B. Whinston, Aiding decision makers with a generalized data base management system, *Decision Sci.* **9**, No. 2 (April 1978).
2. R. Davis, B. Buchanan, and E. Shortliffe, Production rules as a representation for a knowledge-based consultation program, *Artificial Intelligence* **8**, No. 1 (1977).
3. G. W. Ernst and A. Newell, "GPS: A Case Study in Generality and Problem Solving." Academic Press, New York, 1969.
4. R. E. Fikes and N. J. Nilsson, STRIPS: A new approach to the application of theorem proving to problem solving, *Artificial Intelligence* **2** (1971).
5. R. M. Goldenson, "Encyclopedia of Human Behavior," Vol. 1, pp. 592–593. Doubleday, Garden City, New York, 1970.
6. M. Hammer *et al.*, A very high level programming language for data processing applications, *Commun. ACM* **20**, No. 11 (1977).
7. W. D. Haseman and A. B. Whinston, "Introduction to Data Management." Irwin, Homewood, Illinois, 1977.
8. C. W. Holsapple and A. B. Whinston, A decision support system for area-wide water quality planning, *Socio-Econ. Planning Sci.* **10** (1976).
9. A. Newell and H. A. Simon, "Human Problem Solving." Prentice Hall, Englewood Cliffs, New Jersey, 1972.
10. B. Rimland, The autistic savant, *Psychol. Today* **12**, No. 3 (1978).
11. H. A. Simon, The heuristic compiler, *in* "Representation and Meaning" (H. A. Simon and L. Siklossy, eds.). Prentice-Hall, Englewood Cliffs, New Jersey, 1972.
12. M. H. van Emden, Programming with resolution logic, *in* "Machine Intelligence" (E. W. Elcock and D. Michie, eds.), Vol. 8. Halsted Press, New York, 1977.
13. T. Winograd, "Understanding Natural Language," pp. 108–126. Academic Press, New York, 1972.

Chapter 5

FORMALIZATIONS OF PURPOSIVE SYSTEMS

5.00 FORMALIZING PURPOSIVE BEHAVIOR

The decision support systems described in the last chapter all exhibit some degree of purposive behavior. It has been remarked that "a behavior that appears goal-directed, or problem-solving, or error-corrected, or adaptive, or can take variable pathways from where it starts to where it ends has the earmarks of purposive behavior" [7]. With this chapter we begin our exploration of some formalizations that can be used as bases for building computerized purposive systems.

The emphasis in many computer-based information systems is on efficiency, minimizing the machine-related costs of producing data. In considering more purposive computer-based systems, such as those presented in Chapter 4, the emphasis is on building systems that exhibit rational behavior. The result is that the goals or problems presented to the computer are akin to the goals or problems confronting decision makers. In either case these goals or problems demand rational, purposive behavior if they are to be dealt with effectively. For a computer-based system this necessitates formalizations of such behavior. Efficiency is not an unimportant issue when implementing these formalizations. However, efficiency questions *vis-à-vis* purposive systems must be tempered by an understanding of the trend of dramatic hardware advances, of the value of adaptability, and of overall organizational costs rather than machine-related costs.

5.10 THE STATE SPACE APPROACH TO DECISION SUPPORT

The notions of states and operators were outlined in Section 4.13, where it was also shown how they might be used to build problem-solving systems. We shall now investigate the principles and techniques of state space analysis in more detail. Systems that utilize state space analysis will be viewed as decision support systems, in which a decision maker states a problem (goal state) and the system determines whether (and how) the problem can be solved (the goal can be achieved). This determination is made by the state space DSS (SSDSS) in the light of the application-specific information it contains. Note that an SSDSS has a knowledge system (KS), language system (LS), and problem-processing system (PPS).

5.11 Knowledge System for an SSDSS

Before an SSDSS can accept and act on problems (desired or goal situations), it must contain information about the initial state (situation) of the application world and also information as to how and under what conditions states can be altered. Such information is incorporated into the SSDSS knowledge system. Looking first at information about an initial state, it is immediately apparent that some way of describing states must be devised. Whatever the application, we must be able to conceptually identify what is meant by a state for that application. Thus a *state* is a conceptual construct for thinking about and representing knowledge about an application world.

Given that states have been identified in a conceptual sense, they must be operationalized via some descriptive technique. That is, a state must be expressed in terms that can be comprehended by SSDSS software (i.e., its PPS). Examples of various kinds of operational descriptions that are used for representing states include tuples, matrices, predicates, lists, and symbol strings (see Amarel [2] and Nilsson [9] for examples). The particular operational description method selected for a given application is influenced by the nature of the application and is constrained by the information collection ability of the PPS. If, for instance, a PPS has been devised to accept symbol strings only, then states cannot be operationally described as lists. We shall not deal here with methods for physically implementing operational constructs (e.g., a list could be implemented by maintaining its elements in physically contiguous locations or by various uses of pointers [8]).

The KS for an SSDSS must also contain information on how and under what conditions states can be altered. Recall that states are altered by operators. Therefore, for each operator we must have a way to specify the states to which it can be applied and the effect of applying it. Given an application world, we must be able to identify conceptually the pertinent operators for that world. Thus *operator* is a conceptual construct for thinking about, and discussing our knowledge of, some application world. Once an operator has been conceptually identified, it must be operationalized via some descriptive technique. That is, knowledge about an operator must be expressed in terms that are comprehensible to the PPS, which must eventually use this knowledge during problem processing.

Operationally there are numerous ways for describing operator knowledge. The operational description method chosen must be compatible with the previously selected method for representing states. For instance, if states are described in terms of symbol strings, then preconditions for the application of an operator should be described in terms of symbol strings as well; the operator's effect should also be described in terms of symbol strings.

One way to describe operator knowledge operationally is through the use of input–output tables. For each operator there is a table that indicates the states to which the operator can be applied (i.e., permissible "inputs"). For some applications it may happen that we have conceptually identified only one operator. An example of this is a "replacement" or "rewrite" operator, usually denoted by →. If states are operationalized as symbol strings, then the application of the rewrite operator to some permissible input substring S_1 is denoted by $S_1 \rightarrow S_2$. The effect of this operation is to rewrite or replace S_1 by S_2. The usage of a rewrite operator is examined in detail later in this chapter in connection with production systems.

Another method for operationalizing operator knowledge is to declare a function for each operator and to declare preconditions for the application of this function in terms of states. A function takes the current state as an argument and, on execution, returns a description of the new current state. Possible ways for physically implementing tables [8] or computational functions (e.g., subroutine calls) within a knowledge system are well known and are not considered here.

5.12   Language System for an SSDSS

The language system for an SSDSS provides the means for a user to specify the set of states that satisfies the desired goal. That is, the system's user uses the LS to describe what properties a state must have in order to be considered a goal state. In its simplest form such an LS would allow the user to specify a desired goal state in terms of the operational construct(s) used in the KS for representing states. A more elaborate LS would allow the user to indicate goal state properties without being constrained to the use of the KS operational construct(s). The PPS would accept such statements and transform them into an equivalent expression that uses the operational construct(s). The more elaborate versions of LS would have the objective of making it easier (i.e., more English-like) for the system's user to state a problem.

The research emphasis in state space problem-solving systems has not been on providing elaborate language systems. Research has centered on knowledge representation and especially on the problem-solving method itself, taking as given the description of a goal state in terms of the operational construct(s) for state representation. The comparative lack of attention given to LS by state space researchers should not be taken as a sign that they are unaware of the importance of a facile system–user interface [2]. Nor is it indicative of any innate flaw in the state space problem-solving approach itself. An elaborate LS can be added onto an extant SSDSS by incorporating appropriate linguistic transformation software into the PPS.

Regardless of the degree of syntactic nicety a state space LS possesses, we can fit it into the language classification scheme of Chapter 3. Observe first of all that a state space language is nonprocedural, since a problem is posed in terms of the properties of some desired state. Also notice that the problem statement does not invoke one member of a library of models by name. Therefore, with respect to its user–model interface, a state space DSS belongs to the top row of Fig. 3.2. Whether the SSDSS falls into category G, H, or I depends on the way in which the PPS information collection ability is devised with respect to the KS. Since the kinds of reports (or information) that the PPS must obtain from a KS are few and well known, it is reasonable to suppose that most SSDSS fall into category H.

What is the nature of the computation directed by an SSDSS user? The computation consists of an ordered application of various operators that transforms an initial state into some state having the specified goal properties. As noted in the preceding section, the operators might use only simple computations consisting of replacements (i.e., a sequence of assignments or perhaps more properly reassignments). Alternatively, the operator usage may require the execution of a sequence of complex arithmetic or logical functions. The determination of operator sequencing is made by the PPS *after* receiving a problem statement. Thus the PPS does have a model formulation capability. Contrast this was a DSS (middle row of Fig. 3.2), in which all possible models that can be used within the DSS are defined *before* the user's command is received; that is, the system's designer has already formulated those models that will be available to a user. The language system reflects this in terms of what commands are available to a user (e.g., the user invokes model X or Y or Z).

In DSS of the state space variety (or any DSS of the top row of Fig. 3.2) the language system is not restricted by the availability of preformulated models, since model formulation is handled by the PPS in response to a *nonprocedural* problem statement. The PPS does not need to be altered in order to incorporate additional preformulated models (because there are none). To augment its modeling capability the only substantial alteration required is the addition of operator knowledge to the KS. It is possible that additions to the LS lexicon might be necessary to allow for the description of new goal states made possible by the new operator knowledge. However, this does not imply an alteration of the PPS software.

5.13   Problem-Processing System for SSDSS

Although a PPS is software, we are not concerned here with the actual lines of code that constitute it. Attention in this treatise is confined to certain interesting techniques that can be used to furnish one or more of the decision-making abilities that can be displayed by a DSS. These are techniques that can be translated into code by DSS builders. It is vital to bear in mind that there is not necessarily a one-to-one correspondence between a technique and a decision-making ability. A coded technique is a *component* of the system, whereas a decision-making ability is a *property* displayed by the system. An exhibited property can be the result of several components or a component can account for more than one property. As techniques are introduced in this and ensuing chapters, they will be presented in terms of which ability or abilities they provide.

With respect to a state space PPS the technique of interest is that of state space searching. We shall see that this technique furnishes the problem recognition and model formulation abilities of an SSDSS. A state space DSS must, of course, have some information collection ability as well. Since there is no standard technique for handling this ability in

SSDSS and since the development of such techniques has not been a central aim of state space research, the information collection ability of an SSDSS problem processor will receive no further attention here. We simply presume that it exists, so that information (as described in Section 5.11) can be retrieved from the KS and so that information (Section 5.12) can be received through the LS.

The technique of state space searching is conveniently described in graphical terms. A state is represented by a node n_i in the graph. The fact that an operator O_k can be applied to the state depicted by n_i is graphically represented by a directed arc emanating from n_i. This directed arc has O_k as a label and it points to the successor node n_j, where n_j represents the state that results from applying O_k to the state labeled n_i. Given a KS for an application, the initial state gives the root node for a directed graph of the application's state space. The structure of the directed graph is determined by the stored operator knowledge. The entire graph can be constructed as follows:

1. Create the root node.
2. For each node in the graph that has no departing arcs, create all permissible arcs that can emanate from it.
3. If no new arcs were created in step 2, stop. Otherwise, for each arc just created in step 2, create its successor node if that node is not yet in the graph.
4. If no new nodes were created in step 3, stop. Otherwise, go to step 2.

The set of all nodes in the graph gives the application's state space (i.e., the space of all possible states). The state space search problem is one of finding a "path" in the graph that begins at the root node and ends at some node whose corresponding state satisfies some specified goal properties. A path is simply a sequence of nodes connected by arcs, such that each node in the sequence (with the exception of the root) is a successor of the preceding node in the sequence. Note that the path-finding problem becomes nontrivial as the state space becomes very large or even infinite. In such cases it is infeasible to construct the entire graph explicitly.

The principal state space search issue is how to make explicit (i.e., examine) a relatively small portion of the entire graph, such that this "small portion" contains a path ending with a goal node. A related issue arises when there are multiple paths to the same goal node. Is one path "better" than another? The goodness of a path could perhaps be quantified as a function of its length or as a function of the costs of applying the operators along the path. A similar issue arises when the state space contains numerous goal states for a given problem.

For completeness we briefly examine the two major kinds of search procedures that can be used to discover a solution path: uniform searches and heuristic searches. The former refers to search procedures that are applied uniformly (i.e., that are always applied in the same way, making no use of any application-specific or problem-specific information about how possibly to shorten the search). Depth first and breadth first are the most common uniform search methods [9]. A backtracking facility is necessary for depth-first searches. Heuristic searches of a state space are not uniform, but depend on the nature of an application or class of problems.

A heuristic search method makes use of either application-specific or problem-specific information in order to determine a problem-specific search procedure [9]. Thus different problems (or problem classes) are addressed by different search procedures. The logic for how to tailor a search procedure to a specific problem, by taking advantage of problem- or application-specific information, is a part of the PPS. The problem-specific (heuristic) information itself could be passed to the PPS from the user via the LS or from the KS. Thus for the PPS to be able to utilize heuristic information, either the LS or the KS must be extended beyond what was previously discussed.

The activities of a state space problem processor can be summarized as displaying the abilities of information collection, problem recognition, model formulation, and analysis. The technique(s) underlying information collection is not emphasized. In the course of state space search the application of an operator to give a new state amounts to the recognition of a new problem, as long as the new state is not a goal state. Thus the problem recognition ability includes the task of determining which operator to apply when. In the course of discovering a path to a goal node a model has been formulated in the guise of a sequence of operators. As an operator is applied to a particular state, the ability of analysis is demonstrated. That is, some data (a state description) are interfaced with some model (an operator, a module of the overall model that is formulated) in order to produce some facts or expectations (a new state description).

5.20   THE PROBLEM REDUCTION APPROACH
TO DECISION SUPPORT

In the problem reduction approach a user describes a problem that is to be solved. The problem reduction system reduces this problem into subproblems. Each subproblem is then treated as a problem and reduced into further subproblems and so forth. A given problem may be capable of being reduced by more than one reduction operator. The reduction process is repeated until all problems (i.e., the original problem or its subproblems) have been reduced to primitive subproblems. A primitive subproblem is a problem that can be trivially or immediately solved by the system's software. The solutions obtained from the directly solved primitive problems are then used to arrive at the solution to the original problem. A system that uses the problem reduction approach to furnish decision support will be referred to as a PRDSS. We shall examine the KS, LS, and PPS of a PRDSS (see Amarel [2] for more detail and examples) and then comment on the correspondence between problem reduction and the organizational framework for division of information-processing labor.

5.21 Knowledge System for a PRDSS

Before it can begin to solve some problem stated in the LS the PPS must either contain or be able to acquire from a KS the following information:

1. description of each primitive problem,
2. description of each reduction operator, including a specification of the problems to which it can be applied.

If this information is embedded in the PPS, then the PPS is not general. If this information resides in a KS, then the PPS is invariant to application changes. We shall assume that the latter case holds.

Problems can be operationally described in terms of lists, tuples, symbol strings, and so on. A problem can even be described as a state space problem [9]. It is not sufficient merely to have descriptions of all primitive problems in the KS. The KS must also contain the "trivial" solution method for each primitive problem, so that each primitive problem can be directly solved. These "trivial" solution procedures (some of which may actually entail complex calculations) must be specified (e.g., programmed) before a PRDSS user states a problem. They are therefore comparable to the notion of "model building blocks" advanced by Sprague and Watson (Section 3.04).

Knowledge about reduction operators that is also kept in the KS should include not only a description of each operator, but also a coded form of the reduction operator for the PPS to apply, an operational specification of those problems to which the reduction operator can be applied, and an indication of how the solutions to the subproblems resulting from the reduction operator can be used to find the solution to the problem reduced by that operator.

5.22 Language System for a PRDSS

Just as was the case with state space, research in the problem reduction realm has not concentrated on the development of user-oriented languages. The statement of a problem in terms of the operational construct(s) used by the PPS is taken as a starting point. Notice that this problem statement does not specify how the problem is to be solved, nor is it a call to a preformulated model. Therefore a PRDSS falls into the top row of the classification scheme of Fig. 3.2. Its specific category in this row depends on the method used by the PPS for retrieving information from the KS. Since the kinds of reports needed from the KS are stable and few in number, a PRDSS designed according to category H would be reasonable.

5.23 Problem-Processing System for a PRDSS

Information collection must be performed by a PRDSS problem-processing system. Techniques underlying this ability are not examined here. The major contribution of problem reduction from the technical standpoint is its approach to problem recognition and model formulation. Description of this problem reduction technique is greatly facilitated by the use of AND/OR graphs (not to be confused with state space graphs). An AND/OR graph is used to depict the possible ways for reducing a given problem.

The original problem is pictured as a node (the *start* node) in an AND/OR graph. There is one directed arc departing from a problem node for each reduction operator that can be applied to that problem. In Fig. 5.1a we see that three reduction operators could be applied to problem A. That is, there are three methods for beginning to reduce A, any one of which could potentially (as a result of further reductions) yield a solution to A. Reduction operators can be divided into two categories, which we shall call AND reductions and OR reductions. In an AND/OR graph, AND reductions are represented differently from OR reductions.

5.23.1 AND Reductions

The application of an AND reduction operator α to a problem A is fully represented in an AND/OR graph as shown in Fig. 5.1b. Here the reduction operator α when applied to problem A gives three subproblems B, C, and D. If problems B, C, *and* D can be solved, then problem A can be solved. We shall refer to node A1 as a synthesis node.

Having reduced A into three subproblems, there must exist some

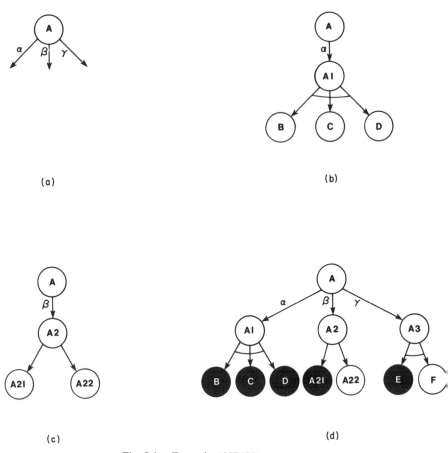

Fig. 5.1.   Example AND/OR structures.

means for synthesizing a solution to A from the solutions of its subproblems. Node A1, intervening between A and its subproblems in the α reduction, highlights the necessity of this synthesis. As explained earlier, in connection with the KS, knowledge about a reduction operator must include sufficient information to enable the synthesis of a solution to the parent problem. Since the A1 synthesis depends on the existence of solutions to A *and* B *and* C, the nodes A, B, and C are often called AND nodes. In an AND/OR diagram, AND nodes are denoted by incoming arcs that are cut by semicircles (e.g., see B, C, D). A node cannot be both an AND node and a synthesis node, although by definition a synthesis node always has AND successor nodes.

5.23.2 OR Reductions

An OR reduction operator β applied to A gives a structure such as that of Fig. 5.1c. In this instance, applying β to A gives two problems, A21 and A22. Notice that neither A21 nor A22 are AND nodes. Applying the β reduction to A tells us that if we solve either A21 *or* A22, then we have a solution to A. For this reason A21 and A22 are called OR nodes. The node A2 is used to suggest a point where heuristic information would be help-ful. Heuristic information associated with the operator β would indicate the conditions under which problem A22 is more likely than A21 to pro-vide a solution (or a faster solution or a better solution) to A, and vice versa. Such information can be useful in AND/OR graph searches to be described shortly.

Observe that an AND reduction operator reduces a problem by *de-composing* it into subproblems, all of which must be solved in order to obtain an answer. It results in AND nodes. In contrast, an OR reduction operator reduces a problem, by providing alternative views, or restate-ments, of the problem. These alternative restatements are typically more explicit or more precise statements of the original problem. Thus we can conceive of an OR reduction operator as reducing a problem by *defining* it more precisely in terms of alternative subproblems, any one of which (when it is solved) gives an answer to the original problem. Such a reduc-tion results in OR nodes only.

Notice that it is permissible to have situations where both an AND operator and an OR operator can be applied to the same node A (see Fig. 5.1d). For a given context it can happen that not all reductions of A will lead to a solution. As discussed in the next section, graph searching con-sists of selecting from among alternative reductions. Thus the heuristic and synthesis nodes in Fig. 5.1d are OR nodes and node A may be thought of as a heuristic node.

5.23.3 Searching an AND/OR Graph

Given a particular problem (e.g., "find profit in 1981") in a particular context (e.g., the current year, the company in question, a current eco-nomic outlook) as a start node, we can use the KS information to draw an AND/OR graph. To generate a complete AND/OR graph for a given start node X, the following procedure can be used:

1.   Apply all *permissible* reduction operators to the original problem denoted by node X. Let $i = 1$ and let X^1 be the set of nodes resulting from this reduction that are neither synthesis nor heuristic nodes.

2. For each element of X^i, $i = 1, 2, \ldots$, apply all permissible reduction operators. The entire set of all nonsynthesis and nonheuristic nodes generated by reductions on the elements of X^i is labeled X^{i+1}. Continue until for some k, $X^k = \varnothing$.

The AND/OR search problem is one of constructing enough of an AND/OR graph to show that the original problem is solvable or unsolvable. Detailed discussion of depth-first, breadth-first, and heuristic search methods appears in Nilsson [9] and is not repeated here. However, a few comments are given concerning the effect of a problem's context on an AND/OR graph in terms of the solution methods (and nonsolution methods) it depicts.

Figure 5.1d shows the effect of applying three reduction operators to A. Notice that the nodes A1, A2, and A3 are OR nodes. It follows that node A can be viewed as a heuristic node. That is, it is a point where it would be helpful to have some heuristic information about which of the three OR nodes is the most promising candidate to examine, as we search the AND/OR graph for a solution method. Suppose that nodes B, C, D, E, and A21 represent primitive problems. Such nodes are traditionally called terminal nodes and they are shaded in Fig. 5.1d. Furthermore, assume that the nonterminal nodes F and A22 are incapable of further reduction.

The application of γ to A is a dead end, because F is not terminal and cannot be reduced and because F is needed to solve A3. Now if the parameters (i.e., the context) of problem A are altered, the γ reduction might result in AND nodes that are all terminals or that consist of some nonterminals all of which can eventually be reduced to terminals. In such a case, the γ reduction would not be a dead end. Returning now to the unaltered problem A, we can see that the α reduction gives a solution method (i.e., solving the primitives B, C, and D and then using their solutions to solve A1). The β reduction also gives a solution method (i.e., A21). Again note that certain alterations in A could result in an A22 that is capable of further reductions. If these proceed to the point of terminal nodes, then there is at least one other solution method for A in addition to the two already shown in Fig. 5.1d.

It is appropriate to pause for a recapitulation of AND/OR graphs. In the foregoing example, α is an AND reduction operator that can reduce problem A to problem A1, where A1 is the problem of combining the solutions of problems B, C, and D to synthesize a solution to A. The OR reduction operator β reduces problem A to problem A2, where A2 is the problem of selecting either problem A21 or problem A22 as the "best" approach to solving A. Figure 5.2 shows a larger-scale AND/OR graph in

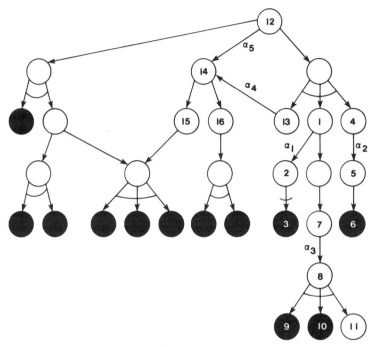

Fig. 5.2.   AND/OR graph with six feasible solution methods.

which the root node has six feasible solution methods. It is important to emphasize that these various solution methods may or may not give the same solutions (i.e., answers) to the root problem. The particular solutions can differ depending on the alternative ways (as embodied in the OR nodes) for restating problems.

Moreover, variations in the context of a problem can result in different AND/OR graphs, even though the same reduction operators are applied to the same root node. Consider the problem "find profit in 1981." The reduction operators that can be applied to this problem can be retrieved from the KS. However, the results of applying these operators may differ according to the problem's context (e.g., the current year, the company, the current economic outlook, etc.). An alternative formalization of the notion of problem reduction would have us view the problem "find profit in 1981" as n distinct problems for each of the n distinct contexts that are possible. For each of these n specialized problems, the KS would have to contain information about the reduction operators that are applicable to it. This could allow us to reduce the number of dead ends in the possible AND/OR graphs. For instance, the γ reduction in Fig. 5.1d would be eliminated, since it is fruitless for that particular context of problem A. Nevertheless, this reduction of the search problem is accompanied by increased knowledge representation problems as n becomes large.

5.23.4   Alternative Expressions of an AND/OR Graph

In this section we briefly examine alternative modes of expressing certain configurations that can arise in an AND/OR graph, thus explaining how certain configurations can arise that do not adhere to the graph construction approach presented in Section 5.23.3. Consider node 1 and the AND reduction operator α_1 depicted in Fig. 5.2. Since α_1 results in only one AND node (3), the synthesis node 2 cannot represent any appreciable synthesis problem. As shown in Fig. 5.3, the graph can be simplified by omitting a trivial synthesis node such as node 2. A similar simplification can be made in the case of an OR reduction that does not give alternative OR nodes. An example is the reduction of node 4 by α_2. Since no heuristic information is needed, the heuristic node 5 can be omitted as illustrated in Fig. 5-3.

Another configuration that can be expressed in a different way is the case of a node that has only one applicable reduction operator, where this

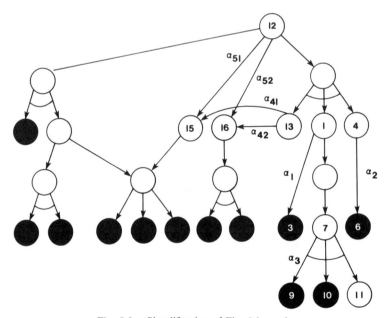

Fig. 5.3.   Simplification of Fig. 5.2 graph.

operator gives an AND reduction. As an example, consider node 7 and reduction operator α_3 in Fig. 5.2. This is sometimes simplified by eliminating node 8 to give the configuration of Fig. 5.3. Since the parent of an AND node is always a synthesis node, the configuration in Fig. 5-3 implies that the problem denoted by node 7 is one of synthesizing the solutions of problems. This is not an unreasonable view. Since no other reduction operators are applicable to node 7, it does not need to be regarded as a heuristic node. Notice that the configuration from node 1 to node 7 could be further simplified as described in the preceding paragraph.

Observe that an OR reduction that results in several OR nodes could be respecified in terms of several different OR reduction operators. Consider the OR reduction of node 12 by α_5 in Fig. 5.2. It may be possible to respecify α_5 in terms of two reduction operators, such that the configuration illustrated in Fig. 5.4 results. Nodes 14a and 14b can then be eliminated, as described earlier, to yield the configuration in Fig. 5.3. This figure also shows the effect of a similar respecification of α_4.

Finally, note that it is possible to draw an AND/OR graph having several start nodes. This is accomplished by combining the graphs of two or more problems that have common subproblem nodes. The resultant AND/OR graph displays solution methods for as many problems as there are start nodes. An example with three start nodes appears in Fig. 5.5. Furthermore, the solution method(s) for the problem represented by any nonterminal node with successors is also given within an AND/OR graph.

All of the alternative expressions presented in this section preserve the customary AND/OR graph restriction that a node cannot have both AND nodes and OR nodes as its immediate successor nodes. In other words, a given nonterminal node cannot be both a synthesis node and a heuristic node.

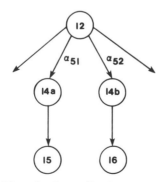

Fig. 5.4. Respecification of α_5.

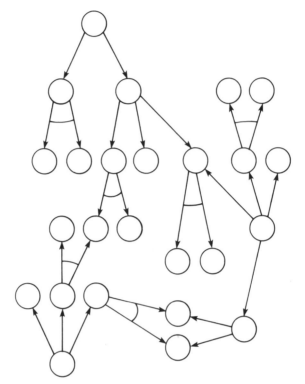

Fig. 5.5. AND/OR graph with multiple start nodes.

5.23.5   Decision-Making Abilities of a Problem Reduction PPS

Techniques for handling information collection, although they must exist, do not constitute the major contribution of problem reduction research. The problem reduction approach to problem solving, together with its various search techniques, allows a PPS to exhibit the abilities of problem recognition, model formulation, and analysis. The major problem recognition task is one of discovering the model and the data that should be interfaced and executed in order to provide a solution to a decision maker's stated problem.

The successive reductions of problems into subproblems may be regarded as a series of problem recognitions. That is, in applying a reduction operator, new problems have been recognized. The problem recognition ability also involves the selection of which path to pursue when a heuristic node is reached, and it thereby controls the model(s) that is eventually formulated. In making such a selection, the problem recognition facet may adopt some uniform search strategy or it may draw on some evaluative ability if heuristic searches are used. At this juncture it may also draw on the PPS information collection ability to gather pertinent contextual information from either a user or the KS.

The problem recognition task ceases when one (or possibly several) feasible model has been formulated. Note that in the course of applying reduction operators, as guided by the problem recognition ability, the system's model formulation ability has been exercised. Thus in a problem reduction technique for problem solving, the model formulation and problem recognition abilities are closely intertwined; and in the case of a heuristic search some evaluation ability may also exist in the PPS. The PPS analysis ability can be separated from the other PPS abilities in terms of the technique(s) that underlies it. That is, problem reduction itself stops when a feasible model has been found (when the problem has been fully reduced).

If the PPS is to be able to return a solution for the problem to a user, it must also employ techniques that give it an analytic ability. It must be able to execute a formulated model, using the primitives (e.g., modules of code) contained in it and the data that the primitives require from a KS. It must also make use of any synthesis information that is included in the formulated model. The problem reduction literature does not concentrate on techniques for supporting the analysis ability. Such techniques lie more in the province of operating systems [5].

5.24 The Correspondence between Problem Reduction and Organizational Information-Processing Framework

In terms of the pictorial formalisms used, an AND/OR graph can be interpreted as a description of the division of information-processing labor in an organization (cf. Chapter 2). Conversely, the organizational information-processing role, by virtue of its information processing, is solving some problem. In fact, the problem addressed by a role could be used to name that role. The correspondences between a role structure and an AND/OR graph are detailed in Table 5.1.

Notice that a role that can be filled in alternative ways corresponds to a node with OR node successors (i.e., what we have called a heuristic node). Similarly, there are other roles (assisted roles) that correspond to synthesis nodes and yet other roles that correspond to terminal nodes. A problem reduction view of an organization would therefore perceive three kinds of roles:

TABLE 5.1

Correspondence between Problem Reduction and Organizational Role Structure

Structure of roles	AND/OR graph
A node represents Expert at solving problem —Expert role (problem solver role) that can be filled in alternative ways —Expert role that consults other experts —Expert role that consults no other expert	A node represents Problem to be solved —Problem with alternative solution methods (node with OR node successors) —Problem that requires solution of other problems (node with AND node successors) —Problem that is directly solvable (terminal node)
Arc Definitional arc points to a way in which an expert role can be filled (i.e., defined) Associative arc points to an expert role from which information is required	Arc Arc emanating from an OR node points to one of a number of alternative problems (one of these alternatives must be solved) Arc emanating from an AND node points to a problem that must be solved

1. the heuristic role, whose information-processing task is one of selecting an appropriate or best role for addressing a given problem, subject to the contextual setting of that problem;

2. the synthesizing role, whose information-processing task is one of synthesizing the results of the work of other roles in order to give a solution to the problem it faces;

3. the primitive (or in other words self-sufficient) role that can immediately, within itself, solve the problem it faces.

A heuristic node in problem reduction is not an essential part of a formulated model, although the selection problem it represents is a crucial ingredient in arriving at a formulation. Similarly, a heuristic role is not an intrinsic participant in an organization's solution method to some problem, but rather an important determinant of what that solution method will entail. A heuristic role may be considered to consist of some set of organizational protocols for channeling a problem in one of several directions, depending on the problem's context. These protocols could conceivably be formal or informal, simple or complex, rigidly or loosely followed, fixed or rapidly changing, and so forth.

A synthesizing role is part of an organization's solution method *per se*, for some given organizational problem(s). It coordinates and controls the way in which other roles are used for a given problem. The most concrete synthesizing roles are handled by persons or automatic mechanisms (e.g., a computer program or even a decision support system). Primitive roles must be concrete, but differ from concrete synthesizing roles in that they are self-sufficient (e.g., the person or group or program that solves its problem without seeking assistance).

The foregoing problem reduction perspective of organizational information processing does not pretend to give a complete view of how an organization works. Nevertheless, we submit that it is a fair and useful framework from the standpoint of studying decision support systems. On the one hand, this view is suggestive of how a DSS might emulate organizational problem solving. On the other hand, this view also indicates how decision support systems could fit into an organization, as primitive (and perhaps even concrete synthesizing) roles.

5.30   A PRODUCTION SYSTEM APPROACH TO DSS

The term "production system," like state space analysis and problem reduction, refers to an application-independent problem-solving technique. Production system research has stemmed from the work of Post [10]. Production systems are presented here in the generic DSS framework. A DSS whose PPS is based on production system techniques will be referred to as a PDSS.

5.31   KS for a PDSS

The knowledge system of a PDSS has two major constituents: a collection of production rules and a "data base." The concept of a production rule is that of an instruction to take a certain action if a certain premise is met. Thus the concept of a production rule (often simply called a production) involves a relationship between two other concepts: a premise and an action. Specific actions and premises are operationally specified in terms of symbol strings. It is customary to operationalize the concept of a production rule in terms of an ordered pair. One element of such an ordered pair consists of a symbol string stating the premise. The other element is a symbol string that states the production rule's action. For ease of exposition we will use the commonplace notation LHS → RHS for indicating a production.

Thus a major portion of the KS for a PDSS consists of a collection of production rules of the form LHS → RHS. These rules may be organized into a certain order as they are inserted into the KS. One should not confuse the symbol → with the implication symbol ⇒ used in logic. The → symbol means that if the premise is satisfied, then the action is taken. A discussion of what is meant by "satisfying" a premise and by "taking" an action is momentarily deferred.

A second major constituent of the KS is what production systems researchers typically call a "data base." This term is used in a loose conceptual sense to indicate some body of information that describes the nature of the application world for which the PDSS will perform its problem solving. The term is not used in an operational sense of implying the use of a data base management technique. To avoid confusion between the production system notion of a "data base" and the subject matter of the field of data base management, we shall hereafter refer to the former as a production system "data base" (PSDB). The latter is introduced in Part III.

According to Davis and King [4] a PSDB "is simply a collection of symbols intended to reflect the state of the world." Attributes of the world state are called *state variables*. So the state variables (i.e., attributes) used to describe one application world can differ from those used to describe another world. At any point during the course of solving a problem, PDSS's production system "data base" will contain a specific value (possibly null) for each of its state variables. Over the course of solving a problem, the contents of the PSDB will change. Such alterations may be viewed as shifts from one specific world state to another.

At a conceptual level the designer of a PDSS knowledge system must ascertain what attributes or state variables are important descriptors of the application world being addressed. There are many possibilities for operationalizing the notion of a PSDB. Perhaps a simple list of tuples [3], one for each state variable that describes the nature of an application world, is the most common. Other techniques that have been used to operationalize a PSDB include graph structures [6] and sequential token streams [11]. Before each problem is posed to the PDSS via its language system, the PSDB portion of the KS may or may not be empty.

Consider first the case of an empty PSDB. When a problem is posed to the PDSS, information from that problem statement is deposited in the PSDB, perhaps in the form of a list of symbols. That is, values are assigned to the PSDB state variables. The problem-processing system takes the state in the PSDB as a starting point and uses productions to alter the PSDB contents repeatedly until it contains a solution. After this solution is reported to the user, the PSDB again becomes empty as it awaits the next problem. In this case, the production system "data base" is comparable to a short-term memory, existing only for the life of a problem.

In some production systems, a PSDB may have a long-term aspect, *in addition* to this temporary memory. That is, it contains other information about an application world that is not specific to only one problem in that application world. Such information is maintained in a PSDB across many problem-solving sessions, so that the PSDB is not empty prior to receiving each problem statement from a user. The existence of this longer-term information diminishes the user's problem statement task.

An interesting research topic related to long-term and short-term memory is the possibility of a PDSS being able to learn. That is, is it feasible to retain in long-term memory the fruits of problem-solving experiences that are lost because of the ephemeral nature of short-term memory? An alternative approach to learning would be to retain information about prior problem-solving experience in the form of productions that are added to the knowledge system's set of production rules. There are many related issues, such as how to assess the utility of a learning capability in various application areas; within an application area, how to determine which problem-solving experiences should be used to learn from and which experiences are less valuable; and how the fact that a particular kind of problem-solving experience is frequently repeated can be used to influence subsequent problem-solving efforts.

5.32 LS for a PDSS

The major contribution of production system research does not lie in the development of an LS for PDSS. (However, as we shall see later, the production system problem-solving technique is very useful in supporting the information collection ability for a DSS problem-processing ability via a language system.) The language system for a PDSS is geared toward allowing a user to specify the initial contents of the PSDB. That is, the user specifies initial values for at least some of the state variables. An example of this may be seen in the PDSS called MYCIN [3].

In MYCIN the PPS prompts the system's user for the data that are inserted into the short-term PSDB. In responding to these promptings the user effectively states a problem that the PPS will attempt to solve through the utilization of productions. Such a language system is non-procedural and is very convenient from a user's viewpoint. The set of permissible expressions in the language is merely the set of all permissible replies that a user can give to the promptings. It should be pointed out that in MYCIN, the PPS can prompt the user for additional information (i.e., state variable values) after the problem-solving process has begun. The particular questions that are asked of the user at a given juncture depend on existing productions and the present status of the PSDB. Thus a user's responses to previous promptings determine the subsequent promptings.

5.33   PPS for a PDSS

The technique(s) for supporting the information-collecting ability of a PDSS problem processor are not standardized, nor are they the central issue in production system research. In the MYCIN system the information collection ability is displayed by the system's ability to ask questions of the user and to accept the user's replies. A reply is converted into an internally comprehensible form and deposited in the KS. The determination of what question should be posed to a user at a given juncture is a part of MYCIN's problem recognition ability.

Techniques underlying a PPS's collection of information from a KS must depend on how the productions and the PSDB are operationalized and implemented. Bear in mind that the information collection ability is not concerned with the determination of which production rule (or which part of the current world state) to access in a given circumstance. It merely executes a retrieval whose necessity has been recognized via the system's problem recognition ability.

A central component of any PDSS problem processor is the interpreter of the system's production rules. The nature of an interpreter can differ markedly from one PDSS to another. Perhaps the simplest kind of interpreter is one that interprets a production rule as a *matching-replacement* rule. Having selected a production, this kind of interpreter examines the present state of the PSDB to see if the state variable values appearing in the production's LHS *match*; if so, a *replacement* action is taken. The state variable values appearing in the production's RHS replace the values of the corresponding state variables in the PSDB. An example of this kind of matching-replacement production system appears in Section 5.35.

There are some interpreters in which this matching-replacement is applied in the opposite direction. Here the interpreter selects a production whose RHS matches some part of the PSDB content. The matching portion of the PSDB is replaced by the production rule's LHS. An example of this type of production system appears in Section 5.36. Production rule interpreters can be more complex than simple matching and replacement (see Davis *et al.* [3] for examples).

From the preceding description it can be seen that not only does an interpreter apply production rules, but also it must determine which production rule to select for application. The problem-solving technique of a production system is to iterate through the cycle of selecting a rule and then applying it. At the start of each cycle the production selection is made according to the criteria defining the interpreter, as well as the PSDB content at that time. It is inappropriate for the interpreter to select a production whose premise is not satisfied by the current PSDB contents. On the other hand, there may be many productions whose premises are satisfied by current PSDB contents. In such a case the selection could be based on an ordering of production rules in the KS, on application of specific selection procedures embedded in the interpreter (implying a nongeneral PPS), or on the use of meta-rules. A meta-rule is an application-dependent strategy for selecting a rule [3]. Meta-rules could be incorporated into the KS to preserve PPS application invariance.

The interpreter's iterative cycling ceases when the PSDB content has taken on some predetermined (i.e., goal) characteristics. The predetermined characteristics depend on the application world and they can be specified in terms of acceptable values for one or more state variables in the PSDB. It is conceivable that the goal characteristics could be stated by a user at the time that the initial short-term PSDB contents are set. But one most frequently finds that goal characteristics are incorporated into the interpreter (or perhaps into the KS) and that these goal characteristics are understood by the system's users. This is the case in MYCIN, where the user does not explicitly state that a diagnosis and treatments are desired. However, the user understands that MYCIN has, as its goal, a PSDB containing a diagnosis and treatments. In the production systems presented in Sections 5.35 and 5.36, goal characteristics are also implicit at the time that initial world states are presented to the systems.

5.34   The Production System Philosophy

The production system philosophy maintains that it is reasonable and possible to capture the knowledge of an expert(s) in some application area in the form of production rules. The rules of the production system represent small parcels of information. Each is a piece of a much larger puzzle. The production system is most effective in its representation when the application being described consists of numerous independent facts. When taken together, these facts allow the interpreter to exhibit a reasonable behavior pattern in an application world (e.g., appropriate responses to different initial PSDB configurations). The philosophy of production systems requires the emphasis of design to be on the construction of the production rules. If the production rules are correctly formulated, then the system will have a behavior consistent with the underlying model. However, the designer should not construct rules solely for the purpose of eliciting a certain behavior. To interpret one rule, knowledge of the other rules is not required; each rule is local.

The PSDB can be as flexible or structured as necessary. It may be restricted in size (only the most recently used pieces of information being maintained), or it may age its data, deleting those elements created more recently than a given number of time units earlier. In any case the PSDB must provide the interpreter with an adequate storage mechanism.

As indicated earlier, interpreters can operate in a variety of ways. Some interpreters perform simple left-to-right replacement by matching the left side of the production rule against elements of the data base and replacing them with the right side of the rule. Other interpreters perform right-to-left replacement. It is conceivable that an interpreter could perform both. Still other interpreters might be additive, not replacing matched symbols, but adding to the data base the symbols on the opposite side. The ordering of the elements of the data base might be controlled by the interpreter. In fact, the interpreter can impose a total ordering on the production rules themselves, in order to specify how ambiguities can be resolved.

Regardless of the technique employed, an interpreter furnishes the problem recognition ability of a PDSS problem processor. It recognizes that the initial world state does not adhere to goal characteristics (i.e., a problem). The constitution of that world state leads the interpreter to select and apply some production. The resultant state of the PSDB is recognized as either a solution or yet another problem. Through the interpreter, new problems are realized, generated or recognized from prior problems until a solution is apparent (or until a time limit is exceeded, or until no new problems can be recognized even though a solution has yet to be found).

Notice that in production systems no computational model is formulated and therefore no subsequent analysis occurs. Thus a PDSS would fit into category L of the classification scheme and it may be described as performing inferential retrieval (recall point 3 in Section 3.13).

Production systems have found application in two separate domains: psychological modeling and decision support. That the former [4] are in fact quite similar in nature to the latter [3, 6] is apparent. Each area is characterized by a large number of independent actions (rules) that combine to form an overall behavior. (In terms of decision support, this is the sum of the knowledge incorporated into the system.) Use of production system concepts and techniques as aids in building decision support systems is the perspective adopted here.

5.35   Generative Grammars as Production Systems

As a first example of a production system, we introduce the notion of grammar [1], which we shall also refer to independently of production systems in later chapters. It should be noted that a generative grammar as a production system has no user in the usual sense of the term. A grammar consists of four objects: a set of *nonterminal* symbols, used by the grammar to represent intermediate steps in the processing; a set of *terminal* symbols, which are symbols in the language produced by the grammar; a set of *production rules*; and a set (usually consisting of a single element) of nonterminal symbols, which may be used to initiate the execution of the production system. The latter are called *start symbols*.

For example, consider the nonterminals: SENTENCE, PRONOUN, VERB, the terminal symbols "he," "she," "eats," "drinks," "sleeps," the initial nonterminal SENTENCE, and the following production set:

(1)   SENTENCE   → PRONOUN VERB
(2)   PRONOUN   → he
(3)   PRONOUN   → she
(4)   VERB   → eats
(5)   VERB   → drinks
(6)   VERB   → sleeps

In generative grammars the PSDB always consists of a single sequential string of symbols, either nonterminals and/or terminals (i.e., there is only one state variable and its possible values are the permitted symbol strings). Initially, the PSDB is empty, and the interpreter will start with a production whose left side contains one of the initial nonterminals. Alternatively, the PSDB could contain one of the initial nonterminal symbols. The interpreter will select arbitrarily (or nondeterministically) one of the production rules, whose left side appears at some point in the PSDB string; this matched portion of the PSDB is then replaced by the right side of the production rule. The execution of the system is terminated whenever no more rules can be applied or the PSDB consists solely of terminal symbols.

Using the grammar defined above, we trace one execution of the production system in Fig. 5.6. Initially the PSDB is empty. We choose production rule (1), since we must start with SENTENCE. After that choice

RULE USED	PSDB
(1)	PRONOUN VERB
(3)	she VERB
(6)	she sleeps

Fig. 5.6.   Simple production sequence.

the rule selection procedure is arbitrary. For this very simple example there are only six possible final configurations of the PSDB (i.e., behaviors of the system), which the alert reader will already have ascertained.

This kind of production system represents the class of left-to-right replacement systems. Rules are applied successively until a final configuration is reached. The set of these final configurations is called the *language* generated by the grammar. The sequence of rules applied in order to generate an element in the language is called that element's *derivation*.

Much research has been conducted on the complexity of languages that have been generated by grammars. Most of this research has been focused on the structure of the production rules. Although the classification schemes are numerous, the simplest (and first) classification scheme is important to the understanding of the behavior of the grammars.

The simplest form of grammar is the *regular* grammar. There are two equivalent forms of regular grammar. The first allows productions of the form: NONTERMINAL → TERMINAL NONTERMINAL and NON-TERMINAL → TERMINAL. The second's productions have the form: NONTERMINAL → NONTERMINAL TERMINAL and NONTER-MINAL → TERMINAL. Regular grammars are also referred to as *finite state* grammars. This is because any "long" derivation will by necessity contain a loop; that is, production rules will be reused.

As an example of a regular grammar, consider a language that consists of only two terminal symbols, a and b. Consider the two production systems characterized by the following two production sets:

(1) A → aA	(1) C → Cb
(2) A → aB	(2) C → Db
(3) B → bB	(3) D → Da
(4) B → b	(4) D → a
(Nonterminals A, B; initial nonterminal is A)	(Nonterminals C, D; initial nonterminal is C)

Each of these systems is regular, because each has one of the two allowable production forms. In Fig. 5.7 the language elements abb and aaabbbb are derived in each system. The reader should verify that the form of the

RULE USED	PSDB	RULE USED	PSDB
(2)	aB	(1)	Cb
(3)	abB	(2)	Dbb
(4)	abb	(4)	abb
(1)	aA	(1)	Cb
(1)	aaA	(1)	Cbb
(2)	aaaB	(1)	Cbbb
(3)	aaabB	(2)	Dbbbb
(3)	aaabbB	(3)	Dabbbb
(3)	aaabbbB	(3)	Daabbbb
(4)	aaabbbb	(4)	aaabbbb

Fig. 5.7.   Right- and left-most derivations of aaabbbb.

language generated by the grammars is "one or more occurrences of a" followed by "one or more occurrences of b," and that each system generates the same language.

However, not all languages are regular. English is not; neither are FORTRAN nor COBOL. For example, in FORTRAN the introduction of "(" in an expression requires the introduction of ")" at a later time. But a regular production system is incapable of such a feat of memory (again because of the concept of finite state grammar). Therefore it is necessary to introduce more complex forms of productions.

Context-free grammars have production rules with a single nonterminal symbol on the left side and any combination of terminals and nonterminals on the right. Figure 5.8 shows a set of production rules for producing arithmetic expressions in FORTRAN. Figure 5.9 gives several sample derivations of this system. The class of context-free languages is a much richer class than regular languages; most programming languages fall into this category. In general, the production system interpreter can select any nonterminal in the production system "data base" for replacement; often,

(1)	$EXP \rightarrow E_1$
(2)	$EXP \rightarrow E_1 + EXP$
(3)	$EXP \rightarrow E_1 - EXP$
(4)	$E_1 \;\; \rightarrow E_2$
(5)	$E_1 \;\; \rightarrow E_2 * E_1$
(6)	$E_1 \;\; \rightarrow E_2 / E_1$
(7)	$E_2 \;\; \rightarrow E_3$
(8)	$E_2 \;\; \rightarrow E_3 ** E_3$
(9)	$E_3 \;\; \rightarrow$ "CONSTANT"
(10)	$E_3 \;\; \rightarrow$ "VARIABLE"
(11)	$E_3 \;\; \rightarrow (EXP)$

Fig. 5.8.   Productions for FORTRAN-like expressions.

RULE USED	PSDB	RULE USED	PSDB
(1)	E_1	(2)	$E_1 + EXP$
(5)	$E_2 * E_1$	(4)	$E_2 + EXP$
(7)	$E_3 * E_1$	(7)	$E_3 + EXP$
(10)	$A * E_1$	(10)	$A + EXP$
(4)	$A * E_2$	(2)	$A + E_1 + EXP$
(7)	$A * E_3$	(6)	$A + E_2/E_1 + EXP$
(11)	$A * (EXP)$	(7)	$A + E_3/E_1 + EXP$
(2)	$A * (E_1 + EXP)$	(10)	$A + B/E_1 + EXP$
(4)	$A * (E_2 + EXP)$	(4)	$A + B/E_2 + EXP$
(7)	$A * (E_3 + EXP)$	(7)	$A + B/E_3 + EXP$
(10)	$A * (B + EXP)$	(10)	$A + B/C + EXP$
(3)	$A * (B + E_1 - EXP)$	(1)	$A + B/C + E_1$
(4)	$A * (B + E_2 - EXP)$	(4)	$A + B/C + E_2$
(7)	$A * (B + E_3 - EXP)$	(7)	$A + B/C + E_3$
(10)	$A * (B + C - EXP)$	(10)	$A + B/C + D$
(1)	$A * (B + C - E_1)$		
(4)	$A * (B + C - E_2)$		
(7)	$A * (B + C - E_3)$		
(9)	$A * (B + C - 3.)$		

Fig. 5.9. Operation of left-to-right interpreter.

however, it is constrained without loss of generality to the leftmost or rightmost nonterminal in the PSDB.

English is not context-free. Therefore two other major classifications of grammars exist. *Context-sensitive* production rules have arbitrary combinations of terminals and nonterminals on both sides of the rule, with the restriction that, for each rule, the number of symbols on the left be less than or equal to the number of symbols on the right. Context-sensitive grammars are for this reason also called *expansive* grammars. *Recursively enumerable* production rules do not have the size limitations. These are the most general form of production rule, and it has been shown that *any* behavior can be simulated by a sufficiently complex recursively enumerable production system [1].

Context-sensitive grammars are much more complex than context-free grammars. Less is understood about them, and hence they are used less in applications. Figure 5.10 gives one use of a context-sensitive system, whose behavior consists of leaving the PSDB in a configuration of a valid date, that is, month/day/year. The notion of context sensitivity enters in selecting a day that is valid for the month in question; for example, we would not want the language element 2/31/80 to appear.

Nonterminals = {DATE, M, M_{30}, M_{31}, Y_1, Y_2, D_{28}, D_{29}, D_{30}, D_{31}}
Terminals = {0, 1, 2, . . . , 9, /}
Productions:
   (1)   DATE → M/Y_1
   (2)   DATE → M/Y_2
   (3)–(78) Y_1 → 00 | 01 | 02 | 03 | 05 | . . . | 99 (Note: No multiple of 4 besides 0)
   (79) Y_2 → 04 | 08 | . . . | 96
   (103)–(105)   M → 02 | M_{30}/D_{30} | M_{31}/D_{31}
   (106)   02/Y_1 → 02/D_{28}/Y_1
   (107)   02/Y_2 → 02/D_{29}/Y_2
   (108)–(111) M_{30} → 04 | 06 | 09 | 11
   (112)–(118) M_{31} → 01 | 03 | 05 | 07 | 08 | 10 | 12
   (119)–(146) D_{28} → 01 | 02 | . . ./28
   (147)–(148) D_{29} → D_{28} | 29
   (149)–(150) D_{30} → D_{29} | 30
   (151)–(152) D_{31} → D_{30} | 31

Fig. 5.10.   Context sensitive grammar for dates.

5.36   Parsing as a Production System

In the preceding section, grammars were used as an example of a production system whose interpreter used left-to-right simple replacement. Here grammars will be used in a different manner, that is, in a production system whose interpreter uses right-to-left replacement.

Parsing is the operation of determining the structure (or syntax) of a language element (string). Thus parsing is a technique of linguistic problem solving. As such we might expect that it could be usefully employed in a DSS problem processor, as a technique for supporting the information collection ability (*vis-à-vis* the LS). If a production system were used in this way, the initial PSDB contents would consist of a user's problem statement (i.e., a string of symbols to be parsed).

Given a grammar (e.g., for a decision support system's LS), it is necessary to determine whether or not some given string was generated by the production rules of the grammar, and also what the production sequence was. For definiteness, let us consider the grammar of Fig. 5.8. Recall that the grammar produces expressions in a procedural programing language such as FORTRAN. Suppose that the initial configuration of the PSDB is ((A − B) * C). We want the behavior of the production system to (1) indicate whether or not the string initially in the PSDB is indeed an element of the language of the grammar, and (2) determine the correct sequence of production rules for generating this string.

Because of their simplicity, regular grammars are relatively easy to parse. Consider the regular grammar of the previous section, whose production rules are as follows:

(1) $C \to Cb$
(2) $C \to Db$
(3) $D \to Da$
(4) $D \to a$

Suppose that the initial configuration of the PSDB is aabbb. We start with the leftmost terminal in the PSDB, and try to match it with the right side of a production rule. The only rule that matches it is (4); performing the replacement, the new configuration of the PSDB is Dabbb. Now we repeat the operation: The leftmost pair of symbols (Da) is matched by the right side of production (3), and this is the only match. Therefore we perform the replacement to produce: Dbbb. Proceeding, the substring Db is matched by the right side of rule (2), and we now have Cbb in the data base. Using rule (1) the PSDB becomes Cb, and another application of rule (1) results in a PSDB consisting solely of the nonterminal C. Since C is one of the initial nonterminals (in fact, it is the only initial nonterminal), we conclude that the string aabbb is an element of the language generated by this grammar. Furthermore, we can read the proper derivation by examining the rules used during parsing; by applying them in the reverse order (i.e., (1), (1), (2), (3), (4)) we arrive at the proper sequence of production rules for generating this string, as the reader can easily verify.

The general form of a parsing production system is to take the initial PSDB configuration, if possible, into one of the grammar's initial nonterminal symbols. In the case of context-free grammars, the situation is complicated by the fact that the leftmost group of symbols in the data base may not always be the candidates for replacement during the parsing process. Therefore the context-free interpreter must have a more complex selection rule than that of the regular interpreter.

Again using the grammar of Fig. 5.8, suppose we have in the PSDB the string $A * (B + C)$, where of course A, B, and C are variables. Beginning the execution of the production system, we see that for the string to begin with a variable, production (10) must be used. Thus the PSDB will become $E_3 * (B + C)$. Now we see that E_3 can be found on the right side of rule (7), so it is replaced by E_2; similarly, E_2 is replaced by E_1 in rule (4) and E_1 by EXP by rule (1). Now the PSDB configuration is EXP $* (B + C)$, and we now have a problem: No production rule has on its right side any expression beginning with EXP. In other words, the string cannot be further altered.

The difficulty arose because we went too far without examining the consequences. So now we must back up to where the PSDB contained E_1

$*$ (B + C). The difficulty here is that no rule has the two consecutive symbols E_1* on its right side. Again we cannot proceed, so we must back up one more step. Before we applied rule (4) the PSDB contained $E_2 * (B + C)$. Now it appears that we can proceed, since the right side of rule (5) begins with E_2*. Our goal then becomes to find a way to identify the remainder of the string with the nonterminal E_1 in order to match rule (5) completely.

The next symbol in the string is "(". Since rule (11) is the only rule to contain parentheses, it is obvious that this is the proper choice. The question becomes, is there enough information to make the match? By pairing the two parentheses, it becomes clear that the new goal is to identify the remainder of the string, namely B + C, with the nonterminal EXP.

The complete parse is shown in Fig. 5.11. Backtracking steps have been eliminated. Notice that the process is as follows: Replace elements in the PSDB string in order to attain a complete right side of some production rule. The interpreter will follow this guideline as long as the result does not lead to a dead end.

5.37 The MYCIN Interpreter

A right-to-left interpreter can also be used in situations where the production rules are not viewed from a linguistic perspective. As an example we shall consider the control architecture of the MYCIN interpreter. Some features (e.g., certainty factors) of this interpreter are not exam-

PSDB	RULE USED
A $*$ (B + C)	
$E_3 * (B + C)$	(10)
$E_2 * (B + C)$	(7)
$E_2 * (E_3 + C)$	(10)
$E_2 * (E_2 + C)$	(7)
$E_2 * (E_1 + C)$	(4)
$E_2 * (E_1 + E_3)$	(10)
$E_2 * (E_1 + E_2)$	(7)
$E_2 * (E_1 + E_1)$	(4)
$E_2 * (E_1 + EXP)$	(1)
$E_2 * (EXP)$	(2)
$E_2 * E_3$	(11)
$E_2 * E_2$	(7)
$E_2 * E_1$	(4)
E_1	(6)
EXP	(1)

Fig. 5.11. Parsing a FORTRAN expression.

ined in this simplified description; refer to Davis *et al.* [3] for a more complete description. Recall that the initial PSDB consists of some patient information (e.g., age, sex, symptoms, test results, etc.) that MYCIN has elicited from a user. Some of the PSDB state variables are null as the problem solving commences. These initially null state variables include those regarding the patient's diagnosis and prescribed treatment. When these two are no longer null, then the system stops and makes its recommendation to the user. Thus a diagnosis–treatment may be regarded as the system's goal.

The MYCIN interpreter works by reducing this goal into subgoals as a depth-first search of an AND/OR graph. There are no explicit reduction operators, but the reductions are implied by MYCIN's productions, together with a right-to-left interpretation of the production rules. Given a production system goal (which may be viewed as a problem node in problem reduction), the interpreter locates every production whose RHS consists of the same state variable that has a null value in the goal. The LHS of each such production is then examined.

Either the LHS premise is verified by the PSDB contents, it is rejected by (contrary to) the PSDB contents, or it refers to some state variables whose values are null in the PSDB. In the first case the goal has been attained, where the production corresponds to an AND reduction operator that gives all terminal nodes. In the second case the RHS of the production definitely does not meet the goal (the production corresponding to a reduction operator that gives a dead end). In the third case a new goal is set up for each state variable with a null value. This corresponds to an AND reduction of the problem that results in some nonterminal AND nodes. Each of these new goals is handled just as was the goal that they resulted from.

If there are *n* productions whose RHS bears on a goal, then in the corresponding AND/OR graph there are *n* arcs emanating from the problem node to OR nodes. Observe that a difference between problem reduction and the right-to-left interpreter of a production system is that in the latter certain information in the PSDB connotes a terminal node (as opposed to the existence of a "model building block" for each terminal node).

5.38 A Production System for Simple Inventory Management

Suppose that the inventory problem is one of managing the stocks of I inventory items. An inventory item is denoted by i, where $i \in \{1, 2, \ldots, I\}$. To keep this example simple, we make the assumption that there is one supplier for each item. The PSDB contains seven state variables for each item i. Each state variable is expressed as a labeled tuple:

STOCK (i, N_i): N_i units of item i are in stock
ONORDER (i, M_i): M_i units of item i are on order
REORDER (i, r_i, l_i): r_i is the reorder point of item i with a re-
                          order quantity of l_i
SENDORDER (i, l_i):   an order of l_i units of item i should be sent
GETORDER (i, l_i): l_i units of item i are received
SALE (i, p_i, q_i): q_i units of item i are sold at price p_i
INVOICE (i, p_i, q_i):   an invoice for q_i units of i at price p_i
                          should be prepared

The interpreter for the inventory production system works on a left-to-right basis, using the *ordered* production rules shown in Fig. 5.12. Each production rule is interpreted as follows. If every state variable on the LHS has a nonnull value in the PSDB and if the condition stated in braces before the right arrow is satisfied, then the values of the state variables on the RHS are entered into the PSDB. Rather than simple matching, the interpreter performs a conditional matching where conditions are shown in braces in Fig. 5.12.

The inventory PSDB has a long-term and a short-term aspect. State variables whose values are maintained between executions of the interpreter are STOCK, ONORDER, and REORDER. Values of the other state variables are retained on a short-term basis only. The interpreter can execute as soon as a user enters either SALE or GETORDER values into the PSDB. Following this stimulus, the interpreter attempts to use each production in the order given in Fig. 5.12. As a result the PSDB will contain values for the initially null SENDORDER and/or INVOICE state

(1) STOCK (i, N_i), REORDER (i, r_i, l_i), ONORDER (i, M_i)

$\{N_i + M_i \le r_i\} \to$ STOCK (i, N_i), REORDER (i, r_i, l_i), ONORDER $(i, M_i + l_i)$,
                SENDORDER (i, l_i)

(2) STOCK (i, N_i), GETORDER (i, l_i), ONORDER (i, M_i)

$\to$ STOCK $(i, N_i + l_i)$, ONORDER $(i, M_i - l_i)$

(3) SALE (i, p_i, q_i), STOCK (i, N_i)

$\{q_i \le N_i\} \to$ STOCK $(i, N_i - q_i)$, INVOICE (i, p_i, q_i)

(4) SALE (i, p_i, q_i), STOCK (i, N_i), ONORDER (i, M_i), REORDER (i, r_i, l_i)

$\{q_i > M_i + N_i\} \to$ ONORDER $(i, M_i + \max(l_i, q_i - (N_i + M_i)))$,
                SENDORDER $(i, \max(l_i, q_i - (M_i + N_i)))$, SALE (i, p_i, q_i),
                REORDER (i, r_i, l_i)

Fig. 5.12. Production rules for inventory management.

variables. These values are used to govern the actions taken (external to the PDSS) as a result of a given stimulus. The interpreter, in determining values for SENDORDER and INVOICE, has also adjusted the values of long-term state variables appropriately. After the interpreter has finished processing for a given stimulus, the values of short-term state variables are set to be null and the PDSS awaits its next stimulus.

5.40 CONCLUSION

In this chapter we have examined three formalized problem-solving approaches that are well known in the field of artificial intelligence. Each was presented in the DSS framework, in order to be suggestive of possible techniques for implementing a generalized PPS. Although the three approaches have some similarities, there are also differences. The state space and problem reduction approaches are summarized in Table 5.2. Both can be described in terms of graphs, but the ways in which the graphs are used belie their fundamentally different orientations. In both approaches the problem solving starts at a root node. For a state space approach the root node connotes the initial state as it exists in the KS. For problem reduction the root node represents a problem (stated via the LS) that a user desires to have solved.

Thus in a state space approach, the PPS works from the initial knowl-

TABLE 5.2

Composition of State Space and Problem Reduction

	State space approach	Problem reduction approach
Node represents	State	Problem
Search to find	Solution path in state space	Solution path in AND/OR graph
Root node represents	Initial state in KS	User-stated problem in LS
End of solution path(s)	Nodes that fit the goal stated by user in LS	Terminal nodes that fit the initial knowledge in KS
Knowledge system	State (initially known in KS)	Problem(s) (initially known in KS)
Problem-solving orientation of PPS	↓ generate	↑ find
Language system	State (goal stated by a user is to achieve this state)	Problem (objective stated by a user is to solve this problem)

edge (in KS) toward the generation of something that fits the user's objective (in LS). We shall refer to this as a top–down or generative orientation toward problem solving. Problem reduction has an opposite orientation. Its PPS works from a user-stated objective of having some problem solved (in LS) toward the discovery of something that fits the initial knowledge (in KS). We shall refer to this problem-solving orientation as being bottom–up. It attempts to verify that there exists knowledge in the KS that allows a problem to be solved. The top–down orientation begins by looking at extant knowledge in the KS and attempts to generate a state in which goals are met. Observe that both orientations result in solution methods to posed problems or goals.

Production systems take one of these two orientations, depending on the nature of the interpreter. Roughly speaking, a left-to-right interpreter has a top–down, generative orientation and a right-to-left interpreter has the opposite orientation. A generative grammar can be used to generate many sentences from a given start symbol, some of which may satisfy a stated goal. A parser begins with some string and attempts to verify that it was derivable from some prestated knowledge (i.e., grammar). MYCIN begins with a problem (or goal) of having a diagnosis–treatment for patient X. Working right to left through the productions, its PPS verifies that the patient's ailments are derivable from some organism. The inventory system was generative; in response to some stimulus it merely generated the appropriate new values for the PSDB.

REFERENCES

1. A. V. Aho and J. D. Ullman, "The Theory of Parsing, Translating and Compiling," Vol. 1. Prentice Hall, Englewood Cliffs, New Jersey, 1972.
2. S. Amarel, On representations of problems of reasoning about actions, *in* "Machine Intelligence" (D. Michie, ed.), Vol. 3. American Elsevier, New York, 1968.
3. R. Davis, B. Buchanan, and E. Shortliffe, Production rules as a representation for a knowledge-based consultation program, *Artificial Intelligence* **8** (1977).
4. R. Davis and J. King, An Overview of Production Systems, *in* "Machine Intelligence" (E. Elcock and D. Michie, ed.), Vol. 8. Halsted Press, New York, 1977.
5. J. J. Donovan, "Systems Programming." McGraw-Hill, New York, 1972.
6. E. A. Feigenbaum, B. G. Buchanan, and J. Lederberg, On generality and problem solving—A case study involving the DENDRAL program, *in* "Machine Intelligence" (B. Meltzer and D. Michie, eds.), Vol. 6. Edinburgh Univ. Press, Edinburgh, Scotland, 1971.
7. R. W. Gerard, The neurophysiology of purposive behavior, *in* "Purposive Systems" (H. von Foerster, J. D. White, L. J. Peterson, and J. K. Russell, eds.). Spartan Books, New York, 1968.

8. D. Knuth, "The Art of Computer Programming," Vol. 1, 2nd ed. Addison-Wesley, Reading, Massachusetts, 1973.

9. N. J. Nilsson, "Problem Solving Methods in Artificial Intelligence." McGraw-Hill, New York, 1971.

10. E. Post, Formal reductions of the general combinational problem, *Amer. J. Math.* **65** (1943).

11. L. G. Tesler, H. J. Enea, and D. C. Smith, The LISP70 pattern matching system, *Proc. Internat. Joint Conf. Artificial Intelligence, 3rd, Stanford, California* (1973).

Part III

DECISION SUPPORT SYSTEMS FROM THE DATA BASE ANGLE

Part III explores data base approaches to constructing decision support systems. Chapters 6 and 7 examine data base techniques for representing (i.e., organizing) knowledge in a KS. The emphasis is on the logical level of knowledge representation, rather than on the ways in which logical representations can be physically implemented. Both conceptual and operational constructs of knowledge representation are presented.

Chapter 8 surveys the kinds of languages that can be used in conjunction with a data base KS. These are presented from the standpoint of the classification scheme developed earlier in Chapter 3. Thus the languages are discussed primarily in terms of what might be called procedurality. That is, how flexible is a language with regard to the richness of procedure (retrieval or computational) available to a user? Moreover, how procedural must a user's problem specification be?

Problem-processing issues for a data base KS are discussed in Chapter 9. Methods for handling the decision-making abilities of information collection, problem recognition, modeling, and analysis are addressed. Extensions to the data base approach for constructing decision support systems are dealt with in Chapter 10.

Chapter 6

CONCEPTUAL AND OPERATIONAL CONSTRUCTS FOR BUILDING A DATA BASE KNOWLEDGE SYSTEM

6.00 INTRODUCTORY COMMENTS

Construction of a knowledge system begins with the selection of techniques for representing elemental pieces of data and for representing their interrelationships. The chosen techniques are then used to define a pattern (a blueprint) according to which actual problem domain data can be organized. This pattern according to which data are organized is often referred to as a *data structure* or a *schema*. As noted in Sections 1.22.1 and 1.23.1, the trend in file management–data base management (DBM) has been toward the invention of techniques that allow the construction of increasingly complex data structures. This complexity is in terms of the data relationships that can be represented.

A frequently drawn distinction in the DBM field is the one between logical data organization and physical data organization. The former views data organization abstractly, whereas the latter views data organization at the level of physical implementation. A physical data organization method is concerned with the relationship between the physical location of a bundle of data in auxiliary memory and the contents of (i.e., data values that make up) that data bundle. Logical organization is unconcerned about where a bundle of data is stored, but is involved with specifying how various data bundles are semantically (i.e., conceptually rather than physically) related to each other. For the most part, our attention here is confined to logical data relationships.

6.01   Logical versus Physical Data Relationships

Physical data organization is concerned with specifying *where* a piece of data is in relationship to other pieces of data. This is accomplished by assigning each piece of data an absolute or relative address by indicating its physical location (in a computer system or a manual system). Thus one piece of data is physically related to a second piece of data by storing them in physically contiguous positions or by storing the address of one piece of data as a part of the second piece of data. The address of one piece of data that is stored within a second piece of data to establish a relationship between the two is called a *pointer;* that is, it points to the first piece of data. There are many variations and combinations of these two basic methods for physically specifying data relationships, such as indexing and pointer arrays (e.g., Haseman and Whinston [5]).

Logical data organization does not descend to this level of detail. Logical data organization utilizes certain *constructs* to specify the relationships among pieces of data without attending to the manner in which the relationships are physically realized. In fact, a logically specified relationship (in terms of some logical construct) can be physically implemented in a variety of ways. Thus a logical data structure *does not* imply a particular kind of physical data organization. For instance, the notion of a list of customers is a logical data organization that may be implemented as a physical list (data on one customer physically succeeds another) or as noncontiguous pieces of data linked by physical pointers.

Unless otherwise indicated, use of the terms "data structure," "data relationship," "data organization" should be understood in the logical sense, without physical connotation. In the preceding paragraph it was mentioned that certain "constructs" are used to specify logical data relationships. These are few in number and they will be introduced and illustrated as needed. In presenting the common varieties of data organization, we begin with tables (otherwise known as logical files or lists). These are the simplest sort of data-structuring techniques, in that they can be described with the fewest conceptual constructs. From this point we progress through increasingly complex types of structures, each involving some new construct or a new use of an already introduced construct.

6.02 Two Levels of Logical Organization

Although it is not customary to do so, we divide logical data organization into two levels: conceptual and operational. These two levels of knowledge representation differ in the constructs that they furnish for describing data and their interrelationships. Conceptual constructs are used to represent knowledge about the world (e.g., about a problem domain, about an organization and its environment) in terms divorced from computer terminology. Operational constructs are data base management terms with which data base structures may be defined.

The strategy of presentation in this chapter is displayed in Fig. 6.1. Conceptual constructs for knowledge representation are introduced. Their striking resemblance to the framework for describing information processing in an organization (Chapter 2) will be apparent. As the operational constructs (i.e., data base terms) are introduced, each one is bound to a corresponding conceptual construct. Readers interested in implementation of constructs and the ways in which they can be bound to various operational constructs should consult data base management textbooks [2, 5, 7].

There are several reasons for this dichotomous approach to describing logical representation, some of which will not be fully appreciated until later chapters. First, it permits an identification of the simple conceptual foundations that underlie DBM terminology. Second, it serves to demonstrate the correspondence between DBM techniques for organizing knowledge and the framework for information processing in an organization. As we shall see in Chapter 10, this correspondence is particularly important for the incorporation of models into a DSS not as a part of its PPS (as is the case with GPLAN and the systems of Chapter 3), but as a

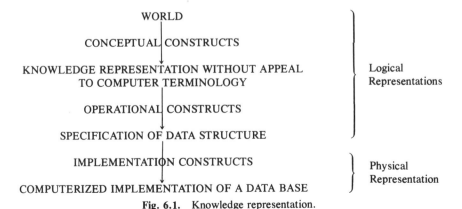

Fig. 6.1. Knowledge representation.

part of its KS. The result is a step toward greater PPS generality. Models can be application specific, just as data can. If these models are incorporated into a PPS, then that PPS must be modified in order to treat a new application. Incorporating models into the KS insulates the PPS from the effects of application changes.

Third, the notion of conceptual constructs, which although not using data base terms can be bound to them, has implications for data base designers and systems analysts. Conceptual constructs provide a stepping-stone to aid in traversing the gap between the world and the data base structures that must be designed to represent it.

Finally, recall that a KS is intended to be used by a PPS. As the abilities of problem processors become more numerous and more highly developed, especially in terms of problem recognition and model formulation, it becomes crucial that the operational constructs used to specify particular data base structures be semantically unambiguous. That is, the same operational construct should not be used to represent semantically distinct conceptual constructs. Otherwise a certain amount of confusion in the PPS results. This point is amplified in Chapter 10.

6.10   CONCEPTUAL CONSTRUCTS FOR REPRESENTING KNOWLEDGE

At a conceptual level, the problem of knowledge representation can be viewed as a problem of representing the relationships among the members of some set of concepts. Here we shall consider two fundamental types of relationship. It is not claimed that these two kinds of relationship account for all conceivable relationships that could exist between concepts. It is, however, fair to say that they are important (i.e., pervasive) and semantically distinct ways for representing relationships between concepts.

Unless otherwise indicated, the term "concept" should be thought of as an indivisible concept. For example, if we are not interested in decomposing customers' names, then 'customer name' is viewed as an indivisible concept. Examples of other concepts that are less abstract than 'customer name' are the actual names of customers, such as 'Bob Smith' or 'Steve Moore.'

6.11   Definitional Relationship between Concepts

The first type of relationship to be considered is of a definitional nature. If reference to a concept X can be construed as being a reference to one of the concepts $X_1, X_2, \ldots, X_n$, then we say that there is a definitional relationship between X and X_i ($i = 1, \ldots, n$). That is, each X_i gives an alternative way of defining X. The choice of one of these alternatives is sensitive to the context in which X is used. This relationship can also be described by saying that X_i is an instantiation or an exemplification of X. For instance, reference to the concept 'company' could mean 'manufacturing company,' or 'service company,' or 'research company,' etc. The latter are instantiations or exemplifications of 'company.' They are alternative ways to 'define' what is meant by 'company.' The instantiation that is chosen depends on the context within which the concept 'company' is used.

Observe that a concept that serves as an instantiation of another concept may have instantiations of its own. Reference to the concept X_1 may be construed as being a reference to one of the concepts $X_{11}, X_{12}, \ldots, X_{1m}$. Returning to the previous example, 'manufacturing company' could be exemplified by 'steel company,' or 'textile company,' or 'paper company,' etc. On yet another level, possible instantiations of 'steel company' are 'U.S. Steel' or 'Inland Steel,' etc.

Notice that it is the definitional relationship between two concepts that establishes their relative degrees of abstractness or concreteness. 'Inland Steel' is more concrete than 'steel company,' which is more concrete than 'manufacturing company,' which is more concrete than 'company.' Taking another example, we said earlier that 'customer name' is a more abstract concept than 'Bob Smith' or 'Steve Moore.' This statement is valid because there is a definitional relationship between 'customer name' and 'Bob Smith' and between 'customer name' and 'Steve Moore.'

Observe that a definitional relationship is a way of referring to the notion of a 'type'–'token' dichotomy [10, 11]. However in the present framework, a 'token' may also be a 'type,' with respect to 'tokens' of its own (X_1 is a 'token' of X, but X_1 is also a 'type' having $X_{11}, X_{12}, \ldots, X_{1m}$ as 'tokens' and so forth). A definitional relationship is also descriptive of the relationship between an attribute and a value with respect to an attribute–value pair [13]. As shown in the foregoing examples, we generalize the notion of attribute–value pairs to include the case where a value is also an attribute, having values of its own.

Finally, we point out that this definitional relationship between concepts is just a generalization of the definitional relationship among roles introduced in Section 2.12.1. That is, the information-processing roles are concepts of a particular kind, and certain roles are related to each other in a definitional manner. It is the definitional relationship that establishes the relative degree of concreteness or abstractness of a role.

6.12   Associative Relationship between Concepts

Thus far we have considered relationships among concepts that consist of one concept having other concepts as its instances or examples. There is another, semantically distinct type of relationship that can exist among concepts. We shall refer to this as an *associative relationship*. An associative connection between two concepts is a nondefinitional relationship, indicating that the two can be associated with each other to yield a meaningful conglomerate. That is, by virtue of associating the two concepts there is a representation of some knowledge that is not present when considering each concept individually.

Each associative connection must specify the nature of the association (e.g., contains, utilizes, possesses, produces, consults, etc.). For example, the two concepts 'company' and 'city' may be associated with one another to indicate that 'company' can be located in 'city.' Another *type* of association between these two specifies that a city can be within a company's sales territory. Thus the same two concepts may be associated in many different ways. Conversely, a particular kind of association (e.g., consults) may be descriptive of the relationship between concepts X and Y, between concepts U and V, etc.

Notice that an associative relationship between concepts is merely a generalization of the associative relationship among roles introduced in Section 2.12.2. That is, the information-processing roles are concepts of a particular kind and certain roles are related to each other in an associative manner. Observe that the specific nature of association between roles is one of consultation, in which one role associates with another by the passage of messages.

6.13   Semantic Distinction between Association and Definition

The distinction between definitional relationships and associative relationships is not an arbitrary one. The key semantic difference is that the two require different kinds of processing in order to be meaningful to a problem processor. With respect to *definitional relationships,* we are interested in finding the *meaning of one concept.* This meaning is established by the problem processor's selection of one of this concept's alternative instantiations; the selected instantiation may itself be a concept (with its own instantiations) whose meaning is determined by the selection of one of its own instantiations. With respect to *associative relationships* we are interested in find the *meaning of a conglomerate of two or more concepts.*

That is, the problem processor must extract a meaning from the combining of two or more concepts via some sort of association. Woods [13] has discussed the importance of this semantic distinction with regard to the representation of English sentences.

The remainder of this chapter focuses on operational constructs that can lead to computerized implementations of the foregoing conceptual constructs. If the semantics of these conceptual constructs is to be maintained on an operational basis, it is imperative that no operational construct be bound to more than one conceptual construct. (For a discussion of this with respect to the use of pictorial semantic networks for representing the semantics of English sentences, see Woods [13].) If this rule is not observed, then the semantic distinctions inherent in the conceptual constructs are lost. This prevents semantic information processing based on the operational (computer-related) constructs. In other words, the semantics of each operational construct must be unambiguous to the automated problem processor, so as to enable it to perform the appropriate variety of processing for each of the semantically distinct constructs.

6.20   SIMPLE FILES AND TABLES

Tables or logical files can be described in terms of four DBM terms: data item type, data item occurrence, record type, and record occurrence. Usage of the word "file" will hereafter denote a logical file. To refer to a physical file, the entire phrase "physical file" will be used. The four DBM terms are operational constructs that allow us to specify how some problem domain's data can be logically organized. The specification of this logical organization (i.e., schema), along with a binding of the operational constructs to implementation constructs, allows the information to be physically represented.

6.21   Item Types and Occurrences

The notion of indivisible concepts is, in DBM, operationalized as *data item types* and *data item occurrences*. An indivisible concept X that has instantiations is called the *data item type X*. For example, the concept of a customer name is operationalized by declaring the data item type: CUSTOMER-NAME. *An indivisible concept* X_i, that is an instantiation of some other indivisible concept X, is called a *data item occurrence* X_i of the item type X. The concept 'Bob Smith,' as an instantiation of the concept 'customer-name,' is operationalized by declaring BOB SMITH to be an occurrence of the item type CUSTOMER-NAME.

Observe that the relationship between a data item type and an occurrence of that type is definitional in nature. Reference to the data item type CUSTOMER-NAME could be a reference to either BOB SMITH, STEVE MOORE, or any other occurrence of CUSTOMER-NAME. The occurrences fix or mark the limits of the item type; they give the possible meanings or values that can be ascribed to an item type.

Consider a request to list a CUSTOMER-NAME. In the course of processing this request, a determination must be made as to what the request really means. Is the request really for BOB SMITH, or STEVE MOORE, or some other customer's name? Which meaning is intended? The selection of a particular instance(s) of CUSTOMER-NAME will depend on the nature of the processing and perhaps on the context in which the phrase is embedded. For instance, the processor may be designed to choose the most conveniently accessible value for CUSTOMER-NAME. This would be analogous to a human processor that selects the first or shortest definition of a word whose meanings are listed in a dictionary. Alternatively, the processor may attempt to determine which customer name is intended on the basis of the context in which the request appears. This is analogous to human utilization of a dictionary to determine the meaning of a word based on the context in which it appears.

The notions presented in this section are summarized in Table 6.1. Horizontally, this table indicates how the operational constructs are bound to the conceptual. Vertically, it suggests that a definitional relation-

TABLE 6.1

Indivisible Conceptual and Operational Constructs

Conceptual construct		Operational construct
1. An indivisible concept X that *has* instantiations	is called	the data item type X
Example: The concept of a 'customer name'	is operationalized	by declaring (in DDL) the data item type: CUSTOMER-NAME.
2. An indivisible concept X_i that *is* an instantiation of some other indivisible concept X	is called	a data item occurrence X_i of the data item type X.
Example: The concept 'Bob Smith' as an instantiation of the concept 'customer name'	is operationalized	by declaring (in DML) BOB SMITH to be an occurrence of the item type: CUSTOMER-NAME

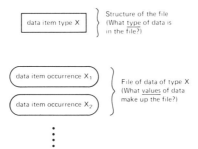

Fig. 6.2. File structure and content.

ship among concepts is akin to the relationship between a data item type and its occurrences. The collection (group or list) of data item occurrences of a data item type is the simplest kind of a *file*. (See Martin [7] for a discussion of ways to organize a file physically.) The relationship between any occurrence in the file and the data item type that describes the file is definitional in nature.

This idea of a simple file may be represented pictorially in a Bachman diagram [9], as shown in Fig. 6.2. The data item type name, enclosed in a rectangle, indicates the *structure* of the file. It tells what *type* of data is in the file. The file itself is composed of occurrences of the named item type. Each occurrence is represented by an encircled value. Figure 6.3 shows examples of three simple files. These files may exist on any of a variety of media, ranging from card or tape to disk or slow core. The physical organization of occurrences within the file may be either sequential or random.

One potential difficulty with representing customer knowledge in the three separate simple files of Fig. 6.3 is how to know, for example, which occurrence of CUSTOMER-NAME is associated with which occurrence

Fig. 6.3. Multiple files.

of CUSTOMER-ADDRESS. If such associations are important with respect to answering users' inquiries, if it is desirable to keep track of which
pieces of customer information belong together, then we can make use of
the operational constructs of a record type and record occurrences in
order to specify a more complex file in place of the three simple files.

6.22   Record Types and Occurrences

Whereas 'customer name' may be treated as an indivisible concept, it is
very often convenient to think (i.e., to conceptualize, to process information) in terms of aggregate concepts that can be decomposed into indivisible concepts as needed. An aggregate concept, then, is a collection of
conceptually related indivisible concepts. Take the concept of a 'customer,' for instance. This could be considered as an aggregate of several
indivisible concepts such as 'customer name,' 'customer address,' 'customer account,' and so on. Assume for the time being that it is indeed
desirable to treat the latter concepts as indivisible. The important point to
notice is that these indivisible concepts are associated with each other in
such a way that, in the totality of their interrelationships, they conjure up
the notion of a customer.

Aggregate concepts are operationalized, in DBM, as *record types* and
record occurrences. An aggregate concept R, which has instantiations
is called the record type R. For example, the aggregate concept of a
'customer' (formed from the indivisible concepts 'customer name,'
'customer address,' and 'customer account') is operationalized by declaring the record type: CUSTOMER. The record type CUSTOMER is a
name for the aggregate of item types: CUSTOMER-NAME, CUSTOMER-
ADDRESS, and CUSTOMER-ACCOUNT. A record type identifies an
associative relationship between its data item types.

An aggregate concept R_i that is an instantiation of some other aggregate concept R is called a record occurrence of the record type R. The
aggregate concept 'Bob Smith, New York, 1000,' as an instantiation of the
concept 'customer,' is operationalized by declaring the tuple (BOB
SMITH, NEW YORK, 1000) to be an occurrence of the record type
CUSTOMER. Note that a record occurrence consists of one data item
occurrence for each data item type existing in the record type. A record
occurrence indicates an associative relationship among its data item occurrences. For instance, BOB SMITH and NEW YORK and 1000 are
associated with each other by virtue of the fact that they form an occurrence of the record type CUSTOMER. The constructs of data item types

and item occurrences by themselves give no means for indicating associative relationships.

Observe that the relationship between a record type and an occurrence of that type is definitional in nature. Reference to the record type CUSTOMER could be a reference to either (BOB SMITH, NEW YORK, 1000) or (STEVE MOORE, CEDAR FALLS, 500), or to any other occurrence of CUSTOMER. Thus the occurrences are the possible meanings, interpretations, or values that can be ascribed to a record type within the knowledge system. An important issue, to be addressed in a later part of the book, is how to determine which of these interpretations are intended by a user's information-processing request.

Table 6.2 summarizes the ideas introduced in this section. The conceptual–operational binding is displayed horizontally, a record type being an aggregate of *types* of data that are conceptually associated with each other. A definitional relationship is depicted vertically. Just as a data item type has data item occurrences, so does a record type have record

TABLE 6.2

Aggregate Conceptual and Operational Constructs

Conceptual construct		Operational construct
1. An aggregate concept R of indivisible concepts $\{X, Y, Z\}$ that *has* instantiations	is called	the record type R
Example: The aggregate concept of a 'customer,' encompassing the concepts {'customer name,' 'customer address,' 'customer amount'}	is operationalized	by declaring the record type CUSTOMER composed of the data item types CUSTOMER-NAME, CUSTOMER-ADDRESS, CUSTOMER-ACCOUNT.
2. An aggregate concept R_i of indivisible concepts $\{X_i, Y_i, Z_i\}$ that *are* instantiations of X, Y, Z, respectively	is called	a record occurrence R_i of the record type R.
Example: The aggregate concept of a particular customer 'Bob Smith, New York, 1000,' as an instantiation of the aggregate concept 'customer'	is operationalized	by declaring 'BOB SMITH, NEW YORK, 1000' to be a record occurrence of the record type CUSTOMER

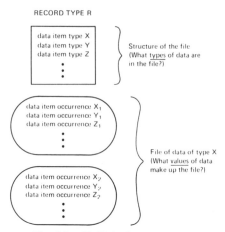

Fig. 6.4.   Multiple data stem types.

occurrences. A collection (group or list) of record occurrences of a particular record type is a *file*.

This kind of file is more complex than that of Fig. 6.2. However, it can be conveniently represented in much the same way. As shown in Fig. 6.4, a rectangle enclosing one or more data item types is used to depict the

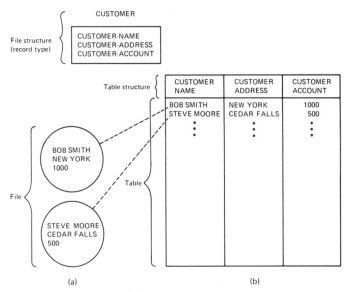

Fig. 6.5.   File-table correspondence. (a) File of CUSTOMERS. (b) Table of customers.

record type consisting of those item types. By indicating which *types* of data appear in the file, the record type gives the file's structure. The file itself is composed of record occurrences, each organized according to that structure. An occurrence in the file is represented by an encircled aggregate of values, one value for each item type in the file's record type.

Figure 6.5a shows how a file of customer information can be pictorially displayed. The record type specifies the file's structure or form. The record occurrences are the file's content. On paper (or a cathode ray tube) it is quite convenient to display a file as a table, where the table headings specify the table's structure and the table's contents follow (see Fig. 6.5b). The interchangeability of the terms "table" and "file" should now be clear. For completeness it must also be mentioned that in DBM circles the term "relation" [4, 7] is often used when speaking of a "table."

Remember that our discussion of files or tables is concerned with the representation of knowledge at an operational (logical) level and not at an implementation (physical) level. The files could be stored in various media and therefore be subject to access methods of a particular medium. Furthermore the file organization could be either random or sequential.

6.23   Multiple Files

The most simplistic kind of data base is one consisting of a group of related files or tables. We say that two files are directly related if they share one or more data item types. Consider, for example, files for the record types of Fig. 6.6. Operationally, CUSTOMER and ORDER are directly related, since they both contain CUSTOMER-NAME. At the conceptual level, the aggregate concept of a customer and the aggregate

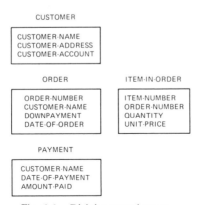

Fig. 6.6.   Disjoint record types.

concept of an order are directly related (i.e., associated) since both are partially made up of the indivisible concept of a customer's name.

Assuming that the CUSTOMER file contains a complete list of all customers, then each occurrence in the CUSTOMER file has zero, one, or more corresponding occurrences in the ORDER file. A correspondence is established by finding an occurrence in the CUSTOMER file and an occurrence in the ORDER file that have the same value for CUSTOMER-NAME.

Similarly, the CUSTOMER file and PAYMENT file are also directly related to each other. The aggregate concept of a customer and the aggregate concept of a payment are directly associated to one another since they have the indivisible concept of customer name in common. Another direct relationship in Fig. 6.6 is between the ORDER file and the ITEM-IN-ORDER file based on the repeated item type ORDER-NUMBER. Given an occurrence of ORDER, we can find zero, one, or more occurrences of ITEM-IN-ORDER whose ORDER-NUMBER value(s) matches that of the ORDER occurrence.

A less direct relationship exists between the two files CUSTOMER and ITEM-IN-ORDER. Although they have no item type in common, both are directly related to the ORDER file. Conceptually, a particular customer is directly associated with a particular order(s), which in turn is directly associated with a particular item(s) in the order, thereby establishing an indirect association between the 'customer' concept and the 'item-in-order' concept.

6.24 File Manipulation

Given a knowledge system whose information is organized into files (like those of Fig. 6.6), an important consideration is how to extract knowledge from those files in response to a user's request. The extracted knowledge is itself typically presented to the user in the form of a table. However, the desired table is rarely identical to any of those already existing as a knowledge system file. A knowledge system's files (i.e., a file system) can be processed or manipulated to produce a desired table by using some combination of the operations of extraction and matching.

Extraction operates on a single file and it has two variations. Horizontal extraction may be thought of as pulling certain occurrences "horizontally" from a file, as shown in Fig. 6.7a. The record occurrences pulled are those satisfying some set of criteria on their data item occurrences (e.g., pull all CUSTOMER occurrences with a CUSTOMER-ACCOUNT of over $750 payable). Vertical extraction (sometimes called splitting) may

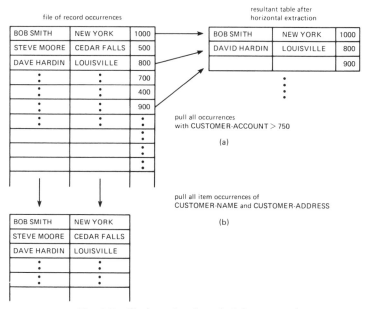

Fig. 6.7.   Horizontal and vertical data extraction.

be viewed as pulling all item occurrences of one or more item types "vertically" from a file to form another file, as shown in Fig. 6.7b. It is not uncommon that both varieties of extraction must be used to produce a desired table.

The matching operation operates on two (or more) of the knowledge system's files each of which has a data item type in common with the other. The matching operation finds all matches in value of occurrences of the common item type. As each match is found, the matched record occurrences are utilized in some way to yield an occurrence in a new file. The ways in which the two record occurrences can be used to give a new record occurrence are numerous, ranging from simple concatenation to updating one matched occurrence with data from the other. Both matching and extraction may be needed to produce a desired file from a given file system.

6.25   Choosing a Logical Structure

The item types appearing in Fig. 6.6 could have been structured into record types other than the four shown, by selecting either smaller or larger aggregate concepts. If we had decided, for example, to treat 'items

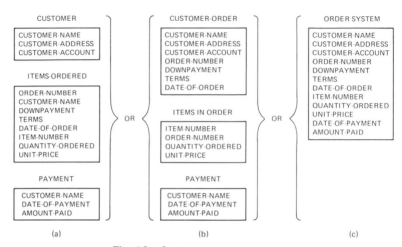

Fig. 6.8. Larger aggregate concepts.

ordered' as a single aggregate concept in lieu of the two aggregate concepts of an 'order' and an 'item in an order,' then the logical structure of Fig. 6.8a would have resulted. Here the record type ITEMS-ORDERED, consisting of the union of item types from ORDER and ITEM-IN-ORDER, has been declared in place of ORDER and ITEM-IN-ORDER.

As another example, suppose that we did not view the knowledge system in terms of the separate (but associated) concepts of a customer and an order. In this event the record type CUSTOMER-ORDER, consisting of the union of item types of CUSTOMER and ORDER, would be declared in place of the record types CUSTOMER and ORDER. This is shown in Fig. 6.8b. At the extreme we could view the knowledge system as arising from just one very large aggregate concept composed of all indivisible concepts. Figure 6.8c shows the single record type that results from the union of all data item types appearing in Fig. 6.6.

Relative to the structure of Fig. 6.6, none of the three alternative structures is a particularly desirable way of organizing our knowledge about an order system. This becomes clear on examining the contents of files defined in these ways. If a customer orders several items on the same order form (i.e., with the same order number), then using the structure of Fig. 6.8a there is one occurrence of ITEMS-ORDERED for each item ordered. But these occurrences have a considerable amount of redundant information. For each item ordered on an order form, values for CUSTOMER-NAME, DOWNPAYMENT, TERMS, and DATE-OF-ORDER are logically (not necessarily physically) repeated. They are not repeated if the structure in Fig. 6.6 is used to store the same information.

Similarly, the structure of Fig. 6.8b forces repetition whenever a customer has more than one order. It does not recognize customer and order as being two separate (albeit associated) concepts. The final structure of Fig. 6.8 is quite cumbersome. Its occurrences are perforce dominated by redundancies. It is left as an exercise for the reader to ascertain how to interpret occurrences of an ORDER-SYSTEM record type.

Not only is it possible to form larger aggregates than those of Fig. 6.6, it is also possible to define smaller aggregates. For example, the 'customer' concept could be replaced by two "smaller" concepts, one for customer location and the other for customer payables. Operationally this would give the record type CUSTOMER-LOCATION, consisting of CUSTOMER-NAME and CUSTOMER-ADDRESS, and the record type CUSTOMER-PAYABLES, consisting of CUSTOMER-NAME and CUSTOMER-ACCOUNT.

Given a group of indivisible concepts, which one of the many alternative logical structures should be chosen for a knowledge system? Although there is no universal rule for finding a "best" logical structure, we can point out several considerations and guidelines to keep in mind when choosing or designing a logical structure. First of all, it should be fairly easy to select a descriptive name for each record type; that is, the record type should be an operationalization of some familiar concept. If name selection is difficult, this may be due to an attempt to aggregate too many indivisible concepts together. Two record types should not have the same name. If this is difficult to avoid, then either declare a single record type consisting of all item types in the two record types with the same name or try to partition this group of item types in various ways until two or more distinguishable aggregate concepts become apparent.

Second, it is usually desirable to avoid large amounts of redundancy in a knowledge system, regardless of whether the KS is a dictionary, a textbook, or a group of files. Therefore, to the extent possible, item types should be aggregated so as to avoid redundancy in record occurrences. This was the reason for declaring the two record types CUSTOMER and ORDER, rather than the single record type CUSTOMER-ORDER that appeared in Fig. 6.8b. Notice that when splitting the CUSTOMER-ORDER file into a CUSTOMER file and an ORDER file, the item type CUSTOMER-NAME remained in both the CUSTOMER and ORDER record types in order to establish the direct relationship between the two. To discover which orders are associated with each customer a matching operation can be used.

A third guideline is that if there is a one-to-one correspondence between the record occurrences of two directly related record types, then these two record types can be combined to form a single record type.

Consider, for example, the two record types CUSTOMER-LOCATION and CUSTOMER-PAYABLES mentioned previously. For a given customer there is one occurrence of CUSTOMER-LOCATION giving the customer's name and address. For that same customer there is one occurrence of CUSTOMER-PAYABLES giving the customer's name and account payable. If these two record types were combined to form CUSTOMER (Fig. 6.6), no redundancy would be introduced and the duplication of customer names in two files would be eliminated.

In devising a logical structure it is advisable (from a physical file organization standpoint) to keep together those item types that tend to be updated at the same time. This is for ease of updating. It is also advisable to keep together those item types whose occurrences tend to be added to the knowledge system at the same time. A formal file design method, called *normalization*, has been proposed by Codd [4]. As a final note, file design need not be exclusively bottom–up, beginning with an enumeration of all item types. A top–down approach could also be used, beginning with an identification of aggregate concepts and culminating with the identification of those indivisible concepts that constitute each aggregate concept.

Once a logical structure has been chosen, each file can be implemented on a particular file medium using a particular file organization technique. For a survey of the major considerations involved in selecting a medium and organization technique, see Burch *et al.* [1]. Notice that logical redundancy can be avoided at the physical level by using pointers.

6.30   ASSOCIATIVE RELATIONSHIP BETWEEN AGGREGATE CONCEPTS

To this point we have considered the notion of two instantiated aggregate concepts that are directly associated with each other via a common indivisible concept. For instance, the aggregate concept of 'customer' could include the indivisible concept of 'customer name' and the aggregate concept of 'order' could also include 'customer name.' We might say that the fact of a nonempty "intersection" of these two aggregate concepts establishes that they are directly associated with one another. Operationally this association is indicated by repeating a data item type in two different record types as shown in Fig. 6.8a.

Now if two aggregate concepts Q and Q' are directly associated via a common indivisible concept q, we would expect that a particular instantiation of Q could be directly associated with an instantiation of Q'. This direct association between two instantiations exists if each has the same instantiation of q. If, for example, 'John Doe' is the instantiation of 'customer name' both in an instance of 'customer' and in an instance of 'order,' then those two instances (i.e., relatively concrete concepts) are directly associated with each other. At an operational level this association is indicated if there is an occurrence of each record type such that the two record occurrences have the same data item occurrence (value) for the repeated (redundant) data item type. Note that this relationship may or may not be physically implemented with redundant values; but from the operational and conceptual perspectives this repetition or redundancy is how direct associative relationships between (record types or record occurrences) aggregate concepts are defined or viewed.

In the remainder of this section we focus on relationships between instantiated aggregate concepts, in which a direct association is not established by redundant use of an indivisible concept embedded within the aggregates. We shall simply *name* a direct association that exists between concepts. For instance, from our world view we know that the notions of customer and order are associated in that a customer can *place* an order. Rather than hinting at this association by the redundant approach discussed earlier, we shall simply and explicitly specify this association at a conceptual level by saying that 'customer' *places* 'order.' Moreover, we will see how to operationalize this conceptual specification of information organization.

Begin with the aggregate concepts 'customer' and 'order,' which consist of ('customer-name,' 'customer-address,' 'customer-account') and ('order-number,' 'downpayment,' 'date-of-order'), respectively. Note that there is no repeated indivisible concept. Nevertheless, we would like to say at the conceptual level that a customer places an order; conceptually there is an associative relationship between 'customer' and 'order' and we shall call it 'places.'

Note the peculiar nature of this associative relationship, namely, that one instance of 'customer' may place many 'orders'; however, one particular instantiation of 'order' cannot be placed by more than one instance of a 'customer.' This is a commonly encountered situation as one attempts to describe the conceptual organization of knowledge in various application areas. We shall refer to this type of associative relationship between two instantiated aggregate concepts as a 1–N association in which one concept is the subject of that association and the other is the object.

A 1–N association between two instantiated aggregate concepts R and R' (subject and object, respectively) means that one instantiation of R may be associated with N ($N \geq 0$) instantiations of R'. However, a given instantiation of R' is conceptually associated with no more than one instantiation of R. Let S name the nature of some 1–N association between

R and R'. Then S can also describe the nature of the associative relationship between R_i, an instance of R, and some R_j, an instance of R'. In fact for any given instance R_i of R there exists a set of instances of R', $_{si}R' = \{_{si}R'_1, _{si}R'_2, \ldots, _{si}R'_{N_i}\}$, such that each member of $_{si}R'$ has an associative relationship with R_i, a relationship whose nature is described by S. The set $_{si}R'$ may be empty; that is, $N_i = 0$. As indicated earlier a 1–N associative relationship S is restricted: If R_i and R_k are any two instances of R, then $_{si}R' \cap _{sk}R' + \varnothing$.

An example will help in visualizing these formalisms. Let R be the aggregate concept 'customer' consisting of ('customer name,' 'customer address,' 'customer account'). Let R' be the concept 'order' consisting of ('order number,' 'downpayment,' 'date-of-order'). Let S be 'places,' describing the nature of a 1–N association between R and R'. The two concepts 'customer' and 'order' are subject and object, respectively, in the context of the 'places' relationship. At a more concrete level, 'places' also describes the nature of an associative relationship between an instance of 'customer' ('Bob Smith,' 'New York,' '1000') and a related instance of the object concept 'order' ('107,' '50,' '110178'). There may be many instances of 'order' associated with this particular customer via the 'places' relationship. However, no instance of 'order' may be associated with more than one instance of 'customer' via the 'places' relationship.

From the previous example it should be clear that just as we have instantiations of a concept R we can also have instantiations of S. If S is a 1–N associative relationship having subject R and object R', then an instance S_i of S is given by the ordered pair $(R_i, _{si}R')$. Thus there are as many instantiations of S as there are instantiations of R. S_i establishes the associative relationship between an instance of R, R_i, and the N_i instantiations of R', $\{_{si}R'_1, _{si}R'_2, \ldots, _{si}R'_{N_i}\}$, that stand in S relationship to one another as subject and objects, respectively. Notice that S_i may be viewed as having a definitional relationship to S. For example, one way of defining or concretizing the notion of 'customer places orders' would be to state that ('Bob Smith,' 'New York,' '1000') places the three orders {('107,' '50,' '110178'), ('148,' '500,' '110978'), ('172,' '900,' '111178')}.

6.31 Operationalizing 1–N Associative Relationships

To recapitulate, 1–N associative relationships between concepts are commonly encountered when we explore how the various concepts pertinent to a given application area are associated with each other. As we shall see in a later section, 1–N associations are sometimes insufficient for describing *all* of our knowledge about the associations among concepts of an application area. Nevertheless we submit that when a 1–N association is recognized between two concepts, it is simple and straightforward just to say so. That is, we merely indicate which concept is the subject, which is the object, and what is the name describing the nature of the subject–object association. Contrast this with the earlier alternative (but more cumbersome) way of thinking about or describing a 1–N associative relationship. This alternative requires that each of two associated aggregate concepts be thought of as encompassing the same indivisible concept. The existence of the repeated indivisible concept is then taken as indicative of some unnamed association between the two aggregate concepts.

If use of a name is more descriptive of an associative relationship than reliance on redundancy, then the question arises of how to operationalize this notion of named 1–N associative relationships. The answer lies in binding it to the operational construct of a "set" type. Thus the notion of *a 1–N association between subject and object concepts is,* in DBM, *operationalized as a "set" type that has an "owner" record type and a "member" record type.* "Owner" and "member" record types of a "set" type are, respectively, the operationalizations of subject and object concepts in a 1–N association.

In DBM, use of the term "set" does not have the same connotation as the commonplace mathematical meaning of a set. The term has become widely used following its appearance as a logical data-structuring construct in the CODASYL DBTG Report [3]. Its origins predate the DBTG Report and stem from the work of Bachman in connection with Integrated Data Store (IDS/1), a commercial software package [6]. To avoid confusion with a mathematical set, we shall hereafter adopt Nijssen's convention [8] of referring to a CODASYL "set" type as a coset. This also precludes confusion of the coset construct with "data sets" as used in the popular DMS Total [12].

As an example of the preceding operationalization, the 1–N association 'places' between the subject concept 'customer' and the 'object' concept 'order' becomes the coset PLACES, having the record type CUSTOMER as its owner and the record type ORDER as its member. Just as we can speak of occurrences of record types, we can also speak of occurrences of a coset. If S is a 1–N associative relationship having subject R and object R', then an instance S_i of S is operationally called an occurrence of the coset S. For this coset S, R_i is called an owner occurrence and $\{_{si}R'_1, {}_{si}R'_2, \ldots, {}_{si}R'_{Ni}\}$ are called its member occurrences with respect to S. Furthermore, in DBM parlance, R_i is said to own $_{si}R_j$ with respect to S ($0 \le j \le N_i$). For example, with respect to the coset PLACES, the record occurrence (BOB SMITH, NEW YORK, 1000) of CUSTOMER is the owner of each of the three member occurrences

{(107, 50, 110178), (148, 500, 110978), (172, 900, 111178)}. Collectively, these four record occurrences constitute an occurrence of the coset PLACES.

The binding of conceptual to operational constructs in the case of 1–N associations is summarized in Table 6.3. Pictorially, a coset is represented in a Bachman diagram as shown in Fig. 6.9a. It is a labeled, directed arc from the owner record type to the member record type. The label indicates the nature of the 1–N associative relationship being represented by the coset.

Figure 6.9b contains two occurrences of the coset PLACES. Each record occurrence is of the type shown in the right margin. The arcs emanating from a particular owner occurrence point to all occurrences of the member record type that are owned by that owner occurrence. Notice

TABLE 6.3

Associative Conceptual and Operational Constructs

Conceptual construct		Operational construct
1. A 1–N associative relationship S between the aggregate concepts R and R', where R is subject and R' is object and where both R and R' *have* instantiations	is called	the coset S having R as its owner record type and R' as its member record type
Example: The 1–N associative relationship 'places' between the subject concept 'customer' and object concept 'order' (customer places order)	is operationalized by	declaring the coset PLACES with record type CUSTOMER as the coset's owner and record type ORDER as the coset's member
2. Given an aggregate concept R_i that *is* an instantiation of R, let $\{_{si}R'_1, {}_{si}R'_2, \ldots, {}_{si}R'_{Ni}\}$ be the set of all instances of R' that have an S relationship to R_i. Then $(R_i, {}_{si}R')$	is called	an occurrence of coset S
Example: The fact that the instantiation of 'customer' ('Bob Smith,' 'New York,' '100') 'places' the 'orders' {('107,' '50,' '110178'), ('148,' '500,' '110978'), ('172,' '900,' '111178')}	is operationalized by	declaring an occurrence of the coset PLACES, in which the record occurrence (BOB SMITH, NEW YORK, 1000) owns the record occurrences {(107, 50, 110178), (148, 500, 110978), (172, 900, 111178)}

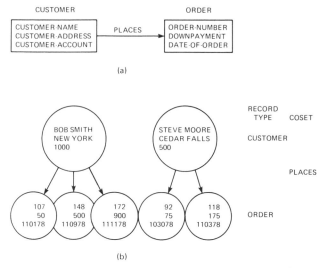

Fig. 6.9. Pictorial representations of a coset and its occurrences. (a) the coset PLACES with owner CUSTOMER and member ORDER. (b) Two occurrences of the coset PLACES.

that for a given member occurrence there is no more than one associated owning occurrence via a particular coset. This is consistent with the notion of a 1–N associative relationship as defined earlier.

Diagrams that depict record types and cosets are referred to as the *logical structure* or *schema* of a data base. Diagrams depicting record occurrences and coset occurrences show the occurrence structure of a data base. An occurrence structure must, of course, be consistent with the logical structure on which it is based. That is, the schema serves as an archetypal pattern or blueprint for constructing an occurrence structure. The former is an operationalization of abstract concepts and associations relative to the latter, which is an operationalization of comparatively concrete concepts and associations.

It must be emphasized that both the schema and the occurrence structure are devices for pictorially describing a data base at the operational level only (recall Fig. 6.1). They imply nothing about how the various operational constructs are implemented. For instance, occurrences of a coset could be implemented in the guise of header and detail records in a sequential file organization. Each header record is the physical realization of an owner occurrence. Each of the detail records that immediately follows a header is the physical realization of a member occurrence. A coset occurrence is implemented as a header, immediately followed by its details. A COBOL Data Division with

STEVE MOORE	CEDAR FALLS	500
92	75	103078
118	175	110378

BOB SMITH	NEW YORK	1000
107	50	110178
148	500	110978
172	900	111178

Fig. 6.10 Header-detail physical file.

FD PLACES-FILE

01 CUSTOMER-RECORD
　　05 CUSTOMER-NAME
　　05 CUSTOMER-ADDRESS
　　05 CUSTOMER-ACCOUNT

01 ORDER-RECORD
　　05 ORDER-NUMBER
　　05 DOWNPAYMENT
　　05 DATE-OR-ORDER

permits a header-detail implementation of the logical structure of Fig. 6.9a. In such an implementation, the physical file depicted in Fig. 6.10 is the materialization of the logical occurrence structure shown in Fig. 6.9b.

The header-detail approach is perhaps the simplest implementation of a coset, but it breaks down when applied to certain logical structures containing many cosets. Other implementations utilize techniques such as linked lists, pointer arrays (which amounts to the use of inverted files), or directory schemes [5, 7]. These techniques do not become ineffective as the logical data structure of cosets and record types becomes complex. Each technique has several variations and it is beyond the purpose of this treatise to consider them here.

6.32 Why Are Conceptual Constructs Significant?

Before proceeding to examine more complex data structures, it is appropriate to pause to reflect on the value of the proposed conceptual constructs (concepts, definitional relationships, associative relationships). We submit that they are valuable additions to the commonplace operational constructs when one is faced with the problem of gathering and converting knowledge about the world into a formal data base schema. As suggested in Fig. 6.1, they aid in bridging the gap between the world and an operational paradigm of that world. This bridging process is the first, and perhaps most crucial, step in building a decision support system's KS.

The value of conceptual constructs may be seen from four related angles. First, they provide a way to structure one's thinking about the world to be represented. They serve as an aid to thinking about the world in an orderly way, and in such a way that these thoughts can be easily converted into an operational specification of the data base. Conceptually, as we view the world, we see that customers place orders and that (on a more concrete level) Bob Smith places three specific orders. Moreover, we see that the concept of a customer is an aggregate of the more elemental concepts of a name, an address, and an amount payable. Through the conceptual–operational bindings described earlier, this conceptual view is operationalized as shown in Fig. 6.9. Second, the conceptual constructs furnish the basis for a methodical approach to data base design to be presented in Section 7.30. Third, the conceptual constructs serve to highlight deficiencies or limitations of extant operational constructs. That is, there are certain ordinary world situations that are captured quite easily with the conceptual constructs but that cannot be represented by usual operational constructs in a straightforward manner. Thus the conceptual constructs provide a starting point and impetus for the development of new, valuable operational constructs that can be bound to the conceptual constructs. The result of such development is logical data base structures that more clearly reflect the worlds they endeavor to represent. Our attention in this chapter is largely confined to situations where commonplace operational constructs suffice. The following chapter examines situations where they are not sufficient and suggests remedies.

A fourth angle from which the conceptual constructs are of value is that they are a generalization of the conceptual framework of an organization as presented in Sections 2.10–2.13. Information-processing roles are just a special variety of concepts. Definitional relationships between information-processing roles are just a special case of definitional relationships between concepts. An associative relationship between information-processing roles is a special case of an associative relationship between concepts, where the nature of the association involves the passage of information and the concepts are organizational roles. The assisted role and assisting role may, for the present, be considered to be subject and object concepts, respectively.

We therefore have a unified view of two areas that are very important to the development of decision support systems: the area of knowledge representation and the area involving the constitution of information-processing labor (be it human or electronic). This unified view is immediately suggestive of the possibility of easily ("naturally") incorporating information-processing knowledge into a knowledge system (KS), thereby divorcing such knowledge from the PPS where it traditionally resides (recall the systems of Chapter 3). This is a step toward a generalized PPS, whose advantages were discussed in Chapter 4.

REFERENCES

1. J. G. Burch, Jr., F. R. Strater, and G. Grudnitski, "Information Systems: Theory and Practice," 2nd ed. Wiley, New York, 1979.
2. A. Cardenas, "Data Base Management Systems," Allyn and Bacon, Boston, Massachusetts, 1979.
3. CODASYL Systems Committee, Data Base Task Group Report, Association for Computing Machinery (April 1971).
4. E. F. Codd, A relational model of data for large shared data bases, *Commun. ACM* **13**, No. 6 (1970).
5. W. D. Haseman and A. B. Whinston, "Introduction to Data Management." Irwin, Homewood, Illinois, 1977.
6. Integrated Data Store I, Honeywell Information Systems Inc., Waltham, Massachusetts.
7. J. Martin, "Computer Data-Base Organization." Prentice-Hall, Englewood Cliffs, New Jersey, 1975.
8. G. M. Nijssen, Two major flaws in the CODASYL DDL 1973 and proposed corrections, *Informat. Syst.* **1** (1975).
9. I. Palmer, Data Base Systems: A Practical Reference, QED Information Sciences, Inc., Wellesley, Massachusetts, pp. 2–15, 2–17 (1975).
10. M. R. Quillian, Semantic memory, *in* "Semantic Information Processing" (M. Minsky, ed.). MIT Press, Cambridge, Massachusetts, 1968.
11. B. Raphael, SIR: A Computer Program for Semantic Information Retrieval, Doctoral Dissertation, MIT, Cambridge, Massachusetts, 1964.
12. TOTAL, Cincom Systems Inc., Cincinnati, Ohio.
13. W. A. Woods, What's in a link: Foundations for semantic networks, *in* "Representation and Understanding" (D. G. Bobrow and A. Collins, eds.). Academic Press, New York, 1975.

Chapter 7

BUILDING A DATA BASE
KNOWLEDGE SYSTEM

7.00 MORE COMPLEX DATA STRUCTURES

Thus far we have considered a logical data structure composed of two record types and a coset. What happens if the world that we are attempting to represent logically is more complicated? The answer is that we take the same approach as in the simpler case, but realizing that a single aggregate concept may participate in many different associative relationships. It may be the subject in some of these relationships and the object in others.

Turning once again to the customer-order world, we can recognize the aggregate concepts of a 'customer', an 'order', an 'inventory item', an 'order line', and a 'payment'. Moreover, we can notice the following 1–N associative relationships among them:

> 'customer' 'places' 'order'
> 'order' 'contains' 'order line'
> 'inventory item' 'appears in' 'order line'
> 'customer' 'makes' 'payment'

The operationalization of this conceptual representation of the customer-order world results in the schema of Fig. 7.1a. CUSTOMER is the owner

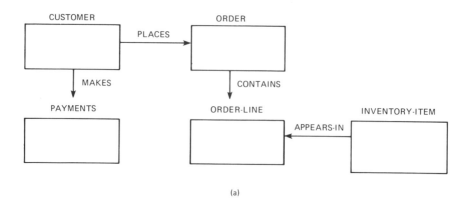

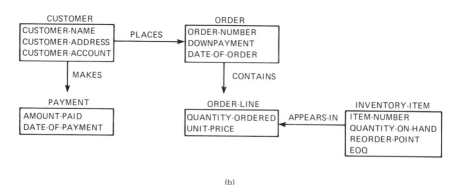

Fig. 7.1. Schema for customer-order world. (a) Schema without data item types. (b) Schema with data item types.

record type for two cosets; ORDER owns one and is the member of another; ORDER-LINE is the member record type of two cosets, but owns none. Although this is a small example, it should be clear that with a few simple constructs one can obtain quite complex schemata, representative of complex world situations.

Having built the schema at an aggregate level, we must now consider the more detailed constitution of each aggregate concept. The 'customer' and 'order' concepts were treated earlier, resulting in the data item types declared in Fig. 6.9a. The concept of a 'payment' may reasonably be considered to consist of 'amount paid' and 'date of payment'. An 'inventory item' is the aggregation of 'item number', 'quantity on hand', 'reorder point', and 'economic order quantity'. Finally, 'order line' is the aggregate composed of a 'quantity ordered' and a 'unit price'. We shall assume that a given inventory item does not have a single fixed unit price, but rather the unit price varies from order to order (i.e., different customers are quoted different prices). Figure 7.1b shows the operational effect of the preceding assignment of indivisible concepts.

The foregoing assignments of indivisible concepts to aggregate concepts, although not seeming unreasonable, may nevertheless seem somewhat arbitrary. Would it, for instance, be "wrong" to include 'item number' and/or 'order number' with the indivisible concepts that constitute the aggregate 'order line'? The answer is that it is not at all wrong in either a conceptual or operational sense. In fact, at the operational level such repetition of data item types has been advocated by Nijssen [13] and it is required in the TOTAL DBMS [15] by the implementation method TOTAL uses.

For the present, we simply note that this repetition is unnecessary. That is, the logical structure of Fig. 7.1b can be practically implemented [7, 11], and from the conceptual side the $1-N$ associations obviate the need for repetition. The "contains" $1-N$ association implies that a given instantiation of 'order line' is associated with no more than one instance of 'order number,' but an instance of 'order number' may be associated with many instances of 'order line'. This is precisely the world situation that we desire to represent. A similar argument holds for the $1-N$ associative relationship 'appears in'. A simple rule for deciding about how to aggregate indivisible concepts is presented in Section 7.30.

7.10   INDIRECT ASSOCIATIONS AMONG CONCEPTS

To this point we have seen two methods for indicating a direct association between two aggregate concepts: repetition of an indivisible concept in two aggregate concepts (Section 6.23) and a $1-N$ named associative relationship between two aggregate concepts. With respect to the first of these, examples of less direct (indirect) associative relationships were discussed in Section 6.23. We shall now examine the kinds of indirect associations than can occur when several $1-N$ associations are used to describe some world situations.

If one selects for examination any two named $1-N$ associative relationships, then exactly one of the following six assertions is true:

(A)   The subject of one statement of association is the object of the other.

(B)   The subject of one associative statement is also the subject of the other, but their objects differ.

(C)   The object of one associative statement is also the object of the other, but their subjects differ.

(D)   Neither the subject nor the object of one association is the same as either the subject or object of the other.

(E)   The subject of one association is the same as the subject of the other, and their object concepts are also identical.

(F)   The subject and object of one association are, *respectively,* the same as the object and subject of the other.

Each of these six cases is dealt with in turn in Sections 7.11 through 7.16. The first four cases are the most commonly encountered when attempting to design a schema. There is an example of each of these four in the customer-order application described in Section 7.00. The fifth case is very useful for a less frequently encountered class of knowledge representation problems. The sixth case is rarely encountered in practice, but is included here for the sake of completeness.

7.11   Case A

Let X, Y, and Z be aggregate concepts having instantiations. If X is the subject of a $1-N$ named association S with object Y and if Y is the subject of a named $1-N$ association T with object Z, then it follows that there is an implied *transitive $1-N$ relationship* from X to Z. This is not a direct $1-N$ named association between concepts X and Z, but rather an implied indirect relationship mediated by the intervening concept Y as the object of S and the subject of T. Where there exists a transitive $1-N$ relationship from X to Z, then any instantiation of X may be indirectly (i.e., transitively) associated with many instances of Z. However, no instantiation of Z may be transitively associated with more than one instance of X. This follows from the fact that T permits no more than one instantiation of Y to be associated with a given instance of Z and S allows no more than one instance of X to be associated with a selected instantiation of Y.

Consider the following two statements made at the conceptual level of knowledge representation:

'customer' 'places' 'order'
'order' 'contains' 'order line'

Observe that 'order' is the object of one of these associative statements and that it is the subject of the other. Since 'places' and 'contains' are

1–N associative relationships, there is at the conceptual level an inescapable implication that 'customer' and 'order line' are indirectly associated in a 1–N fashion.

As shown in Fig. 7.2a, the transitive 1–N relationship from 'customer' to 'order line' is operationally represented by CUSTOMER owning ORDER which owns ORDER-LINE. The occurrence structure shown in Fig. 7.2b clearly reflects the transitivity of the relationship between a customer and an order line. Occurrences of CUSTOMER and occurrences of ORDER-LINE are associated with each other indirectly through occurrences of ORDER. This occurrence structure also illustrates at an operational level that for any occurrence of CUSTOMER we can find the N occurrences of ORDER-LINE that are indirectly associated with it (e.g., $N = 5$ for BOB SMITH). However, for any occurrence of

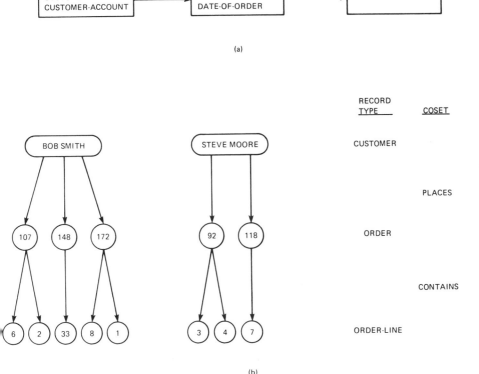

Fig. 7.2. Transitive 1–N relationship.

ORDER-LINE there is no more than one occurrence of CUSTOMER transitively related to it.

As a footnote, it must be pointed out that the occurrence structure of Fig. 7.2b does not contain data item occurrences for all data item types appearing in the schema. For reasons of brevity each record occurrence shows the value of only one data item type, namely, the data item type that appears first in the corresponding record type. This shorthand is adopted in many of the examples that follow.

The notion of an implied 1–*N* transitive association can be extended to situations where there is more than one mediating concept. Suppose that the following three statements are made at the conceptual level of knowledge representation:

'customer category' 'classifies' 'customer'
'customer' 'places' 'order'
'order' 'contains' 'order line'

There is an implied 1–*N* transitive association from 'customer category' to 'order line'. This is mediated by the concepts 'customer' and 'order'.

7.12   Case B

Let *X*, *Y*, and *Z* be aggregate concepts having instantiations. If *X* is the subject of a 1–*N* named association *S* with object *Y* and if *X* is also the subject of a named 1–*N* association *T* with object *Z*, then (in the absence of additional information) nothing more can be said about the relationship between concepts *Y* and *Z*. That is, the relationship between *Y* and *Z* is very "weak," because the fact that *X* is the subject of both *S* and *T* implies nothing more about the relationship between *Y* and *Z*.

Consider the following two statements made at the conceptual level of knowledge representation:

'customer' 'makes' 'payment'
'customer' 'places' 'order'

There is a weak indirect relationship between 'payment' and 'order'. A particular payment and a particular order are related to each other only insofar as they are directly associated with the same customer. Nothing more than this is implied. For a particular customer, this weak indirect relationship has nothing to say about any possible relationships between that customer's orders and that customer's payments. To put it another way, a particular order of a given customer is not more closely related to any one of that customer's payments than it is to any other of that customer's payments.

Operationally, the schema for this example appears as shown in Fig. 7.3a. The occurrence structure of Fig. 7.3b illustrates that for any order (say, 92) we can determine what payments ($50, $85) have been made by the customer (STEVE MOORE) who placed that order. However, for a given CUSTOMER occurrence, we are unable to say that one ORDER occurrence is more closely associated with a particular PAYMENT occurrence than is some other ORDER occurrence. Contrast this with the

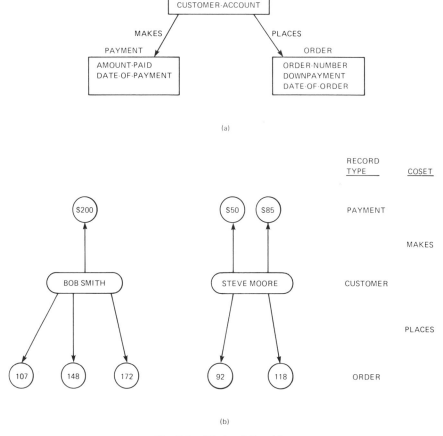

(a)

(b)

Fig. 7.3.   Weak relationship.

"stronger" kind of indirect association depicted in Fig. 7.2. There the two indirectly related concepts are 'customer' and 'order line'. If we look at any occurrence of ORDER-LINE, the coset configuration forces it to be more closely associated with one occurrence of CUSTOMER than with any other occurrence of CUSTOMER. Looking at any occurrence of CUSTOMER, we see that the coset configuration forces it to be more closely associated with some subset of the set of all ORDER-LINE occurrences than it is with any other such subset. Thus the indirect association involved in case B is weaker (or more loose) than the indirect association involved in case A, in the sense that comparatively few implications can be drawn from it.

This notion of a weak indirect association can be extended to situations where the mediating concept is the subject of more than two direct $1-N$ associative relationships. In this event any pair of its objects have a weak indirect association. Furthermore, a transitive $1-N$ association may be combined with a weak indirect association, as shown in Fig. 7.1b. In this example not only are payments and orders weakly associated, but so are payments and order lines because of the transitive $1-N$ association between customers and order lines. For a given occurrence of ORDER-LINE, the cosets can be used to find the unique occurrence of CUS-TOMER associated with it, plus all occurrences of PAYMENT for that CUSTOMER occurrence. But no member of this group of PAYMENT occurrences is more closely associated with the given ORDER-LINE occurrence than is any other.

7.13 Case C

Let X, Y, and Z be aggregate concepts having instantiations. If X is the subject of a $1-N$ named association S with object Y and if Y is also the object of a named $1-N$ association T with subject Z, then it follows that there is an implied $M-N$ *relationship* between X and Z. The concept Y mediates this indirect relationship in such a way that an instantiation of X can be indirectly associated with N (≥ 0) instances of Z and an instantiation of Z can be indirectly associated with M (≥ 0) instances of X.

This kind of relationship is implied by the facts that S allows many (N) instances of Y to be directly associated with a given instance of X and that for each of these instantiations of Y, T permits a direct association with no more than one instance of Z. Similarly, T permits many (M) instances of Y to be directly associated with a given instantiation of Z and, for each of these instantiations of Z, S allows a direct association with no more than one instance of X.

Consider the following two statements made at the conceptual level of knowledge representation:

'order'   'contains'   'order line'

'inventory item'   'appears in'   'order line'

Note that 'order line' is the object of both of these associative statements. This implies an $M-N$ relationship between 'order' and 'inventory item'. In other words, an order may refer to many inventory items (one in each of its many order lines) and an inventory item may be referred to in many orders (by appearing in many order lines). At the level of instantiations, the indirect association between a particular order and a particular inventory item is established by directly associating each with the same instance of 'order line'. Conversely, a particular order line, through its two direct associations, identifies a certain (order, inventory item) pair.

The operationalization of this $M-N$ association, in terms of record types and cosets, is shown in Fig. 7.4a. The occurrence structure of Fig. 7.4b clearly shows the $M-N$ indirect association between orders and inventory items. Each occurrence of ORDER is indirectly associated with

(a)

(b)

Fig. 7.4. $M-N$ relationship.

one or more occurrences of INVENTORY-ITEM through the medium of ORDER-LINE occurrences. And each occurrence of INVENTORY-ITEM is indirectly associated with possibly many occurrences of ORDER through the medium of ORDER-LINE occurrences. Order number 107 contains two order lines, one of which refers to six units of ITM-20 and the other to two units of ITM-22. Note that ITM-24 is referred to in two orders: eight units are requested by order number 172 and three units are requested by order number 92.

7.13.1 Extensions

The notion of indirect M–N associations can be extended to the case where there are more than two associative statements having the same object. Consider, for example:

> 'order' 'contains' 'order line'
> 'inventory item' 'appears in' 'order line'
> 'status' 'describes' 'order line'

Examples of instantiations of 'status' include 'backordered', 'shipped', etc. The ''describes'' association indicates that an instance of 'status' may describe many instances of 'order line', but no instance of 'order line' is associated with more than one instantiation of 'status' at a time.

Taken together, the three statements imply an indirect tertiary M–N association (i.e., L–M–N). A particular instance of 'order line' is associated with one instance of 'order', one instance of 'inventory item', and one instance of 'status'. It follows that a given instance of 'order' may be associated with many ('inventory item', 'status') instance pairs. A given instantiation of 'inventory item', since it may be associated with many order lines, may be associated with many ('order', 'status') pairs. Similarly, if a particular instance of 'status' is associated with L instantiations of 'order line', then it is indirectly associated with L ('order', 'inventory item') instantiation pairs. Operationally, the added fact that 'status' 'describes' 'order line' would cause Fig. 7.4a to be amended to contain the coset DESCRIBES with STATUS as its owner record type and ORDER-LINE as its member.

Another extended case of indirect M–N association appears when we have the following direct 1–N associations:

> X S Y
> Z T Y
> W U X

where W, X, Y, Z are aggregate concepts and S, T, U are association names. Because of the indirect (transitive) 1–N association from W to Y

and the direct 1–N association with subject Z and object Y, there is an M–N indirect association between W and Z.

An example of an operational structure resulting from this kind of situation appears in Fig. 7.1b. Customers are indirectly related to inventory items in an M–N fashion, because of the 1–N transitivity from customers to order lines.

7.13.2   Direct M–N Associative Relationship

Thus far we have presented M–N associations as indirect relationships implied by a particular configuration of two 1–N direct associations. In the course of stating all important 1–N direct associations for some application area, the important M–N relationships between pairs of concepts are often captured automatically (albeit indirectly) by the 1–N named associations. Occasionally, however, one may encounter two concepts (say, X and Z) that cannot be conceived as having a 1–N named association with each other; nor do the associative statements show that they have an indirect, implied M–N relationship. Nevertheless, they may be related in the real world, such that one instance of X is conceptually associated with many instantiations of Z and one instance of Z is associated with many instantiations of X.

Suppose that we are confronted with the two concepts 'supplier' and 'part.' A named 1–N association cannot be specified between these two because one supplier could supply many parts and, at the same time, a part could be supplied by many suppliers. It is clear that these two concepts have an M–N associative relationship, but the kinds of associative relationships presented so far (direct 1–N association, transitive or indirect 1–N association, indirect weak association, indirect M–N association) do not permit us to capture this fact at the conceptual level. A simple solution is to introduce *a second kind of direct associative relationship: a direct M–N association.*

A direct M–N association will be indicated by a colon intervening between the two concepts (e.g., 'part' : 'supplier'). The order of the concepts is irrelevant. Since this is not a direct 1–N association, the association does not have a clear-cut subject and a clear-cut object. In a direct M–N association, the two concepts are balanced in the sense that we do not have a situation where one of them is primary (subject) while the other is subsidiary (object). If it is desired to give a name to the 'supplier' : 'part' relationship, one must be careful to avoid a name that gives an impression that one concept dominates (is primary relative to) the other; otherwise the relationship is easily mistaken for a direct 1–N association.

The relationship 'part' : 'supplier' can be operationalized with the record types and cosets shown in Fig. 7.5a. Note that a direct $M-N$ association can be operationalized with the same variety of logical structures as an indirect $M-N$ association. The only difference is that the NULL record type is not the operationalization of any concept, nor are the cosets C1 and C2 operationalizations of direct $1-N$ associations named at the conceptual level. As illustrated in Fig. 7.5b, the $M-N$ association between suppliers and parts is fully captured by occurrences of the intervening NULL record type.

Although the above operationalization of a direct $M-N$ association is straightforward and simple, the issue of a new operational construct for treating this kind of association more concisely deserves attention. In the operationalization of Fig. 7.5a, two previously introduced constructs (coset and record type) were used to handle the direct $M-N$ association. Is it possible to conceive of a new operational construct that can treat a direct $1-N$ association? No such construct appears in the CODASYL approach to data structuring [3, 11]. From the standpoint of implementation this new operational construct presents no appreciable difficulty. The construct would need to have a name and a notational convention for incorporating it into schematic diagrams.

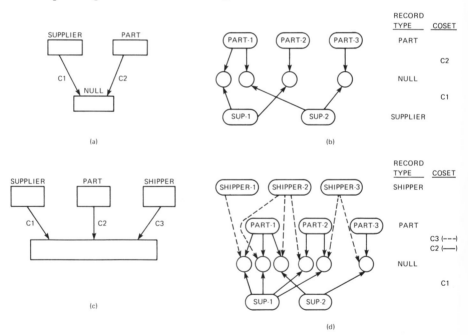

Fig. 7.5. Use of a null record type.

A commercial system that employs a novel construct for operationalizing a direct $M-N$ association is MDBS [12]. The operational construct used is called a "many-to-many set," which we shall simply refer to as an mm set. Pictorially, an mm set is depicted as an undirected arc between the two participating record types. In MDBS an mm set is named; one record type is arbitrarily called its 'owner' and the other record type is called its 'member.' In practice, both direct $M-N$ associations and indirect $M-N$ associations are encountered often. The indirect variety, appearing automatically as a result of direct $1-N$ named associations, does seem to arise somewhat more frequently.

Although it is more rare than *direct M-N* associations, we sometimes encounter a direct $L-M-N$ association existing among three concepts. Consider ('part' : 'supplier' : 'shipper'), for example. This can be operationalized by using a null intervening record type as shown in Fig. 7.5c. A corresponding occurrence structure is shown in Fig. 7.5d. Notice that two NULL occurrences are needed to represent the fact that SUP-1 is associated with PART-1. This is because the (PART-1, SUP-1) occurrence pair is associated with both SHIPPER-1 and SHIPPER-2, and a given occurrence of SHIPPER can be associated with many (PART, SUPPLIER) occurrence pairs via NULL occurrences. Clearly, the $L-M-N$ direct association can be generalized for the case of a direct association among more than three aggregate concepts. To date, commercial systems offer no operational constructs that reflect $L-M-N$ (or . . . $-L-M-N-$ . . .) *direct* associations without forcing us to contrive null record types.

In those systems that do not recognize the notion of direct named associations among aggregate concepts (i.e., logical file systems), there can be no operational construct that is bound to the now existent conceptual construct of an explicit $L-M-N$ direct association. This does not mean that the above 'part'-'supplier'-'shipper' example cannot be handled. It is easily handled by defining a record type for each of these concepts, plus an additional record type consisting solely of data item types that already appear in the other three record types. A key is a data item type (or group of data item types) that invariably takes on a different value for every occurrence of the record type of which it is a part. The additional record type cited earlier consists of a key from each of the three record types: PART, SUPPLIER, and SHIPPER. It is an analogue of the NULL record type in Fig. 7.5c, because it too operationally establishes an indirect relationship (recall Section 6.23) among PART, SUPPLIER, and SHIPPER. This indirect relationship stems from redundant use of data items types rather than cosets owning the same null record type.

7.14   Case D

Let W, X, Y, Z be aggregate concepts having instantiations. Suppose that W and X are, respectively, subject and object of the direct 1–N association S. Suppose also that Y is the subject of the direct 1–N associa-

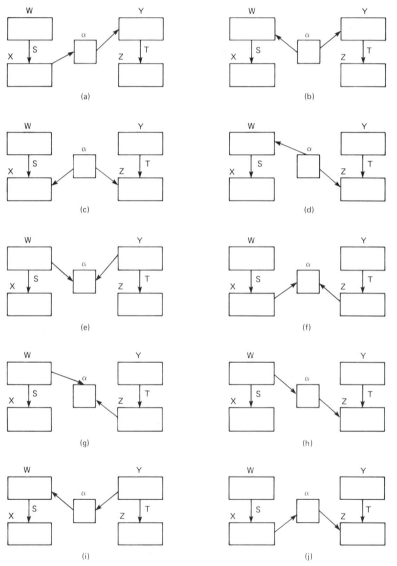

Fig. 7.6. Types of remote indirect relationships.

tion T having object Z. In the absence of any further information, there is no evidence that either W or X is in any way associated with either Y or Z. However, with additional information about other aggregate concepts and other 1–N associations, it may be possible to establish that a *remote* indirect relationship exists between W or X, and either or both of Y and Z. From this juncture onward the term "indirect" refers to a relationship that is operationalized with two cosets. If more than two cosets are used, the relationship is called a remote indirect relationship or simply a remote relationship.

Some relationships of this "very indirect" or remote kind were briefly discussed earlier in connection with cases A through C. We shall now examine more closely the possible kinds of remote relationships that can occur. The important point to note here is that a *remote indirect relationship between two concepts is only as strong as the weakest indirect relationship that is a part of it*. Figure 7.6 displays, at the operational level, the possible types of remote indirect relationships. These differ according to the way in which some concept α is related to concepts W, X, Y, Z.

The situation of Fig. 7.6a was described in Section 7.11. Note that the only indirect relationships that appear here are 1–N transitive associations (there are three of them). Thus a somewhat remote 1–N transitive association exists between W and Z. Figure 7.6b has a logical structure containing two kinds of indirect relationships: 1–N transitive (e.g., α to X) and weak (W to Y). Because of the weak relationship between W and Y, the remote relationship between W and Z, as well as that between X and Z, is weak. In Fig. 7.6c there is a weak indirect relationship and two M–N indirect relationships. The former dominates the latter in such a way that the remote relationships between X and Y and between W and Y are weak.

For Fig. 7.6d, notice that from α to X there is a 1–N transitive association, between α and Y there is an M–N indirect relationship, and between W and Z there is a weak indirect relationship. It follows that the remote relationships between X and Y and between W and Y are weak. The two weak indirect relationships and the indirect M–N relationship of Fig. 7.6e imply that the remote relationship between W and Z, as well as that between X and Z, is weak. There is no weak relationship in the logical structure of Fig. 7.6f. Therefore the remote relationships between W and Y and between W and Z are of the M–N variety.

Figure 7.6g has one each of the three kinds of indirect relationships presented in cases A through C. Notice that the remote relationship between Y and W is of the M–N variety, whereas the remote relationship between X and Z (or Y) is weak. Figure 7.6h has the same three kinds of indirect relationships. The two indirect relationships between W and Y are 1–N transitive (W to Z) and indirect M–N (between α and Y). Since M–N

is the "weaker" of these two, the remote indirect relationship between W and Y is the $M-N$ variety. Between X and Z there is a weak indirect relationship (between X and α) and a $1-N$ transitive association (W to Z). Therefore the remote relationship between X and Z (or Y) is of the weak variety.

In Fig. 7.6i the weak indirect relationship between α and Z means that any remote relationship of either X or W to either Y or Z must be weak. Notice that the logical structure of Fig. 7.6j has two $1-N$ transitive associations and one indirect $M-N$ relationship. Because of the position of this $M-N$ relationship, the remote relationship between either W or X and either Y or Z is of the $M-N$ variety.

It should be clear that relationships that are more remote than those depicted in Fig. 7.6 are common. The nature of such a relationship is again determined by the weakest indirect relationship that is a part of the overall remote relationship. As we have seen, the strongest indirect relationship is a $1-N$ transitive association, followed by an indirect $M-N$ relationship and then a weak indirect relationship.

7.15   Case E

Cases A through D are commonly encountered during the design of logical structures. Case E is less common, but nevertheless very useful in certain situations. Let X and Y be two aggregate concepts having instantiations. If S is a direct $1-N$ association with subject X and object Y, and if T is a direct $1-N$ association with the same subject and object, then there is an *indirect reflexive relationship* from X to itself. This indirect relationship is mediated by the intervening concept Y, as the object of both S and T.

Where an indirect reflexible relationship exists, an instantiation of X (X_0) may be reflexively associated with many other instances of X. This set of instances may be partitioned into those obtained when viewing X_0 as the subject instance of S and those obtained when viewing X_0 as the subject instance of T. These two subsets are formally expressed as

$$\{X_i|_{T_i}Y \cap_{S_0} Y \neq \varnothing,$$

where $_{T_i}Y = \{_{T_i}Y_1, \ _{T_i}Y_2, \ \ldots , \ _{T_i}Y_{M_i}\}$ and $_{S_0}Y = \{_{S_0}Y_1, \ _{S_0}Y_2, \ \ldots , \ _{S_0}Y_{N_0}\}\}$, and

$$\{X_j|_{S_j}Y \cap \ _{T_0}Y \neq \varnothing,$$

where $_{S_j}Y = \{_{S_j}Y_1, \ _{S_j}Y_2, \ \ldots , \ _{S_j}Y_{N_j}\}$ and $_{T_0}Y = \{_{T_0}Y_1, \ _{T_0}Y_2, \ \ldots , \ _{T_0}Y_{M_0}\}\}$, respectively. Thus an indirect reflexive relationship from X to X is similar to an indirect $M-N$ relationship except that subject concepts are identical in the reflexive case.

At the conceptual level, suppose that we are confronted with an assembly application in which many parts (i.e., components, products) are to be assembled. A given part needs certain quantities of other parts in order to be assembled. A given part may also be used in particular quantities for assembling other parts. This is the well-known material requirements planning (MRP) application [6]. At a concrete level we may know that

> part A needs 2 of part B, 3 of part C, and 1 of part D;
> part B needs 5 of part E and 4 of part F;
> part C needs 6 of part F, 9 of part G, and 3 of part H, etc.

Concrete descriptions such as this are simple, but how to describe this situation at the abstract level may not be immediately apparent.

First, discover the concepts (not associations) involved. Examination of the above example reveals two concepts: 'part' and 'part quantity'. Next, we must find and state any direct $1-N$ associations that exist among the concepts. Notice that a part needs or uses various quantities of various parts. So we assert that 'part' 'needs' 'part quantity'. Operationally, this gives the logical structure shown in Fig. 7.7a and the occurrence structure (for the above example) of Fig. 7.7b.

The direct association 'needs' is treated here as a $1-N$ relationship. Operationally, this forces us to create two occurrences of PART-QUANTITY that have the value of 3. That is, the instantiation '3' of 'part quantity' associated with the instance 'A' of 'part' is being viewed as a distinct concept from the instantiation '3' that is associated with the instance 'C' of 'part'. This view violates none of the construct definitions, nor any of the binding conventions, that have been previously presented.

Although 'needs' is a legitimate $1-N$ named association, it does not completely describe how 'part' and 'part quantity' are related. In Fig. 7.7b we see that part A needs 2, 3, and 1 as part quantities, but these are part quantities of what? This question is answered by declaring another direct $1-N$ association having 'part' as subject and 'part quantity' as object. Since a single part is used for a given part quantity and since a given part may be used for many part quantities, we can state that 'part' 'is used for' 'part quantity'. For example, part F is used for two part quantities: namely, 4 (needed by part B) and 6 (needed by part C). On the other hand, a given instance of 'part quantity' such as 3 (needed by part A) is associated with only one instance of 'part' (i.e., part C).

Operationalizing this second $1-N$ association from 'part' to 'part quan-

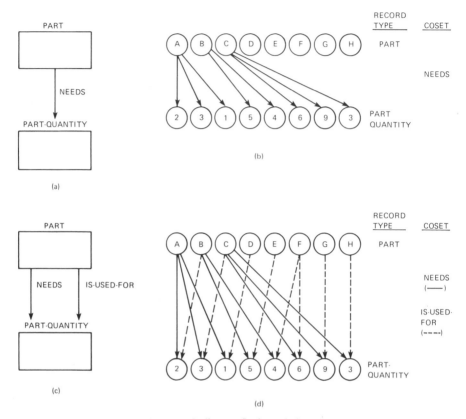

Fig. 7.7. Indirect reflexive relationship.

tity' gives the logical data structure shown in Fig. 7.7c. The corresponding occurrence structure appears in Fig. 7.7d. Coset occurrences for NEEDS are indicated with solid arrows and coset occurrences for IS-USED-FOR are indicated with broken arrows. Looking at the occurrence B of PART in this occurrence structure, we can easily determine that it needs 5 of E and 4 of F and that it is used for (in quantities of 2) assembling part A.

7.16   Case F

This case is rarely encountered in practice but is included here for the sake of completeness. Let X and Y be two aggregate concepts having instantiations. Suppose that X is the subject of a direct $1-N$ association S having Y as its object. Also suppose that Y is the subject of a direct $1-N$ association T having X as its object. The result is an *indirect circular 1-N relationship* between X and X (and also between Y and Y). That is, given an instantiation of X (X_0), there may be many other instances of X associated with it. More precisely, the set of instantiations of X having an indirect circular $1-N$ relationship with X_0 is $\{X_i | X_i \in {}_{T_j}X \text{ and } Y_j \in {}_{S_0}Y\} \cup \{X_i | X_0 \in {}_{T_j}X \text{ and } {}_{S_i}Y \cap Y_j \neq \varnothing\}$. The first set in this union may have many elements, but the second set can have no more than one. Just as the reflexive relationship was similar to an indirect $M-N$ relationship, the circular $1-N$ relationship is similar to a $1-N$ transitive association. The difference is that in the circular case the subject of each direct association is the object of the other, whereas in the transitive case the subject of only one direct association can be the object of the other.

   Consider the following two statements made at the conceptual level of knowledge representation:

> 'computer vendor' 'services' 'accounting firm'
> 'accounting firm' 'audits' 'computer vendor'

We assume that these are $1-N$ direct associations. That is, no accounting firm is serviced by more than one vendor and no vendor is audited by more than one accounting firm. The indirect circular relationship between computer vendors (and the circular relationship between accounting firms also) is visualized at the operational level as shown in Fig. 7.8a. An example occurrence structure appears in Fig. 7.8b.

   Given an occurrence of COMPUTER-VENDOR, say, TWO BIT INC., the circular relationship allows us to find all computer vendors audited by the accounting firms serviced by TWO BIT INC. These make up the set of the first term in the previously described union. For TWO BIT INC., the second term of the union consists of the computer vendor that services the accounting firm that audits TWO BIT INC.

   Given an occurrence of ACCOUNTING-FIRM, say, FIRM-1, the circular relationship permits us to find all accounting firms serviced by the computer vendors audited by FIRM-1. These are FIRM-2, FIRM-3, and FIRM-4. We can also see that FIRM-1 is indirectly related to FIRM-4 in another way. FIRM-4 audits the computer vendor that services FIRM-1. Thus it is important to realize that, in a circular $1-N$ relationship, various instances of X (e.g., 'accounting firm') can be related to a given instance (e.g., 'TWO BIT INC.') of X in one or both of the two ways indicated by the union stated earlier.

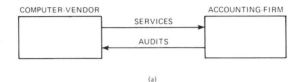

(a)

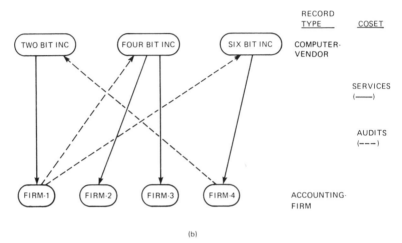

(b)

Fig. 7.8.   Indirect circular 1–N relationship.

7.20 THE MAJOR VARIETIES OF LOGICAL DATA STRUCTURES

A summary of the kinds of direct and indirect relationships presented thus far appears in Table 7.1. These can be used in identifying the major varieties of logical data structures: disjoint structures, linear structures, cyclic structures, tree structures, and network structures.

A disjoint structure (Fig. 7.9a) consists of record types with no cosets. The corresponding occurrence structure merely consists of flat files or tables. The record types may or may not contain duplicate item types. If they do not, then the record types (and the concepts they are derived from) are unrelated. If there are duplicate item types, then the record types (and the aggregate concepts they are derived from) are related. However, none of the direct relationships is named. The remaining varieties of logical data structuring reflect a conceptual view of the world that makes use of named associations between aggregate concepts.

TABLE 7.1

Direct and Indirect Relationships

Direct relationships via	Indirect relationships via
The appearance of an indivisible concept as part of two aggregate concepts (Section 6.23)	Various indivisible concepts duplicated in various aggregate concepts (Section 6.23)
A 1–N named association between two aggregate concepts (Sections 6.30, 6.31)	A 1–N transitive relationship (Section 7.11)
	A weak indirect relationship (Section 7.12)
	An indirect M–N relationship (Section 7.13)
	Remote indirect relationships (Section 7.14)
	A reflexive indirect relationship (Section 7.15)
	A circular indirect relationship (Section 7.16)
An M–N named (i.e., direct) relationship between two aggregate concepts (Section 7.13)	

A linear data structure is the result of a conceptualization whose only indirect relationships are 1–N transitive associations. In operational terms, a linear structure is identified by two major restrictions. First, no record type is the owner of more than one coset and no record type is the member of more than one coset. Second, there is one record type that owns a coset but is not the member of a coset. This second restriction implies that one record type is the member of a coset but does not own a coset. An example of a linear structure is shown in Fig. 7.9b. A corresponding occurrence structure is depicted in Fig. 7.10b. By relaxing one or both of the linear structure restrictions other varieties of logical structures are obtained.

Relaxing the first restriction on linear structures somewhat gives a tree structure. In operational terms, a tree structure is identified by the same restrictions as a linear structure *except* that a record type is here allowed to be the owner of many cosets. Note that this relaxation implies that there may be many record types, each of which is the member of a coset but does not own a coset. An example of a tree structure appears in Fig. 7.9c and a corresponding occurrence structure appears in Fig. 7.10c. Because of the way tree structures are defined, it is clear that any linear structure is a special (i.e., restricted) case of tree structuring.

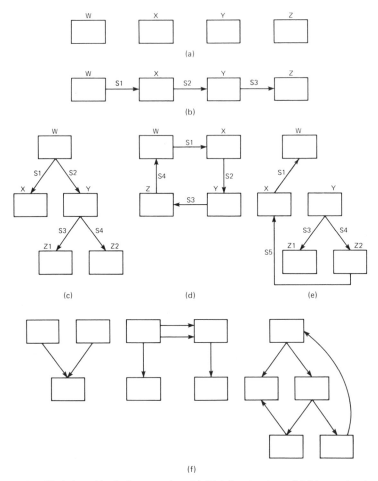

Fig. 7.9. Varieties of logical structuring. (a) Disjoint structure. (b) Linear structure. (c) Tree structure. (d) Cyclic structure. (e) Linear structure as a special (i.e., restricted) case.

A nonlinear tree structure will be referred to as a *strictly* tree structure. Observe that a strictly tree structure results from a conceptual description that contains at least one weak indirect relationship and may contain many $1-N$ transitive associations. In the example of Fig. 7.9c there are two weak indirect relationships and two $1-N$ transitive associations. The two remote indirect relationships (X to $Z 1$ and X to $Z 2$) are akin to that described in Fig. 7.6i.

Removing the second restriction on linear structures and retaining the first permits a cyclic structure such as that shown in Fig. 7.9d. An exam-

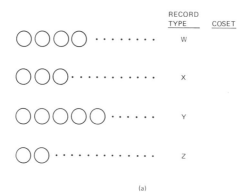

(a)

Fig. 7.10a.   Occurrence structure for Fig. 7.9a.

ple of a corresponding occurrence structure is shown in Fig. 7.10d. This definition of cyclic structure does not exclude linear structures, the latter being a special (restricted) case of the former. A nonlinear cyclic structure will be referred to as a strictly cyclic structure. Just as was the case with linear structures, a cyclic structure results from a conceptual description that exclusively contains 1–*N* transitive associations. One exception to this is the very simple case where there are only two record types in the cyclic structure (see Fig. 7.8a). This very simple cyclic structure results from a conceptual description having one indirect circular relationship. Note that any remote indirect relationship existing in a cyclic structure is of the form shown in Fig. 7.6a.

The tree and cyclic structures represent two paths of departure from strictly linear structures. A third variety of logical structure is obtained by

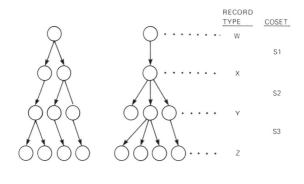

(b)

Fig. 7.10b.   Example occurrence structure for Fig. 7.9b.

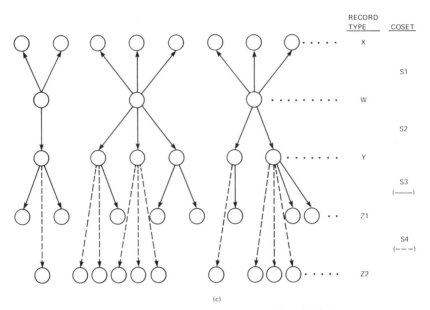

Fig. 7.10c.   Example occurrence structures for Fig. 7.9c.

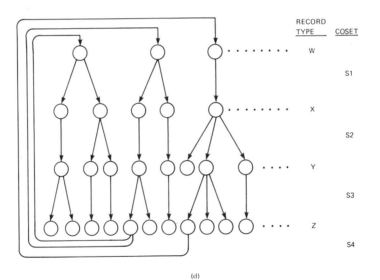

(d)

Fig. 7.10d.   Example occurrence structure for Fig. 7.9d.

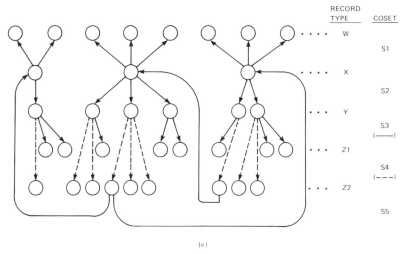

RECORD
TYPE   COSET

W

S1

X

S2

Y

S3
(——)

Z1

S4
(———)

Z2

S5

(e)

Fig. 7.10e.   Example occurrence structure for Fig. 7.9e.

relaxing both restrictions on linear structures, such that the only restriction remaining is that no record type can be the member of more than one set. Here again a linear structure is a special (i.e., restricted) case of this variety of structure. An example of this kind of structure appears in Fig. 7.9e. Structures of this tree–cyclic variety consist of the combination of a tree and a cyclic structure. Figure 7.10e displays an example occurrence structure. In passing we note that cyclic structures and tree–cyclic structures are infrequently encountered in practice.

If no restrictions are placed on the number of cosets that a record type can own, or on the number of cosets that a record type can be the member of, then network structures are permitted. Therefore trees, cyclic structures, tree–cyclic structures, linear structures, and disjoint structures are special (i.e., restricted) cases of the network variety of logical data structuring.

Any structure that does not adhere to one of these previously introduced varieties will be called a strict network. Three strictly network structures are illustrated in Fig. 7.9f. A strictly network structure results from a conceptual description that contains at least one indirect (or direct) $M-N$ relationship or at least one indirect reflexive relationship. One or more of the other indirect relationships may also be present.

An understanding of these varieties of logical structuring is important when assessing the knowledge representation mechanisms furnished by alternative data base management systems. If, for example, a given conceptual description is such that a network structure is called for, we would probably not want to use a data base system that supports tree structures only. On the other hand, if we have a data base system that can handle network structures, then a conceptual description that results in a tree structure or a disjoint structure is easily accommodated.

Of these varieties of logical structuring, systems that support either the disjoint view, the tree view, or the network view are the most prominent. Examples of systems that take the disjoint view of knowledge representation are relational systems (e.g., System R [2], although the System R implementation resembles network implementations) and inverted file systems such as ADABAS [1]. It must be emphasized that we are here referring to the logical view of knowledge representation and not to the ways in which that view can be implemented. Also it should be noted that various researchers and vendors utilize terms other than "record type," "record occurrence," "coset," etc., to name these operational constructs.

An example of a system that supports the tree variety of logical structuring is SYSTEM 2000 [14], although coset constructs are not explicitly stated or named. HDBS [5] supports tree schemata through the explicit use of cosets. The IMS [9] approach uses tree structures that are logically linked to give effectively a network view. Systems that support the network view of logical structuring include IDS [10], IDMS [8], DMS 1100 [4], and MDBS [12]. There is another major system that supports a network view, except that it does not permit a network structure derived from a conceptual description that has one or more 1–*N* transitive associations. This system is TOTAL [15]. Operationally, TOTAL does not permit a schema to contain any substructure of the form shown in Fig. 7.11a. This limitation can be skirted by creating an artificial record type as shown in Fig. 7.11b.

Finally, several words of caution (i.e., qualification) are in order when considering the various logical data structuring views. Recall that logical data structures (schemata) exist at the operational level of knowledge representation. Different vendors and researchers use different terms and different notations to represent the operational constructs that have been presented in this chapter.

A formal statement of a schema is made in terms of what is often called a data description language (DDL) [3]. Each data base system has its own version of a DDL. Although a DDL typically deals primarily with the operational level of knowledge representation, in some systems there is no clearly drawn distinction between the operational and implementation levels of knowledge representation. That is, when the KS designer formally states the desired logical structure, he or she is also required to make decisions as to how this structure will be implemented.

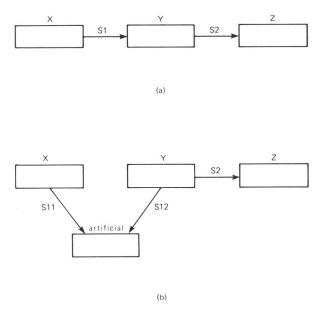

(a)

(b)

Fig. 7.11.   Using an artificial record type in place of a 1–*N* transitive relationship.

Another point to be careful about is that it is erroneous to claim that any one of the varieties of logical structuring is more efficient than another. Efficiency depends on implementation methods used and on the nature of the particular application area being addressed. It is entirely possible for two different logical views (e.g., disjoint versus network [16]) to have practically identical underlying implementations. On the other hand, two data base systems, each supporting network views, could have substantially different implementations. When considering efficiency issues, it is vital to remember that there are tradeoffs between storage efficiencies, processing efficiencies, and labor efficiencies (recall Section 1.03.2).

One sometimes hears or reads claims to the effect that one data-structuring view is "more natural" than another. Although "naturalness" is generally regarded as a desirable property, its specific attributes or dimensions are commonly left unexplained; nor is there a widely accepted objective measure of the degree of naturalness possessed by a given variety of logical data structure. Dubious, or perhaps even meaningless, claims of "naturalness" should be considered in the above light. An appropriate response is: "Naturalness to whom?"

7.30   A DESIGN PROCEDURE

The emphasis in this chapter has been on conceptual and operational levels of knowledge representation. Conceptual constructs and operational constructs have been introduced and have been bound together. There was an examination of the various kinds of indirect relationships that can exist, given the conceptual constructs. Depending on which of these indirect relationships appear in a conceptual description of some application, binding produces a schema that strictly conforms to one of the major varieties of logical data structuring.

Knowledge of conceptual and operational constructs (and their bindings) is, however, only the set of tools that are available for constructing a particular logical structure. Knowledge of the possible varieties of logical structure shows us the possible forms (i.e., architectural styles) that our particular logical structure could assume. What is missing is a procedure or method for using the "tools" to construct a schema that is appropriate for a particular application. An analogy to carpentry is appropriate here. The novice carpenter may understand the uses of the various tools but may lack a knowledge of how to organize the usage of these tools in various construction projects. Construction methods are either distilled from experiences or acquired by adopting the methods of experienced carpenters.

It is usually the case that students of data base design learn how to use the operational "tools" of schema design through experience (i.e., trial and error). They eventually develop a knack for schema design. The methods (or "knack") of experienced data base designers are rarely articulated or written down. Unlike the experienced carpenter, whose methods can be observed, the experienced schema builder's work is largely mental and unobservable to others. There is little literature about *how* to transform knowledge of an application area into a schema, compared to literature on the nature of the *operational tools* for building a schema.

In this section we introduce a *schema design procedure that makes use of both the conceptual and the operational constructs* presented earlier. The procedure is straightforward and simple to use, but by no means is it simplistic. It is not claimed that the procedure gives the "optimal" data structure (e.g., most "efficient," most "natural") for every application problem. It has, however, been tested by numerous students in dealing with diverse applications. In each instance an appropriate logical structure was produced. Moreover, reactions toward the procedure, as a valuable method for organizing one's approach to schema building, have been favorable. The procedure is not a complete substitute for experience in schema design, but it can save a good deal of trial and error. A schema generated by this procedure is, of course, subject to refinement.

The design procedure, when confronted with a particular application or "world," is as follows:

1.   Identify and name all indivisible concepts that have instantiations. No two indivisible concepts can have the same name. A data item type is declared for each of the indivisible concepts.

2.   In this step aggregate concepts are generated. The aggregations will be based on the existence of "nearly" 1–1 associations between indivisible concepts. A 1–1 association is merely a 1–N association in which $N = 1$. A "nearly" 1–1 association is loosely used to describe situations where there is a 1–1 relationship for all but a "few" of the instances of the two concepts involved. Consider the concepts 'customer name' and 'customer address'. For the most part a given customer name is associated with only one customer address and vice versa. However, since exceptions can occur (e.g., a customer with two addresses or two customers with the same address) we refer to the relationship as nearly 1–1. When such exceptions begin to become the rule, then the relationship is 1–N ($N > 1$) or M–N ($M, N > 1$).

(a)   Select an indivisible concept from those identified in the first step.

(b)   From the pool of indivisible concepts remaining, find all other (if any) indivisible concepts that have a 1–1 or nearly 1–1 association with the selected concept. This entire set of indivisible concepts, which pairwise have at least nearly 1–1 associations, will henceforth be treated as an aggregate concept. Give a name to this aggregate concept that is descriptive of the notion represented by the set of indivisible concepts and their interrelationships (e.g., pairwise, the indivisible concepts 'customer name', 'customer address,' and 'customer account' have at least nearly 1–1 relationships. Collectively, we can say that they represent the notion of a 'customer'). Usually, a descriptive name is readily apparent. No two aggregate concepts can have the same name.

(c)   Remove the indivisible concept(s) just aggregated in step 2b from further consideration. If there are no unaggregated indivisible concepts remaining, proceed to step 2d. Otherwise select one of the remaining indivisible concepts and go to step 2b.

(d)   At this stage there should be no unaggregated indivisible concepts, although some aggregates may consist of only one indivisible concept apiece. At the operational level, declare a record type for each aggregate concept. At the operational level a nearly 1–1 relationship forces us

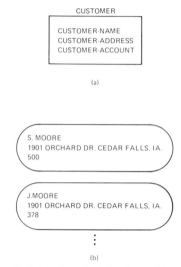

(a)

(b)

Fig. 7.12. Nearly 1–1 relationship.

to admit a small amount of redundancy into our occurrence structure. As an example, consider the record type for 'customer' shown in Fig. 7.12a. If two customers have the same address, then the two occurrences of Fig. 7.12b will appear in the occurrence structure. Notice that the same address appears twice in the occurrence structure. Thus we can say that a nearly 1–1 relationship is a 1–1 relationship with some redundancy.

3.   We are now prepared to identify and name all direct 1–N associations existing between pairs of aggregate concepts. But we shall also make use of the idea of a "nearly" 1–N association. A "nearly" 1–N association is a 1–N association that has some redundant instantiations of the object concept. An example at the operational level is shown in Fig. 7.4b. Note that ORDER-LINE is the member of the coset CONTAINS. There are two occurrences of this record type that have 3 as the quantity ordered; if the unit price for each of these two occurrences is also identical in value, then "contains" is a nearly 1–N association. That is, there is one case of two identical instantiations of the object concept. If declaration of a 1–N association from a subject concept to an object concept forces us to have "many" redundancies among the instantiations of an object concept, then it may be more appropriate to consider the association between the two concepts as being M–N rather than nearly 1–N.

(a)   Find all 1–N or nearly 1–N associations between aggregate concepts. For each of these, name the 1–N association and write out its subject and object. No two 1–N associations can have the same name.

(b)   At the operational level declare a coset to correspond with every named 1–N association. Eliminate any coset that is not required because of the existence of transitive (possibly remotely transitive) 1–N associations.

4.   If there are no unassociated aggregate concepts, proceed to step 5. Otherwise, for each of the remaining unassociated concepts do the following:

(a)   Select the aggregate concept that is, in a conceptual sense, most closely related to the unassociated concept. Declare a direct M–N relationship between the two.

(b)   Operationally, incorporate this M–N relationship into the schema either by the use of a null record type (recall Fig. 7.5) or by the use of an mm set.

5.   At this point a review of the resultant schema should be undertaken. This review should address the following questions and should revise the schema accordingly.

(a)   Are there any indivisible concepts that were omitted in step 1?

(b)   Is it desirable to collapse two record types into one by eliminating the coset between them and introducing redundancies into occurrences of the occurrence structure for the resultant record type?

(c)   Is it desirable to decompose a record type into two record types in order to eliminate redundancies in the occurrence structure for the original record type? The two resultant record types would be related either by a coset or by the operationalization of a direct M–N association.

Other points for review could be added to step 5. The review issues are intended for "fine tuning" the schema that emerges from step 4. The answers to these review questions depend on a knowledge of how the operational constructs are implemented and how the data base will be used (i.e., what kinds of reports will need to be produced from it, how often, and how fast).

It should be mentioned that the procedure is still workable if the notions of "nearly" 1–1 and "nearly" 1–N relationships are dropped. At the end of step 4 one would still have a logically correct schema, a schema whose occurrence structure would contain no data redundancies at the level of item occurrences or at the level of record occurrences. If such an approach is taken, one should pay close attention to (b) and (c) of step 5. Depending on the implementation, the storage cost of a complete elimination of all redundancy at the logical level may become quite high.

Table 7.2 summarizes steps 1–4 in the guise of questions that the schema builder should ask himself or herself.

TABLE 7.2

The Design Procedure

---

1. Have all indivisible concepts been listed?
2. Given an indivisible concept q, does another indivisible concept r have a 1–1 or almost 1–1 relationship with q? That is, given a value of q, is there usually only one value of r related to it, and given a value of r is there usually only one value of q related to it? Partition the set of indivisible concepts into aggregates, such that a 1–1 or nearly 1–1 relationship exists among all pairs in an aggregate.
3. Given an aggregate concept X, does another aggregate concept Y have a 1–N or almost 1–N relationship with X? That is, given an instance of X, are there possibly many instances of Y associated with it, and given an instance of Y is there usually only one instance of X associated with it? Name all 1–N or almost 1–N associations, indicating the subject and object. Omit any 1–N associations not needed because of the existence of 1–N transitive associations.
4. If any unassociated aggregate concepts remain, establish a direct M–N relationship between each unassociated concept and the aggregate concept with which it is most nearly related, in a conceptual sense.

7.31   An Example of Schema Design

Consider the following scenario: A retailer of machine parts maintains a number of warehouses in various cities. Each warehouse has its own manager. Warehouses are supplied through a network of suppliers. Each part is assigned a part number. In each city in which either suppliers or warehouses are located, a local trucking firm has been contracted to provide shipping facilities. Furthermore, each state in which business is transacted has its own regulatory agency. The goal is to design a data structure for an inventory system that includes all the above information. The inventory information itself consists of the per unit value and quantity of each type of part stored in each warehouse, classified by the original supplier.

The first step in the design procedure is to identify the indivisible concepts. Many have been explicitly stated above; others are implicit (i.e., can be inferred from the description), and some have yet to be clarified. For instance, what information is to be collected on the local trucking firm in each city? For our purposes, the only relevant information is the name of the firm and its telephone number. Similarly, we identify suppliers by name, telephone, and address; and warehouses by number and address. Note that some concepts are already being aggregated into groups (step 2).

The set of indivisible concepts is listed in Fig. 7.13. For each concept

CONCEPT	ABBREVIATION
warehouse number	WNUM
warehouse manager	WMGR
warehouse street address	WSTR
city	CITY
state	STAT
zip code	ZIP
supplier name	SNAM
supplier telephone	STEL
supplier street address	SSTR
local trucking firm	LTF
firm's telephone	TTEL
part number	PNO
part description	DESC
per unit value	VAL
quantity stored	QTY
state agency	AGNC
agency's address	ADDR

Fig. 7.13.   Indivisible concepts.

an abbreviation or synonym is defined, solely for the purpose of facilitating the discussion.

The next phase in the design procedure is to form aggregates of 1–1 or nearly 1–1 related concepts. Some of these relationships are obvious: WNUM (see Fig. 7.13) is related to WMGR and WSTR; SNAM is related to STEL and SSTR, etc. What about CITY and WNUM? There is no proscription on having several warehouses located within a single city; thus this is not 1–1 or nearly 1–1. However, since one local trucking firm (LTF and TTEL) is dealt with exclusively in each city, it is possible to associate CITY, LTF, and TTEL in an aggregate group.

One possible aggregation is shown in Fig. 7.14. It must be noted that this is not the only possible aggregation, nor is it necessarily the first aggregation obtained in the design process. Rather, it is the result of several evaluations and reworkings, generally involving the division of large aggregate groups into smaller groups. In the present case, the aggregate Q (VAL and QTY) was formed separately from any other aggregate, because these concepts did not readily fit into a 1–1 relationship with any other concept.

The third phase is to establish 1–N and nearly 1–N relationships between the aggregate groups. One of the simplest is the relationship between C (cities) and S (states). Each state may have several cities in it, but each city is part of only one state. Similarly, each warehouse W is part of

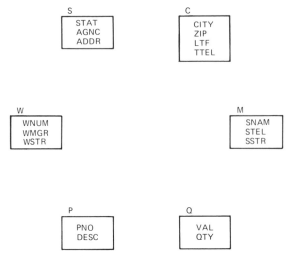

Fig. 7.14.　Aggregate groups.

just one city C, but each city C can contain several (i.e., 0, 1, or more) warehouses. Thus between each pair of aggregates the relationship must be analyzed.

The result of this analysis is shown in Fig. 7.15. The aggregate groups are the boxes, and the relationships have for convenience been numbered. It is possible to stop at this point; however, many of the relationships depicted are redundant, because of the transitive nature of 1–N associa-

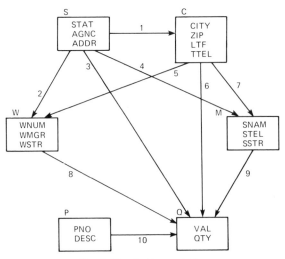

Fig. 7.15.　1–N associations.

tions. Eliminating many of these, the schema of Fig. 7.16 emerges (with some slight repositioning).

Of course, it is not necessary to eliminate all the 1–N associations. Consider association 2, between states S and warehouses W. This is eliminated in Fig. 7.16, because 2 is captured by 1 and 5. However, 2 could convey information not obtainable directly through the transitive link. For example, the ordering of information might be different. In general, redundant associations have the operational effect of increasing the storage requirements of the system while decreasing the processing requirements.

The final step in the design process is to establish M–N relationships between the unassociated concepts and the main body of the data structure. In this case there are no unassociated concepts, and so no M–N associations need be created. However, it is possible to establish such associations when other types of information must be presented.

For example, the data structure of Fig. 7.16 allows us to determine which suppliers (M) have supplied parts (P). But it does not allow us to determine which suppliers have the potential of supplying certain parts. This is an M–N relationship between parts P and suppliers M, since each part may be supplied by many suppliers, and each supplier could supply many parts. This structure is shown in Fig. 7.17. The M–N relationship

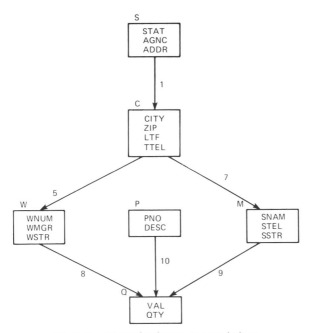

Fig. 7.16.   Nonredundant 1–N associations.

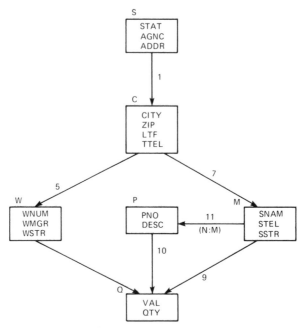

Fig. 7.17. Final schema.

must be handled with the artificial record type approach (Fig. 7.5), except in the case of MDBS [12], which allows direct representation of this kind of relationship. Figure 7.17 uses the MDBS $N:M$ set construct (i.e., an mm set) in which M is arbitrarily used as the owner.

The fine tuning next performed should be undertaken at several levels. The designer of the structure must verify that the structure does indeed match the description of the application. Someone cognizant of the application should also review the schema, to ascertain whether or not the schema completely captures the data processing involved in the application.

REFERENCES

1. *ADABAS*, Software Ag, Reston, Virginia.
2. M. M. Astrahan *et al.*, System R: A relational approach to data base management, *ACM Trans. Data Base Syst.* **1**, No. 2 (1976).
3. CODASYL Systems Committee, *Data Base Task Group Report*, Association for Computing Machinery (April 1971).
4. DMS 1100. Sperry Univac Division, Sperry Rand Corporation, Blue Bell, Pennsylvania.
5. HDBS, Micro Data Base Systems, Inc., Lafayette, Indiana.

6. D. Garwood, Stop: Before you use the bill processor . . . , *Production and Inventory Management* **2** (1970).
7. W. D. Haseman and A. B. Whinston, "Introduction to Data Management." Irwin, Homewood, Illinois, 1977.
8. IDMS, Cullinane Corporation, Wellesley, Massachusetts.
9. *IMS/VS*, IBM Corp., White Plains, New York.
10. Integrated Data Store II, Honeywell Information Systems Inc., Waltham, Massachusetts.
11. J. Martin, "Computer Data-Base Organization." Prentice-Hall, Englewood, Cliffs, New Jersey, 1975.
12. *MDBS*, Micro Data Base Systems, Inc., Lafayette, Indiana.
13. G. M. Nijssen, Two major flaws in the CODASYL DDL 1973 and proposed corrections, *Informat. Syst.* **1** (1975).
14. SYSTEM 2000, MRI Systems Corp., Austin, Texas.
15. TOTAL, Cincom Systems Inc., Cincinnati, Ohio.
16. D. Tsichritzis, A network framework for relation implementation, *in* "Data Base Description" (B. C. Douque and G. M. Nijssen, eds.). North Holland Publ., Amsterdam, 1975.

Chapter 8

LANGUAGE SYSTEMS FOR DATA BASE KNOWLEDGE SYSTEMS

8.00 INTRODUCTION

This chapter deals with language systems that can be used in a DSS that has a data base KS. The discussion of these language systems is organized on the basis of the classification scheme of Chapter 3. We begin by examining retrieval-only language systems, proceding from category J through category L. This is followed by discussion of languages for directing computations in DSS with a data base KS. We present these beginning with those that fall into the bottom row of Fig. 3.2 and finishing with those of the top row.

It is vital to remember that a LS deals with the linguistic facilities available to a decision maker for use in stating a problem. The details of how the PPS "understands" and utilizes a problem statement are deferred until Chapter 9. In this chapter we deal only with how to state a problem and the major effects of stating it, and not with how those effects are realized. The style of presentation adopted in this chapter is consistent with that of the preceding chapters. The languages can be viewed from conceptual, operational, and implementation levels. The former two are emphasized here.

8.10 LANGUAGES FOR DIRECTING RETRIEVAL

Recall that languages for directing retrieval result in no executions of computational models. Nevertheless, they can result in reports that furnish valuable support for decision makers where the KS consists of a data base. Category J languages are commonly referred to as data manipulation languages (DML). A DML typically exists within a procedural host language such as COBOL or FORTRAN and can be considered as providing an extended-COBOL or extended-FORTRAN. Category K languages provide the means for invoking the execution of a preexisting DML program. With category L languages the user instigates the automatic creation of a DML program by stating the characteristics of a desired report.

8.11 Category J Languages

As indicated in Chapter 3, languages of this category are procedural and flexible. A DML allows a user, knowledgeable in the host language, to specify a procedure that constructs a desired report from a given data base. The syntax of one DML can differ markedly from the syntax of another. The various data manipulation languages do, however, have a conceptual commonality. That is, if we begin with a conceptual representation of knowledge, as presented in Chapters 6 and 7, then we can investigate how to undertake retrieval of some subset of the conceptually represented knowledge. This undertaking can proceed quite apart from the use of a specific DML syntax that permits an operational specification of retrieval processes. Both the conceptual and operational levels of procedural problem statements are examined here. Implementations of various data manipulation languages are beyond the present scope, being based on the language of implementation (e.g., assembler languages) and the implementation methods used for the data base.

8.11.1 Conceptual View of Procedural Data Base Retrieval

Remember that, conceptually, knowledge about some application area is represented as a pool of aggregate concept instantiations, each composed of instantiations of indivisible concepts. The aggregate concept instantiations are meshed together via instances of direct $1-N$ (and perhaps $M-N$) associations. Confronted with this highly intertwined mesh of instantiations and their associations, a retrieval problem consists of directing our attention to certain desired aggregate instantiations and then extracting instances of particular indivisible concepts from them.

This focusing of attention on certain strands (or paths) in the conceptual knowledge mesh does not happen all at once. Rather, it is a *process* that may be somewhat likened to a word association game, where the next word to appear is one that is related to the last word. However, retrieval is not the following of a random path of associations, nor does it necessarily involve the traversal of a habitual, well-worn path of associations. A retrieval process involves the discovery of a path(s) satisfying some prespecified criteria (i.e., goal conditions).

The discovery of such a path (remember that in category J this discovery is procedural) within the knowledge mesh depends on our ability to utilize three kinds of operations. We shall refer to these three operations as finding, activating, and extracting. A retrieval procedure can be specified in terms of finding a particular instantiation of any given aggregate concept, activating a given aggregate instantiation, and extracting the instantiation of a particular indivisible concept from any *activated* aggregate instantiation. Finding and extracting should be clear, but activation deserves further comment.

If we conceive of a knowledge mesh as being *passive* (an unlighted maze), then retrieval may be thought of as involving an *activating* or "lighting" of some pathway in the mesh; the information along this active, lighted path can then be viewed and returned as a report. We shall say that an instantiation of some concept X is on the activated path if, in the retrieval procedure, it has been declared to be either

(1)   the active instance of concept X (i.e., the current "definition" of X),

(2)   the active subject instance of some $1-N$ association having X as its subject,

(3)   the active object instance of some $1-N$ association having X as its object, or

(4)   an active instance of some $M-N$ association having X as participant.

It is by activating instantiations in these ways that an activated path in the otherwise passive knowledge mesh is defined. It is assumed that the directing of attention in a retrieval process is sufficiently *focused* that, at a given instant, any concept X can have no more than one active instance, nor can any $1-N$ association have more than one active subject instance and one active object instance, nor can any $M-N$ association have more than one active instance for each participating concept.

In the following examples it is assumed that we are confronted by a knowledge mesh conforming to the concepts and associations used to represent the customer-order world in Section 7.00. A very simple retrieval might have as its goal a report of the customer Bob Smith's account. Conceptually, the procedure for retrieving this would be to *find* the instance of 'customer' having 'Bob Smith' as the instance of 'customer name'. This 'customer' instance is *activated* as the active (or current) instance of 'customer.' The instantiation of 'customer account' is then *extracted* from the active instance of 'customer'.

Consider the retrieval whose goal is to produce a report of the order numbers of all orders placed by Bob Smith. Conceptually the retrieval procedure would be to find the instance of 'customer' having 'Bob Smith' as the instance of 'customer name'. This instance is made the active instance of 'customer'. Since we are interested in Bob Smith's orders, we declare the active subject instance of 'places' to be the same as the active instance of 'customer'. We now find an instantiation of 'order' that is associated with the currently active subject instance of 'places.' Having found such an instance of 'order', we can activate it as the current object instance of 'places'. The instantiation of 'order number' residing in this active object instance of 'places' is extracted for the report. We can now find another instance of 'order' that is associated with the active subject instance of 'places', activate it, and extract from it. This continues until all 'order' instances associated with 'Bob Smith' via the 'places' association have been found, activated, and subjected to extraction.

The last retrieval problem that is considered at a conceptual level is the procedure for producing a report of each item number and its quantity ordered for order number 777. First, find the instance of 'order' having an order number of 777. Make this the active instance of 'order' and also the active subject instance of the 'contains' association. Find an instance of 'order line' associated with the active subject instance of 'contains' and activate it as the current object instance of 'contains'. Now declare the active object instance of 'appears in' to be the same as the active object instance of 'contains'. Since 'contains' is a 1–*N* association, the *unique* subject instance of 'appears-in' that is associated with the active object instance of 'appears in' is readily found and activated to be the current subject instance for 'appears in'. The instantiation of 'item number' for the active subject instance of 'appears in' is extracted, as is the instantiation of 'quantity ordered' for the active object instance of 'contains'. These go into the report.

We now find another instance of 'order line' that is associated with the active subject of 'contains'. This newly found instance is activated as the current object of 'contains' and the procedure continues as before, with different activated instances for 'appears in' and the extraction of another item number and quantity ordered. We continue looping through this procedure until all instances of 'order line' associated with the active subject instance of 'contains' have been found and dealt with. If we desired to produce a similar report for order number 778, we would find the appropriate instance of 'order'. It would become the active instance of 'order' (replacing the instance having 777) and we would proceed just as we did for order number 777.

8.11.2   Operational View of Data Base Retrieval

Retrieval procedures are operationalized as sequences of statements in a DML-extended host language. Because of the variation among data manipulation languages, a stylized DML is used here. Although its syntax may differ from that used here, the retrieval specification of a particular DML (e.g., see the appendix of this chapter) is overshadowed by the same conceptual processes of finding, activating, and extracting. A retrieval procedure written in this stylized DML should be readily translatable into another DML. The set of commands that we shall use for operationalizing the conceptual processes appears in Table 8.1. Underlined arguments must be specified by the LS user; values of other arguments are returned to the user's program after a command's execution.

At the operational level, retrieval involves navigation through an occurrence structure in order to find and activate a path from which data values will be extracted. As the various DML commands are introduced, pictorial examples are used to illustrate the commands' effects *vis-à-vis* the activation of a path. The occurrence structures for the examples in this section conform to the schema of Fig. 7.1. In these illustrations all shaded record occurrences are currently inactive. When an occurrence is activated as the current occurrence of a record type or as the current

TABLE 8.1

Stylized DML Commands

---

(1)   FIND-RECORD (<u>record-type-1</u>, <u>data-item-type</u>, <u>data-item-value</u>, failure-flag)
(2)   FIND-FIRST-MEMBER (<u>coset-1</u>, failure flag)
(3)   FIND-NEXT-MEMBER (<u>coset-1</u>, failure flag)
(4)   FIND-MEMBER (<u>coset-1</u>, <u>data-item-type-in-member</u>, <u>data-item-value</u>, failure-flag)
(5)   ACTIVATE-OWNER-BASED-ON-MEMBER (<u>coset-1</u>, <u>coset-2</u>, failure-flag)
(6)   ACTIVATE-OWNER-BASED-ON-RECORD (<u>coset-1</u>, <u>record-type-1</u>, failure-flag)
(7)   ACTIVATE-MEMBER-BASED-ON-MEMBER (<u>coset-1</u>, <u>coset-2</u>, failure-flag)
(8)   ACTIVATE-OWNER-BASED-ON-OWNER (<u>coset-1</u>, <u>coset-2</u>, failure-flag)
(9)   ACTIVATE-MEMBER-BASED-ON-RECORD   (<u>coset-1</u>,   <u>record-type-1</u>,   failure-flag)
(10)   ACTIVATE-MEMBER-BASED-ON-OWNER (<u>coset-1</u>, <u>coset-2</u>, failure-flag)
(11)   EXTRACT-VALUE-OF-RECORD (<u>record-type</u>, <u>data-item-type</u>, value, failure-flag)
(12)   EXTRACT-VALUE-OF-MEMBER (<u>coset-1</u>, <u>data-item-type</u>, value, failure-flag)
(13)   EXTRACT-VALUE-OF-OWNER (<u>coset-1</u>, <u>data-item-type</u>, value, failure-flag)

---

owner or member occurrence of a coset, the shading is removed and the occurrence is labeled to indicate the nature of its activation. The labeling convention used is CR for the currently active record occurrence of its record type, CO for the current owner occurrence of a coset, and CM for the current member occurrence of a coset. As we shall shortly see, a given occurrence may be active in more than one of these capacities during a particular retrieval. It should be noted that CODASYL systems do not use CO and CM indicators; they provide only one currency indicator per coset, which makes the DML programming somewhat more cumbersome.

The four FIND commands serve to indicate the kinds of 'finding' that we might want to undertake. Commands for other, but similar, 'finding' tasks (e.g., FIND-LAST-MEMBER, FIND-FIRST-RECORD, etc.) could also be bound to the concept of 'finding'. FIND-RECORD is a command to find the record occurrence of record-type-1 that has the specified data-item-value for the indicated data-item-type. If no such occurrence exists, then the failure-flag is turned on. An example of the usage of this command (see Fig. 8.1) is

FIND-RECORD ('CUSTOMER', 'CUSTOMER-NAME', 'BOB SMITH', FLAG).

If after executing the command, FLAG is not on, then the record occurrence of CUSTOMER whose value for CUSTOMER-NAME is BOB SMITH has been found. (Quotes are used around arguments in this and following examples indicate that the argument is a literal, rather than a variable, in a host language.) There are no preconditions that must be satisfied prior to using the FIND-RECORD command. Thus it is typically the first kind of DML command that appears in a retrieval procedure. It locates the beginning of a path in an occurrence structure. In some commercial systems, application of the FIND-RECORD operation is restricted to a subset of the total set of record types.

Remember from the examples of conceptual retrieval that finding an instance was always immediately succeeded by activating it in some way. Therefore a convenient convention is that use of any of the four opera-

Fig. 8.1. Finding a record.

tional FIND commands is automatically accompanied by an activation of the occurrence that is found. The record occurrence that is found by FIND-RECORD is automatically activated as the current occurrence of its record type. The record occurrence found by either FIND-FIRST-MEMBER, FIND-NEXT-MEMBER, or FIND-MEMBER is automatically activated as the current member occurrence of the coset appearing in the command's argument list. Bear in mind that, even though a 'find' is pointless without subsequent activation, it is in many cases necessary to perform additional activations during a retrieval procedure.

The FIND-FIRST-MEMBER command finds the 'first' member record occurrence (i.e., record occurrence of a member record type) that is owned by the *current* owner record occurrence of the indicated coset-1. The current or active occurrence of the owning record type for coset-1 can have many member occurrences. This set of member occurrences can be ordered in one of a number of ways (e.g., LIFO, FIFO, ascending order on the basis of respective values some data item type, etc.). The ordering convention for a coset is declared during the specification of the data base schema. Since the member occurrences can be ordered it is reasonable to have a command that finds that first member occurrence. There is a precondition that must be satisfied before FIND-FIRST-MEMBER can be used: There must be an occurrence of the owner record type of coset-1 that has been activated as the current owner of coset-1. When the first member occurrence is found by this command, that occurrence automatically becomes the current member occurrence of coset-1.

The FIND-NEXT-MEMBER command finds the next member record occurrence (following the *current* member record occurrence) that is owned by the *current* owner record occurrence of coset-1. The precondition that must be met before using this command is that there must be an occurrence of the member record type of coset-1 that has been activated. When the next member record occurrence is found, it is activated as the new current member occurrence of coset-1. Figure 8.2 depicts the effect on a retrieval path of applying FIND-FIRST-MEMBER and then FIND-NEXT-MEMBER. The example assumes a starting point in which the customer record occurrence for Bob Smith has been activated as the current owner of the coset PLACES.

The FIND-MEMBER command does not necessarily find the first (or the next) member occurrence (for the current owner of coset-1), but one that has the indicated data item value for the stated data item type. Thus FIND-MEMBER appears to access directly a specific member record occurrence, whereas FIND-FIRST-MEMBER and FIND-NEXT-MEMBER can be used in conjunction to access sequentially the member occurrences of some coset that are owned by the currently active owner occurrence. A

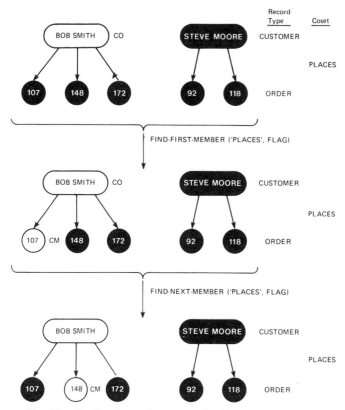

Fig. 8.2.   Finding first and next records of a coset occurrence.

precondition for the usage of FIND-MEMBER is that some occurrence of coset-1's owning record type must be the current owner. The member occurrence found by this command is automatically activated as the current member occurrence for coset-1. Many data manipulation languages have restrictions on which data item types can be used as a basis for finding a member occurrence. An example of FIND-MEMBER is given in Fig. 8.3.

Note that the last three kinds of FIND commands have the precondition that coset-1 must have a currently active owner. However, neither they nor the FIND-RECORD command have the effect of activating some record occurrence as the current owner of a coset. This activation is accomplished by the second group (5–10) of commands in Table 8.1. Unlike the FIND commands, these commands are bound to a single conceptual operation, namely, activation. They involve no finding or extract-

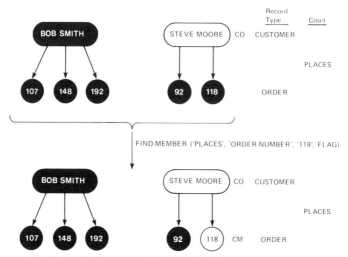

Fig. 8.3.   Finding a particular member in a coset occurrence.

ing. There is no finding in the sense of finding some record occurrence, although they do look at some record occurrence that was previously found and activated. The DML syntax used here is largely self-explanatory.

Command (5) activates as the owner of coset-1 the record occurrence that is the currently active member of coset-2. Clearly, the precondition for this command is the existence of a currently active member of coset-2. It should also be clear that the owner record type of coset-1 must be the member record type of coset-2 in order for this to be a meaningful command. Command (6) is similar to (5), except that the occurrence activated as the owner of coset-1 is the same as the currently active occurrence of record-type-1. In the logical structure record-type-1 must be the owner of coset-1. A precondition to the application of (6) is that there must exist an active occurrence of record-type-1.

Figure 8.4 contains a five-step procedure that utilizes the foregoing activation commands to find the first order line of Steve Moore's first order. Command (7) can be used to lengthen this path in the occurrence structure to include the inventory item that appears in the order line. This command activates as the member of coset-1, the record occurrence that is the currently active member of coset-2. Coset-1 and coset-2 must have the same member record type. As a precondition for the application of (7), there must exist a current member of coset-2. Observe that an occurrence that has been activated as the current member of coset-1 can be owned by at most one occurrence of coset-1's owning record type. There is no choice involved here as there is when confronted by several member occurrences for a given owner occurrence. Therefore we shall permit command (7) to have the additional effect of activating a current owner of coset-1. The occurrence that is thus activated is the one that owns (via coset-1) the currently active member of coset-1. Figure 8.5 contains an example showing the usage and effect of ACTIVATE-MEMBER-BASED-ON-MEMBER. Figure 8.4f is taken as a starting point for this example.

Command (8) activates, as the current owner occurrence of coset-1, the record occurrence that is currently the active owner occurrence of coset-2. The precondition for this command is that coset-2 must have a current owner. The command can be used only if coset-1 and coset-2 have the same owner record type in the data base schema.

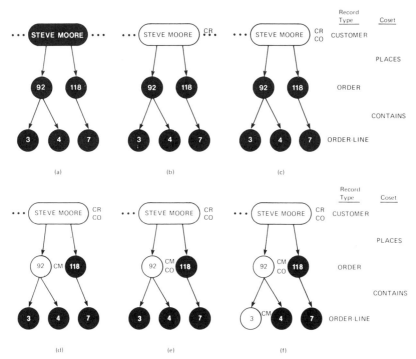

a) FIND-RECORD('CUSTOMER', 'CUSTOMER-NAME', 'STEVE MOORE', FLAG) → (b)
(b) → ACTIVATE-OWNER-BASED-ON-RECORD('PLACES', 'CUSTOMER', FLAG) → (c)
(c) → FIND-FIRST-MEMBER('PLACES', FLAG) → (d)
(d) → ACTIVATE-OWNER-BASED-ON-MEMBER('CONTAINS', 'PLACES', FLAG) → (e)
(e) → FIND-FIRST-MEMBER('ORDER', FLAG) → (f)

Fig. 8.4.

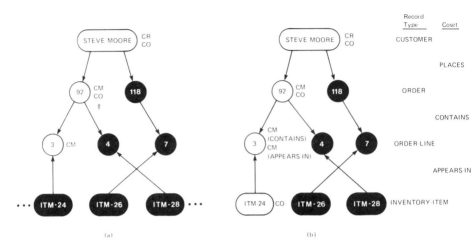

(a)

(b)

(a) ACTIVATE-MEMBER-BASED-ON-MEMBER ('APPEARS-IN', 'CONTAINS',
FLAG) → (b).

Fig. 8.5.

The ACTIVATE-MEMBER-BASED-ON-RECORD command takes the currently active occurrence of record-type-1 and makes it the currently active member occurrence of coset-1. The occurrence that owns (via coset-1) this newly active member occurrence is itself activated to become the current owner of coset-1. Since there is no possibility of more than one owner of the active member occurrence, it is unnecessary to have a 'find' command that chooses one of several owners. The precondition for usage of command (9) is the existence of a currently active occurrence of record-type-1. Notice that legitimate usage of this command requires that record-type-1 is the member record type of coset-1.

An example utilizing commands (8) and (9) appears in Fig. 8.6. Here the activated path consists of occurrences for the order 118 and the customer Steve Moore. Note that the latter occurrence is the current owner for the coset MAKES in Fig. 8.6d. We are therefore poised to use commands (2), (3), or (4) to rummage through the payments that have been made by the customer that placed order 118. Thus we have a way of activating the payment occurrences that are weakly related to the occurrence of a given order.

The final activation command of the stylized DML activates, as the current member of coset-1, the record occurrence that is the current owner of coset-2. An additional effect of this command is the activation of a current owner occurrence for coset-1; the occurrence thus activated is the record occurrence that owns (via coset-1) the current member of

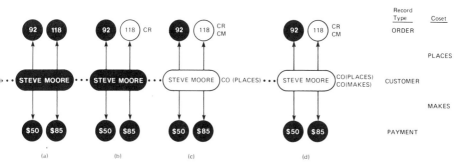

(a) FIND-RECORD('ORDER', 'ORDER-NUMBER', '118', FLAG) → (b)
(b) → ACTIVATE-MEMBER-BASED-ON-RECORD('PLACES', 'ORDER', FLAG) → (c)
(c) → ACTIVATE-OWNER-BASED-ON-OWNER('MAKES', 'PLACES', FLAG) → (d)

Fig. 8.6.

coset-1. The precondition for command (10) is the existence of a currently active owner for coset-2. It should be clear that this command can be used only if the owner record type for coset-2 is also the member record type for coset-1. Suppose that it is desired to activate the occurrence of a customer who has ordered a given inventory item (say, ITM-24). Figure 8.7 shows how command (10) can be used in accomplishing this.

Observe that commands (5), (7), (8), and (10) are the key mechanisms for activating paths through the various indirect relationships discussed in Chapter 7. Command 5 is used in activating a path through the operationalization of a transitive 1–N relationship, where the path activation begins with a subject instance (i.e., an owner occurrence, operationally speaking). Path activation in the opposite direction through an operationalized 1–N transitive relationship employs command (10). An example of the former is the activation of a path from a customer to an order line (Fig. 8.4). An example of the latter is the activation of a path from an order line to a customer (Fig. 8.7). Commands (5) and (10) are similarly employed in activating paths through indirect circular 1–N relationships that have been operationalized. This is readily apparent when we view such a relationship as a 1–N transitive relationship that has wrapped around on itself.

In order to generate a path through the operationalization of a weak indirect relationship, command (8) is used (recall Fig. 8.6 in this connection). Path activation through operationalized *indirect* M–N relationships depends on command (7), as shown in Fig. 8.5. A discussion of path generation through *direct* M–N relationships is deferred until Section 8.11.3. Commands (7) and (8) are also used in path activation in the case of an indirect reflexive relationship. This is easily seen when we view such a

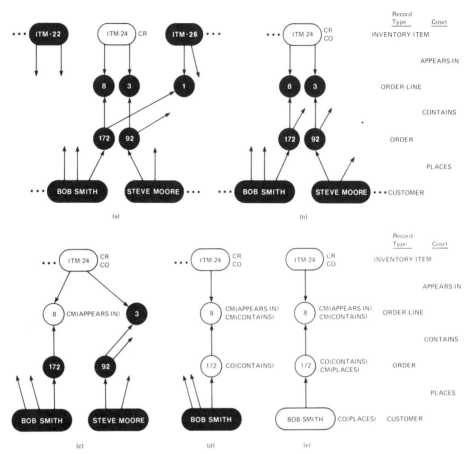

FIND-RECORD('INVENTORY-ITEM', 'ITEM-NUMBER', 'ITM-24', FLAG) → (a)
  (a) → ACTIVATE-OWNER-BASED-ON RECORD('APPEARS-IN',
  'INVENTORY-ITEM', FLAG) → (b)
    (b) → FIND-FIRST-MEMBER('APPEARS-IN', FLAG) → (c)
    (c) → ACTIVATE-MEMBER-BASED-ON-MEMBER('CONTAINS', 'APPEARS-IN',
    FLAG) → (d)
    (d) → ACTIVATE-MEMBER-BASED-ON-OWNER('PLACES', 'CONTAINS',
    FLAG) → (e)

Fig. 8.7.

reflexive relationship as having a weak aspect (record type that owns two cosets) and a $M-N$ aspect (record type that is the member for two cosets).

The last three commands in Table 8.1 are for the actual extraction of data from an activated record occurrence. The particular extraction command that can be used for a given occurrence depends on the nature of that occurrence's activation. If the occurrence from which we desire to extract data is the current occurrence of its record type, then command (11) is used. The record type and the data item type of interest are specified by the user. The value of that data item type for the current record occurrence of record-type-1 is an output of the command's execution, being held in whatever host language variable appears as the command's third argument. A precondition for the execution of (11) is, of course, the existence of a currently active occurrence of record-type-1.

Command (12) is used if the occurrence that we want to extract data from is the current member of a coset. Thus a precondition is that the user-specified coset-1 must have a currently active member. Command (13) is similar except that the value of data-item-type in the current owner of coset-1 is extracted. It is possible that a record occurrence is only partially instantiated (i.e., values for one or more of its data item types have not yet been assigned). For any of the extraction commands, an attempt to extract a value that does not exist in the active record occurrence results in the failure flag being turned on.

As mentioned previously, DML is used within a host language. For a given schema, such as the one in Fig. 7.1, the range of possible user-directed retrievals in a DML-extended host language is quite wide. Thus far we have seen how the DML commands can be used for path construction and data extraction, independent of a host language. Notice that the DML by itself has no convenient facilities for iteration or branching. These are furnished by its host language (e.g., FORTRAN, COBOL, PL/1).

Figure 8.8 contains an example of a retrieval procedure that demonstrates the interaction of a DML with its host language. In this example a report is produced that contains complete information about every order that has been placed by the customer whose name is read into the host language variable: c-name. The logical structure of Fig. 7.1 is assumed. Non-DML statements in the host language appear in lower-case letters; DML commands and literals are capitalized. Host languages differ, of course, in syntax. The host syntax used in Fig. 8.8 is stylized to represent clearly iteration, branching, and I/O facilities. Although specific formats are ignored in this example (since they are well known), they are an indispensable element of the host languages I/O facilities. Figure 8.9 shows the report that is produced if Bob Smith is the value read into the variable c-name.

In this section we have discussed, at an operational level, a category J language interface (LS) for a DSS whose knowledge system is a data base. The stylized DML presented here is rooted in the same conceptual operations as the data manipulation languages of various commercial data base

host language variables: c-name, flag, value-1, value-2, value-3
flag off

comment: input a customer's name and write it out as the first line of the report

read c-name
write 'CUSTOMER NAME:', c-name

comment: activate the appropriate occurrence of CUSTOMER

FIND-RECORD ('CUSTOMER', 'CUSTOMER-NAME', c-name, flag)
if flag on then go to output-1
ACTIVATE-OWNER-BASED-ON-RECORD ('PLACES', 'CUS-TOMER', flag)
if flag on then go to error

comment: find the first order for the current customer

FIND-FIRST-MEMBER ('PLACES', flag)
if flag on then go to output-2

comment: extract and write values from the current member of PLACES; as-sume that each occurrence of ORDER is fully instantiated, so that there is no need to check the flag following extraction.

loop-1:   EXTRACT-VALUE-OF-MEMBER ('PLACES', 'ORDER-NUMBER', value-1, flag)
EXTRACT-VALUE-OF-MEMBER ('PLACES', 'DOWNPAY-MENT', value-2, flag)
EXTRACT-VALUE-OF-MEMBER ('PLACES', 'DATE-OF-ORDER', value-3, flag)
write 'ORDER NO.', 'DOWNPAYMENT', 'DATE'
write value-1, value-2, value-3

comment: activate this order as the current owner of CONTAINS and find the first order line for this order

ACTIVATE-OWNER-BASED-ON-MEMBER ('CONTAINS', 'PLACES', flag)
if flag on then go to error
FIND-FIRST-MEMBER ('CONTAINS', flag)
if flag on then to to error
write 'ITEM NO.', 'QUANTITY', 'UNIT PRICE'

comment: extract values from the order line just found, activate the inventory item that owns this order line and extract its inventory number

loop-2:   EXTRACT-VALUE-OF-MEMBER ('CONTAINS', 'QUANTITY-ORDERED', value-2, flag)
EXTRACT-VALUE-OF-MEMBER ('CONTAINS', 'UNIT-PRICE', value-3, flag)
ACTIVATE-MEMBER-BASED-ON-MEMBER ('APPEARS-IN', 'CONTAINS', flag)
if flag on then go to error
EXTRACT-VALUE-OF-OWNER ('APPEARS-IN', 'ITEM-NUMBER', value-1, flag)

comment: the order line information is written beneath the previously written headings: ITEM NO., QUANTITY, UNIT PRICE

                            write value-1, value-2, value-3

comment: activate the next order line for the current order; if this activation fails (i.e., ther is no 'next' order line) then proceed to activate the next order for the current customer, otherwise go to loop-2 to extract information about this 'next' order line.

                            FIND-NEXT-MEMBER ('CONTAINS', flat)
                            if flag off then go to loop-2
                            FIND-NEXT-MEMBER ('PLACES', flag)
                            if flag off then go to loop-1
                            stop

output-1:   write 'THERE IS NO CUSTOMER BY THE NAME OF', c-name
                            stop
output-2:   write 'NO ORDERS FOR THIS CUSTOMER EXIST IN THE DATA BASE'
error: stop

Fig. 8.8. Using DML within a host language.

management systems. In directing the retrieval of data, a DML user has explicitly specified the steps in a retrieval procedure (i.e., the user has written a program to perform retrieval). Writing the DML program is a problem-solving task. Later discussions will indicate that this problem-solving task can be automated as a part of a PPS.

CUSTOMER NAME: BOB SMITH

ORDER NO.	DOWNPAYMENT	DATE
107	50	110178

ITEM NO.	QUANTITY	UNIT PRICE
ITM-20	6	25
ITM-22	2	200

ORDER NO.	DOWNPAYMENT	DATE
148	500	110978

ITEM NO.	QUANTITY	UNIT PRICE
ITM-22	3	210

ORDER NO.	DOWNPAYMENT	DATE
172	900	111178

ITEM NO.	QUANTITY	UNIT PRICE
ITM-24	8	100
ITM-26	1	300

Fig. 8.9. Report generated from code of Fig. 8.8.

Although writing DML programs is by no means an overly difficult task, it does require a certain degree of programming skill that is developed through study and practical experience. It can be time-consuming (although this tends to diminish as skill increases) and it can become an onerous or even boring occupation (this tends to increase as skill increases). Certainly, a high-level decision maker should not be expected to be a skilled DML programmer in order to obtain a report; some staff personnel may have such skills. Regardless of the level of skill, the time and boredom factors provide a motivation for finding methods to reduce the amount of programming effort required to effect a retrieval.

One possibility for reducing programming effort is find a DML syntax that is easier to use. For instance, a DML with a moderate number of simple commands is probably easier to learn and use than a DML having a comparatively small number of relatively complicated commands. A second, and perhaps more substantive, approach to reducing the DML programming effort is to make additional, but more powerful, DML commands available. A more powerful DML command than those already presented is one that could accomplish a task that would otherwise require the use of several of the earlier, less powerful commands. We shall refer to these more powerful commands as macro commands. Macro commands have the same generality as less powerful DML commands; the usage is not restricted to a single-application world. The macro commands have the effect of making the DML less procedural.

One useful group of macro commands is related to path creation through the various kinds of indirect relationships that can be operationalized in a schema. Consider the logical structure in Fig. 8.10a, expressive of an indirect 1–N transitive association from X to Z. It should be clear that a sequence of DML commands can be devised that, beginning with an active owner of S, will result in the activation of some member of T that is *indirectly* related with the active owner of S. Depending on the sequence, the activated member of T may be the first member occurrence of T that is indirectly related to the active owner of S, it may be a next member occurrence, or a member occurrence having a specified data value for one of its data item types.

Regardless of the application world, the logic for activating the first member occurrence of T, indirectly owned by the current owner of S, is unchanged. Which occurrence of Z is the first member of T indirectly owned by the active owner of S depends on the ordering conventions of both S and T. Notice also that this activation sequence activates an occurrence of Y as the current member of S and the current owner of T. Rather than repeatedly writing out the same sequence of commands (differing only in their arguments) for various application worlds, a macro command

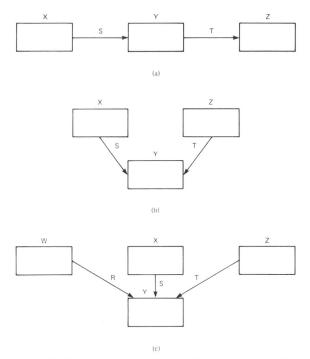

Fig. 8.10.   Structures for use with macro commands.

could be used. This macro command to find the first indirect member reduces programming effort.

Similar macro commands that find the next indirect member and find a particular indirect member containing a specified data value are quite conceivable. These latter two would have the expected, albeit unspecified, effect of activating the proper occurrence of Y as the active member of S and the current owner of T. Macro commands of this sort are not encountered in commercial DBM systems, despite the facts of their easy implementability and their wide applicability.

Consider Fig. 8.10b. It is often desirable to activate, as the current owner of T, some occurrence of Z that has an indirect $M\text{-}N$ relationship with the current owner of S. As was the case with the foregoing macro commands, we may want to activate the first (subject to the ordering of S, but not the ordering of T!) indirectly related occurrence of Z, a next indirectly related occurrence of Z, or an indirectly related occurrence of Z that contains a specified data value. This implies at least three additional macro commands that could reduce programming effort and that are easily implementable. These too are absent from prominent commercial DBM systems.

Macro DML commands for a structure such as the one of Fig. 8.10c could go a step beyond those for Fig. 8.10b. One such command would activate the first (subject to the ordering of S) occurrence of W that is indirectly related to the current owner of S, as well as the first occurrence of Z that is indirectly related to the current owner of S. The proper occurrence of Y would automatically be activated as the current member of R, of S, and of T. Commands for activating next occurrences or other particular occurrences of both W and Z would be similar. A variation of these commands would allow the extraction of data values from a pair of occurrences of W and Z that are indirectly related to a given occurrence of X. Other macro commands for the other kinds of indirect relationships may also prove to be fruitful topics for investigation.

A different variety of macro command that could reduce programming effort would replace certain commonly encountered loops that iteratively activate and extract. A very common task (recall Fig. 8.8), for example, involves activating the first member of a coset for the coset's current owner and extracting a data value from the active member; then the next member is activated and its value for the same data item type is extracted, and so on, until all members of the current owner have been examined. Following each extraction the extracted value is either written or placed in an array for later processing. The DML commands utilized for this task and their sequence are unchanged from one application to another. The task is therefore a prime candidate for a macro command that, when executed, would result in a host language array filled with data values extracted from the record occurrences owned by some current owner occurrence. A variation of this macro command would allow the user to indicate parametrically the conditions (e.g., a range of values) that a data value must satisfy in order to be retrieved into the array.

Aside from macro DML commands and syntax simplifications, another significant approach to reducing DML programming effort is to create a LS in which the need for programs in directing retrieval has been eliminated. These are language systems of categories K and L; they are examined in Sections 8.12 and 8.13.

8.11.3   *Data Base Loading: The Inverse of Retrieval*

Although we shall not deal with it as extensively as retrieval, it is appropriate to pause for a consideration of the conceptual operations employed in putting data into a data base. Stylized DML commands for loading data must be introduced. These DML commands are used to write the programs that create and maintain (i.e., update) a data base KS. In overseeing the writing and usage of these programs, systems analysts must take data integrity and data security considerations into account [2].

The fundamental loading task is one of building new strands in the knowledge mesh by creating a new instance of some aggregate concept and establishing the proper associative connections between it and other aggregate instances already in the mesh. Clearly, the establishment of these conceptual connections depends on some additional information that indicates which of the preexisting instantiations should be associated with the newly created instance.

The loading task can be operationalized by introducing two additional stylized DML commands:

(14)   CREATE-AND-STORE (record-type-1, value-array, flag)
(15)   ESTABLISH-MEMBERSHIP (record-type-1, coset-1, flag)

The former creates an occurrence of record-type-1 and stores values from the host language variable value-array into that occurrence. This newly created occurrence becomes the current record occurrence of record-type-1. The CREATE-AND-STORE command has no preconditions. The second new DML command makes the current occurrence of record-type-1 a member of the coset occurrence of the currently active owner of coset-1, thereby establishing its membership in coset-1. The newly established member could automatically be made the current member of coset-1. Command (15) assumes that the stated record-type-1 is the member of coset-1 in the schema. Preconditions for application of the ESTABLISH-MEMBERSHIP command are the existence of a currently active occurrence of record-type-1 and a current owner of coset-1.

Returning to the customer-order world, suppose that Bob Smith has made a payment of $100 on 050179. A new occurrence of PAYMENT should be created. This is accomplished as shown in Fig. 8.11. The payment should be reflected by a $100 reduction in the value of CUSTOMER-ACCOUNT in the Bob Smith record occurrence. Another group of DML commands is needed to allow us to make alterations in stored data values. These may be thought of as the inverses of the EXTRACTION commands in Table 8.1:

(16)   STORE-VALUE-IN-RECORD (record-type-1, data-item-type, value, flag)
(17)   STORE-VALUE-IN-MEMBER (coset-1, data-item-type, value, flag)
(18)   STORE-VALUE-IN-OWNER (coset-1, data-item-type, value, flag)

Command (16) stores the indicated value as the data value for data-item-type in the currently active occurrence of record-type-1. Commands (17) and (18) do the same for the currently active owner of coset-1 and currently active member of coset-1, respectively. Continuing the example

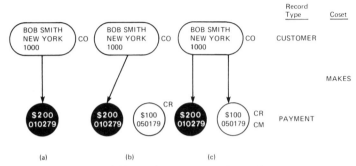

host language variables: value-array(2), value-1, flag

comment: assume a) is our starting point, so the current owner of MAKES has already been activated

comment: read $100 and 050179 into value-array(1) and value-array(2) respectively

     read value-array

comment: the following command gives b)

     CREATE-AND-STORE ('PAYMENT', value-array, flag)

comment: the following command gives c)

     ESTABLISH-MEMBERSHIP ('PAYMENT', 'MAKES', flag)

Fig. 8.11.   Data loading.

in Fig. 8.11, the customer account of Bob Smith is updated by the following program fragment:

     EXTRACT-VALUE-OF-OWNER ('MAKES', 'CUSTOMER-ACCOUNT', value-1, flag)
     value-1 = value-1 minus value-array(1)
     STORE-VALUE-IN-OWNER ('MAKES', 'CUSTOMER-ACCOUNT', value-1, flag)

Other commands that are sometimes useful for updating are those that can be viewed as doing the opposite of commands (14) and (15). The opposite of creating a record occurrence is deleting a record occurrence. Deletion could be accomplished by deleting the current occurrence of a record type or the occurrence that is the current member of a coset or the occurrence that is the current owner of a coset. The opposite of establishing membership is the removal of the current member of an indicated coset. That is, the record occurrence that is the current member is no longer an element in any occurrence of the indicated coset. This removal of membership does not, however, imply a deletion of the record occurrence.

8.11.4   DML for a Data Base Having Direct M–N Associations

The DML commands used to treat a data base, derived from conceptually direct $M-N$ associations, depend on how such associations have been operationalized. If a direct $M-N$ association is operationalized by the use of an intervening null record type, then the DML commands introduced in the preceding two sections are sufficient. Macro DML commands for dealing with the logical structures of Figs. 8.10b and 8.10c are particularly valuable if this operationalization is used.

However, if we use an operationalization of direct $M-N$ associations that more nearly mirrors the concept of a direct $M-N$ association, then additional DML commands are needed to deal with the new operational construct(s). For example, one approach [7] to operationalizing a direct $M-N$ association between record types X and Z makes no use of cosets; instead a named mm set is declared between X and Z. In the MDBS schema definition, either X or Z is arbitrarily declared to be the mm set's 'owner' and the other record type is declared to be its 'member.' The interesting implication of this 'owner-member' terminology for mm sets, as well as for cosets, is that all of the DML commands introduced previously can use mm sets interchangeably with cosets as arguments (e.g., either a coset or an mm set can be used as the first argument of FIND-MEMBER). However, the 'owner-member' terminology does not reflect the conceptual parity between X and Y.

Even though the previously introduced DML commands can still be used in systems with mm sets, they are insufficient. Additional DML commands are needed to process the 'owners' of an mm set. Since a 'member' occurrence in an mm set can have numerous owners, commands such as FIND-FIRST-OWNER, FIND-NEXT-OWNER, FIND-OWNER are needed (see the appendix to this chapter).

DML commands for retrieval from a data base derived from conceptually direct $L-M-N$ (or . . . $-L-M-N-$ . . .) associations, depend on the method of operationalization. If an intervening null record type is used (Fig. 7.5c), the previously introduced DML suffices. Suppose, however, that we have a new operational construct enabling us to represent concisely a direct $L-M-N$ association by simply giving it a name and stating the record types that participate in it. This construct will be referred to as a plex and will be pictured as shown in Fig. 8.12. The plex occurrence structure depicted in Fig. 8.12b is derived from the same world knowledge as the occurrence structure of Fig. 7.5d.

Entry into a plex occurrence structure requires an activation of one of the record occurrences participating in it. The occurrence thus activated

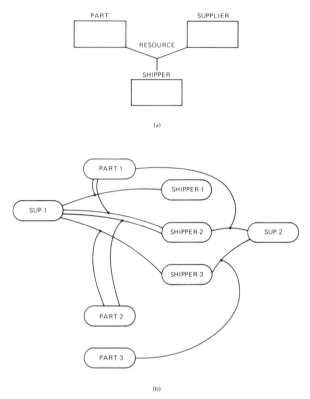

Fig. 8.12.   Plex structuring. (a) Logical structure of the RESOURCE plex. (b) Corresponding occurrence structure for the RESOURCE plex.

will be referred to as the current entry occurrence. As might be expected, stylized DML commands for accomplishing this activation are

ACTIVATE-ENTRY-BASED-ON-RECORD (plex-1, record-type-1, flag)
ACTIVATE-ENTRY-BASED-ON-OWNER (plex-1, coset-1, flag)
ACTIVATE-ENTRY-BASED-ON-MEMBER (plex-1, coset-1, flag)
ACTIVATE-ENTRY-BASED-ON-ENTRY (plex-1, plex-2, flag)

Referring to Fig. 8.1b, suppose that the PART-2 occurrence has been activated as the current entry occurrence of the RESOURCE plex. Notice that it is directly associated with two pairs of occurrences: (SUP-1, SHIPPER-2) and (SUP-1, SHIPPER-3). Each such pair is a complement of PART-2 in the RESOURCE plex. In fact, each record occurrence in the plex has a set of associated complements (e.g., PART-1 has three complements, SHIPPER-3 has two complements, etc.).

Having activated an entry occurrence, a retrieval process could proceed to find (and activate) the complements of the current entry occurrence. Conceivable DML commands for the plex include FIND-FIRST-COMPLEMENT, FIND-NEXT-COMPLEMENT, and FIND-COMPLEMENT. The latter would find a complement having some specified data value(s). Execution of one of the FIND commands results in activating the found record occurrences as the current complement. The existence of a current complement suggests further DML command such as ACTIVATE-RECORD-BASED-ON-COMPLEMENT, ACTIVATE-OWNER-BASED-ON-COMPLEMENT,   ACTIVATE-MEMBER-BASED-ON-COMPLEMENT,   ACTIVATE-ENTRY-BASED-ON-COMPLEMENT. The obvious extraction commands for use with a plex are EXTRACT-VALUE-FROM-ENTRY and EXTRACT-VALUE(S)-FROM-COMPLEMENT.

8.11.5   Retrieval from a Collection of Logical Files

Remember that a data base composed of a collection of files has as its schema disjoint record types. Conceptually, there are no explicitly recognized 1–N or M–N associations. The possibilities of direct and indirect relationships among aggregate concepts are inherent in the repetition of indivisible concepts as elements of the various aggregate concepts. Thus there is no knowledge mesh as in the case of explicit associations. Instead the KS is conceived as a set of aggregate instantiations partitioned into mutually exclusive and collectively exhaustive subsets. There is one subset (i.e., file) for each aggregate concept having instantiations.

Conceptually, retrieval from a collection of files involves the generation of a new file (and possibly intermediate files) that is the report desired by a user. This generated file is new in the sense that (1) it consists of some subset of the existing instances of an aggregate concept or (2) it consists of instances of a new aggregate concept that did not previously exist in the conceptual world view captured in the KS. The newly generated file (and any intermediate files) is usually only temporarily a part of the KS, disappearing when its contents are reported to a user.

Whereas retrieval in the case of a knowledge mesh involved the activation of passive paths, retrieval in the case of a partitioned knowledge set involves pattern matching. Specifically, there are four basic kinds of operations each of which results in a temporary file that did not previously exist: extraction of desired aggregate instantiations from a file; formation of the union of two files, each of which consists of instantiations of the same aggregate concept; extraction of all instances of some specified indivisible concept (or group of indivisible concepts) from a file; and matching of the aggregate instantiations of one file with those of another file, on the basis of identical instances of their common indivisible concept(s).

Recall that the *concept* of a file (i.e., a partition of the knowledge set) is *operationally referred to* as a table or as a relation or simply as a file. The foregoing retrieval operations are operationalized in our stylized DML as

(1′) EXTRACT-OCCURRENCES (record-type-1 or temp-file-1, data-item-type, data-value-range, temp-file-2, flag),

(2′) UNION (record-type-1 or temp-file-1, temp-file-2, temp-file-3, flag),

(3′) SPLIT (record-type-1 or temp-file-1, data-item-type(s), temp-file-2, flag),

(4′) MATCH-AND-CONCATENATE (record-type-1 or temp-file-1, record-type-2 or temp-file-2, data-item-types, temp-file-3, flag).

The use of record-type as an argument indicates a file that is not transitory in the data base; temp-file is used as an argument to name a temporary file.

The operations executed by commands (1′)–(4′) were briefly and informally introduced in Section 6.24. Horizontal extraction is accomplished by EXTRACT-OCCURRENCES, i.e., temp-file-2 consists of every occurrence of the record-type-1 file (or temp-file-1) whose occurrence of data-item-type falls in the indicated data value range. In Fig. 6.7a the resultant table (call it temp-file-a) is generated by EXTRACT-OCCURRENCES ('CUSTOMER', 'CUSTOMER-ACCOUNT', '>750', temp-file-a, flag).

The UNION command is used to form the set-theoretical union of two files. Usage of the command is restricted to aggregates with the same structure, i.e., the same data item names appear in each. The purpose of UNION is to provide an inverse operation to EXTRACT-OCCURRENCES. Operationally, redundant occurrences are omitted from the resultant temp-file-3.

The SPLIT command selects a subset of data item names, the occurrences of which are copied into the new file (temp-file-2). This new file then has a structure consistent with those data item names selected. This is the vertical extraction process described in Section 6.24. The table in Fig. 6.7b can be produced by SPLIT ('CUSTOMER', 'CUSTOMER-NAME', 'CUSTOMER-ADDRESS', temp-file-b, flag), where temp-file-b is the name given to the new table.

Before considering the matching command, let us convert the schema of Fig. 7.1b into a schema with no explicit associations. In general (and in the absence of reflexive or circular relationships) such a conversion is accomplished as follows:

1.   For each record type that owns a coset but is the member of no cosets, identify its key. Recall that a record type's key is a data item type (or group of data item types) that always takes on a different value for every occurrence of the record type.

2.   If no such record type exists, then stop. Otherwise, do the following for each record type X treated in step 1:

   (a)   Insert the key of X into each record type that is the member of a coset owned by X.

   (b)   Destroy all cosets having X as the owner.

3.   Go to step 1.

The conversion for the schema of Fig. 7.1b is traced in Fig. 8.13.

Caution must be exercised in any attempt to reverse this conversion procedure. We cannot proceed from a schema with no explicit associations to a schema with explicit associations without additional information. For example, ORDER and ORDER-LINE in Fig. 8.13c have a common data item type (ORDER-NUMBER), thereby leading us to suspect that they are directly related. However, it is impossible to ascertain the nature of this relationship from the schema of Fig. 8.13c alone. Before we can revert to a schema having an explicit, direct association between ORDER and ORDER-LINE, we must have additional information as to whether an order can be related to many order lines, or whether an order line can be related to many orders, or both. This must be answered at a conceptual level; it cannot always be concluded from an examination of the occurrences of a disjoint logical structure (even if they exist).

Returning to the stylized DML consider the command MATCH-AND-CONCATENATE ('ORDER', 'ORDER-LINE', 'ORDER-NUMBER', temp-file-e, flag) as applied to the schema of Fig. 8.13c. Each time an ORDER-LINE occurrence is found that has a value for ORDER-NUMBER matching the ORDER-NUMBER value for an occurrence of ORDER, the two record occurrences are concatenated (dropping the duplicate order number) to form an occurrence in temp-file-e. The collection of all such concatenations constitutes temp-file-e.

Commands (1')–(4') can be used in various sequences with varying arguments in order to direct retrieval from a disjoint schema. For example, a report similar to that of Fig. 8.9 results from the retrieval procedure specified in Fig. 8.14a. The procedure assumes the schema of Fig. 8.13c. The report itself (contents of temp-file-j) is shown in Fig. 8.14b. The fundamental difference between commands (1)–(13) and (1')–(4'), aside from the different kinds of schemata they are used for, is that the former deal with individual occurrences one at a time. In contrast, commands

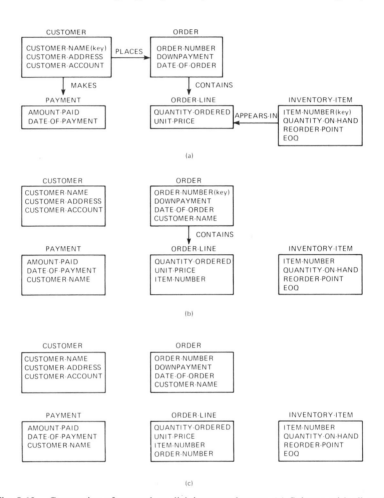

Fig. 8.13. Conversion of network to disjoint record types. (a) Schema with all explicit associations. (b) Schema after first iteration of conversion procedure. (c) Schema after second (final) iteration of conversion procedure.

(1′)–(4′) govern operations on entire groups of record occurrences. The latter are therefore suggestive of macro commands that could reduce programming effort in the case of structures with explicit associations.

EXTRACT-OCCURRENCES, as an operational command, is just as applicable to schemata like that of Fig. 8.13a as it is to disjoint structures. EXTRACT-OCCURRENCES (record-type-1, data item-type, value-range, temp-file, flag) can concisely replace the following procedure, host language variables: flag, cust-name, temp-file-f, tem-file-g, temp-file-h, temp-file-i, temp-file-j

read cust-name

flag off

EXTRACT-OCCURRENCES   ('CUSTOMER',   'CUSTOMER-NAME', cust-name, temp-file-f, flag)

if flag on, then go to message-1

SPLIT (temp-file-f, 'CUSTOMER-NAME', temp-file-g, flag)

if flag on, then go to error

write 'CUSTOMER-NAME:', temp-file-g

MATCH-AND-CONCATENATE ('ORDER', temp-file-g, 'CUSTOMER-NAME', temp-file-h, flag)

if flag on, then go to message-2

MATCH-AND-CONCATENATE ('ORDER-LINE', temp-file-h, 'ORDER-NUMBER', temp-file-i, flag)

if flag on, then go to error

SPLIT (temp-file-i, 'ORDER-NUMBER' 'DOWNPAYMENT' 'DATE-OF-ORDER' 'QUANTITY-ORDERED' 'UNIT-PRICE' 'ITEM NUMBER', temp-file-j, flag)

if flag on, then go to error

write 'ORDER NO.', 'DOWNPAYMENT', 'DATE', 'QTY OF ITEM', 'UNIT PRICE', 'ITEM NO.'

write temp-file-j

stop

message-1:   write 'THERE IS NO CUSTOMER WITH NAME', cust-name

stop

message-2:   write 'THIS CUSTOMER HAS PLACED NO ORDERS'

stop

error: write 'ERROR'

stop

(a)

CUSTOMER NAME: BOB SMITH

ORDER NO.	DOWNPAYMENT	DATE	QTY OF ITEM	UNIT PRICE	ITEM NO.
107	50	110178	6	25	ITM-20
107	50	110178	2	200	ITM-22
148	500	110978	3	210	ITM-22
172	900	111178	8	100	ITM-24
172	900	111178	1	300	ITM-26

(b)

Fig. 8.14.   DML example for disjoint structure.

which deals with the occurrences of record-type-1 one at a time:

```
          flag off
          FIND-FIRST-RECORD (record-type-1, flag)
          if flag on, then go to finish
loop-1:   EXTRACT-VALUE-OF-RECORD (record-type-1, data-item-type,
          value-1, flag)
          if flag on, then go to finish
          if value-1 is not in value-range, then go to loop-2
```

comment: extract all n values from the current record occurrence and write them onto the temp-file

```
          EXTRACT-VALUE-OF-RECORD (record-type-1, data-item-1, val-1,
          flag)
          .
          .
          .
          EXTRACT-VALUE-OF-RECORD (record-type-1, data-item-$n$, val-$n$,
          flag
          write val-1, . . . , val-$n$ onto temp-file
loop-2:   FIND-NEXT-RECORD (record-type-1, flag)
          if flag off, go to loop-1
finish:   continue
```

The same command can also replace a similar procedure that uses FIND-FIRST-MEMBER and FIND-NEXT-MEMBER in lieu of FIND-FIRST-RECORD and FIND-NEXT-RECORD. Note that the above procedure is a way of implementing (1′) as a macro command for nondisjoint schemata and may very well differ from the implementation used in the case of an operationally disjoint schema.

The use of SPLIT as a macro command for schemata with explicit associations is straightforward. The procedure that it would replace (and that could be used to implement it) is obvious and not given here. MATCH-AND-CONCATENATE could also serve as a macro command for schemata with cosets, replacing procedures involving some of the activate commands. Of course, no matching actually occurs, since all associations between two record types are explicit in terms of cosets. (Indeed the data-item-types argument would be replaced by a coset argument.) The net result would be a file consisting of concatenations of owner occurrences with each of their member occurrences. The availability of (1′)–(4′) as macro DML commands for use in retrieval from schemata with explicit associations implies that retrieval from such schemata entails procedures that are at least as simple or concise as retrievals from disjoint schemata.

It is interesting to note that MATCH-AND-CONCATENATE corresponds not only to certain commonly used DML retrieval procedures in the case of schemata with direct associations. This command is also descriptive of a DML loading procedure in the case of schemata with cosets. Suppose that all CUSTOMER occurrences have been loaded into a data base with the schema of Fig. 8.13a but that no other occurrences have been loaded. In order to load occurrences of PAYMENT and establish their proper associations with CUSTOMER occurrences, a short DML procedure using commands (14) and (15) can be written as follows:

        host language variables: value-array, cust-name

comment: read the first occurrence of the PAYMENT input file; the value of its CUSTOMER-NAME is inserted into cust-name

        read value-array, cust-name

comment: 'match'

        FIND-RECORD ('CUSTOMER', 'CUSTOMER-NAME', cust-name, flag)
        ACTIVATE-OWNER-BASED-ON-RECORD ('MAKES', 'CUSTOMER', flag)

comment: 'pseudo-concatenation'

        CREATE-AND-STORE ('PAYMENT', value-array, flag)
        ESTABLISH-MEMBERSHIP ('PAYMENT', 'MAKES', flag)

Observe that the appropriate input file for such a program is precisely a file having as its schema the record type PAYMENT in Fig. 8.13c. In order to accomplish its loading, the DML procedure 'matches' each occurrence of the PAYMENT input file with an occurrence of CUSTOMER; when the 'match' is found the program proceeds to 'concatenate' the matched occurrences by creating an occurrence of the record type PAYMENT (as it is defined in Fig. 8.13a) and establishing its membership in the coset MAKES. Of course, this establishment of membership is not a true concatenation in the sense in which we have heretofore used the term. It may be thought of as a pseudo-concatenation in much the same way that the 'matching,' performed when MATCH-AND-CONCATENATE was viewed as a macro retrieval procedure, was a pseudo-matching.

As a final point, remember that commands (1')–(4') are stylized. Many programming languages such as FORTRAN or COBOL are equipped for directing the retrieval from a disjoint data base, but the commands they provide are not at the relatively macro level of commands (1')–(4'). Nevertheless, the usage of a traditional programming language in retrieval of data from files entails the production of new files via the extraction of record occurrences, splitting, and matching with concatenation (or with elimination or updating or merging in the event of data loading and maintenance).

Recall that the "relational" data base view [4] requires a user to view conceptually and operationally the data base as a collection of disjoint files (i.e., "relations"). Relational data base systems would make use of the relational albegra [4,6] as a DML. Its commands allow a user to specify procedural retrievals in a vein similar to the foregoing stylized DML. The principal operations in the relational algebra are division (akin to EXTRACT-OCCURRENCES), projection (akin to SPLIT), union, and joining (akin to MATCH-CONCATENATE).

8.12   Category K Languages for Retrieval from a Data Base KS

Unlike a DML, languages of category K are not procedural. We have seen that within category J there are degrees of procedurality; with the addition of macro commands, a DML is positioned farther to the right in category J. Although a user's programming effort is reduced, some procedurality is still required. The procedurality is virtually eliminated in category K languages. This elimination occurs at the cost of language flexibility. That is, the user has considerably less flexibility in terms of the retrievals that can be directed. On the other hand, the language for directing retrieval is quite simple compared to a DML; it consists of invoking the execution of some already programmed procedure.

Since they are nonprocedural, category K languages not only are easier to use but can be described much more briefly than DML (hence the brevity of this section). The commands of a category K language are application specific. Furthermore, the DML procedure used in executing a command is dependent on the schema used in the KS. The DML procedure itself constitutes part of the PPS information collection ability. If the schema is altered then the DML procedure for a particular command may need to be revised correspondingly, in order to produce the report required by that command. Such a revision to the PPS is made by the builder of the DSS.

Consider, for example, a command to produce a report of the order information for a stated customer. The user of a category K language for the customer-order application would direct this retrieval by a command such as EXECUTE ORDER-REPORT ('BOB SMITH'). Notice that this nonprocedural command requires no knowledge on the part of the user as to the logical structure of information in the knowledge system. If the KS logical structure is the one shown in Fig. 8.13a, then the PPS would contain a DML procedure like that of Fig. 8.8. This procedure would be executed in response to the preceding command. However, if the KS logical structure is like that of Fig. 8.13c, then a DML procedure similar to the one in Fig. 8.14a would be embedded in the PPS.

Because the user of a category K language is not required to have a particular conceptual or operational view of how knowledge is represented in the KS, the operational commands included in the language have conceptual counterparts that are unrelated to conceptual knowledge representation methods. The conceptual counterpart of EXECUTE ORDER-REPORT is one of a "black box" that accepts a customer's name and provides an order report for that customer. Other commands would be the operationalizations of other black boxes. For instance, the notion of a black box that furnishes a report of all items in inventory could be operationalized in a category K language as EXECUTE INVENTORY-REPORT.

Because of the application-specific nature of category K languages, a general and stylized syntax for these languages is not given. In a decision-making application where the kinds of reports needed are stable and not excessive in number, a DSS having a category K language is appropriate. It should be realized that the need for a new kind of report necessitates a new command, which in turn necessitates the incorporation of a new DML program into the PPS. With category J languages, the need for a new kind of report does not require a change in the LS (nor in the PPS).

8.13 Category L Languages for Retrieval from a Data Base KS

Languages of category L are nonprocedural, but they are more flexible than category K languages in terms of the retrievals that they permit a user to direct. Their flexibility derives from the fact that they are not application specific. This also means that it is possible to present a stylized, archetypal language in discussing category L languages at the operational level. The user of this language is, for the most part, unconcerned with the logical structure of the KS. Unlike category K languages, the *PPS for a category L language is invariant to schema alterations (and therefore to application areas)*.

Conceptually we might view the retrieval task as one of presenting to a single black box (regardless of the nature of the desired report) the description of an aggregate concept whose instantiations are to be generated by the black box. This aggregate concept may have no existence beyond the scope of a particular retrieval (i.e., it has no existence in the knowledge mesh or knowledge set schema). The method of generation could be via any one of the four approaches described in Section 3.13. The description of the aggregate concept is in terms of indivisible concepts that are known to exist (in the schema of a knowledge mesh or knowledge set). To allow for selective retrieval, the description may also include conditions that an instantiation of the aggregate concept must satisfy in order to appear in the report. These include conditions on the values of indivisible concepts and conditions on the nature of the association between two indivisible concepts.

As an example, suppose that a report is desired subject to the aggregate concept composed of a 'teacher name' and a 'student name'. Since a teacher could be associated with students in more than one way (e.g., teachers teach students, teachers advise students), our description of the preceding aggregate concept should be conditioned by one of the associations. One conditioning would give a report of the teachers and the students they teach, whereas the other would give a report of the teachers and the students they advise. In the case of category K this conditioning concept is inherent in the selection of one specialized black box (EXECUTE ADVISING-REPORT) versus another (EXECUTE TEACHING-REPORT) and in providing certain inputs to the specialized black box (e.g., 'Bob Smith' in the case of the EXECUTE ORDER-REPORT black box). For category J, conditioning is inherent in the activity of selecting one path versus another.

The stylized, archetypal language for category L consists of all statements of the following form: DISPLAY <find clause> <conditional clause>. In its simplest form the find clause is simply a list of the data item types that constitute a virtual record type. That is, the record type need not actually exist in the KS. It is, however, the schema of the report being produced. The conditional clause is a Boolean expression stating conditions that must be true for an occurrence of the virtual record type before it can be included in the report. Terms in this expression involve conditions on values of data item types or on the nature of association between occurrences of data item types in the virtual record type. It should be noted that the LS may be interactive (e.g., if there are several associations between two data item types but none is specified in the user's request, then the system may prompt the user for this additional information).

As an example of the usage of the above language, a report of order information for Bob Smith would be obtained by stating: DISPLAY ORDER-NUMBER, DOWNPAYMENT, DATE-OF-ORDER, ITEM-NUMBER, QUANTITY-ORDERED, AND UNIT-PRICE FOR CUSTOMER-NAME='BOB SMITH'. The beginning of a conditional

clause is denoted the words FOR, WHEN, or HAVING. The report produced by this command resembles that of Fig. 8.14b. In order to obtain a
list of all customers who have ordered ITM-26, the find and conditional
clauses are altered to give: DISPLAY CUSTOMER-NAME WHEN
ITEM-NUMBER='ITM-26'. Figure 8.15 shows retrieval statements with
various compound conditional clauses. The language does not limit a user
to equalities; terms in a Boolean expression may also involve the use of
inequalities, greater-than (or less-than) conditions, etc. Conditional terms
may be grouped by using parentheses. The kinds of Boolean expressions
appearing in these examples can be compounded into more complex conditional clauses.

Notice that, from a user's standpoint, none of these commands depends on an appreciation of data base schemata. Utilization of the language
does not depend on whether a user should happen to subscribe to a disjoint view (Fig. 8.13c), a view recognizing explicit associations (Fig.
8.13a), or some other view of knowledge organization. All that is required
aside from a working knowledge of the application world is a list of the
data item types and (see Example 7) a way for distinguishing among
multiple associations between two data item types. Possible multiple associations are defined as the KS schema is defined. This is straightforward
if we use cosets; a coset (or path of cosets) defines a distinct association
between two data item types. If the schema does not use cosets, a named
association can be defined in terms of the record types that establish a
direct or indirect relationship between two data item types.

Observe that the stylized language presented in this section provides a
much simpler (less time-consuming and less cumbersome) way for directing retrieval than a DML. Unlike the specialized languages of category K,
there is great flexibility in the reports that a user can obtain. This flexibility approaches that allowed by the DML. For any DML retrieval program
on any schema, there is a more or less equivalent problem statement(s) in
the category L language presented here.

A language permitting nearly the same retrieval flexibility as, and having a somewhat similar appearance to, the stylized language presented
here has been implemented in the GPLAN system [5] and has been studied in a variety of applications. Although its user need not have such a
view of knowledge representation, this language is implemented to operate on network schemata. Another useful language is MDBS.QRS [8],
which can respond to queries directed at network schemata that include
mm sets. The result of such queries is effectively a "relation" (i.e., a file)
that is generated from a network. The "relational calculus" of Codd [3],
plus certain of its derivative languages (e.g., SEQUEL [1]), is also nonprocedural and quite general, even though the relational calculus syntax is

by no means English-like. There are other nonprocedural retrieval languages that are not quite as flexible as the foregoing languages (e.g., working on tree, but not network, schemata). Other important characteristics of category L languages are their capacity for noise words (e.g., OF THE in Example 4 of Fig. 8.15), for synonyms (e.g., allowing abbreviations of data item type names), and for user control of the format of a report.

8.20 LANGUAGES FOR DIRECTING COMPUTATIONS IN THE CASE OF DATA BASE KS

We now turn our attention to the nine categories of Fig. 3.2. They are examined row-wise beginning at the bottom. Some of the languages mentioned (e.g., FORTRAN) are not used exclusively as user interfaces to decision support systems that have a data base KS. Treatment of the nine categories is relatively brief because the languages suitable for categories A–C are well known and those used for categories D–I are not particularly complex. Bear in mind that, although languages of categories D–I ultimately result in some retrieval, the retrieval method(s) employed is beneath a user's level of awareness. That is, the user of a language from the middle or top row draws no horizontal distinctions within a row.

8.21 Languages for Stating a Model Explicitly

Categories A–C use programming languages such as FORTRAN, PL/1, or COBOL as hosts for retrieval commands. We have already seen how these programming languages were used as DML hosts, but in that capacity their computational, calculating facilities were not used to affect the values appearing in a report. In categories A–C, their computational mechanisms are employed by a user to give a procedural statement of the model. The execution of the model results in the desired report. The calculations embodied in the model must utilize data and these data can be retrieved from a data base. Therefore the procedural specification of computations is appropriately interspersed with commands to perform needed retrievals. The difference between categories A and B and C is in terms of the language used to perform the retrievals, and not in terms of the computational aspects of a host language.

An example of a LS falling into category A is a FORTRAN host language that is both used to state computational models and extended by a DML as described in Sections 8.11.1–8.11.5. An example of a category B language system is FORTRAN, where it is used to specify calculations and where it makes calls on a library of subroutines (implemented with DML) in order to accomplish retrieval. If FORTRAN were extended by the addition of a DISPLAY command (possibly in a subroutine form) like the one discussed in Section 8.13, then we would have an example of a category C language system. Another way to obtain a category C LS, of perhaps more limited computational power, is to alter the stylized language of Section 8.13 to include arithmetic expressions as terms in the find clause and conditional clause [e.g., DISPLAY EMPLOYEE-NAME AND (EMPLOYEE-HOURS ∗ EMPLOYEE-RATE) FOR EMPLOYEE-RATE ÷ STARTING-RATE < 2.5] [8].

1. DISPLAY A FOR B = x AND C = y
   e.g.: DISPLAY ORDER-NUMBER FOR CUSTOMER-NAME = 'BOB SMITH' AND ITEM-NUMBER = 'ITM-20'
   —report of order numbers of all orders placed by Bob Smith that included ITM-20
2. DISPLAY A FOR B = x OR C = y
   e.g.: DISPLAY CUSTOMER-NAME FOR CUSTOMER-ACCOUNT > '750' OR DATE-OF-ORDER > '010179'
   —report of all customers having accounts of over 750 or having ordered since 010179, or both; note that the use of EOR in place of OR would function as an exclusive 'or'.
3. DISPLAY A HAVING ALL OF THE FOLLOWING B (x, y, . . .)
   e.g.: DISPLAY CUSTOMER-NAME HAVING ALL OF THE FOLLOWING ITEM-NUMBER ('ITM-22', 'ITM-26')
   —report of all customers that have ordered both ITM-22 and ITM-26
4. DISPLAY A HAVING ANY OF THE FOLLOWING B (x, y, . . .)
   e.g.: DISPLAY CUSTOMER-NAME HAVING ANY OF THE FOLLOWING ITEM-NUMBER ('ITM-22', 'ITM-26')
   —report of all customers that have ordered either ITM-22 or ITM-26, or both
5. DISPLAY A HAVING (ALL OF THE FOLLOWING B (x, y, . . .) FOR THE SAME C) AND . . .
   e.g.: DISPLAY CUSTOMER-NAME HAVING (ALL OF THE FOLLOWING ITEM-NUMBER ('ITM-22', ITM-26') FOR THE SAME ORDER-NUMBER)
   —report of all customers having ordered both ITM-22 and ITM-26 in the same order
6. DISPLAY A FOR B < C
   e.g.: DISPLAY ITEM-NUMBER AND EOQ FOR QUANTITY-ON-HAND ≤ REORDER POINT
   —report of all items (and their economic order quantities) whose quantity on hand is less than or equal to that item's reorder point
7. DISPLAY A AND B FOR REL
   e.g.: DISPLAY TEACHER-NAME AND STUDENT-NAME FOR ADVISING
   —report of teachers and the students they advise; replacement of ADVISING by the TEACHING association would give a different report consisting of teachers and the students they teach

Fig. 8.15. Sample queries.

8.22   Languages for Invoking Models

The programming burden for categories A–C is reduced if the programming language has available to it a library of computational modules that can be called as needed during a procedural specification of the overall model. Examples of such modules are square root computation, random number generation, matrix operations, etc. If this library idea is pushed to the extreme, then we find ourselves in the middle row of Fig. 3.2. Here the language systems permit a user to invoke any one of a number of prespecified (preprogrammed) models from a library of models. Implementationally, these models may be integrated by the use of common modules.

Unlike the bottom row, decision support systems of the middle row cannot always be categorized as being either D, E, or F by merely observing their language systems. The distinction lies in the type of retrieval language utilized in the preprogrammed models, and this is not often ostensible in a LS that invokes models. Belonging to category D are systems whose models utilize DML for retrieval. Models in a category E decision support system accomplish retrieval by invoking specialized report generators. Retrieval by the models incorporated into a category F system is effected by using a generalized, nonprocedural retrieval command such as DISPLAY.

An example of a category F system is one where the language system still uses the DISPLAY command but where the find and conditional clauses are permitted to contain the names of models available to the PPS. These models may be thought of as functions (which are underlined) in the following examples:

DISPLAY CUSTOMER-NAME FOR SUM (AMOUNT-PAID) > '1000'
DISPLAY CUSTOMER-NAME, AVERAGE (DOWNPAYMENT)
DISPLAY CUSTOMER-NAME, STANDARD-DEVIATION (AMOUNT-PAID)

In each case a simple function is invoked to operate on data that have been retrieved by the DISPLAY command. If arithmetic expressions are included with functions in the find or conditional clauses, then we have a system on the borderline between categories C and F; for instance, DISPLAY ITEM-NUMBER AND SUM (QUANTITY-ORDERED * UNIT-PRICE FOR SAME ITEM-NUMBER).

This elaboration of the DISPLAY command to allow the invocation of functions is very useful, providing those functions are simple in terms of their retrieval needs. Notice that a simple function such as AVERAGE requires the retrieval of only *one* file (e.g., all downpayments of a customer) at the *start* of each time that it executes. For the above example,

AVERAGE would be executed once for each customer. A model that requires complexly conditioned retrieval of various data at various points during its execution cannot be easily handled as the above functions. Data retrievals, for models having more complex retrieval needs, are directed from within the model rather than in the LS.

A stylized language that serves to illustrate the user interface for decision support systems of categories D–F (in the case of more complex models) can be obtained by slightly modifying the retrieval language of Section 8.13 as follows: <model name> <conditional clause>. Rather than DISPLAY, a command begins with the name of a model that exists in the DSS. Since the model chosen determines the types of data appearing in the report, a find clause is unnecessary (i.e., null). The conditional clause is used to condition the data that will be used by the invoked model as it executes. Some sample statements in this language include the following:

REGRESSION FOR W VERSUS X, Y, AND Z . . .
WATER-SIMULATION FOR RIVER-NAME = 'WABASH', DATE = '110180', . . .

The data item types and/or data values appearing in the conditional clause are used in the model's parameterized retrieval commands. This model–data base interface is examined more closely in Chapter 9.

8.23 Directing a Computation by Stating Its Results

A category A, B, or C decision support system enables a user to take a "do-it-yourself" approach to directing computations. This is an approach characterized by flexibility in determining what is to be accomplished and by effort that is possibly time-consuming and tiring. A category D, E, or F decision support system allows a user to select one of a number of prefabricated computational procedures. This approach is characterized by inflexibility in determining what can be accomplished, but also by the ease and rapidity with which calculations can be directed.

A category G, H, or I decision support system allows a user to adopt a "make-a-wish" approach to directing computations. This approach is characterized both by flexibility in determining what is to be accomplished and by an ease and rapidity of effort. The stylized archetypal language presented for category L works equally well as a LS for systems of these last three categories. It must be understood, however, that the report specified by this new use of the DISPLAY command is the result of the execution of some computational model. Once again the find clause gives the schema of the report and any information appearing in the report must be consistent with the conditions detailed in the conditional clause.

Even though categories G, H, and I can have the same stylized LS, they differ according to the manner in which models are interfaced with the data base. A DSS of category G has models, each of which contains its own DML retrieval procedures. For category H the models only invoke one or more of a set of preprogrammed, specialized, report generators. For category I systems, all models utilize a single nonprocedural, generalized report generator to accomplish all retrievals.

Finally, there is a vertical variation among systems within each of the last three categories. Near the bottom of any of the three categories are those systems whose KS and PPS give them few alternative ways for generating a desired report. That is, a user's specification of a desired report is tantamount to the selection (invocation) of a model. If the model must be formulated, then the DSS would lie closer to the top axis of Fig. 3.2 (farther from those systems in which a model is explicitly invoked). A DSS also lies closer to the top if its PPS and KS permit many alternative formulations that could fulfill a user's requirements. Such systems must have some mechanism for recognizing which alternative formulation should be used to solve the user's problem.

Observe that the statement of a desired report is essentially a statement of certain goal criteria. The DSS attempts to arrive at a knowledge state (i.e., report) satisfying the goal criteria by transforming an initial knowledge state (i.e., data base contents) via an appropriately formulated model (i.e., sequence of operators or modules). From a different perspective, the user's statement may be viewed as a problem that is not immediately solvable (i.e., for which no formulated executable model exists in the system). This problem is successively reduced into subproblems until a set of subproblems is found, such that each of its elements is directly solvable via either retrieval or the execution of some module (i.e., model building block) existing within the DSS.

8.30   APPENDIX: COMMANDS USED WITH MDBS

The DML commands enumerated here are among those used within MDBS. The MDBS DML has been selected for inclusion because the logical structuring features of MDBS are more extensive than those available in other major commercial DBM systems currently on the market. Thus the MDBS set of DML commands performs a wider range of tasks than that of other DBM systems. The following is not a complete list of the MDBS DML commands, but it is representative of the commands available.

Whenever a DML command is executed, a message flag is set to a numeric value from 0 to 225. A nonzero value of the message flag after execution of a DML command indicates that a special condition occurred during that execution. This may be an error condition (the command was used incorrectly) or it may indicate other conditions, such as the fact that the last member occurrence of a coset occurrence has already been found. A message flag is a host language variable; its value can be used to control subsequent processing in a DML program.

Data item type is abbreviated as dit, record type as rt, and coset (also mm set) as st. Lowercase arguments refer to a data base schema. Uppercase arguments are variables or data blocks in the host language. A message flag is denoted by MF.

List of Commands

Classification	Command name	Command arguments	Interpretation
Finding	FFM	st	Find the first member occurrence for the current owner of st. If there is no such member, then MDBS sets MF to have a value of 255.
	FNM	st	Find the next member occurrence for the current owner of st. Which occurrence is next depends on the ordering convention used for members of st. If there is no next member, MF becomes 255.
	FMSK	st, IVALUE	Find the member occurrence, for the current owner of st, having a sort key value that matches the contents of IVALUE. If no such occurrence exists, MF becomes 255.
	FFO	st	Find the first owner occurrence for the current member of st. If none exists, MF becomes 255.
	FNO	st	Find the next owner occurrence for the current member of st. Which occurrence is next depends on the ordering convention used for owners of st. If there is no next owner, MF becomes 255.
	FOSK	st, IVALUE	Find the owner occurrence, for the current member occurrence of st, having a sort key value that matches the contents of IVALUE. If no such occurrence exists, MF becomes 255.

List of Commands (continued)

Classification	Command name	Command arguments	Interpretation
		There are six additional find commands.	
Activation	SOM	st-1, st-2	Set the current owner of st-1 to be equal to the current member of st-2.
	SMM	st-1, st-2	Set the current member of st-1 to be equal to the current member of st-2.
	SOO	st-1, st-2	Set the current owner of st-1 to be equal to the current owner of st-2.
	SMO	st-1, st-2	Set the current member of st-1 to be equal to the current owner of st-2.
		There are ten additional activation commands.	
Extraction	GFM	dit, st, IDATA	Get the data value of the field dit from the current member of st, and put that value into IDATA.
	GFO	dit, st, IDATA	Get the data value of the field dit from the current owner of st, and put that value into IDATA.
		There are six additional extraction commands.	
Creation	CRS	rt, IDATA	Create an occurrence of the record type rt and store the contents of IDATA into that occurrence.
Establishing membership	AMS	rt, st	Add the current occurrence of record type rt as a member in the set (i.e., coset or mm-set) occurrence of st whose owner is the current owner of st.
Storing	SFM	dit, st, IDATA	Store the contents of IDATA into the dit field of the record occurrence that is the current member of st.
	SFO	dit, st, IDATA	Store the contents of IDATA into the dit field of the record occurrence that is the current owner of st.
		There are six additional storage commands.	
Deletion	DRM	st	Delete the record occurrence that is the current member of st.
		There are three additional deletion commands.	
Removing membership	RMS	st	Remove the current member of st from the occurrence of st in which it participates.

REFERENCES

1. D. D. Chamberlain and R. F. Boyce, SEQUEL: A Structured English Query Language, ACM-SIGFIDET Workshop (1974).

2. CODASYL Systems Committee, Data Base Task Group Report, Association for Computing Machinery (April 1971).
3. E. F. Codd, A Data Base Sublanguage Founded on the Relational Calculus Process, ACM-SIGFIDET Workshop (1971).
4. E. F. Codd, A relational model of data for large shared data bases, *Commun. ACM* **13**, No. 6 (1970).
5. W. D. Haseman and A. B. Whinston, "Introduction to Data Management." Irwin, Homewood, Illinois, 1977.
6. J. Martin, "Computer Data-Base Organization." Prentice-Hall, Englewood Cliffs, New Jersey, 1975.
7. MDBS, Micro Data Base Systems, Inc., Lafayette, Indiana.
8. MDBS.QRS, Micro Data Base Systems, Inc., Lafayette, Indiana.

Chapter 9

PROBLEM-PROCESSING SYSTEMS FOR DATA BASE KNOWLEDGE SYSTEMS

9.00 OVERVIEW

The problem-processing systems (PPS) addressed in this chapter depict methods that are presently employed to make use of knowledge that is organized in a data base fashion. Remember that a PPS is the software that bridges the gap between a language system (LS) and a knowledge system (KS), where we are presently concerned with data base knowledge systems and the language systems applicable to them. We shall examine the nature of this bridging software for each of the DSS categories, according to the PPS abilities depicted in Fig. 2.3. The discussion is primarily at the operational level, identifying and describing techniques that underlie the notions of information collecting, problem recognizing (or adapting), model formulating, and analyzing. It is beyond the scope of this treatise to present the actual lines of code that are used to implement the described techniques.

9.10 PROBLEM PROCESSING FOR RETRIEVAL—ONLY DSS

The next three sections consider problem-processing systems for the data base DSS of categories J, K, and L. Thus these PPS do not have

230

model formulation or analysis abilities in the sense in which we have been using these terms, and only for category L is there any appreciable adaptive or problem-recognizing ability on the part of the PPS. It is interesting to note that as the language systems become simpler (from a user's viewpoint), the corresponding problem-processing systems become more complex. More of the problem-solving effort is shifted from the user to the decision support system.

9.11   PPS for Category J

Since a user-written retrieval program, employing DML, constitutes the user's problem statement in category J systems, it is clear that the PPS includes the host language compiler and the software for executing each DML command. The compiler accepts the user's problem statement as input and proceeds to translate it into an internally comprehensible form (i.e., object code). Thus the compiler embodies the system's information collection ability with respect to the user. With respect to the data base, the information collection ability is realized through the DML software. This software is the code that actually performs the tasks stated in the user program's DML commands.

For a detailed discussion of compiler techniques refer to Donovan [6] and Knuth [7]. Briefly, compilation has two aspects: parsing and translation. As we have seen in Chapter 5, parsing involves the utilization of productions to determine whether a string belongs to a language (i.e., whether the user's problem statement is a valid expression in the language) and to recognize the structure of the string (i.e., its derivation). The derivation is used as a guideline for translating the string into an internally comprehensible form (e.g., machine language code in the case of a host language compiler such as FORTRAN).

The appearance of the software for a particular DML depends on the nature of the commands in the DML and on the manner in which the data base has been implemented. The language used in implementing DML software can be low level (e.g., a particular machine's assembler or machine languages) or comparatively high level (e.g., FORTRAN). The former approach makes a data base system highly machine dependent, although individual releases may be available for various machines. The latter approach allows a data base management system (DBMS) to be easily installed on any machine that has a compiler for the high-level language. However, the object code produced in this way for a given machine is probably not as efficient as the object code resulting from an equivalent system programmed in the machine's assembler language.

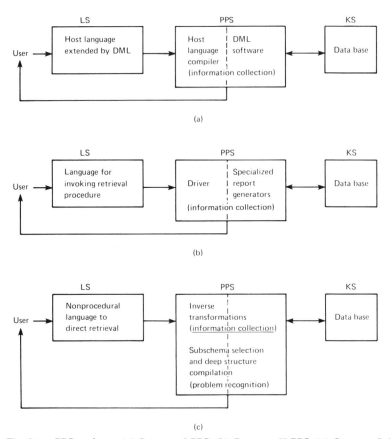

Fig. 9.1. PPS variants. (a) Category J PPS. (b) Category K PPS. (c) Category L PPS.

An overview of a category J PPS is provided in Fig. 9.1a. Notice that its only substantial ability is that of information collection. No model formulation is involved and therefore there is no analysis in the sense of interfacing collected information with a model during the model's execution. Furthermore, there is no problem recognition ability of a very high order. One could argue that the compiler recognizes a problem and adapts to it (by converting it to object code) in the course of collecting information from the user. But this is of a relatively low order, compared to the problem recognition that has been performed by the user (i.e., the decision maker).

In writing the DML program, the user has already recognized the retrieval problem and explicitly indicated how it is to be solved (i.e., how to adapt to the problem). In the course of collecting this information, the compiler translates the user's recognitions into an executable form. Upon execution the desired report is sent to the user.

The reader may find it useful to think of this act of execution as a low-order display of an implementation ability, predicated on a low-order display of a formulation (or design) ability. That is, the compiler in arriving at the object code has designed a plan for implementation that is subsequently executed by the operating system. Although they are somewhat similar, the activities of designing a plan for implementation and designing a model for analysis have different purposes and should not be confused (recall the earlier discussion of Fig. 4.4).

We say that the above design and implementation activities are of low order because they do not involve design and implementation with respect to the global decision problem faced by the man–machine decision-making system as a whole. They refer only to problems that are internal to the PPS itself, as it endeavors to demonstrate one or more of the seven decision-making activities in a global sense. As we progress through this chapter, the reader may find it helpful to identify lower-order abilities that manifest in the various problem processors. However, little more is said about low-order abilities in the following sections.

9.12 PPS for Category K

A category K problem processor (see Fig. 9.1b) consists of a group of report generators that are applicable to the particular data base schema of the KS. It may also include a driver program that, for a given user's statement, calls the appropriate report generator. In the absence of a driver, a desired report generator is directly invoked by a user's statement. Clearly, the major problem recognition ability resides with the user. The user, in recognizing which specialized report generator to invoke, has recognized what the retrieval problem is and how it is to be solved.

9.13 PPS for Category L

Unlike the previous two categories, the user of a category L system does not recognize a retrieval problem in any appreciable detail. The user merely states the criteria that must be satisfied by a displayed report. Thus the retrieval problem of obtaining a needed report has been only partially recognized, in that the user has not thought through how to adapt to (i.e., to satisfy, to solve) it. It is up to the PPS to complete the user's

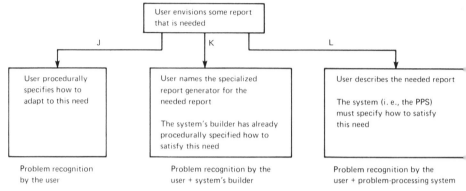

Fig. 9.2.   Different treatments of problem recognition.

line of thought. The ability to complete the problem specification down to the point where a procedure has been recognized constitutes the problem processor's problem recognition ability. (At a lower order, the procedure is typically translated into an equivalent procedure in a lower-level language that is directly executable.) Figure 9.2 summarizes the distinction between the three retrieval categories, in terms of where the high-order problem recognition is performed.

Universal techniques for operationalizing the information collection and problem recognition abilities in category L systems are not readily identifiable. In order to provide a flavor of how these abilities can be operationalized we shall examine the techniques used in one PPS of this category, namely, DSS-Q. DSS-Q is an experimental system (implemented in FORTRAN) that utilizes a network DBMS. The labeling within the PPS of Fig. 9.1c reflects these techniques. Bear in mind that other systems could use other techniques.

9.13.1   Information Collection

In DSS-Q, information collection from a user is accomplished by a preparser whose output is subjected to certain inverse transformations. The preparser decomposes a string (e.g., DISPLAY X AND Y FOR Z = a) into its constituent "tokens" (e.g., the preceding string has the following eight tokens: DISPLAY, X, AND, Y, FOR Z, =, a). Inverse transformations are applied to give a string that is used internally (within the PPS) as a basis for arriving at a fuller (i.e., procedural) recognition of the retrieval problem.

Before discussing the value of inverse transformations, it is necessary to describe briefly the major aspects of a transformational grammar (see

Chomsky [2] for details). A transformational grammar consists of a set of production rules (also called phrase structure rules) and a set of transformational rules. Recalling Section 5.35, the production rules can generate a number of strings. A string generated by the phrase structure rules of a transformational grammar is called an underlying (or deep structure) string and its phrase structure is determined by the rules used to generate it. Consider the abstract example in Fig. 9.3a; here a production system has generated the string 'd x for $y < z$' having the phrase structure as shown. Recall that upper-case letters are used for nonterminals. Now suppose that this is a deep structure string generated from the phrase structure rules of some transformational grammar. It may then be possible to subject this string to one or more transformational rules, resulting in a new string.

Technically speaking, a transformational rule is applied to the phrase

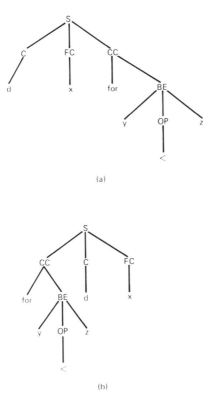

(a)

(b)

Fig. 9.3. Transformation example. (a) Phase structure for the string d x for $y < z$. (b) Phase structure resulting from the transformation C FC CC → CC C FC.

structure of some string, resulting in a new phrase structure. Consider the simple transformation C FC CC → CC C FC. Applying this to the phrase structure of Fig. 9.3a gives the phrase structure shown in Fig. 9.3b. Notice that the underlying string has been transformed into: for $y < z\,d\,x$. This derived string may now serve as the underlying string for some further transformation (e.g., CC C FC → CC , C FC would yield the derived string: for $y < z, d\,x$). Some transformational rules may be optional in that they do not need to be applied whenever they are applicable. Other transformational rules are obligatory; they must be applied whenever they are applicable.

The language that can be generated from a given transformational grammar consists of all strings that can be derived by applying permissible transformational rules to all underlying strings generated from the phrase structure rules. Obligatory transformations must be observed. A string in the language generated from a transformational grammar is called a surface structure string. A string that is both a derived string and an underlying string in the generation of some surface string will be referred to as an intermediate string. Because of the existence of optional transformations, a particular deep string may have numerous surface strings. On the other hand, transformations allow two different deep strings to be used to generate the same surface string (with the same phrase structure) [2].

In building a PPS we are interested not in generating the strings of some language but in discovering their derivations. If we consider the permissible strings in a LS to be those generated by some transformational grammar, then it is necessary to identify *inverse transformations* that take surface strings or intermediate strings into deep structure strings. When the deep structure of some surface string has thus been found, parsing can proceed as discussed in Section 5.36.

Now suppose that during the DSS design we have sketched out some language system that is easy to use, sufficiently expressive, and of sufficient generality. But suppose that we are unable to write out the grammar for this LS or that the grammar turns out to be context sensitive or recursively enumerable. Compared to context-free grammars, context-sensitive and recursively enumerable grammars are not as well understood in terms of parsing algorithms. Parsing algorithms for many context-free grammars have been successfully studied [1].

Thus if the grammar of an LS is not easily identifiable or is not a well-studied context-free grammar, then we are at a loss when the time comes to operationalize the PPS information collection ability. A solution lies in the identification and use of inverse transformations that can convert a string of the LS (i.e., a surface structure string) into an underlying deep string, where every deep string is a sentence in the language of some well-studied context-free grammar. Using this approach, the LS is not constrained to being one of those languages generated by a context-free grammar for which a parsing algorithm has been devised. Other language systems that are perhaps richer in expressive power or more English-like or easier for the user can be used. Such language systems are also extensible through the addition of new inverse transformations.

The preceding approach was adopted in DSS-Q. Its information collection ability is operationalized via the application of inverse transformations to LS string, yielding deep structure expressions that are used in the discovery of appropriate retrieval procedures. The inverse transformations are implemented as sections of code in the problem processor. The inverse transformations used in DSS-Q are general in that they are applicable regardless of the application area.

An alternative treatment of inverse transformations would incorporate them into the system's KS. The PPS would have a section of code for accessing and applying these inverse transformations. This would permit the utilization of application-specific inverse transformation while maintaining PPS invariance and generality. In other words, inverse transformations would be added to or deleted from a data base just as other data.

As a related issue, it should be noted that transformational grammar and other types of generative grammars (recall Section 5.35) are important in research into the psychology [4] and philosophy [3, 5] of mental behavior. The implication, of their contributions to such research, for the design of decision support systems constitute an interesting topic, but it is beyond the scope of this discussion.

Furthermore, a formal parsing technique for transformational grammars, called an augmented transition network, has been developed by Woods [9]. This allows the parsing and translation process to be fully automated, in the sense of a language compiler. A problem with this approach is that language extensions and modifications require major changes in the "compiler." This does not arise in the DSS-Q approach, since each transformation is a module to the PPS.

9.13.2   Problem Recognition

Problem recognition in DSS-Q may be thought of as taking a deep structure expression as its starting point. It culminates with the specification of a procedure for performing the desired retrieval. For ease of explanation, we shall consider operationalization of the DSS-Q problem recognition ability in terms of subschema selection and deep structure compilation.

Before a retrieval procedure can be specified it is necessary to identify

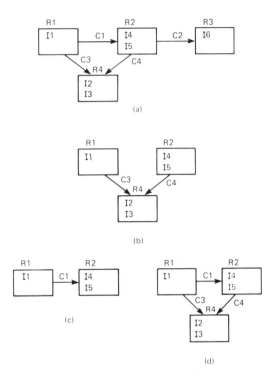

Fig. 9.4.   Subschema examples.

the relevant cosets and record types. That is, a subschema containing all data item types appearing in the deep structure string is determined. For present purposes a subschema should be viewed as what remains after a schema has been masked to omit some of its data item types, record types, and/or cosets. For example, the schema of Fig. 9.4b is a subschema of the schema in Fig. 9.4a.

Suppose that a user's problem statement (e.g., DISPLAY I1, I5 FOR I4 = x) results in a deep structure expression having the item types I1, I4 and I5. Two distinct subschemata that contain these data item types are shown in Fig. 9.4b and 9.4c. Just as a DML programmer must select one of the subschemata prior to writing a DML program that retrieves occurrences of I1 and I5 for I4 = x, so must the PPS select one of the subschemata. There are several ways to govern the selection. These include

(1)   determining the relevant subschemata and interacting with the user to find out which one of them should be selected,

(2)   allowing the user to indicate in the problem statement which of the multiple associations is to be selected (recall Section 8.13), and

(3)   the utilization of application-specific inverse transformations that would, for instance, give a deep string containing the cosets of the desired subschema.

The first two methods are supported in DSS-Q.

The determination of relevant subschemata (as in the preceding method 1) may appear to be a simple task in the example of Fig. 9.4. However, it is by no means trivial to automate. Remember that subschema determination must be general, capable of finding all subschemata in possibly complex network schemata for any set of data item types. The DSS-Q implementation of subschema determination finds all subschemata that contain no loops. It would find the subschemata of Figs. 9.4b and 9.4c but not that of Fig. 9.4d. Thus a request for a report of all students taught by the teacher that advises student Z (recall the student–teacher example from Section 8.13) is not handled directly in DSS-Q. The request can, however, be handled if it is decomposed into the two simpler requests of displaying the teacher that advises student Z (suppose that teacher Y is displayed) and then displaying the students taught by teacher Y.

Subschema determination is a recursive process. Therefore the use of automatic backtracking is a crucial aspect of finding the subschemata that contain some set of data item types $\{d_1, d_2, \ldots, d_n\}$. In Fig. 9.5 there is a step-by-step illustration of the notion of backtracking in the context of a simple depth-first procedure. The point of this example is not to advocate this technique but to illustrate backtracking in a simple context. The objective is to find all subschemata of the schema in Fig. 9.5a that contain the data item types d_1, d_2, d_3, d_4. Each subschema is specified in terms of the cosets it contains. At each step in Fig. 9.5b there is a list of data item types currently in the subschema, a goal of finding a way to include some data item type in the subschema, and proposed cosets for effecting this inclusion.

The proposed cosets at each step either succeed or fail. If there is success, then a new data item type goal is addressed with the intent of more fully specifying a subschema (e.g., step 3 to step 4) or of finding another subschema (e.g., step 11 to step 12). If a step fails then the proposed cosets are never again considered as a way for meeting the goal of incorporating the indicated data item type into that step's current subschema. On failure, an attempt is made to find other, previously unconsidered, cosets that might satisfy the goal for the current subschema. If such cosets are found, they become the proposed cosets that are considered in the next step (e.g., step 6 to step 7).

If no previously unconsidered cosets for the goal and subschema are found, then we back up to a different subschema, formed by dropping the

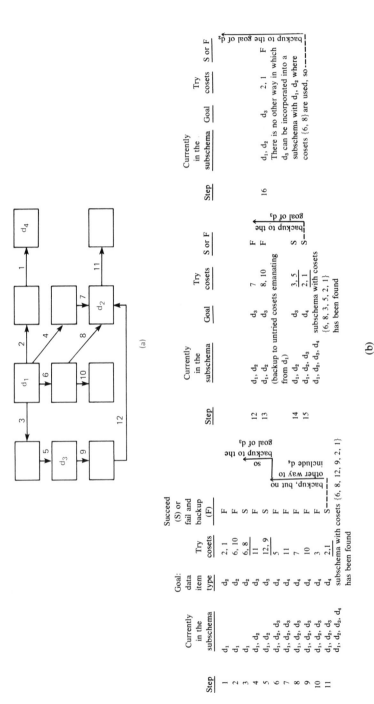

Fig. 9.5. Depth-first procedure for finding subschemata. (a) Schema. (b) Finding subschemata.

last data item type from the current subschema. We then have the new goal of trying to incorporate this dropped data item type into the reduced subschema (using cosets other than those already considered for this goal and subschema). As an example, after step 16 the data item type d_2 is dropped and we back up to a new current schema of d_1 only. When carried to completion, the example in Fig. 9.5b yields three subschemata in addition to the two that are shown: $\{4,7,12,9,1,2\}$, $\{4,7,3,5,2,1\}$, and $\{3,5,9,12,2,1\}$.

Since it is handled within the PPS, all of this backtracking during subschema determination is automatic. The data item types in a deep string are treated as a sequence of goals:

The goal is inclusion of d_1 in the subschema.
The goal is inclusion of d_2 in the subschema.
The goal is inclusion of d_3 in the subschema.
The goal is inclusion of d_4 in the subschema.

In this sense the foregoing depth-first subschema determination resembles the PLANNER approach to problem solving (recall Section 4.12 and see Winograd [8]).

Other subschema determination techniques are possible. A breadth-first approach is employed in DSS-Q (see Section 9.40). Thus the first subschema found is the smallest in terms of the number of cosets it contains. If this subschema does not contain the relationship desired by a user, the next smallest subschema is found, and so forth. Alternatively, if the user's problem statement indicates desired relationships, these are taken into account during subschema determination.

Once a subschema has been selected, the PPS compiles the deep-structure expression by (1) parsing that expression and (2) utilizing the derivation found in parsing and the selected subschema to transform the deep-structure string into object code. The parsing is straightforward, since deep-structure expressions are sentences generated from a well-studied context-free grammar. The parsing algorithm is impervious to changes in the application area. The context-free grammar itself does not change from an application to the next, with the exception of some of its terminal symbols (i.e., the data item types and the relationship names).

The derivation discovered in the parse, together with the pertinent subschema, is used by the PPS to generate object code that is subsequently interpreted in order to carry out the desired retrieval. Even though it is automated, this is similar to the task performed by the user of a category J system. For the category J user must also utilize a recognition of the appropriate subschema, an understanding of which data item types are to have their occurrences retrieved, and an understanding of which data item types are to be used in conditioning the retrieval (and the nature of that conditioning) in order to devise a correct retrieval procedure. The problem processor of a category L system must have similar capacities in order to specify a retrieval procedure (i.e., object code).

Notice that determination of the parse and subschema are necessary and sufficient conditions for the construction of a retrieval procedure. This construction process is invariant to the application area. The object code produced by the transformation aspect of the deep-structure compiler is the culmination of problem recognition. It constitutes a procedural statement of how to accomplish the retrieval. One must be careful not to confuse this compilation of an internal, nonprocedural statement (a deep string) with the compilation of an external (i.e., user-stated), procedural statement as in category J systems.

In DSS-Q the object code produced by deep structure compilation contains no DML. All DML usage occurs in the interpreter's code (review Fig. 9.1c). It is this interpreter that constitutes the PPS information collection ability with respect to the KS. The object code from the deep structure compilation serves as the source code for the interpreter. Execution of the interpreter with this source code results in the desired report.

We can summarize the category L problem processor by noting that the system responds to a user's statement by recognizing what the retrieval problem is and how to adapt to it. The user's request is viewed as creating a disequilibrium (an unfulfilled demand) in the decision-making system. The PPS adapts (by specifying an appropriate procedure for directing retrieval) in order to abolish the disequilibrium to fulfill the demand.

9.20   PROBLEM PROCESSORS FOR COMPUTATIONALLY ORIENTED DSS

Retrieval-only decision support systems are concerned with the design of plans to govern retrieval, but they do not deal with the design of plans (i.e., models) to govern the analysis of data. Throughout this treatise the term "model" is used in the sense of a computational model, a model that specifies some calculations used in operations research, management science, normative economics, etc.

In the remainder of this chapter we explore the problem processors or computationally oriented decision support systems. Thus we shall consider operationalizations of the abilities of model formulation and analysis, in addition to information collection and problem recognition. We consider first the PPS for systems falling into the bottom row of Fig. 3.2. This is followed by an examination of problem processors for systems of the middle and highest rows of the classification scheme.

9.21 PPS Where Models Are Explicitly Stated

The constitutions of problem processors for categories A, B, and C are depicted in Fig. 9.6. Information collection from the user is, in every case, accomplished by a host language compiler. In this respect a PPS of any of these three categories resembles the PPS of category J (Section 9.11), except that the compiler's capacity to handle computational statements is now utilized.

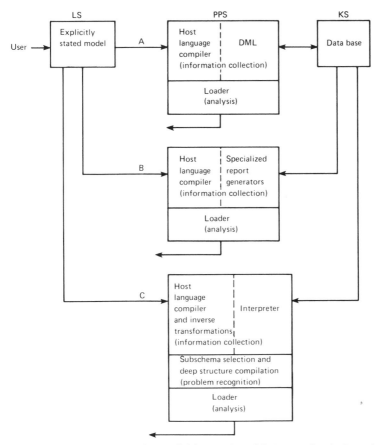

Fig. 9.6. Problem processors for explicitly stated models (categories A, B, and C).

A category C problem processor may also include an inverse transformation (and preparser) component, since computational language compilers (e.g., FORTRAN) are not equipped to deal with generalized, nonprocedural requests for data base retrieval. A straightforward way to integrate the compiler and the inverse transformation component (ITC) into a single system is to treat the ITC as an operating system routine (existing as object code) that can be accessed from the host language. This generalized report generation routine would also include code for the subschema selection, deep-structure compilation, and interpreter. Thus a user's problem statement is interspersed with calls to a generalized report generator.

As far as information collection from the data base is concerned, categories A, B, and C use the methods described in Sections 9.11, 9.12, 9.13.2, respectively. High-order problem recognition for category A is done by the user. In category B the system's builder has aided in the problem recognition by specifying the allowable retrieval procedures in the guise of specialized report generators. The specialized report generators are invoked from a computational host language via traditional subroutine facilities. The PPS itself aids in problem recognition for category C systems by generating retrieval procedures. All problem recognition involving computations and all model formulation are performed by the user.

Recall that the term "analysis" is used to describe the activity of interfacing some data with a model in order to obtain some facts or expectations. For the problem processors of Fig. 9.6, this activity is performed primarily by an operating system's load and execute routines. For category A the compiled model, together with the object code of any needed DML commands, is loaded and control is transferred to the loaded code in order to execute it. For category B the compiled model, together with executable code of any specialized report generators that it invokes, is loaded for execution. For category C the compiled model and the generalized report generator are loaded and executed. There is a clear correspondence between this automated analysis and human analysis, wherein some data (obtained from memory or from outside sources) are utilized in the execution of some mental model in order to arrive at some facts or expectations.

9.22   PPS Where Models Are Invoked

Information collection from a user in category D, E, or F systems bears a certain similarity to the same ability in category K systems (Section 9.12). In the latter a driver was used to set parameter values properly and then transfer control to a prefabricated and specialized report generator. In the former, a driver is used to set parameter values as implied by the user's statement and then transfer control to the desired prefabricated model. The three categories where a model is invoked by a user differ from each other primarily in terms of the manner in which information is collected from the data base *by the model* (not by the user, as in Section 9.21). These are illustrated in Fig. 9.7.

In category D systems information is retrieved from a data base as discussed in Section 9.11, except it is the model that directs the retrieval and not the user. Appropriate DML commands are embedded in each prefabricated model's code. Data base retrieval for category E systems is accomplished as described in Section 9.12, with the exception that it is the model that directs the retrieval. Embedded in a prefabricated model's code are calls to specialized report generators. Since they contain DML

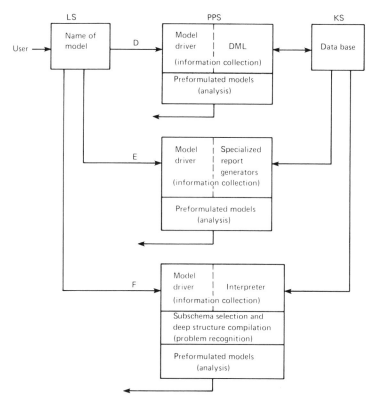

Fig. 9.7. Problem processors for invoked models (categories D, E, and F).

commands, these report generators are sometimes called DML extraction routines (extracting reports from the data base). The preformulated model itself contains no DML commands.

For category F systems, data base retrieval can be accomplished as described in Section 9.13.2, except that retrieval is directed from within a preformulated model rather than by a user. The DML commands are embedded in the generalized report generator's *interpreter*. So with respect to retrieval, only category F problem processors display an appreciable degree of problem recognition and adaptation. With respect to model specification, none of the three categories have problem processors that perform problem recognition, nor do they display a model formulation ability. The problem recognition involved in arriving at a procedural model specification, for a particular problem facing the decision-making system, is instigated by the user and relies on model code created by the DSS builder. The model formulation ability is also absent from the PPS. It is the system builder that fabricates models in advance.

As indicated in Fig. 9.7, the PPS analysis ability is exercised by executing the code of some preformulated model. For each of the three categories, there is a transfer of control from the model driver to the executable code of the desired model. Note that this analysis ability is contingent on the existence of information-collecting and model-formulating abilities within the decision-*making* system (recall Section 2.22). In the next section we examine the design of decision *support* systems that possess model formulation abilities.

9.23 PPS with Model Formulation Abilities

Problem processors for systems of categories G, H, and I are the topic of this section. The principal attribute that distinguishes these systems from those discussed earlier is their model formulation ability. Since this is an ability that is not displayed by extant decision support systems having data base knowledge systems, the discussion in this section is less detailed (less technique oriented) than that of the preceding sections. Nevertheless it does provide an overview that foreshadows Part V of this treatise. There we examine techniques that can be used to operationalize both the model formulation ability and the problem recognition ability that goes along with it.

As depicted in Fig. 9.8, categories G through I differ from one another primarily in terms of the data retrieval method that they use. For category G, retrieval is accomplished by the use of DML commands in the formulated model. If the formulated model invokes specialized report

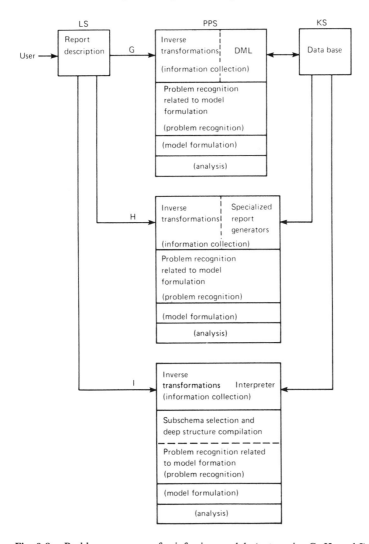

Fig. 9.8.   Problem processors for inferring models (categories G, H, and I).

generators, then the PPS is of category H. In systems of category I, all retrieval by a formulated model is accomplished by the use of a generalized report generator. Note that only in this last category does a PPS have any problem recognition abilities related to information collection from the data base.

In all three categories information collection from a user must accept problem statements in the respective language systems and convert them into an internally comprehensible form. Since these language systems closely resemble the LS for category L, the information collection ability for category G, H, and I problem processors could be operationalized using a technique similar to that of category L (e.g., inverse transformations). However, the problem recognition that occurs for the deep structure string does *not* involve subschema selection. The system must formulate a model on the basis of the deep structure string, rather than conduct a retrieval. The formulated model, in its turn, will direct some retrieval using one of the three approaches described in the preceding paragraph.

Given a deep string, the task of the PPS is to recognize the appropriateness (or the lack thereof) of a formulated model as a basis for analysis that is pertinent to the user's desires. There must also be a recognition of what data are to be retrieved from the data base (and when) for use in the analysis. The actual retrieval of these data is accomplished by the PPS information-collecting ability during the exercise of (i.e., at the request of) the analysis ability.

There are at least two major approaches to recognizing the appropriateness of a formulated model. One consists of examining a model after it has been formulated and discarding it if it is deemed inappropriate in light of the deep string. If it is discarded then another model is formulated and examined to determine whether it can meet the user's need (i.e., successfully lead to a restoration of the DSS equilibrium), and so forth. The second approach is to intertwine the recognition and formulation activities. That is, the ability to recognize the appropriateness of a model is used to govern the formulation activity, such that the model that is formulated is necessarily appropriate. This governing process could take the form of a series of problem recognitions (adaptations) that tend to reduce the problem until no further problem is recognized. A further, complicating factor is the recognition and selection of which formulated model to use when there are several that are appropriate. A related issue concerns the identification of optimum models within the constraints of the existing model formulation ability.

Some insights into the requirements of a model formulation ability can be garnered by viewing the human model formulation used in connection with systems of categories A through F. The human model formulator, beginning with a set of modules, must have a knowledge of how these modules can interact with each other. The nature of this interaction is seen in the way in which one module can obtain information from (or provide information to) other modules. It should be clear that an automatic model formulator must also have access to a set of modules (information-processing roles) and a body of knowledge about how these modules can interact with each other (the associative connections among roles).

If there are several modules that could furnish the kind of information needed by some other module, then the human designer must have the knowledge that allows a recognition of which of them is appropriate for dealing with a given problem. If a PPS is to emulate this problem recognition, governing the model formulation, then it too must have access to a body of knowledge concerning which module to select (i.e., how to define an information-processing role) for a given problem.

This kind of modeling knowledge, together with the other modeling knowledge (the modules themselves and knowledge of their interaction), must be incorporated into the DSS. First of all, observe that this requires a formal way for expressing modeling knowledge. Modules are expressed easily enough in terms of some programming language. However, formalisms for other modeling knowledge are not so obvious. These are examined in later chapters. Second, modeling knowledge will change from one application area to another, and even within an application area over time. If the objective is a generalized problem processor, then the modeling knowledge cannot be incorporated into the PPS. It must be incorporated into the KS. This raises the question of techniques for storing such knowledge. For instance, can modules and other formally expressed modeling knowledge be stored in a data base? This question is addressed in subsequent chapters.

The human designer of a model must also be able to distinguish between the case where a module needs information from another module and the case where a module can simply make use of already extant information. In governing the model formulation, the PPS problem recognition ability must also be able to distinguish between problems (module input needs) that are solved by a retrieval and those that necessitate the use of a module (or group of modules). This aspect of problem recognition must make use of the data base schema and the already mentioned modeling knowledge.

Note that there are primarily two approaches to treating the retrieval that must accompany the execution of a formulated model and these have different implications for the operationalization of the PPS analysis ability. In one approach all retrieval is instigated from within the modules that form a model. Systems in any of the categories G through I could adopt this approach. The analysis ability would be operationalized as a loader that loads the (object code) modules of the formulated model and transfers control to that model.

An alternative approach consists of instigating retrieval from outside of the modules that make up a model. That is, the formulated model consists not only of a sequence (possibly with looping and branching) of modules but also of retrieval commands, such that prior to the execution of a module all reports needed by that module (other than those that are outputs of other computational modules) are retrieved from the data base. These reports are accessed as needed by read statements in the module's code. Unlike the intramodule retrieval approach, this extra-module approach requires the PPS to recognize (prior to analysis) just what retrievals are necessary.

In the intramodule approach the PPS only performs the retrievals. In the extra-module approach the PPS both specifies the retrieval to be performed and later performs it. This retrieval specification could be in the form of DML or invocations to specialized report generators or a report description that is subsequently acted on by a generalized report generator. In terms of implementing a PPS, the latter type of specification is probably preferable to the other two. It affords more generality and flexibility than specialized report generators and it is more easily specified than a DML procedure. For the extra-modular retrieval approach the analysis ability would involve coordinating the loading and execution of modules with performance of the specified retrievals. If a category I system employs the extra-modular approach, then it may be convenient to consider the generalized report generator as a (noncomputational) module that is loaded along with the computational modules. In any event, analysis depends on the availability of a statement (generated by the PPS formulation and recognition abilities) of which modules to execute, when to execute each module, and what retrieval to perform before the execution of each module. We shall refer to such a statement as the analysis statement that has been generated for a user's problem statement.

The natures of analysis and the analysis statement become more lucid when they are conceived as corresponding to an operating system and its job control language (JCL), respectively. In a JCL we can request the operating system to "get" certain files from auxiliary memory. Either program files (corresponding to modules) or data files (corresponding reports retrieved for use as inputs to a module) can be obtained in this way. Furthermore, a JCL allows us to load and execute an object program that has been obtained. The read statements in that program input the data that the program needs, by reading it from one or more of the previously obtained data files (by means of module input reports).

When the program (a module) has completed its execution, another object program (corresponding to the next module in the formulated model) is loaded, the data files (corresponding to module input reports) it needs are obtained, and the program is executed. Note that the file(s) produced by the write statements in a program can be saved following the program's execution and can serve as a data file(s) for subsequent programs. This corresponds to using the output report of one module as an input report to another, and as such it is a realization of module interaction.

Utilizing JCL in the above manner of (1) obtaining data files needed by a program; (2) obtaining, loading, and executing the program; (3) saving its output data file for later use by other programs (or as a final output for viewing by the JCL user); and (4) repeating the process with another program, corresponds to an analysis statement employing extra-module retrieval. If a JCL is utilized without commands that get the individual data files used by each program, then it corresponds to an analysis statement for intramodule retrieval. Such a JCL usage presumes that the programs have, within themselves, a method for obtaining any needed data files other than those that are output from previously executed programs.

From the foregoing considerations it should be clear that in building a model formulating PPS, one must employ a variety of techniques. Techniques for operationalizing information collection have received extensive coverage in this and earlier chapters. Specific techniques for operationalizing the analysis ability become apparent on a study of operating systems. Although it is beyond the scope of the present discussion to review operating system techniques, we do point out that the PPS correspondence to operating system "gets" utilizes data base retrieval techniques, and these have been discussed earlier. The mechanics of implementing program (or module) loading and execution are well known in the operating system field (see Donovan [6], for example).

Techniques for operationalizing the model formulation and problem recognition abilities in the event of a data base KS are not well known. Much of the remainder of this treatise involves the identification and application of such techniques.

9.30 SUMMARY

In this chapter we have investigated techniques that can be used in constructing problem processors for decision support systems having data base KS. At a conceptual level we differentiated among various categories of problem processors in terms of the language systems they employ and, in the case of computations, in terms of the language used by a model in directing retrieval. We also saw the similarities and differences of the various categories in terms of the decision-making abilities that their respective problem processors exhibit. Finally, within each category it is possible to differentiate further among its problem processors in terms of how the characteristic abilities of that category are operationalized and implemented.

9.40   APPENDIX: A CATEGORY L PROCESSING EXAMPLE

In this section we trace the processing performed by DSS-Q for an example problem. Although the example deals with retrieval only, it should be noted that DSS-Q also enables the user to direct computations by invoking a model by name (category E), by allowing arithmetic expressions in a problem statement (limited category C), and by using functions (limited category F) in a problem statement. The example depicted here is not particularly complex, but it does illustrate the inner workings of the PPS.

Suppose that the KS contains information organized according to the data base structure of Fig. 9.9. The sample problem is one of obtaining a

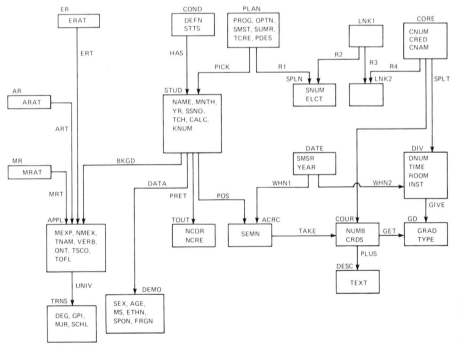

Fig. 9.9.   Sample schema.

report containing the name (NAME), course number (NUMB), and credits (CRDS) of all students for the semester (SMSR) beginning in month 8, whose names begin with "A," where the year (YEAR) is '79, and the course is not a management ('MGMT') course. There are several ways to express this problem in the DSS-Q language, one of which is

FOR SMSR = 8 DISPLAY NAME NUMB CRDS FOR NAME =
'A' YEAR = 79 NUMB .NE. 'MGMT'

Figure 9.10a shows the output of the preparser; notice that there are 18 tokens. The code number identifies the nature of the token (1 denotes a keyword such as FOR, 2 denotes a data item type such as SMSR, 3 denotes an alphanumeric literal such as "A," 4 denotes a numerical value such as 79). The value of a token consists of a unique number for keywords (e.g., 7 for FOR and 11 for =), the data item type names for data item types, positions in a storage list for literals (e.g., 'MGMT' is at position 2 in the literal list), and a real number for numerical values. The final column of this table contains the name of the record type that con-

CODE	VALUE	RECORD	CODE	VALUE	RECORD
1	7		1	201	
2	SMSR	DATE	1	6	
1	11		2	NAME	STUD
4	8.00		1	6	
1	201		2	NUMB	COUR
2	NAME	STUD	1	6	
2	NUMB	COUR	2	CRDS	COUR
2	CRDS	COUR	1	7	
1	7		2	SMSR	DATE
2	NAME	STUD	1	11	
1	11		4	8.00	
3	1		1	9	
2	YEAR	DATE	2	NAME	STUD
1	11		1	11	
4	79.00		3	1	
2	NUMB	COUR	1	9	
1	12		2	YEAR	DATE
3	2		1	11	
			4	79.00	
			1	9	
			2	NUMB	COUR
			1	12	
			3	2	
			0	0	
(a)			(b)		

Fig. 9.10. (a) Output from preparser. (b) Output from inverse transformations.

tains the indicated data item type. Observe that there are only three different record types here; thus when the system has found a subschema that contains these three, it can proceed to deep-structure compilation. The result of applying certain inverse transformations is shown in Fig. 9.10b. Notice that the string has been reordered and that additional keyword values have been inserted (e.g., the keyword with value 9 indicates the AND keyword).

DSS-Q uses a recursive breadth-first search technique for subschema determination. Steps in determining the smallest subschema are shown in Fig. 9.11. These steps are portrayed graphically in Fig. 9.12. A step is identified by two record types (under the FROM and TO headings in Fig. 9-11). The initial step is from $\emptyset$ to DATE. This is the parent step for steps 2 (DATE-ACRC) and 3 (DATE-DIV). These in turn are parents of other steps. The third column of Fig. 9-11 shows the number of record types, containing desired data item types, that have been included in the subschema denoted by the step. Step 5, for example, denotes that subschema consisting of the coset from ACRC to COUR and the coset from DATE to ACRC; it therefore includes the record types DATE, ACRC, and COUR. This is easily visualized (see Fig. 9.11 or 9.12c) by beginning at step 5, noting that its parent step is step 2, and noting that the parent of step 2 is the parentless step 1. Two of the record types in this subschema (DATE and COUR) contain desired data item types. As soon as the system reaches a step having a 3 in the third column (for this example) a usable subschema has been found.

As shown in Fig. 9.12 the steps are taken in a breadth-first fashion. As each step is taken, the new record type that is added to the subschema is

STEP	PARENT STEP	NUMBER	FROM	TO
1	0	1		DATE
2	1	1	DATE	ACRC
3	1	1	DATE	DIV
4	2	2	ACRC	STUD
5	2	2	ACRC	COUR
6	3	1	DIV	CORE
7	3	1	DIV	GD
8	4	2	STUD	TOUT
9	4	2	STUD	PLAN
10	4	2	STUD	COND
11	4	2	STUD	DEMO
12	4	2	STUD	APPL
13	4	3	ACRC	COUR

SUBSCHEMA FOUND.

Fig. 9.11. Finding the schemata.

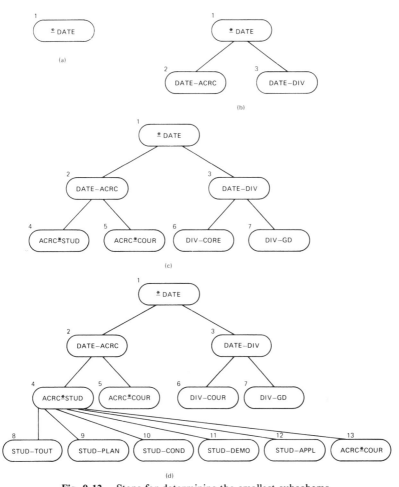

Fig. 9.12.   Steps for determining the smallest subschema.

checked to determine whether it contains a desired data item type. If so, this is reflected in the table of Fig. 9.11; it is indicated pictorially by an asterisk in the step node. The key to understanding the graphs in Fig. 9-12 is to bear in mind that *each step node identifies a different* subschema. How and why the first seven steps are taken (through Fig. 9-12c) is clear if the schema of Fig. 9.9 is examined. Through step 7, seven different subschemata have been found, none of which contains three record types having desired data item types.

In keeping with the breadth-first strategy, the steps having step 4 as a parent are examined next. From Fig. 9.9, the genesis of step nodes 8 through 12 is clear; we refer to these as natural descendants. None of them proves to contain a desired data item type. If one of them had contained a desired data item type, then the PPS would have found a usable subschema having three cosets. Are there any other descendants for step node 4 that give subschemata of this same size? There is one and it appears as step 13. It is determined by a recursive (backtracking) procedure based on the following rule: If no natural descendant of a node X, which contains an asterisk, gives a usable subschema, then backtrack to the parent step of X and make each of its descendant steps a descendant step of X as well.

In the example, step node 4 has an asterisk but none of its natural descendant's gives a usable subschema. Therefore the PPS backs up to step 2. Its descendant is ACRC–COUR. This becomes step 13 and its subschema consists of three cosets (from ACRC to COUR, from ACRC to STUD, and from DATE to ACRC). Since the subschema of step 13 contains three record types having desired data item types, it can be used for retrieval. If this subschema does not contain the relationships desired by the user, then the subschema determination continues from where it left off by examining the descendants for step 5. The subschema is depicted in Fig. 9.13.

If the subschema implied by step 13 is acceptable to the user, then deep-structure compilation begins. In DSS-Q this compilation entails the application of further inverse transformations to the deep string of Fig. 9.10b, giving a "deeper" string. The result of these inverse transformations is not shown here. It is basically a reordering of the deep string with respect to the subschema and the data item types that appeared in the conditional clause of the original problem statement. The effect is a more efficient object code.

The deep (i.e., deeper) string is subsequently parsed, the derivation (and subschema) being used to arrive at the internal object code that is executed by the interpreter. The object code for the present example is given in Fig. 9.14a and the report that it produces appears in Fig. 9.14b. It

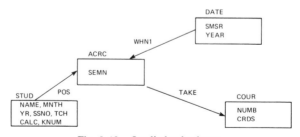

Fig. 9.13. Implied subschema.

(a)

LEFT OPERAND	DEPTH	LEFT OPERAND CODE	RIGHT OPERAND CODE	OPERATOR	RIGHT OPERAND
YEAR	1	2	4	11	79.00
SMSR	1	2	4	11	8.00
NAME	3	2	3	11	
NUMB		2	3	12	1
			6	9	2
4		6	6	9	3
5		6	6	9	2
6	4	6	6	7	1
			2	6	7
			2	6	CRDS
			2	6	NUMB
					NAME

(b)

NAME	COURSE NUMBER	CREDIT HOURS
ABBOTT, LINDA G.	ECON 640	2
ABBOTT, LINDA G.	PSY 585	3
ABRAHAM, PAULA L.	ECON 640	2
ADAMS, REBECCA	ECON 640	2
ADAMS, REBECCA	AS 681	3
AGNEW, DAVID C.	ECON 640	2
ALBURN, LAURA	ECON 513	4
ALEXANDER, MATTHEW J.	ECON 513	4
ALEXANDER, MATTHEW J.	AS 681	3
ALLEN, AMIR H.	ECON 513	4
ALLEN, AMIR H.	AS 681	3
ANDREWS, DAVID E.	ECON 513	4
ANDREWS, DAVID E.	AS 681	3
ARTHUR, RICHIE J.	ECON 513	4
ARTHUR, RICHIE J.	AS 681	3
AUSTIN, WILLIAM C.	ECON 513	4
AUSTIN, WILLIAM C.	AS 681	3

Fig. 9.14. (a) Internal object code. (b) Report.

is beyond the current scope to give a detailed discussion of the meaning of this code for the DSS-Q interpreter. Figure 9.14a is included merely to give a notion of what object code looks like.

REFERENCES

1. A. V. Aho and J. D. Ullman, "The Theory of Parsing, Translating and Compiling," Vol. 1. Prentice-Hall, Englewood Cliffs, New Jersey, 1972.
2. N. Chomsky, "Aspects of the Theory of Syntax." MIT Press, Cambridge, Massachusetts, 1965.
3. N. Chomsky, "Cartesian Linguistics." Harper, New York, 1966.
4. N. Chomsky, "Language and Mind." Harcourt, New York, 1972.
5. N. Chomsky, "Problems of Knowledge and Freedom." Random House, New York, 1972.
6. J. J. Donovan, "Systems Programming." McGraw-Hill, New York, 1972.
7. D. Knuth, "The Art of Computer Programming," Vol. 1, 2nd ed. Addison-Wesley, Reading, Massachusetts, 1973.
8. T. Winograd, "Understanding Natural Language." Academic Press, New York, 1972.
9. W. A. Woods, Augmented Transition Networks for Natural Language Analysis, Rep. No. CS-1, Harvard, 1969.

Chapter 10

EXTENSIONS

10.00 INTRODUCTION

This chapter explores some enhancements to the arsenal of tools available for constructing decision support systems that have data base knowledge systems (KS). These are presented primarily at an operational level. The term "enhancement" is used with respect to the constructs and techniques covered in the four preceding chapters and it refers to ways of extending DSS capabilities beyond those already discussed. The extensions explored in this chapter are language system (LS) enhancements and KS enhancements.

A language (and related problem processor elements) is introduced that has capabilities beyond the instigation of a report. This language could be used for addressing a variety of tasks such as KS loading, information transferral among distributed knowledge systems, dynamic data base restructuring, and intermodule communication. The KS enhancements make use of the same operational constructs for knowledge representation that were presented in Chapters 6 and 7. However, these constructs are utilized in nontraditional ways in order to introduce more levels of abstraction within a data base and to organize the elements of a module pool into a network.

10.10   LANGUAGE EXTENSIONS

We have already discussed a general, nonprocedural language for retrieving data from a data base. This language can replace DML retrieval
procedures. We have also seen that DML procedures are used to load data
into a data base. An obvious question is whether the notion of a generalized, nonprocedural language can be extended to encompass loading, as
well as retrieval. Recalling that loading is the inverse of retrieval, we can
see that loading has the effect of scattering the data from a file into an
occurrence structure, whereas retrieval has the effect of pulling together
(into a file) data that is scattered about in an occurrence structure.

Another task that can be performed with DML, but that cannot be
directed through the generalized, nonprocedural language introduced earlier, is that of data base restructuring. Restructuring refers to the addition
or deletion of data item types, record types, or cosets for an existing
schema. A common approach to restructuring is to write DML routines
(or alternatively, retrieval statements in a category L language) that will
dump all data organized according to the current structure into a collection of files. The schema is redefined to reflect the new structure. The files
with dumped data then serve as inputs to DML load programs that are
written to take the new logical structure into account.

An alternative restructuring method that saves a good deal of programming effort is available in a few commercial systems (e.g., MDBS
[9]). In this approach DML restructuring commands are used (e.g., a
command to add a record type to the schema, delete a coset, etc.). Rather
than writing and revising programs to dump and reload data base contents, a single DML program using the restructuring commands is written.
Since no dumping or reloading of data is required, we refer to the restructuring as dynamic. Any physical reorganization of record occurrences
caused by the new logical structure is handled automatically by the execution of the restructuring commands. Even though this extension to the
customary DML commands is quite useful, it is of interest to investigate
whether this restructuring approach can be improved. Can a general,
nonprocedural language that performs retrieval and loading be enhanced
to handle dynamic restructuring as well?

A third kind of useful language extension becomes apparent when we
look more closely at the passage of information between two modules in a
model. Suppose that some module X produces an output file(s) O_x. The
schema of O_x is specified by the format(s) used by the write statement(s)
of X. Furthermore, suppose that some module Y needs information from
O_x as an input. The format(s) used by Y's read statement(s) is a statement

of the schema of the file from which Y expects to retrieve data. If the input schema for Y is compatible with the output schema for X, then the information transferral from X to Y is straightforward. The two are compatible if the schema expected by Y is a mask of the schema used by X.

If the two are not compatible, then some intermediate processing is needed before X's outputs can be accessed by Y. Can this processing be generalized (i.e., so that it works for any two modules) and specified concisely and nonprocedurely? If so, modules in a module pool could be designed independently of each other, without prior coordination of their input and output formats. In other words, data organized according to the output schema of one module could be reorganized into the input schema expected by another module.

None of the foregoing extensions involve tasks performed directly by a decision maker. However, these are tasks that are performed either by the PPS or by the administrator of the DSS. In the following sections, a generalized "mapping" language that accounts for all of these tasks (plus retrieval) is outlined. It is referred to as a mapping language because retrieval and every one of the extended tasks that it addresses entail a mapping of data from one logical structure to another. The language is general in the sense that it allows us to specify a map from any network schema (source schema) into another network schema (target schema).

10.11   A Generalized Mapping Language for Network Schemata

The present description of the generalized mapping language (GML) has been extracted from Bonczek and Whinston [4]. For more details about the GML, the reader should consult the original source. The language itself has a linguistic formulation involving inverse transformations and a context-free deep structure grammar. The surface language is nonprocedural and has, as a subset, retrieval capabilities comparable to the stylized category L language presented in Chapter 8.

To reinforce the notion of mapping, five examples of the mapping process are presented. They depict the kinds of mapping situations that can be expected to arise in practice. The examples are also suggestive of what a mapping language should permit us to express. With this background we proceed to define a generalized data base mapping language and discuss its processor. The issue of specifying the mapping of relationships is also examined. The mapping description closes with a discussion of its value to DSS builders and administrators. Refer to Bonczek and Whinston [4] for notes on implementation.

10.11.1 Mapping Examples

The examples presented can be categorized into four mapping problems. These are retrieval for display, simple data base loading, data base compaction, and data base expansion. The first two are, respectively, special cases of the latter two.

Example 1: Retrieval Maps

The problem is to map selected items from an arbitrary network data base into items of a single record type (Fig. 10.1). This kind of map is typical of the data base retrieval problem, where the target data base record type is a sequential output file for display at the user's terminal. In the example depicted in Fig. 10.1, the data items TNAME and SNAME of the source data base are mapped into OTN and OSN, respectively, of the target data base.

The problem with the retrieval class of data base maps appears in the specification of the proper relationships to employ while performing the retrieval. In the example of Fig. 10.1, there are two possibilities for the relationship between STUDENT and TEACHER: the relationship ADVISOR or the pair of cosets GIVE and RECEIVE. The mapping language must have the ability to specify desired relationships between the record types in the source data base.

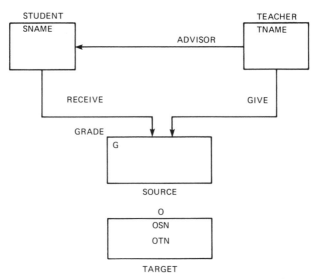

Fig. 10.1. Sample source and target for retrieval mapping.

Example 2: Load Maps

Here we consider the problem of mapping data items from a single record type into a network data base, by reversing the target and source data bases of Fig. 10.1. This process is similar to that performed during the loading of data into the (target) data base from a (source) sequential file. In practice, this problem most often arises when converting a file manipulation system into a network data base environment. Information stored in the source data base (file), for data items OTN and OSN, is mapped into the target data items TNAME and SNAME, respectively.

Again the problem arises of specifying the relationships to employ in the map; however, now the possibilities are part of the target data base. The proper relationships among the target record types must be chosen to reflect properly the implicit relationship between the source data items.

Example 3: Compaction Maps

Suppose the source data base of Fig. 10.2 is unnecessarily detailed for required applications, and it is desired to compress the data base into the schema of the Fig. 10.2 target data base. In this example the source data base indicates both professors and graduate instructors who teach courses, while the target does not draw distinctions between professors and graduate instructors. Here the data item mappings are PNAME to INAME, GNAME to INAME, CNAME to NAMC, SNUM to NUMS, PSAL to ISAL, and GSAL to ISAL.

The interaction among the relationships is clearly more complicated in this situation. Consider the target relationship DIVIDE. It has as its source counterpart the relationship SPLIT. But the target relationship TEACH has two counterpart relationships in the source data base: PT and TP for professors and GT and TG for graduate instructors. Moreover, the target relationship SPRV corresponds to the source relationship SUPERVISE for professors but has no counterpart for graduate instructors. The mapping language must provide the capabilities for specifying complex sets of relationships for both the source and target data bases.

Example 4: Expansion Maps

This is a reprise of Example 3 (Fig. 10.2), but with the source and target data bases reversed. In this case the data base is to be expanded by adding more relational information to it. Some criterion must exist for partitioning the occurrences of INST in the source data base into professors and graduate instructors. The criterion could be that graduate instructors' salaries are below 5000 (ISAL < 5000). In effect, what must be performed are two conditional maps, the first mapping instructors with ISAL < 5000 to graduate students, the second mapping instructors with

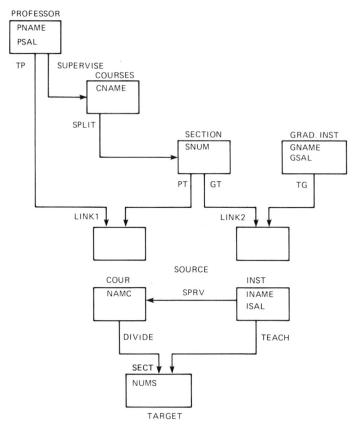

Fig. 10.2.   Sample source and target for compression mapping.

ISAL $\geq$ 5000 to professors. It is clear that conditional data selection capability is required.

Example 5: Maps with Functions

In Fig. 10.3 we see a map in the same class as that of Example 1 (i.e., retrieval). It is desired to map the source data item D# into OD# and to have the target data item AVER represent the average weekly salary of the employees in the given department. The weekly salary for each employee can be computed from the stored information, namely, by RATE * HOURS. An averaging function could then be applied to produce the desired value. In any event, it is advantageous for the mapping language to permit computational expressions.

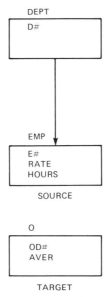

Fig. 10.3. Sample source and target for mapping with functions.

10.11.2 The Generalized Mapping Language and Its Processor

As described earlier, the problem is to map data described by one data base schema into items defined in a second data base schema. It is, of course, allowable for the source and target schemas to be the same, that is, mapping information from one data base into itself. The specification of the schema definitions is not strictly a part of the mapping process. Thus throughout this discussion, all schemata referred to are assumed to have been previously defined.

The mapping language is generated by a transformation grammar. As such, the discussion of Chapter 9 applies. The base grammar is presented in Fig. 10.4. Its form (Uniquely Invertible (1,1) Simple Precedence; see Aho and Ullman [1]) makes expressions in the deep language simple to parse.

However, this deep language is useless as a user-oriented language. For instance, the required prototype expressions for mapping the previous Examples 1 and 3 are as follows:

Example 1

$$\text{MAP} \equiv \text{TNAME} \equiv \text{SNAME} \quad \text{WRT}$$
$$\text{SOURCE INTO @ OTN @ OSN WRT}$$
$$\text{TARGET} \quad \text{RELATING} \quad \{\equiv \text{RE-}$$
$$\text{CEIVE} \equiv \text{GIVE}\} \text{ TO } [\equiv \text{NIL}]$$

⟨Q⟩   → MAP ⟨DE⟩ WRT ⟨SCH⟩ | MAP ⟨DE⟩ WRT ⟨SCH⟩
            RELATING ⟨R⟩   (command)
⟨DE⟩   → ⟨DE$_1$⟩ ⟨DE⟩ ⟨DE$_2$⟩ | ⟨DE$_1$⟩ WRT ⟨SCH⟩ INTO ⟨DE$_2$⟩ |
            ⟨DE$_1$⟩ FOR ⟨COND⟩ WRT ⟨SCH⟩ INTO ⟨DE$_2$⟩   (data expr.)
⟨DE$_1$⟩   → ≡ ⟨ARG⟩
⟨DE$_2$⟩   → ⟨DE$_3$⟩
⟨DE$_3$⟩   → @ ⟨A$_7$⟩
⟨SCH⟩   → schema name   (schema)
⟨R⟩   → {⟨R$_0$⟩} ⟨R⟩ [⟨R$_0$⟩] | {⟨R$_0$⟩} TO [⟨R$_0$⟩]   (relationships)
⟨R$_0$⟩   → ⟨R$_1$⟩
⟨R$_1$⟩   → ⟨R$_1$⟩ ≡ ⟨SET⟩ | ≡ ⟨SET⟩
⟨SET⟩   → set name
⟨COND⟩   → ⟨CC⟩
⟨CC⟩   → ⟨CE⟩ | ⟨CE⟩ ∧ ⟨CC⟩   (cond. clause)
⟨CE⟩   → ⟨A$_1$⟩ ⟨REL⟩ ⟨A$_0$⟩ | (⟨LE⟩)   (cond. expr.)
⟨LE⟩   → ⟨LE$_0$⟩   (logical expr.)
⟨LE$_0$⟩   → ⟨LE$_0$⟩ ∨ ⟨LE$_1$⟩ | ⟨LE$_1$⟩
⟨LE$_1$⟩   → ⟨LE$_2$⟩
⟨LE$_2$⟩   → ⟨LE$_2$⟩ ∧ ⟨LE$_3$⟩ | ⟨LE$_3$⟩
⟨LE$_3$⟩   → ⟨LE$_4$⟩
⟨LE$_4$⟩   → ¬ ⟨LE$_4$⟩ | (⟨CE⟩)
⟨REL⟩   → = | ≠ | < | ≤ | > | ≥   (relational ops.)
⟨ARG⟩   → ⟨A$_0$⟩   (argument)
⟨A$_0$⟩   → ⟨A$_1$⟩   (arith. expr.)
⟨A$_1$⟩   → ⟨A$_1$⟩ + ⟨A$_2$⟩ | ⟨A$_1$⟩ − ⟨A$_2$⟩ | ⟨A$_2$⟩
⟨A$_2$⟩   → ⟨A$_3$⟩
⟨A$_3$⟩   → ⟨A$_3$⟩ * ⟨A$_4$⟩ | ⟨A$_3$⟩ / ⟨A$_4$⟩ | ⟨A$_4$⟩
⟨A$_4$⟩   → ⟨A$_5$⟩
⟨A$_5$⟩   → ⟨A$_5$⟩ ↑ ⟨A$_6$⟩ | ⟨A$_6$⟩
⟨A$_6$⟩   → ⟨UF⟩ ⟨A$_6$⟩ | ⟨A$_7$⟩
⟨UF⟩   → SIN | COS | TAN | ASIN | ACOS | ATAN | ALOG |
            ALOG10 | EXP | SQRT | AVE | MAX | MIN | NUMB |
            SUM   (functions)
⟨A$_7$⟩   → data items | constants | ⟨LA⟩ ⟨RP⟩
⟨LA⟩   → (⟨A$_0$⟩   (left paren)
⟨RP⟩   →)   (right paren)

Fig. 10.4. Productions of the prototype grammar. Symbols enclosed in <> are the
nonterminals of the grammar; the rest are terminal symbols. The vertical lines represent
alternatives.

Example 3

MAP≡PNAME≡PSAL≡GNAME
≡GSAL≡CNAME≡SNUM   WRT
SOURCE INTO @ INAME @ ISAL @
INAME   @   ISAL   @   NAMC   @
NUMS   WRT   TARGET   RELA-
TING   {≡PT≡TP}{≡GT≡TG}{≡SUP-
ERVISE}{≡SPLIT} TO [≡TEACH][≡
TEACH][≡SPRV] [≡DIVIDE]

Clearly, transformations are needed to make this language accessible to users.

The simplest transformation to apply to the prototype language is the removal of the symbols $\equiv$ and @ from the language. This is possible, since the meaning of the resulting phrases can be deduced directly from the context of the expression. Another transformation would allow the map statement to be expressed in a much freer form. For example, the new form might allow a construction such as

MAP $e_1, \ldots, e_N, r_1, \ldots, r_M$ WRT S1 INTO $d_1, \ldots, d_N, R_1, \ldots, R_M$ WRT S2

where e_1 is a source expression, r_1 is a source relationship group, d_1 is a target data item, and R_i is a target relationship group. The form of this expression is (MAP) $e^N r^M$ (WRT S1 INTO) $d^N R^M$ (WRT S2), which clearly defines a context-sensitive language [1]. Another feature of the transformation would allow the conditional FOR clause to be split up into several clauses, each being allowed to occur anywhere in the statement.

It is usually clear from context that if two conditional expressions are written down together, then both must be satisfied. Thus a transformation can be introduced to eliminate the operator in conditional expressions. Also, noise words (i.e., words that add no meaning to the expression), such as THE and AND, can be added to mapping language statements without any difficulty. These are just examples of the kinds of transformations that can be defined.

Because of the complex nature of the transformational language, it is virtually impossible to characterize the language in a standard form, such as a BNF definition. We can, however, present the language in terms of examples of its use. One possible realization of three of the mapping examples described earlier is as follows:

Example 1

Map the TNAME and SNAME items, plus relationships RECEIVE and GIVE of SOURCE, into OTN and STN of TARGET

Example 2

Map OTN STN TARGET into TNAME SNAME RECEIVE GIVE SOURCE.

Example 3

Taking SOURCE to TARGET, map PNAME to INAME, GNAME to INAME, PSAL to ISAL, GSAL to ISAL, CNAME to NAMC, and SNUM to NUMS, relating PT and TP to TEACH, GT and TG to TEACH, SUPERVISE to SPRV and SPLIT to DIVIDE

A clear advantage of transformational grammars is that new transformations can be added to the language without changing the underlying structure. In terms of computer implementation, this feature is very important. New code, representing the new transformation, can be added to the problem processor without modifying the previously existing routines. In this way, the mapping language can grow and develop in step with the needs of its users.

10.11.3 The Mapping of Relationships

The specification of relationships in GML parallels the development discussed in Chapter 8. The problem is compounded by the need to specify relationships in both the source and target data structures. The user may choose to specify the cosets in the mapping command.

However, the PPS can also guide the user through the relationship specification. This processing can be viewed as a special kind of inverse transformation on the surface structure. The actual transformation would take a deep structure language expression and remove all or part of the relationship information in the expression. In effect, the transformation is acting like a projection of a deep structure expression into a surface structure having no relationships. The inverse of the projection cannot be computed directly without additional information. In this case, the additional information must be supplied by the user.

We now show sample dialogues for each of the maps presented for Examples 1 and 3. The mapping statements are reformulated without using relationships. The processor's statements are given on the left side of the page, the users responses on the right.

Example 1
   MAP TNAME, SNAME wrt SOURCE into OTN, OSN wrt TARGET
   Would you please
   provide the relationships?   NO

Choose how OTN and OSN should be related:
   1: TEACHER advises STUDENT
   2: TEACHER gives GRADE,
       STUDENT receives GRADE   2

Example 3
   MAP PNAME, PSAL, GNAME, GSAL, CNAME, SNUM of
   SOURCE into INAME, ISAL, INAME, ISAL, NAMC, NUMS of
   TARGET
   Would you please
   provide the relationships?   NO

Choose how INST and COUR should be related (through SPRV):
For PROFESSOR:
    1: PROFESSOR supervises COURSES
    2: PROFESSOR has LINK1,
        SECTION has LINK1,
        COURSES split into SECTIONS   1
For GRAD.INST
    1: GRAD.INST has LINK2,
        SECTION has LINK2
        PROFESSOR has LINK1,
        PROFESSOR supervises COURSES
    2: GRAD.INST has LINK2,
        SECTION has LINK2,
        COURSES split into SECTIONS   No relationship

Choose how INST and SECT should be related (through TEACH):
For PROFESSOR:
    1: PROFESSOR has LINK1,
        SECTION has LINK1
    2: PROFESSOR supervises COURSES,
        COURSES split into SECTIONS   1
For GRAD.INST
    1: GRAD.INST has LINK2,
        SECTION has LINK2   1

Choose how COUR and SECT should be related (through DIVIDE):
    1: PROFESSOR supervises COURSE,
        PROFESSOR has LINK1,
        SECTION has LINK1
    2: COURSE splits into SECTIONS   2

Note that zero, one, or more relationships can be chosen by the user at any stage of the processing. This is why even when unique relationships exist between record types, as is the case above between GRAD.INST and SECTION, the opportunity for choice must be presented to the user, since "no relationship" is a valid response. Further, it would be desirable to replace the clumsy construction PROFESSOR has LINK1, SECTION has LINK1 with something like PROFESSOR TEACHES SECTION. Here the superrelationship TEACHES is composed of the two binary relationships TP and PT. The same construction would apply for relationships GT, TS.

When the source and target data bases are both very large, the automatic relationship determination process can become quite lengthy and involved. Relationship chains can become so long that a user presented with the chains would still find it difficult to choose among them. In this case, the total relationships can be gradually unfolded, several steps at a time, until the full chain is decided on. The effect is similar to the application of a branch and bound procedure on the generation of nodes in a decision tree, except that here the heuristic evaluation function is determined by user interaction.

This same kind of interactive inverse projection transformation can be used for other missing deep-structure language elements. In particular, a user might forget to, or choose not to, include either the SOURCE, or TARGET, or both schema names in the statement of a mapping function. Such a user would be asked to supply them; if unable to do so, the user would be prompted to choose among all schemata known to the data base system.

10.11.4   Other Views of Mapping

Several recent papers have appeared discussing aspects of the mapping problems. Two of these are discussed in this section and compared to the proposed language in terms of capability and usefulness.

Shu *et al.* have defined a mapping language CONVERT [12]. Although the language is designed to operate primarily on tree schemata, full network capability is possible via a relational "join" operation. The CONVERT language maps data organized according to a tree schema into a data base that is also defined in terms of a treelike logical structure and includes computational facilities similar to those described earlier.

The following example has been adapted from Shu *et al.* [12]. Consider the mapping problem defined in Fig. 10.5. In the target data base, the SUPPORT records are employees with no educational degrees, the SR records are employees with their first degree earned 15 or fewer years ago, and the SC records are for employees who earned their first degree more than 15 years ago. The required CONVERT statements to perform this mapping are as follows:

```
IEMP(D#,E#,ENAME, SEX, DYR)
←CASE(EMP.EDUC.DEG=NULL OTHERS)
   GRAFT(SELECT(E#,ENAME, SEX, 0 FROM EMP)
   ONTO DEPT (D#,E#):DEPT.E#=EMP.E#),
   GRAFT(SELECT(E#,ENAME, SEX, MIN(EMP.
   EDUC.YR FOR UNIQUE EMP.E#)
   FROM EMP) ONTO DEPT(D#,E#):DEPT,E#
   =EMP.E#));

SUP←SELECT (D#,E#,ENAME, SEX FROM IEMP:
   IEMP.DYR = 0);
```

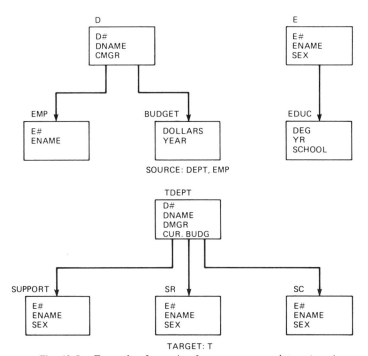

Fig. 10.5.   Example of mapping from two sources into a target.

TSR←SELECT(D#,E#,ENAME, SEX FROM IEMP:
  IEMP.DYR≠ 0 AND 1980-IEMP.DYR>15);

TSC←SELECT (D#,E#, ENAME, SEX FROM IEMP:
  1980-IEMP.DYR≦15);

TDEPT(D#,DNAME, DMGR, CUR.BUDG)
←SELECT(D#,DNAME, DMGR, DOLLARS FROM
DEPT:
  DEPT.BUDGET.YEAR= 1974);

T←GRAFT(SUP,TSR,TSC ONTO DEPT:TDEPT.D#
  PREVAIL SUP.D#,TSR.D#,TSC.D#);

The first statement determines the proper educational classification for each employee. The next three divide these classes into separate forms (record types). The final two copy the departmental information and the last one unifies all the separate forms.

The proposed generalized mapping language statements for performing the map are as follows:

MAP D# DNAME DMGR DOLLARS FOR YEAR=1980 WRT SOURCE INTO D#
DNAME DMGR CUR.BUDG WRT TARGET

MAP D#, EMP.E#, E.ENAME, E.SEX FOR EMP.E# = E.E.#, NUMBER OF DEG=0
WRT SOURCE INTO D#, SUPPORT.E#, SUPPORT.ENAME, SUPPORT.SEX
WRT TARGET

MAP D#, EMP.E#, E.ENAME, E.SEX FOR EMP.E# = E.E.#, MIN YR≤1965 WRT
SOURCE INTO D#, SR.E#, SR.ENAME, SR.SEX WRT TARGET

MAP D#, EMP.E#, E.ENAME, E.SEX FOR EMP.E# = E.E.#, MIN YR≥1965 WRT
SOURCE INTO D#, SC.E#, SC.ENAME, SC.SEX WRT TARGET

There are several points to notice in this example. First, the CON-
VERT language is much more procedural than the mapping language. A
user of CONVERT must pay much more attention to details that do not
have a direct bearing on the map, such as the definition and manipulation
of intermediate data structures. Further, the specification of the language
does not suggest general implementation algorithms. Moreover, the introduction of network data structures would necessitate in CONVERT the
introduction of new operators, such as SLICE and CONSOLIDATE [12],
whereas no such constructions are necessary in the generalized mapping
language.

In another approach to mapping, Navathe and Fry [10] define and
classify the operations that restructuring functions must include. Again,
their work is directed toward treelike data bases, although the classifications can be applied to network structures also. Mapping operations are
classified in three groups: naming, grouping, and relating. Three levels of
abstraction are considered: the schema level, the instance level, and the
value level.

The proposed generalized mapping language includes all the operations defined by Navathe and Fry [10]. Consider, first of all, the schema
level operations. Renaming the data, compression of record types, expansion of record types have all been demonstrated in the preceding examples. Grouping operations that involve the combining of data items from
various record types have also been used in the examples. The relating
operations are implemented by the relationship determination process.
Similarly, the generalized mapping language satisfies all the criteria of the
other two levels of abstraction.

10.11.5   Uses of a Mapping Language within a DSS

Several uses of a mapping language within a decision support system
were alluded to in Section 10.10. These are now reexamined in the light of
the foregoing mapping language discussion. Notice, first of all, that the
retrieval language presented in Chapter 8 is functionally a special case of
the mapping language. That is, the retrieval statement "DISPLAY data
items FOR conditions" has the same effect as the mapping statement:

MAP data items FOR conditions WRT DATA-BASE INTO data items WRT OUTPUT-FILE. The implication is that the mapping language could serve as a DSS language system, with the mapping processor being included in the PPS. Notice that the "DISPLAY" statement could be used with the mapping processor by means of a straightforward inverse transformation that takes it into the "deeper" "MAP" statement.

Inclusion of the mapping processor in a PPS provides other (than retrieval) interesting possibilities without a need for any additional software. These possibilities are not of immediate interest to the system's user, but rather to the system's designer and administrator. For the administrator, the tasks of data base loading and restructuring are greatly simplified. For the designer, the mapping processor offers a method for information transferral within a distributed data base system and a method for handling intermodule communication. All these possibilities are furnished by the same software.

As discussed in Chapter 8, data base loading is customarily accomplished by writing DML programs. A DML load program is a procedural specification of how the data, organized according to some record type (i.e., some file) or possibly organized according to some linear structure (e.g., in a header-detail file), is reorganized into a network data base. So, conceptually, loading is a kind of expansion mapping and it can therefore be operationally realized in terms of mapping statements. The input file containing data to be loaded is the source, the data base is the target, and the entire loading process is governed by a nonprocedural mapping statement.

The issue of restructuring was also addressed in Chapter 8. Conceptually, restructuring entails the mapping of data organized according to the current network schema into a data base organized according to a restructured schema. Certain data manipulation languages allow this restructuring to be dynamic, albeit procedural. Nonprocedural, dynamic restructuring can be accomplished via mapping statements in which the current data base is the source and the restructured schema defines the target. If the restructuring involves the introduction of new data item types for which there are no corresponding data item types in the source, then null data item types are mapped into the new target data item types. The result is an allocation of space for values of these new target item types in all affected record occurrences. The appropriate values can then be loaded as indicated in the preceding paragraph.

We turn now to the usage of the mapping language to accomplish information transferral within a logically distributed data base. The phrase "logical distribution" indicates a situation in which administrators in various locales are responsible for the creation and maintenance of their own local portions of a global data base, but a user in one locale can access data maintained at another locale. Situations of this variety could arise on any of a variety of machine configurations (e.g., Asenhurst and Vonderoke [2], Canady *et al.* [7], Farber [8]). Local data bases may or may not be situated on the same hardware. They may or may not use words of the same size or the same character codes. We shall examine the distribution strictly from the logical angle; resolving physical or hardware incompatibilities at the implementation level is not addressed here (see Anderson *et al.* [3] and Schneider [11]). Rather, the focus is on how the mapping language can be used to resolve incompatibilities in the schemata of various locales.

There are several potential sources of interlocale disparities. One is the usage of different data base management systems. We shall assume that all local data bases within a global data base use the same data base system (i.e., all use the same DDL and the same DML). If there are hardware disparities within the global context, then the data base management system used must be largely machine independent. Either the DBMS is implemented in a language compilable on all of the involved hardware or several implementations of the DBMS exist (e.g., TOTAL), each one tailored to specific hardware. The disparity of principal interest here consists of interlocale differences in logical structure.

There are four classes of data base distribution [6], differentiated in terms of the stability and uniformity of local schemata. With respect to stability, static schemata do not change over some time horizon, whereas volatile structures do change. There is structural uniformity if every locale adopts the same schemata, and there is nonuniformity if they do not. The four classes of distribution are as follows:

(1) static and uniform schemata,
(2) static but nonuniform schemata,
(3) volatile but uniform schemata, and
(4) volatile and nonuniform schemata.

Methods for using the mapping language and processor to accommodate each of these situations are explored in [6]. The basic approach involves mappings in which the target data base's schema is a subschema mask of the user's local data base. The source is some other local data base(s).

An important question is, "Who is the user of the mapping language?" The user may be the decision maker, who knows (or is told by the DSS) that the desired data are in another locale. Alternatively, a PPS with greater problem recognition capabilities may recognize the desired source data base(s) without being explicitly told what it is; that is, the decision maker may be unaware of the distributed nature of the knowledge system.

As discussed in earlier chapters, the user may be a module, requiring information from the KS. Observe that there are two ways to use mapping in this situation. One involves embedding mapping statements within the module code. The other, more flexible, approach is to have the PPS map information from the data base into a temporary "data base" having the schema expected by the module's input statements. This approach is more flexible in that it permits the module to be executed with data from different sources on different occasions. It does, however, require greater "intelligence" on the part of the PPS, which must determine which of the sources is appropriate on a given occasion.

In addition to its potential for aiding the DSS builder in designing a module–data base interface approach, the mapping language is also potentially useful in designing an approach to handling the intermodule interfaces within a formulated model. Suppose that module B needs information from module A before it can execute. If the output schema of module A is the same as the input schema of module B, then there is relatively little difficulty in message passing between these two information processors.

If the schemata do not match (i.e., the two information processors do not "speak" the same language), then the problem of message passing becomes more difficult. The information from A must be translated into a form that is palatable to B. Conceptually, some mapping must take place. The mapping language and processor provide a basis for operationalizing this mapping task. The output of module A is the source data base and the target data base is used as input to module B. The mapping is carried out after the execution of module A and before the execution of module B. The mapping statement for interfacing a pair of modules could be stored by the DSS designer in the KS, so that the PPS can access it as needed.

In summary, it appears that general mapping languages (and their processors) can be usefully applied within a DSS context. From the foregoing discussion, it should be clear that there is room for more research on mapping and on how to utilize it within decision support systems.

10.20   DATA BASE EXTENSIONS

In the last chapter we saw that it is advisable to retain modules in the KS in order to protect the generality of the PPS. If the KS is a data base, then the question arises of how to use data base techniques to store modules. Data bases have customarily been used to hold empirical and computed knowledge. In the remainder of this chapter we shall see how the well-known data base constructs can be used for the storage of procedural knowledge. The discussion is based on ideas contained in Bonczek *et al.* [5]. As a starting point it is shown how the data base constructs can be used in a novel way to introduce numerous levels of abstraction into a data base.

10.21 Abstraction Levels

Remember that conceptually, definitional relationships can represent a world in which there are concepts that have additional concepts as instantiations, and where these additional concepts have still other concepts as instantiations—and so forth. Traditional data base management is not sufficiently sophisticated to operationalize these conceptual possibilities in a straightforward, unambiguous manner. We have seen that a record type and its occurrence is an operationalization of a definitional relationship between two levels of concepts. But in traditional data base management there are only two levels of abstraction: the record type and its record occurrence (the logical structure and the data base itself). Note that it is the definitional relationship that establishes the connection between these two levels of abstraction.

10.21.1 Record Types That Are Also Record Occurrences

In this section we shall see how to extend the representative power of traditional data base management, to permit the operational representation of many levels of abstraction. The approach taken involves no operational constructs beyond those already introduced. All that is needed is a slight modification of the way in which they are used: A record occurrence is allowed to be a record type, having occurrences of its own. In other words, we allow a record type to be treated as a record occurrence of another (more abstract) record type that exists on a higher level of abstraction. The latter record type is referred to as a higher-level record type with respect to the former.

This feature of multiple data base abstraction levels allows a *given* record type to be considered as being both

(1) relatively abstract with respect to its occurrences, and

(2) relatively concrete with respect to the record type of which it is an occurrence.

This added data base structuring capability mirrors conceptual representations of the world, where there are various levels of abstraction. A formal description of the abstraction level feature appears in Bonczek *et al.* [5]. (In Bonczek *et al.* [5] abstraction levels are referred to as levels of "resolution.") Observe that the way in which cosets are used is unchanged. A coset is still a named 1–*N* relationship between two record types.

The abstraction level feature can be illustrated through the following example drawn from Winograd [14]. Consider data about cars, where it is desired to capture the relationship of specific weights and specific colors with specific cars. It is further desired to capture the fact that color and weight are properties of cars. Notice that 'color' is a concept that has instantiations (e.g., 'red', 'blue', etc.); operationally, COLOR is a record type as shown in Fig. 10.6a. Also note that 'property' is a concept that has instantiations, one of which is 'color'. Thus, operationally, we treat PROPERTY as a record type and 'COLOR' as one of its occurrences (see Fig. 10.6b). Thus COLOR is both a record type and a record occurrence.

Figure 10.7 shows the three levels of abstraction for the preceding example. The 'red', 'blue', '1 ton', '2 ton', and 'car 1', 'car 2', and 'car 3' concepts are operationalized on the lowest level of abstraction within the data base: level 1. The 'car', 'color', and 'weight' concepts are operationalized on abstraction level 2; each has instantiations that give occurrences on level 1. Some record types of level 2 are also record occurrences with respect to a higher level of abstraction. The 'most abstract' concept is 'property' and it is operationalized on level 3.

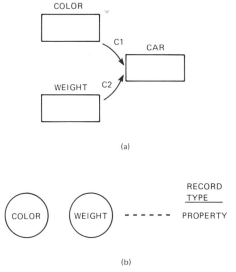

Fig. 10.6. COLOR as a record type and a record occurrence.

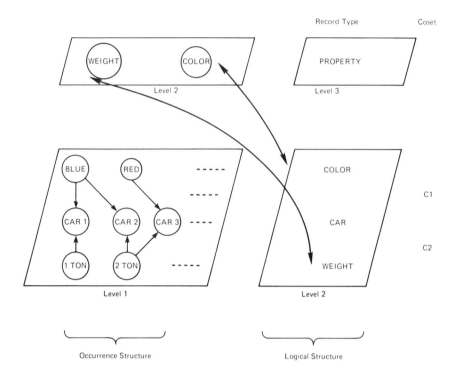

Fig. 10.7. Three abstraction levels.

In general, the most abstract data base level consists of record types only. The most concrete level consists of record occurrences only. Intermediate abstraction levels are composed of record types, one or more of which are also record occurrences. Level 1 information, then, is related to level 3 information by means of those level 2 entities that display the characteristics both of types and of occurrences. These Janus-faced entities are concrete in one context (i.e., relative to higher levels) and abstract in another context (i.e., relative to lower levels). They look both upward and downward in the multilevel network.

Of course, cosets and/or coset occurrences are still used to establish "horizontal" relationships on a level of abstraction. On the highest abstraction level, cosets are used. Coset occurrences are used on the lowest level. Either or both may be used on intermediate levels. Furthermore, it is possible to declare cosets in which the two participating record types are from different levels of abstraction, providing there is a meaningful associative relationship between the two corresponding concepts.

10.21.2   Value of Multilevel Networks

The reader may have noticed that it would be possible to squeeze a conceptual representation containing many levels of abstraction into an operational representation having only the two traditional abstraction levels. The approach would be to operationalize some of the definitional relationships with cosets. An example, using the preceding car information, is shown in Fig. 10.8. All definitional relationships except those between the two lowest levels of abstraction are represented by cosets (S1 and S2). The result is a data base having only the two traditional levels of abstraction. A disadvantage of this approach of squeezing three (or more) conceptual levels of abstraction into two levels is that we are forced to use two distinct methods (the coset and the record type–occurrence dichotomy) to operationalize a single kind of relationship (i.e., definitional).

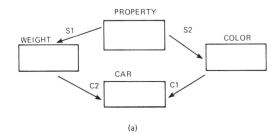

(a)

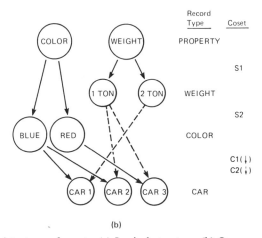

(b)

Fig. 10.8.   Inconsistent use of cosets. (a) Logical structure. (b) Occurrence structure.

Observe that such an approach compromises the semantic integrity of the coset construct and this can necessitate asymmetric processing. Recall that the coset was reserved for operationalizing an associative connection among concepts. It was not reserved for operationalizing the definitional relationship between a concept and its instantiations. Using the coset in both ways leads to two incongruities: First, a single operational construct would be used to denote two semantically distinct kinds of conceptual relationships; and second, a single kind of conceptual relationship (the definitional) would be *required* to be operationally denoted in two different ways. These incongruities are not inherent in the information to be stored. They are forced on the data base designer by limitations inherent in traditional network notation. The desirability, practicality, and reasonableness of such a practice are questionable. The data base extension described in the previous section does not suffer from these incongruities.

Suppose that a data base is to be used as the KS of a DSS whose generalized problem processor ventures beyond mere retrieval and update. This processor's value derives from its capacity systematically to discern the semantics of what it perceives. Thus the semantics of one construct should be distinct from the semantics of another construct. As Woods [15] has pointed out, there is an important semantic distinction between exemplifying or defining a concept on one hand, and specifying a structural or functional relationship (association) between that concept and another concept on the other hand. This distinction leads to different processing requirements, because of the different semantics. In the next section, the preceding distinction becomes even more significant as the topic of representing modules within a data base is discussed.

Another advantage of the multilevel network over the traditional two-level network is that the former requires fewer cosets. This can lead to implementation efficiencies. Contrast Fig. 10.7 with Fig. 10.8b. Notice that both methods use four record types and, correspondingly, they necessitate identical numbers of record occurrences. However, the traditional approach uses four cosets, whereas the multilevel approach needs only two. These additional cosets require the storage of additional pointers, which are not needed in the multilevel approach. A straightforward implementation of the multilevel approach is to store the record type and record occurrence information of a Janus-faced entity in essentially the same location. Not only does this result in storage savings relative to the traditional two-level network, but it also results in access that is no less efficient (by virtue of the smaller number of cosets to be traversed). These advantages become more important as the number of abstraction levels increases.

We close this section by pointing out the correspondence between a multilevel network and the "generalization abstraction" for relational data bases, as proposed by Smith and Smith [13]. They maintain that 'generalization' is "perhaps the most important mechanism we have for conceptualizing the real world."

10.22 Representation of Models with Data Base Constructs

One method for incorporating models into a data base treats each module as a record occurrence. These occurrences can be partitioned into groups according to the types of information-processing tasks they perform. Modules that perform the same type of processing task (i.e., solve the same problem) constitute occurrences of a record type. The record type is indicated by the task performed (i.e., by the problem solved). Although these modules perform the same type of task (producing the same types of outputs), they differ in their processing methods, their problem-solving approaches, and, perhaps, their input requirements. One module may give a different solution from another module in the same group, though both modules attack the same problem (the same type of information-processing task).

Modules that are occurrences of some record type define alternative ways for addressing the information-processing problem represented by that record type. For example, several modules, each of which performs regression, differ in the solution algorithms employed. Each module may be viewed as an alternative for defining regression; each gives a solution to a regression problem. Or suppose that there are several alternatives to estimate, or define the concept of, the cost of a water treatment facility. Each cost module is treated as an occurrence of a cost record type.

The record type–record occurrence constructs provide a straightforward mechanism for representing information-processing roles that can be performed by other roles. The most concrete roles (the modules of code) exist at the lowest level of data base abstraction. More abstract information-processing roles exist on higher levels.

Construction and execution of a desired model is based on *modifying* and *combining* various known information-processing roles. The occurrence structure of a multilevel network can implicitly store knowledge of allowable modifications and combinations. Using the described module storage method, allowable modifications (redefinitions) of an information-processing role are inherent in networks' abstraction levels. Allowable combinations (associations) among information-processing roles can be implicitly represented by cosets. An elaboration follows.

There may be many ways to define the notion of total cost (TC); the TC information-processing role, or concept, is modifiable in context with its utilization. We propose that alternative definitions of a concept be treated as occurrences of the record type for that concept. There may be numerous levels of conceptual abstraction. If there are n ways to define total cost, then there may (on a different level) be alternative ways to define each of these n. In Chapter 2 we said a role may be capable of being performed by other roles, themselves capable of being performed by yet other roles. The conceptual levels of abstraction, *vis-à-vis* information-processing roles, are operationalized as a data base abstraction level by using the approach outlined. The result is a single structural technique (the record type–record occurrence relationship) implicitly used to represent allowable modifications of information-processing roles.

Another structural technique, using cosets, can represent allowable combinations of information-processing roles. Figure 10.9 contains a simple example. Here the USES coset indicates the association between the TC information-processing task and the elementary cost (EC) information-processing task. On level 2, TC1 *uses* EC1 and EC2. TC1 is solved if EC1 and EC2 are solved.

The occurrences of TC and EC may or may not be modules. For

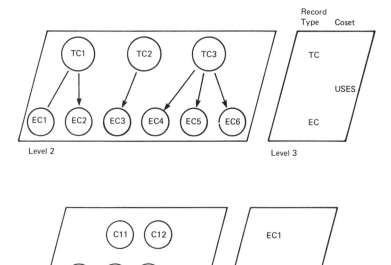

Fig. 10.9. Multiple abstraction levels for modeling information.

instance, TC1 may or may not have occurrences on a lower level of abstraction. It does not in Fig. 10.9. On the other hand, EC2 does have occurrences (C21, C22, C23) on level 1. These occurrences designate modules and are on the lowest abstraction level. The module may be a program module or a mental module.

If it is a program module, the code need not be stored in the record occurrence. The record occurrence could consist of the module name, a description of its problem-solving performance, data concerning the size of the module code, and a method to obtain the module code for execution. This code may even exist in a different computer system. The occurrence could also indicate how to instigate the module's execution and obtain its results from some other computer system. This alternate approach could utilize the mapping language.

If the module designated by an occurrence at the lowest level of abstraction is a mental module, then there is no code involved. The information-processing task is performed mentally and the occurrence must indicate how to contact the person (or group) that executes the task. The mental modules feature allows construction of models that are not entirely formal, as well as allowing the use of nonformalized, subjective problem solving combined with formal problem solving.

Further research will be needed to formulate a detailed implementation of models represented in a data base fashion particularly when some modules are nonformal, as well as when some program modules exist in other computer systems. However, the foregoing approach does provide for unambiguous model representation. This incorporation amounts to a statement of all models that can be used by a decision support system to answer user queries. Any record occurrence defines a problem. By looking at its occurrences—if any—and the coset occurrence(s) it owns—if any—we have a model(s) that can give the solution to the problem. In Fig. 10.9 EC4 can be used by another problem solver (TC3), or it can be used on a stand-alone basis, solving the EC4 problem alone.

All models are implicit, but unambiguously represented, in the multilevel network structure. Let us try to squeeze the models of Fig. 10.9 into a data base having only the two traditional levels of abstraction. This can be accomplished by the logical structure (see Fig. 10.10). From the perspective of the PPS, though, this structure is ambiguous, since a single construct (the coset) is used to represent information about both the modification and the combination of information-processing tasks. The relationship between TC and EC is associative; it describes how their instantiations can be meaningfully combined. The relationship between EC and C (although represented by an identical operational construct) is definitional. Instances of C are alternatives for defining an instance of EC; they are the ways instances of EC can be filled (i.e., modified) during the construction of a model.

Forced structural ambiguity leads to asymmetric processing. If a PPS is to be involved in model formulation, it must be able to distinguish the two activities of (1) choosing an alternative definition of a problem solver and (2) combining problem solvers. The PPS must process each activity differently. A straightforward method to permit discernment of the distinction is to operationalize each with a different technique, as in Fig. 10.9.

Forcing model representation into the limited, two-level data base (as in Fig. 10.10) requires the PPS to be able to process the same operational construct in two very different ways. It may also necessitate additional data storage to indicate how each coset is to be interpreted by the PPS. Conversely, since the approach illustrated in Fig. 10.10 must use two different operational constructs to represent the same type of concept (i.e., definitional relationship), the PPS must possess two different methods to discern a single kind of fact (i.e., the existence of a definitional relationship) from a data base of models.

One additional comment concerning the multilevel data base approach of model representation: In the example in Fig. 10.9, no occurrence of EC was used by more than one occurrence of TC. Suppose instead that an M–N relationship existed between EC and TC; that is, an instance of EC could be shared by several instances of TC. Such a situation is handled either by substituting an mm set for the USES coset or by the invention of an intervening record type (see Chapter 7 for a description).

If the second of these two treatments is adopted, it is interesting to consider storing intermodule maps in occurrences of the intervening record type. For either treatment, some directional indicator is needed so the PPS can determine which role is assisting and which role is assisted.

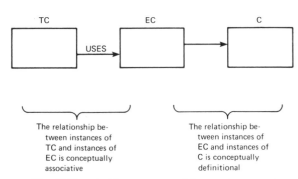

Fig. 10.10.   Ambiguous usage of the coset construct.

There is a possibility of recursion between occurrences of two record types—an issue for future research.

10.30 CONCLUSION

This chapter has emphasized directions for further research where decision support systems have data base knowledge systems. We have also provided at least skeletal descriptions of possible approaches to these research issues. Approaches are presented in a stimulating spirit; they are not final pronouncements.

Extensions, such as those discussed, make various enhancements to decision support systems possible; their capabilities are limited, though, because they all take a data base knowledge system as the starting point. Other interesting DSS enhancements become apparent when we look at schemes other than a data base for representing knowledge in a knowledge system. These are the subject of the final sections in this book. Part IV presents a DSS that uses a predicate calculus KS as its starting point. Part V shows how both data base techniques and predicate calculus expressions can be utilized in a KS and the consequent effect on problem-solving capabilities of the PPS.

REFERENCES

1. A. V. Aho and J. D. Ullman, "The Theory of Parsing, Translating and Compiling," Vol. 1. Prentice Hall, Englewood Cliffs, New Jersey, 1972.
2. R. L. Asenhurst and R. H. Vonderoke, A hierarchical network, *Datamation* (February 1975).
3. R. D. Anderson *et al.*, The data reconfiguration service—An experiment in adaptable process to process communication, *Proc. Symp. Problems in the Optimization of Data Commun. Syst.,* Palo Alto (October 1971).
4. R. H. Bonczek and A. B. Whinston, A generalized mapping language for network data structures, *Internat. J. Informat. Syst.* **2,** No. 2 (1977).
5. R. H. Bonczek, C. W. Holsapple, and A. B. Whinston, Design and implementation of an information base for decision makers, *Proc. Nat. Comput. Conf., Dallas* (1977).
6. R. H. Bonczek, C. W. Holsapple, and A. B. Whinston, Information transferral within a distributed data base via a generalized mapping language, *The Comput. J.* **21,** no. 2 (1978).
7. R. H. Canady, D. Harrison, E. L. Ivie, J. L. Ryder, and L. A. Wehr, A back-end computer for data base management, *Commun. ACM* (October 1974).
8. D. J. Farber, A ring network, *Datamation* (February 1975).
9. MDBS User's Manual, Micro Data Base Systems, Inc., Lafayette, Indiana.
10. S. B. Navathe and J. P. Fry, Restructuring for large data bases: Three levels of abstraction, *ACM Trans. Data Base Syst.* **1,** No. 1 (1975).

11. G. M. Schneider, DSCL—A data specification and conversion language for networks, *Proc. ACM SIGMOD Workshop, San Jose* (May, 1975).
12. N. C. Shu, B. C. Housel, and V. Y. Lum, CONVERT: A high level translation definition language for data conversion, *Commun. ACM* **18,** No. 10 (1975).
13. J. M. Smith and D. C. P. Smith, Database abstractions: Aggregation and generalization, *ACM Trans. Data Base Syst.* (June 1977).
14. T. Winograd, "Understanding Natural Language." Academic Press, New York, 1972.
15. W. A. Woods, What's in a link: Foundations for semantic networks, *in* "Representation and Understanding" (D. G. Bobrow and A. Collins, eds.). Academic Press, New York, 1975.

Part IV

FORMAL LOGIC APPROACH TO DECISION SUPPORT

Formal logic has its roots in antiquity. It is a powerful tool for modeling human thought processes. It allows for quite complex expressions to be constructed using a small set of operations. The parallel to general computer software should be evident.

There are many operationalizations of formal logic. The first-order predicate calculus presented here is one of the most widely used. The resolution form of proof theory presented in Chapter 12 is but one of many proof methodologies. The direct application of formal logic to decision support is made in Part V.

Chapter 11

THE LANGUAGE AND KNOWLEDGE SYSTEMS OF A DSS BASED ON FORMAL LOGIC

11.00 INTRODUCTORY REMARKS

As noted in Chapter 6, a blueprint (or schema) for organizing problem data is required in the construction of a knowledge system (KS) for a decision support system (DSS). The constructs for a (conceptual) schema may be complex, as in data base management, or they can be simple. It has been argued that a simple collection of schema constructs is "better" than its more complex counterpart in that deceptively complex data structures can be supported using direct combinations of the single schema constructs [1].

Formal logic is a well-known technique for expressing statements (or facts) about a problem domain. Its rules were understood in antiquity, the foremost example still extant being Euclid's *Elements* (ca. 320 B.C.). Formal logic has the additional property that its (operational) constructs are few in number and quite innocuous in appearance. That these simple constructs are sufficient for the formulation of the entire realm of mathematics demonstrates conclusively the richness available in formal logic.

This chapter presents formal logic in some detail. Unfortunately, this knowledge is not as widely known as it could be. For a complete treatment, the reader should consult any one of the many introductory texts on logic (e.g., Copi [3] and Kleene [5]). We begin with a discussion of the conceptual use of formal logic, followed by its operational counterpart, the predicate calculus. Finally, language system (LS) elements for formal logic are presented. The problem-processing system (PPS) for formal logic is described in Chapter 12.

11.10   CONCEPTUAL FRAMEWORK

Each of us believes that our existence is governed by logic. Logic is the basis for coherent speech, writing, and actions. It rules over all managerial processes, including the more abstract, as well as the mundane, aspects of decision making. We want to believe that our legislative and judicial bodies behave "logically." In short, logic is an important part of our everyday existence.

In order to formalize logic, it is necessary to examine so-called logical processes and extract from them whatever universal rules are in use. Operationally, this amounts to a determination of operands and operators germane to the logical process. Conceptually, the process of "logical thought" must be simulated in such a way that the underlying thought processes are visible and the whole is formally consistent.

Many individuals will not accept the concept of a formalization of logical thought processes. However, this is most often on nonmathematical grounds. These individuals fear exposure of not being "logical" in their decision-making processes. Others may avoid a formalization to shield biased or discriminatory decision making. These behavioral problems are discussed in Copi [3].

11.11   Axioms

The conceptual building block for formal logic is the *axiom*. The axiom represents a formalization of a statement, fact, or assertion that is germane to a particular problem area. The axiom is not atomic—it is composed of one or more operational constructs. However, at the conceptual level the axiom is treated as a single entity.

Our axioms have the additional property of being "true." If the statement "It is raining" is presented as an axiom, then we must accept it as a fact that indeed it is raining. There can be no recourse to empirical evidence when it comes to axioms. One can think of this usage of axioms as "hypothetical," in that they represent facts that can be empirically tested. Thus in situations where the axiom is empirically "true," the reasoning provided by formal logic will be "correct."

The concept of "truth" is very important in formal logic. It establishes the justification of formal logic: that the axioms are reasonable in their assertions. The statement "It is raining" may or may not be valid at a particular point in time. However, if it is taken as an axiom, then any reasoning that uses the axiom is valid only when the axiom itself is valid. Thus in logic we can make hypothetical arguments, whose axioms are subject to validation. But when the axioms have been validated, the reasoning will be correct.

Of course, establishing the truth of an axiom does *not* use formal logic in any way. Indeed this action is external to the process of formal logic, and independent of it as well. Similarly, reasoning via formal logic is also external to the (operational) constructs of logic. If we express our use of formal logic as a language, then the establishment of the truth of axioms, as well as reasoning with these axioms, must be done in a distinct language (called by some the metalanguage [5]).

11.12   Axiom Sets

Obviously, an axiom set is simply a collection of axioms. However, when dealing with more than one axiom simultaneously, it is possible to encounter contradictions. We say an axiom set is *consistent* if it contains no contradictions.

For example, consider the statements "It is raining" and "It is not raining". It is doubtful that any empirical evidence would support both of these statements as being "true" simultaneously. Thus any axiom set that contained both of these statements as axioms would not be consistent. The statements "It is raining" and "The sun is shining" can both be true simultaneously, and the axiom set consisting of just these two statements is consistent.

Unfortunately, consistency cannot be checked by examining only pairs of axioms. Consider the following three statements: "The Dow Jones Average is up 5 points", "The Standard & Poor's Average is down 7 points", and "The Dow Jones Average and the Standard & Poor's Average always move in the same direction". Assuming for a moment that all three of these statements have been established as "true," then each of the three possible pairs of axioms are consistent; but taking all three together, the axiom set is inconsistent.

In general, if an axiom set consists of n axioms, then there are $2^n - 1$

combinations of these axioms that must be checked for consistency. Of these, *n* consist of a single axiom, which, of course, corresponds to determining the validity of that particular axiom.

The importance of consistency is that from an inconsistent set of axioms *any* conclusion can be drawn. Thus concluding that "It is raining" from the three preceding stock market axioms is correct reasoning in formal logic. This is because our reasoning mechanism involves a "material implication" [3]. In other words, for an implication to be false (not true), the premises or antecedents must all be true, but the conclusion must be false.

A digression is in order here. The axiom "The Dow Jones Average and the Standard & Poor's Average always move in the same direction" is not one that most people consider as "true." In fact, it is only necessary to find a single day for which one rose and the other fell to establish that the statement is false. On the other hand, we might note that the statement is true 63% of the time. The temptation is to define a random variable X for the statement, with $P(X$ is true$) = .63$. This is *not* permissible in formal logic. Our logic is "two-valued"; i.e., a statement is either true or false (not true).

Some statements cannot be assigned a value of true or false. For example, a command such as "Buy 20 shares of AT&T at $50 a share" is in itself neither true nor false. However, it can be decomposed into different elements. One element is a statement whose truth value can be determined: "Some person or collection of persons is offering to sell 20 shares of AT&T at $50 or less per share". The other is an operator (cf. Chapters 5, 14): "Buy them!". This is similar to the operation of a state space system. This idea is expanded in Chapter 12.

11.13   Model Theory

Given a particular statement (which we denote by the letter B), we want to determine if B is a *valid consequence* of some axiom set $\{A_1, A_2, \ldots, A_n\}$. We say B is a valid consequence of $A_1, A_2, \ldots, A_n$ if B is "true" whenever the axioms $A_1, A_2, \ldots, A_n$ are *all* "true." The steps involved in determining whether or not a statement is a valid consequence of some axiom set is called a deduction (or proof).

Model theory is a particular deductive technique, which requires identifying all possible methods of making the axiom set "true" and then observing to see whether or not the statement being validated is true for every such method. As such, it is actually a facet of a problem-processing system for formal logic. However, it is useful for expository purposes to discuss this technique briefly here in its conceptual sense and in Section 11.25 in its operational sense.

An example will clarify the technique. Consider the following statement, plus three axioms that comprise the axiom set:

B: "Either it is cloudy, or I can paint the house".
A_1: "If it is raining, then it is cloudy".
A_2: "If it is cloudy, then I can't paint the house".
A_3: "Either it is raining, or I can paint the house".

Informally speaking, there are only two ways in which this axiom set can be made consistent, i.e., two methods for making the axiom set "true" (see Section 11.24 for formal details):

(1)   "It is raining, it is cloudy, and I can't paint the house".
(2)   "It is not raining, it is not cloudy, and I can paint the house".

In (1), "it is cloudy"; in (2) "I can paint the house". Thus in each case statement B will be true. Thus we can conclude that B is a valid consequence of axioms A_1, A_2, and A_3.

Model theory is usually presented as defining the various concepts of validity, consistency, and valid consequence. However, in a practical sense, model theory is computationally expensive, even in medium-sized applications (a dozen or more axioms).

11.14   Proof Theory

Proof theory uses a "rule of inference" to relate axioms and derived statements into a "proof." It invokes the same rules and forms as the logical statements on which it acts. Although best described in operational terms (see Chapter 12), some of the conceptual features can be noted here.

In proof theory a number of expressions are used repeatedly. These expressions are called *axiom schemata*. They represent the form (i.e., structure, syntax) of particular axioms. Instantiation of a particular axiom to an axiom schema, assuming that they are structurally equivalent, is necessary for the construction of a proof. The axiom schemata are useful in the creating of new axioms and axiom schemata by means of the inference process.

The single "rule of inference" that is used in proof theory is called in Latin *modus ponens,* which means affirmative method. It states that if A is either an axiom or inferred statement, and "If A, then B" is another axiom or inferred statement, then we can infer B as a "true" statement. In this rule, A and "If A, then B" is called the premise(s), and B is the conclusion.

For example, let A represent "It is raining" and B mean "It is cloudy". "If A, then B" is simply "If it is raining, then it is cloudy". The rule of inference allows us to conclude that "It is cloudy", when we assume "It is raining" and "If it is raining, then it is cloudy". This is, of course, what our innate common sense would dictate.

11.15   Learning

A proof (or deduction) involves a series of steps, using axiom schemata and the rule of inference, that begin with elements of the axiom set and terminate with the valid consequence desired. In cases where the axiom set is stable (not changing), this proof can be used to justify the creation of a new axiom schema and its inclusion in the axiom set. This learning process will prove useful whenever a similar result needs to be proven. In such a case, the new axiom schema can be applied directly, without necessitating the inference of all the intermediate steps.

There is an analogy here between a proof and a path through the data base. As stated in Chapter 9, a path search is a goal-oriented search through the data base schema to determine an ordering of the sets and record types that will provide the desired information (i.e., answer the user's query). A proof involves the same elements: a search to find appropriate axiom schemas on which to use the rule of inference; an ordering of these axiom schemata, axioms, and derived statements; and goal-directed processes. Here a goal is a desired valid consequence. Moreover, paths in the data base can be saved (learned), so that future processing will not have to invoke the path-finding processor. Similarly, proofs can be saved (learned), so that certain future processing need not invoke the goal-directed deductive processes.

11.20   OPERATIONAL CONSTRUCTS

The primary operational construct in formal logic is the predicate symbol. A predicate represents a concept, whose internal structure is of no importance or interest to the current application. As with data base management, the identification of such concepts is often a nontrivial task, in that many formalizations exist for a particular problem. The operational level of formal logic is usually called the *predicate calculus.*

Predicates are related by operators (functions). These operators can be composed to create predicate expressions of arbitrary complexity. Furthermore, in the predicate calculus concepts can be *quantified,* an operation with no correspondent in data base management. This term indicates that a concept is being treated not as a single occurrence, but as representing the set of all such occurrences. This new fact allows for incomplete statements of fact in formal logic, which are awkward, if not impossible, to represent in data base structures. For example, a statement like "Customer Jones places Order 1312" is easily captured in data base terms; but a statement such as "Some customer has placed Order 1312" is not. "Some customer" is a quantified instance of the concept "customer," and this kind of statement is very naturally represented in the predicate calculus.

Predicate calculus is a well-defined and universally accepted technique. The notations are more or less standard. Processing techniques have been mathematically established as "correct." Finally, the PPS for a predicate calculus based DSS provides a proof of correctness for each action it takes (an automatic audit trail).

11.21 Predicates

Traditionally, the predicate symbol is the lowest level of definition in the predicate calculus, i.e., no meaningful internal structure is assigned to predicate symbols. If P is a predicate symbol, then P represents a fact or idea that is indivisible. For example, P might represent the statement "Today is Sunday". We do not further analyze the structure of the statement (for the predicate calculus).

Predicate symbols may also occur with arguments, such as $Q(x)$ or $R(s,t,w)$. In predicate calculus there are two types of arguments: constants and variables. The set of constants in the application area being considered is called the *domain of discourse.* Often the domain of discourse is only implicitly specified in a given problem. Variables play the usual role of representing one or more of the allowable constants in the domain of discourse. We shall follow the usual convention of using uppercase letters for predicate symbols, lowercase from the beginning of the alphabet for constants (such as a, b, c), and lowercase letters from the end of the alphabet for variables (e.g., w, x, y). When describing real applications, both the predicate symbols and constants will reflect the terminology of the application, the context usually being sufficient to discriminate between them.

A predicate such as $Q(x)$ can be interpreted as stating "x has property

Q''. So, if the single-place predicate $M(x)$ is interpreted as "x is a model", then we might state the facts that "regression is a model" and "linear programming is a model" by M(regression) and M(linear programming). It should be clear that it is allowable for a predicate symbol to take on many different arguments as above. However, it is incorrect for predicate symbols to appear with a different number of arguments in the same application. So $P(a)$, $P(x)$, and P(simulation) are correct, whereas $T(a)$, $T(z,b)$, and T cannot appear together.

11.22   Predicate Symbols and Record Types

There is a direct correspondence between predicate symbols and record types in a data base. To see the correspondence, suppose that record type TRANSACTION has data items AMOUNT, DATE, and SALES-PERSON. An occurrence of this record type might have \$35.95 on 7/15/80 sold by Jones. Let us now define a predicate symbol $T(x,y,z)$, which we will interpet as "a transaction of \$$x$ on date y is made by salesperson z". The foregoing occurrence would then be represented simply as $T(35.95, 7/15/80, \text{Jones})$. Any record type can be treated in this way, along with its occurrences. This concept is further developed in Chapter 13.

However, the predicate calculus differs from the data base in its use of the occurrence information. The data base representation of information is achieved by the presence or absence of occurrences. In the predicate calculus, information is evaluated through a special function, called an interpretation.

11.23   Interpretations

An interpretation I is a function mapping all the instantiated predicate symbols that are defined for an application into a set consisting of the letters t and f; in symbols, I: {predicate symbols} $\rightarrow$ {t,f}. For example, suppose that P stands for "It is raining" and Q stands for "It is snowing." There are four possible interpretations of these two predicate symbols:

$$I_1(P) = t, \quad I_1(Q) = t, \quad I_2(P) = t, \quad I_2(Q) = f,$$
$$I_3(P) = f, \quad I_3(Q) = t, \quad I_4(P) = f, \quad I_4(Q) = f.$$

It is customary to interpret t as "true" and f as "false." Then interpretation I_1 says that both P and Q are true, i.e., "It is raining" and "It is snowing" are both true. I_2 says that it is raining but not snowing; etc. The situation is compounded when predicate symbols have arguments. Suppose that the domain of discourse consists of three constant terms: regression, simulation, and Mozart. Then if $M(x)$ is a predicate symbol, every interpretation must assign a value of t or f to each of M(regression), M(simulation), and M(Mozart). The readers should take the time to ascertain that there are eight ($=2^3$) possible interpretations of these three predicate expressions.

Which interpretation is "correct"? In predicate calculus, no facility exists for determining the correct interpretation. But to humans, often there is an interpretation that makes more or less "sense" than others. In the preceding example, we would seldom choose I_1 as correct, since only in rare instances does it rain and snow at the same time. Similarly, if $M(x)$ means "x is a model," then we would like to have M(regression) and M(simulation) be interpreted as true, whereas M(Mozart) should be false. If, however, $M(x)$ means "x is a musician", then we should like to select the opposite interpretation. But in doing this we have stepped beyond the boundaries of the predicate calculus. The problem is one of context. The value of M(Mozart) ("true" or "false") is only relevant in the context of how that predicate expression is used.

11.24   Predicate Operators

Thus we are led to consider operations on predicate expressions. The basic data base operation was relating occurrences via cosets. Predicate calculus contains four binary operators and one unary operator. These are as follows:

Symbol	Operation	English rendering
↔	Equivalence	$P \leftrightarrow Q$ is read as: P is equivalent to Q
⇒	Implication	$P \Rightarrow Q$ is read as: P implies Q
∧	Conjunction	$P \wedge Q$ is read as: P and Q
∨	Disjunction	$P \vee Q$ is read as: P or Q
~	Negation	$\sim P$ is read as: not P

The five operators are actually functions mapping the predicate expressions and their interpretations into $\{t,f\}$. The operators are defined by the following tables (often called truth tables):

$P \leftrightarrow Q$	$I(P) = t$	f
$I(Q) = t$	t	f
f	f	t

$P \Rightarrow Q$	$I(P) = t$	f
$I(Q) = t$	t	t
f	f	t

$P \wedge Q$	$I(P) = t$	f
$I(Q) = t$	t	f
f	f	f

$P \vee Q$	$I(P) = t$	f
$I(Q) = t$	t	t
f	t	f

$\sim P$	$I(P) = t$	f
	f	t

The tables can be read as follows: Take for example ↔. If $I(P) = t$ and $I(Q) = t$, then $I(P ↔ Q) = t$. If $I(P) = t$ and $I(Q) = f$, then $I(P ↔ Q) = f$, etc.

The operators can be summarized as follows. Equivalence means both sides of the equivalence have the same interpretation. An implication is true if both sides are true or if the antecedent (left side) is false. This means that in the predicate calculus, a false expression can imply anything and the implication will be true. Another way of viewing a statement such as $P ⇒ Q$ is by noting that if $I(P) = t$ and $I(P ⇒ Q) = t$, then it must follow that $I(Q) = t$.

A conjunction is true only if both expressions within the conjunction are true. If either or both sides of the conjunction are false, the conjunction is false. A disjunction is true if either side or both sides are true. This is the inclusive disjunction, as opposed to the exclusive disjunction, where $I(P) = t$ and $I(Q) = t$ means $I(P \lor Q) = f$. Negation simply produces the complementary value.

We now extend our notation by introducing parentheses for forming more complex predicate expressions involving the five operators. We also define an order of precedence for the operators, where ~ is performed before $\lor$ before $\land$ before $⇒$ before ↔. So $P \lor Q ⇒ R ↔ {\sim}T \land U$ can be restated with parentheses as $(((P \lor Q) ⇒ R) ↔ (({\sim}T) \land U))$.

11.25   Operational Model Theory

Consider the predicate calculus expression (or formula) $P \lor {\sim}P$. This is by our convention equivalent to $P \lor ({\sim}P)$. Note that since P appears without arguments, we do not have to consider a domain of discourse for the formula. Since there is only a single predicate symbol in the formula, there are only two possible interpretations: $I_1(P) = t$ and $I_2(P) = f$. Let us compute the value of the formula under each of the interpretations.

If $I_1(P) = t$, then by definition $I_1({\sim}P) = f$. Thus we are taking the disjunction of two terms, the first with value t, the second with value f. Again by definition, "t" $\lor$ "f" will have the value t. Thus we must conclude that $I_1(P \lor {\sim}P) = t$. Now consider $I_2(P) = f$. By the same argument, $I_2({\sim}P) = t$, and so $I_2(P \lor {\sim}P) = t$.

Now under all possible interpretations of the predicate symbols in the formula (in this case two), the formula evaluates to t. Whenever this occurs we say that the formula is *valid,* or more formally that it is a tautology. Thus we have proved that $P \lor {\sim}P$ is a valid formula of the predicate calculus. Note that we have not assigned P any meaning to this

$$I_1(P) = t \qquad \begin{array}{l} (P) \leftrightarrow (\sim(\sim(P))) \\ (t) \leftrightarrow (\sim(\sim(t))) \\ (t) \leftrightarrow (\sim(f)) \\ (t) \leftrightarrow (t) \\ \boxed{t} \end{array}$$

$$I_2(P) = f \qquad \begin{array}{l} (P) \leftrightarrow (\sim(\sim(P))) \\ (f) \leftrightarrow (\sim(\sim(f))) \\ (f) \leftrightarrow (\sim(t)) \\ (f) \leftrightarrow (f) \\ \boxed{t} \end{array}$$

Fig. 11.1. Proof of the validity of $P \leftrightarrow \sim\sim P$.

point. Thus P stands for any proper predicate expression. So without any further analysis we can conclude that the following are valid:

$$Q \lor \sim Q$$
$$R(a,y) \lor \sim R(a,y)$$
$$(P \land T(w,z) \Rightarrow V(z)) \lor \sim(P \land T(w,z) \Rightarrow V(z))$$

In other words, $P \lor \sim P$ is a valid axiom schema.

Let us examine some other formulas and test their validity. First consider $P \leftrightarrow \sim\sim P$. Again there are two possible interpretations, summarized in Fig. 11.1. The figure shows a treelike substitution of truth values for expressions in the formula. On each successive line a different subformula is evaluated and its value indicated. To read through the evaluation of I_1, in the formula each occurrence of P has the value t. Working from the right, the value of $\sim$"t" is "f", hence the second line. Again, $\sim$"f" is "t", and we are left with "t" $\leftrightarrow$ "t", which of course evaluates to t.

The bottom line of this analysis is that under all possible interpretations, $P \leftrightarrow \sim\sim P$ has the value t. Hence it is a valid formula.

Now consider the more complex formula $(P \Rightarrow Q) \leftrightarrow (\sim P \lor Q)$. There are four possible interpretations, all of which are considered in Fig. 11.2. This formula also is valid. We can interpret the validity of this formula in the following way: An equivalence is true when both sides have the same truth values; hence for all possible interpretations, $P \Rightarrow Q$ and $\sim P \lor Q$ have the same truth value, i.e., they are logically equivalent. The equivalence of these two formulas will be very important to us later (see Section 11.32). Important valid formulas are summarized in Table 11.1; it is left as an exercise for the reader to establish validity in each case.

Next, let us analyze the formula $Q \land \sim Q$. As before, there are two possible interpretations of Q. Figure 11.3 shows that each of these leads to

$$I_1(P) = t, \quad I_1(Q) = t \qquad \begin{array}{c} (P \Rightarrow Q) \leftrightarrow ((\sim P) \vee Q) \\ (t \Rightarrow t) \leftrightarrow ((f) \vee t) \\ (t) \leftrightarrow (t) \\ \boxed{t} \end{array}$$

$$I_2(P) = t, \quad I_2(Q) = f \qquad \begin{array}{c} (P \Rightarrow Q) \leftrightarrow ((\sim P) \vee Q) \\ (t \Rightarrow f) \leftrightarrow ((f) \vee f) \\ (f) \leftrightarrow (f) \\ \boxed{t} \end{array}$$

$$I_3(P) = f, \quad I_3(Q) = t \qquad \begin{array}{c} (P \Rightarrow Q) \leftrightarrow ((\sim P) \vee Q) \\ (f \Rightarrow t) \leftrightarrow ((t) \vee t) \\ (t) \leftrightarrow (t) \\ \boxed{t} \end{array}$$

$$I_4(P) = f, \quad I_4(Q) = f \qquad \begin{array}{c} (P \Rightarrow Q) \leftrightarrow ((\sim P) \vee Q) \\ (f \Rightarrow f) \leftrightarrow ((t) \vee f) \\ t \leftrightarrow t \\ \boxed{t} \end{array}$$

Fig. 11.2. Proof of the validity of $(P \Rightarrow Q) \leftrightarrow ((\sim P) \vee Q)$.

the conclusion that $Q \wedge \sim Q$ has the value "*f.*" In other words, this formula is invalid, since under all possible interpretations it evaluates to "*f.*"

Determining the validity of formulas that contain predicate symbols with arguments is somewhat more complicated, especially when variables appear in the formula. If $P(x)$ is a predicate symbol with a single argument, then $I(P(x))$ for some interpretation I is a function of x, i.e., as x is replaced by all the different constants in the domain of discourse, I is evaluated. Using the variable x in this way is called *free*, and we say that x is a free variable.

Consider a domain of discourse with three constants: a, b, and c. We

TABLE 11.1

Some Valid Formulas

(1) $P \vee \sim P$
(2) $P \leftrightarrow (\sim \sim P)$
(3) $(P \leftrightarrow Q) \leftrightarrow [(P \Rightarrow Q) \wedge (Q \Rightarrow P)]$
(4) $(P \Rightarrow Q) \leftrightarrow (\sim P \vee Q)$
(5) $\sim(P \vee Q) \leftrightarrow [(\sim P) \wedge (\sim Q)]$
(6) $\sim(P \wedge Q) \leftrightarrow [(\sim P) \vee (\sim Q)]$
(7) $\sim(P \wedge \sim P)$
(8) $(P \vee (Q \wedge R)) \leftrightarrow ((P \vee Q) \wedge (P \vee R))$
(9) $(P \wedge (Q \vee R)) \leftrightarrow ((P \wedge Q) \vee (P \wedge R))$

$$I_1(Q) = t \quad \begin{array}{c} Q \wedge (\sim Q) \\ t \wedge (\sim t) \\ t \wedge f \\ \boxed{f} \end{array}$$

$$I_2(Q) = f \quad \begin{array}{c} Q \wedge (\sim Q) \\ f \wedge (\sim f) \\ f \wedge t \\ \boxed{f} \end{array}$$

Fig. 11.3.   Demonstration of invalidity of Q $\wedge$ ~Q.

will define two predicate symbols $H(x)$ and $D(y)$. There are 64 possible interpretations for this problem, for each interpretation must assign a value of "t" or "f" to each of the six expressions $H(a), H(b), H(c), D(a), D(b), D(c)$. Since we have two values we can assign to each of these six items, we must have $2 \times 2 \times 2 \times 2 \times 2 \times 2 = 2^6 = 64$ possible assignments. So, even for a small problem like this, using diagrams like those in Figs. 11.1–11.3 to determine the validity of formulas can be difficult.

11.26   Quantification

When using predicates with arguments, two new operators can be employed. These are $\forall$ and $\exists$. $\forall$ is called the universal quantifier, and is read "for all." The formula $\forall x P(x)$ states that "for all (every) x in the domain of discourse, x has property P." This clearly can be assigned a value of t or f under an interpretation. $\exists$ is called the existential quantifier and is read "there exists." The formula $\exists y Q(y)$ states that "there exists at least one y in the domain of discourse such that y has property Q."

The two quantifiers are most often used to express general knowledge in terms of predicate formulas. For example, let $D(w)$ represent "w is a data item" and $R(x,y)$ stand for "x is a record type that contains data item y." Then the statement, "Every data item belongs to some record type" can be expressed as $\forall s\, (D(s) \Rightarrow \exists t(R(t,s)))$. This reads "for all (every) s, if s is a data item, then there exists (is some) t for which t is a record type containing data item s."

There are several important things to note about this formula. The variables s and t are called *bound* variables, since they are bound to their respective quantifiers. Notice also that each quantifier, being an operator, has a scope indicated by the parentheses. When clear from the context, these parentheses will be omitted. Finally, note that in the interpretation of our data base system, the formula would evaluate to true. However, this does not preclude the existence of other interpretations for which this

TABLE 11.2

Valid Quantified Expressions[a]

(10)	$\sim\forall x(P(x)) \leftrightarrow \exists x(\sim P(x))$
(11)	$\sim\exists x(P(x)) \leftrightarrow \forall x(\sim P(x))$
(12)	$\forall x\ \forall y(Q(x,y)) \leftrightarrow \forall y\ \forall x(Q(x,y))$
(13)	$\forall x(P(x)) \leftrightarrow \forall y(P(y))$
(14)	$\exists x(P(x)) \leftrightarrow \exists y(P(y))$
(15)	$\forall x(P(x)) \lor Q \leftrightarrow \forall x(P(x) \lor Q)$
(16)	$\exists x(P(x)) \lor Q \leftrightarrow \exists x(P(x) \lor Q)$
(17)	$\forall x(P(x)) \land Q \leftrightarrow \forall x(P(x) \land Q)$
(18)	$\exists x(P(x)) \land Q \leftrightarrow \exists x(P(x) \land Q)$
(19)	$\forall x(P(x)) \land \forall x(Q(x)) \leftrightarrow \forall x(P(x) \land Q(x))$
(20)	$\forall x(P(x)) \lor \forall x(Q(x)) \leftrightarrow \forall x\ \forall y(P(x) \lor Q(y))$
(21)	$\exists x(P(x)) \lor \exists x(Q(x)) \leftrightarrow \exists x(P(x) \lor Q(x))$
(22)	$\exists x(P(x)) \land \exists x(Q(x)) \leftrightarrow \exists x\ \exists y(P(x) \land Q(y))$
(23)	$\forall x(P(x)) \Rightarrow P(\hat{a})$
(24)	$P(\hat{a}) \Rightarrow \exists x(P(x))$

[a] The term $\hat{a}$ stands for any constant in the domain of discourse.

formula is false. The problem then is to determine what information (predicate expressions) must be included in this formula to make it valid under all interpretations.

There are, however, a number of useful valid formulas concerning quantifiers, which we will use in Section 11.32. These are given in Table 11.2. The first of these (which is numbered 10, following the scheme of the previous table) states that "not all x have property P" is equivalent to "some x does not have property P." The second says "it is not true that at least one x has property P" is equivalent to "all x do not have property P." The other formulas can be interpreted in a similar manner.

One major problem that arises in the use of quantifiers is the evaluation of $I(\exists x P(x))$ and $I(\forall x P(x))$ for a specified interpretation I. It is often the case that the domain of discourse is very large (e.g., transactions over a one-year period for a large company) or even infinite (the integers). In these cases it is infeasible, if not impossible, to establish the value under the interpretation by examining each element of the domain of discourse. Consider $I(\exists x P(x))$. Suppose that we have examined the first 10,000 elements of the domain of discourse and have not yet found an element a such that $P(a)$ is true. We cannot conclude that $I(\exists x P(x))$ is false, because the 10,007th might be true. The same argument can be used with $I(\forall x P(x))$. This points out the limitation of the direct evaluation method of computing interpretations. Another technique, proof theory, is presented in Chapter 12.

11.27   Axiom Sets--Operational Details

Often in application problems, there is a certain set of knowledge that guides the processing of the problem in question. Such prestated knowledge is referred to as a set of axioms. In general, an axiom is some piece of information that we believe is true.

For example, consider the statement: If Company A fires Mr. Jones, then its stock will increase in value. For this statement to be considered an axiom, we must believe in its validity at all times. Let the predicate symbol P stand for: Company A fires Mr. Jones, and let the predicate symbol Q stand for: The value of Company A's stock increases. Then the axiom in question can be represented in predicate calculus by the expression $P \Rightarrow Q$. Most importantly, when we use this axiom, we will restrict ourselves to those interpretations that make the expression evaluate to t.

To formalize this process, we now define a valid deduction: Let P_1, $P_2, \ldots, P_n$ be n axioms expressed in predicate calculus. We say "From $P_1, P_2, \ldots, P_n$ we conclude Q is a valid deduction," and notate it by $P_1, \ldots, P_n \vdash Q$, if and only if for all interpretations I such that $I(P_1) = t$, $I(P_2) = t, \ldots, I(P_n) = t$, it follows that $I(P_1 \wedge P_2 \wedge \cdots \wedge P_n \Rightarrow Q) = t$.

In the preceding example, we want to know whether the following is a valid deduction: If Company A fires Mr. Jones (P), then its stock will rise (Q). Mr. Jones is fired. Therefore we conclude that the stock will rise. In symbols, $(P \Rightarrow Q)$, $P \vdash Q$. Figure 11.4a demonstrates the four possible interpretations of P and Q. Note that only the first interpretation makes both $P \Rightarrow Q$ and P have the value t. Thus this is the only interpretation

$$
\begin{array}{c c c c}
 & P & Q & P \Rightarrow Q \\
(1) & \boxed{t} & t & \boxed{t} \\
(2) & t & f & f \\
(3) & f & t & t \\
(4) & f & f & t \\
\end{array}
$$

(a)

$$
\begin{aligned}
((P \Rightarrow Q) \wedge\ & P) \Rightarrow Q \\
((t \Rightarrow t) \wedge\ & t) \Rightarrow t \\
t \wedge\ & t \Rightarrow t \\
t\ & \Rightarrow t \\
& t
\end{aligned}
$$

(b)

Fig. 11.4.   Using model theory in deductions.

that need be considered. Figure 11.4b indicates the evaluation of $((P \Rightarrow Q) \wedge P) \Rightarrow Q$, which has the value t. Thus under the interpretation in question, the formula has the value t. Therefore we can conclude that this is an example of valid deduction.

Consider the following example: If we reduce our selling price, then demand for our product will increase. Demand has increased. Therefore we must conclude that the selling price has been reduced.

To analyze the problem, let R represent "Reduce selling price" and let D represent "increased demand." The problem can now be stated symbolically as $R \Rightarrow D$, $D \vdash R$. The four possible interpretations of D and R are indicated in Fig. 11.5a. Note that interpretations (1) and (3) have the requisite property of evaluating both $R \rightarrow D$ and D as t. But as Fig. 11-5b demonstrates, under interpretation (3) $((R \Rightarrow D) \wedge D) \Rightarrow R$ evaluates to f. Because of this fact the reasoning used to conclude that selling price has been reduced is invalid.

It is important to note that this kind of analysis does not directly concern itself with the truth or falsity of axioms. The axiom "Decreasing the price will increase the demand" may be true under the appropriate economic conditions. The predicate calculus is not concerned with the validity of this statement under the prevailing conditions. If you believe that the axiom is in fact valid, then it can be used in a deduction (or argument) and the deduction can then be analyzed as demonstrated in this section.

11.30   A LANGUAGE SYSTEM FOR PREDICATE EXPRESSIONS

In many instances [2, 7], the language system (LS) for a predicate calculus based KS is simply the predicate calculus itself, or an extension of it. In such systems users express their requests as a predicate formula, and the system validates this expression using the KS.

For example, suppose that a KS contained predicate expressions such as TRANS (1131, Smith, $400), TRANS (1427, West, $255), etc. Each expression represents a transaction consisting of an invoice number, a salesperson, and an amount. To determine what transactions Smith has made, a user of this system might enter: $\exists x \, \exists y \, (\text{TRANS}(x, \text{Smith}, y))$. This expression would be tested for validity; if it is true, then Smith indeed has made some transactions, and the values of x and y that make the expression true are the desired outputs of the system.

A more flexible LS would allow statements in a language of higher level than predicate calculus. Some of the difficulties in achieving this goal

$$
\begin{array}{c}
\underline{R \quad D \quad R \Rightarrow D} \\[4pt]
(1) \quad t \quad \boxed{t} \quad \boxed{t} \\
(2) \quad t \quad f \quad f \\
(3) \quad f \quad \boxed{t} \quad \boxed{t} \\
(4) \quad f \quad f \quad t
\end{array}
$$

(a)

$$
\begin{array}{c}
((R \Rightarrow D) \wedge D) \Rightarrow R \\
((f \Rightarrow t) \wedge t) \Rightarrow f \\
t \quad \wedge \; t \; \Rightarrow f \\
t \quad\quad \Rightarrow f \\
f
\end{array}
$$

(b)

Fig. 11.5.   Using model theory in invalid deductions.

are presented in the next section. Then a "normal form" for predicate calculus statement is defined, and techniques are discussed for translating predicate expressions into this form. Finally, a method for maintaining a predicate-based KS using data base management constructs is presented.

11.31   Stating Arguments as Predicate Expressions

There is, unfortunately, no algorithm for translating statements in English into predicate calculus expressions. This is due primarily to the ambiguousness inherent in the English language, as well as the variety of ways in which a single thought can be expressed. The purpose of this section, then, is to state some guidelines for this task, illuminating some of the pitfalls as they occur.

One of the more difficult parts of the translation process is the identification of the units that will become predicate symbols. Using the definition, these should be indivisible thoughts, for which any further subdivision is unnecessary for the given problem. For example, consider the statement "Prices will rise if demand increases." This can be interpreted in many ways. For example, we could let the predicate symbol A represent the entire sentence. You may say, "The sentence has more structure than that!" but in some context this might be the proper choice. Another possible interpretation is similar to the expression derived in Section 11.27: Let P stand for "Prices will rise" and D for "Demand increases"; then the English statement is rendered $D \Rightarrow P$. A third translation might define $R(x)$ to be "x has increased (or risen)"; then the statement is simply $R(\text{demand}) \Rightarrow R(\text{prices})$. It is impossible to determine in isolation which of these three translations is "better"; each is valid for certain purposes. It is necessary then to examine the entire problem or argument to establish the proper set of predicates.

Another difficulty can arise in determining the operators involved in the English sentence. "If . . . then . . ." kinds of sentences clearly can become implications, and equivalences are usually fairly easy to identify. Conjunctions and disjunctions must be carefully examined before the translation is made. For example, consider the following instruction that might be issued in a data base environment: "Delete the transactions of salespersons Smith and Jones." In data base terms, this appears to say to delete those occurrences whose salesperson data values are Smith and Jones. But no single occurrence will have salesperson equal to both Smith and Jones, only one or the other. Hence the proper analysis is to delete those occurrences for which salesperson is either Smith or Jones, clearly a disjunction. Another way of analyzing the same sentence using conjunction is "Delete the transactions for salesperson Smith *and* delete the transactions for salesperson Jones." The structure of the source statements must be fully understood before the translation can be made.

Another difficulty is that often in English arguments are not completely stated. Sometimes the premises of the arguments are fully expressed and the conclusion left unsaid. Sometimes the conclusion has not yet been deduced (e.g., clues in a murder mystery). More often, one or more of the premises of the argument or deduction are not explicitly written down. There are many reasons for this. In everyday conversation, it would soon become tedious to repeat all the antecedents to our statements; this habit carries over to written arguments as well. Sometimes the premises are so obvious to us that we do not see the need to write them down (e.g., the nonnegativity constraints in a linear programming problem). The argument can be so complex that we cannot easily identify what our premises are. Sometimes the premise itself can be controversial, and hence it is omitted intentionally in order not to draw attention to it. Finally, premises can be omitted intentionally for purposes of innuendo: to make it obvious to the listener or reader what the missing premise is and to lead the listener or reader to draw his or her own conclusion.

It was noted earlier that the predicate calculus can be used to establish the validity of a deduction or argument, using the techniques discussed in Section 11.27. However, this still will not determine whether or not the argument is "sound." Validity of $P_1, \ldots, P_n \vdash Q$ means that Q follows logically from the premises $P_1, \ldots, P_n$. The soundness of the argument means that it is valid *and* that each of the premises are "true." The "truth" of the premises must be established either by previous deduction or by common consent; otherwise the argument is not sound. For example, consider "If today is the 31st day of the month, it is the last day of the month." This is by all reasonable standards a "true" implication. Its use in the deduction: "Today is February 31. Therefore it is the last day of February" leads to a valid statement, although clearly unsound logic.

In dealing with predicate symbols that take arguments, it is important to establish the domain of discourse from the beginning. The domain need not be explicitly stated, but should be implicitly recognized in order properly to regard quantified expressions. It is also important to consider the case of the domain being empty. For example, consider "All angels have wings." If we let $A(x)$ mean "x is an angel," and $W(x)$ mean "x has wings," the statement is rendered as $\forall x(A(x) \Rightarrow W(x))$. If there are no angels, then this statement is "true." On the other hand, $\exists x(A(x) \Rightarrow W(x))$, which in words is "at least one angel has wings," is false if there are no angels. When translating from English, it is necessary to establish whether or not the statements imply the existence of elements of the domain. In the preceding example, "If today is the 31st day of the month, it is the last day of the month" led to unsound arguments, since all months do not have 31 days. A better rule is "If this month has 31 days, *and* today is the 31st day of the month, then it is the last day of the month."

In general, quantifiers can be difficult to translate. "Some" and "all" often in English convey more meaning than $\exists$ and $\forall$. "Some accountants are crooks" is usually interpreted as meaning "some but not all accountants are crooks." When we say "people have landed on the moon" we have a case where the quantifier is not stated at all. But it is clear that we mean "some" people, not "all" people. On the other hand, "people die" must be interpreted as "all people die." Similarly, it is important to analyze closely sentences that contain words like "a," "an," or "any": "a shipment just arrived" (some shipment, certainly not all); "a client needs pampering" (all clients are implied here). "Any worker can become foreman": if $W(x)$ is "x is a worker" and $B(x)$ is "x can become foreman," then this is $\forall x[W(x) \Rightarrow B(x)]$; but "if any worker can become foreman, Smith can": $[\exists x(W(x) \Rightarrow B(x))] \Rightarrow B(\text{Smith})$. These few examples will serve to indicate the complexity of the translation process. For further examples see Kleene [5] and Ruby [6].

11.32   Skolem Normal Form

Skolem normal form [4] is a distillation of two other normal forms, conjunctive normal form and prenex normal form. It involves a transformation of the predicate expression into a more easily processed version. The resultant expressions, called clauses, form the basis for most predicate calculus based PPS.

Prenex normal form of a predicate expression involves the migration of all quantifiers to the left of the expression. A formula in this form will begin with quantifiers and terminate with predicates and operators only. For each predicate calculus expression there is a unique (up to names) prenex normal form equivalent.

The steps involved in translating a particular expression into prenex form use some of the 24 valid formulas presented in Tables 11.1 and 11.2. The algorithm is as follows:

Step 1: Use formula (3) to eliminate all ↔ from the given expression. Next, use (4) to eliminate all ⇒. At this stage the expression will involve only ∨, ∧, and ~.

Step 2: Use (2) to eliminate double negatives; use (5) and (6) (known as De Morgan's laws) to distribute ~ over subexpressions; and use (10) and (11) to distribute ~ over all quantifiers. This step should be repeated until none of these valid formulas can be applied. At this stage all ~ should immediately precede predicate symbols.

Step 3: Use formulas (15–22) to move quantifiers to the left of the subexpressions. Notice that in some instances, i.e., (20) and (21), a renaming of variables is required.

Figure 11.6 provides an example of the algorithm.

A formula in prenex form is said to consist of a prefix (the quantifiers) and a matrix (the remaining expression). The next part of this transformation process involves reorganizing the matrix into conjunctive normal form. In conjunctive normal form, an expression consists of a conjunction of subformulas, each subformula consisting of predicates, ∨, and ~.

		Formula used
	[∀x ($T(x) \Rightarrow \exists y(R(x,y)))] \vee [\sim\forall x$ ($\exists y(R(x, y)) \Rightarrow$ $P(x)$)]	
Step 1:	[∀x ($\sim T(x) \vee \exists y(R(x,y)))] \vee [\sim\forall x$ ($\sim\exists y(R(x, y)) \vee$ $P(x)$)]	(4)
Step 2:	[∀x ($\sim T(x) \vee \exists y(R(x,y)))] \vee [\quad \exists x \sim (\sim\exists y(R(x, y)) \vee$ $P(x)$)]	(10)
	[∀x ($\sim T(x) \vee \exists y(R(x,y)))] \vee [\quad \exists x (\sim\sim\exists y(R(x, y)) \wedge$ $\sim P(x)$)]	(5)
	[∀x ($\sim T(x) \vee \exists y(R(x,y)))] \vee [\quad \exists x$ ($\exists y(R(x, y)) \wedge$ $\sim P(x)$)]	(2)
Step 3:	[∀x (∃y ($\sim T(x) \vee$ $(R(x,y)))] \vee [\quad \exists x$ ($\exists y(R(x, y) \wedge$ $\sim P(x)$)))]	(16, 17)
	∀x[(∃y ($\sim T(x) \vee$ $R(x,y)))] \vee (\quad \exists w$ ($\exists y(R(w,y) \wedge$ $\sim P(w))))$	(15)
	∀x[∃w ((∃y ($\sim T(x) \vee$ $R(x,y))) \vee (\qquad \exists y(R(w,y) \wedge$ $\sim P(w))))]$	(16)
	∀x[∃w (∃y(($\sim T(x) \vee$ $R(x,y)) \vee (\qquad R(w,y) \wedge$ $\sim P(w))))]$	(21)

Fig. 11.6.   Prenex normal form.

There is only a single step involved in taking the prenex form matrix into conjunctive normal form:

Step 4: Use formulas (8) and (9) to distribute $\wedge$ and $\vee$; reorganize into the proper form.

The modification of the expression of Figure 11.6 into conjunctive normal form is as follows:

$$\forall x \; \exists w \; \exists y[(\sim T(x) \vee R(x,y)) \vee (R(w,y) \wedge \sim P(w))]$$

Step 4:
    Use rule 8 with $P = (\sim T(x) \vee R(x,y)), Q = R(w,y), R = \sim P(w)$

$$\forall x \; \exists w \; \exists y[(\sim T(x) \vee R(x,y)) \vee R(w,y)] \wedge [(\sim T(x) \vee R(x,y)) \vee \sim P(w)]$$

or, by dropping some parentheses,

$$\forall x \; \exists w \; \exists y[\sim T(x) \vee R(x,y) \vee R(w,y)] \wedge [\sim T(x) \vee R(x,y) \vee \sim P(w)]$$

The final transformation of a formula in prenex–conjunctive normal form to Skolem normal form is accomplished by eliminating all existential quantifiers and existentially quantified variables. This is done by the expedient trick of substituting functions for these variables. The arguments of the functions, called Skolem functions, are those universally quantified variables in whose scope the existential quantifier appears.

More formally, suppose that variables x_i, $i = 1, 2, \ldots, n$, are the quantified variables in a particular formula in prenex–conjunctive normal form, which have been labeled in the order of their appearance (from left to right) in the prefix of the formula. Note that in a predicate expression involving no quantifiers, $n = $ zero. Suppose that x_j is an existentially quantified variable. Then in the matrix we replace all occurrences of x_j with a Skolem function f_j. The arguments of f_j are those universally quantified variables x_k, $k < j$.

In the previous example, w is preceded by x, so we can replace w with $f_2(x)$ in the matrix; similarly, y is also preceded by x, so we replace y with $f_3(x)$. The Skolem normal form of the expression is

$$[\sim T(x) \vee R(x,f_3(x)) \vee R(f_2(x),f_3(x))] \wedge [\sim T(x) \vee R(x,f_3(x)) \vee \sim P(f_2(x))]$$

Note that we can completely drop all quantifiers at this point. Any variable that appears in a formula in Skolem normal form by definition is universally quantified. For another example of this process, the Skolem normal form of $\exists v \; \forall w \; \forall x \; \exists y \; \forall z, Q(v,w,x,y,z)$ is $Q(f_1(\quad), w,x,f_4(w,x),z)$. Note that f_1 has *no* arguments, i.e., f_1 is a constant.

An interesting correspondence between Skolem functions and paths through a data base is given in Chapter 13.

11.33   A DB Structure for Predicate Expressions

The importance of Skolem normal form derives from its simplicity. A formula in Skolem form can be viewed as a (sequential) list of clauses, which as a whole form a large conjunction. Each individual clause consists of predicate symbols $\vee$ and $\sim$. Quantifiers have been completely eliminated. This form of expression is useful for both information storage and processing.

A simple data structure for representing predicate calculus expressions in Skolem form is given in Fig. 11.7a. The CLAUSE record type contains the set of clauses, each of which must be satisfied in a particular interpretation. The record type APPEARS has as its data items the "sign" of a particular predicate symbol in a particular clause (whether the predicate is negated or not), plus the arguments of the predicate itself. The

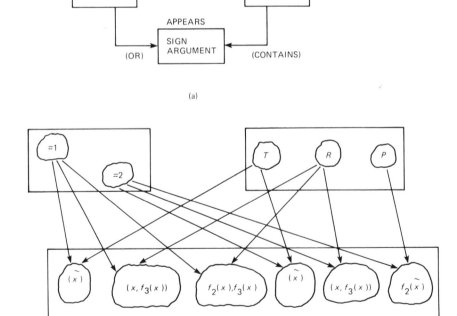

(a)

(b)

Fig. 11.7.   (a) DB structure. (b) Occurrence structure.

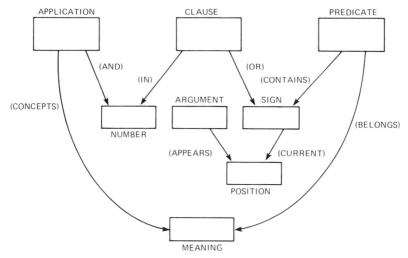

Fig. 11.8. Extended DB structure.

coset connecting CLAUSE and APPEARS is labeled OR, since each occurrence of APPEARS represents a predicate appearing in a clause, and these predicates (or literals) in the clause are "or-ed" together. PREDICATE and CONTAINS have clear meaning.

Figure 11.7b shows the occurrence structure for the Skolem normal form of the expression first presented in Fig. 11.6. Note that there are two clauses, three predicate symbols, and a total of six appearances.

A more elaborate data structure is indicated in Fig. 11.8. This data base structure allows multiple applications of predicate-based information to be maintained. This is an *M–N* relationship with both clauses and predicates, since a particular application will have many clauses, while a particular clause can be pertinent in more than one application; the same applies to predicates.

REFERENCES

1. A. F. Cardenas, "Data Base Management Systems," Allyn and Bacon, Boston, Massachusetts, 1979.
2. E. F. Codd, A data base sublanguage based on the relational calculus, *Proc. ACM SIG-FIDET Workshop on Data Description, Access, and Control, San Diego, California* 1971.
3. I. M. Copi, "Introduction To Logic." MacMillan, New York, 1961.

4. M. Davis and H. Putnam, A computing procedure for quantification theory, *J. ACM* **7**, 3, 201–215 (1960).
5. S. C. Kleene, "Mathematical Logic." Wiley, New York, 1967.
6. L. Ruby, "The Art Of Making Sense." Lippincott, Philadelphia, Pennsylvania, 1954.
7. N. H. Van Emden, Computation and Deductive Information Retrieval, Research Rep. CS-77-16, Department Of Computer Science, Univ. of Waterloo (1977).

Chapter 12

PROBLEM-PROCESSING SYSTEMS FOR PREDICATE CALCULUS

12.00 INTRODUCTION

The four primary functions of a problem-processing system (PPS) for a decision support system are information collection, problem recognition, analysis, and model formulation (cf. Chapter 3). In a predicate calculus-based DSS there are a number of difficult problems that must be considered. These problems, which do not arise in data base knowledge system (KS) storage schemes, are caused by the richness of expression available in the predicate calculus. This chapter examines some of these problems in order to indicate viable solutions. For a more complete treatment see Chang and Lee [2].

Information collection is complicated by the nature of the PPS for the predicate calculus. The predicate calculus requires that its PPS be inherently nondeterministic, i.e., there is no algorithmic way to select the appropriate solution to a stated problem without backtracking and/or parallel operation. Some heuristic techniques have been suggested [2,8]. These suffer from the defect of being either inefficient or, even worse, incomplete. A PPS for the predicate calculus is incomplete if there are some "true" statements that cannot be mechanically derived from an axiom set.

The central processes of the PPS comprise the problem recognition phase. There are many variants to the basic idea, but all are based on the resolution principle of Robinson [9]. This proof technique combines clauses, as defined in the previous chapter, in such a way as to provide a proof by contradiction of the desired statement. The principle is complicated by predicates with arguments, and these complications lead to other techniques and algorithms.

The PPS facets of analysis and model formulation are not discussed in this chapter. These topics are reserved for Part V.

The predicate calculus-based PPS is a kind of mechanical theorem-proving system [2], in that the user's query is taken as a theorem that is to be proved from the existing axiom set. It is thus important to review the principle of proof briefly. A proof is a partial ordering of axioms, arranged in a linear list, that, together with some rule or rules of inference, derive the desired result. For example, in Chapter 11 the rule of modus ponens was introduced. In symbolic terms, it states that if A and $A \Rightarrow B$ are axioms, then we can conclude (or prove) B. A formal statement of the proof is

(1) A axiom
(2) $A \Rightarrow B$ axiom
(3) B modus ponens

We may require all proofs to have this form. The "axioms" used in the proof can also be previously derived (learned) results: Suppose that A, $A \Rightarrow B$, and $B \Rightarrow C$ are axioms. Then we can prove C:

(1) A axiom
(2) $A \Rightarrow B$ axiom
(3) B modus ponens, lines 1, 2
(4) $B \Rightarrow C$ axiom
(5) C modus ponens, lines 3, 4

12.10   INFORMATION COLLECTION

The information collection activities of a PPS involve two sources— the knowledge system and the user. In a predicate calculus DSS, each of these requires special processing. The processing involved can, in the case of the knowledge system, be related to problems previously encountered. However, when collecting information from the user, a philosophical controversy arises that cannot be resolved by recourse to previously discussed material.

Naturally, most of the information collection is of a nature that directly parallels the development of data base DSS. Indeed, if the predicate expressions are maintained in a data base structure, then most of Chapter 9 applies. These aspects of information collection will not be repeated here. The same remarks apply to the user–PPS interface.

12.11   Collection from the KS

The fundamental problem of information collection from the KS is the selection of the axiom or derived fact to next use in the continuation of the proof. For definiteness, consider the following scenario: We are currently at the nth step in the proof, having derived the predicate expression B. This is not the final step, i.e., B is not the desired result of the exercise. Furthermore, suppose that there are k possible continuations (i.e., expressions that can be combined with B to form a new expression for the $n + 1$st step). Call these k expressions $A_1, A_2, \ldots, A_k$.

One of these k expressions must be selected and the proof continued. There is no way of knowing *a priori* which of the expressions leads to proofs of the desired result. In fact, it is possible that none of these continuations will allow the derivation of the desired result (i.e., the desired result may be false for the given axiom set). This problem is enlarged on in the next section.

The solutions to this problem are similar to those described previously in Chapter 5. The simplest technique is a breadth-first search of all of the clauses, building an evaluation tree as indicated in Fig. 12.1. Each node of the tree is expanded in turn (i.e., all possible continuations from that node are added as descendants of the node, until the desired result is obtained). This technique has the advantage of always finding the *shortest* proof, i.e., the proof that involves the fewest steps. This is not to say that breadth-first search is the most efficient search; many times it is one of the slower search techniques available. For details the reader should consult Nilsson [8].

In the tree depicted in Fig. 12.1, the node R represents the previous step in the proof. It has two possible continuations, B and C. Each of these is added to the tree. Then B is evaluated, and each continuation $A_1, \ldots, A_k$ is added. This is the situation shown in Fig. 12.1. The next processing step would be to determine the possible continuations from node C.

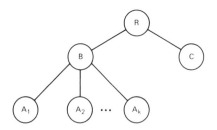

Fig. 12.1.   Evaluation tree.

Alternatively, depth-first searching could be used. One of the k candidate expressions is chosen and the proof is continued. At each step there are three possibilities: the desired result is derived, in which case the proof is concluded; the derived result can be further continued, in which case one of its possible continuations is chosen and the process is repeated; or there is no further continuation. In this case, backtracking is called for, to a step in the current proof fragment for which one of several possible continuations had been selected. At this point, another continuation is selected and the process is restarted.

Using the previous example, from node R only one continuation is evaluated, say node B. Next, node B is evaluated to produce node A_1. A_1 is subsequently processed. If a descendant of node A_1 leads to a proof, the process terminates. If A_1 produces no possible continuations, backtracking to node B occurs, and B is evaluated to produce continuation A_2.

Depth-first searching sometimes leads to "quick" proofs, especially if the selection process can be guided in some way. Often the process is quite slow and resource consuming. Furthermore, both depth-first and breadth-first search techniques are exhaustive search methods, not attempting in any way to eliminate unproductive continuations *a priori*.

Thus one is led to various heuristic selection techniques. These for the most part attempt to hasten the search process by eliminating certain expressions from the list of possible extensions. The danger with such heuristic techniques is that unless some care is taken, these techniques are potentially incomplete, i.e., they might eliminate certain "true" facts from the "provable" facts.

One simple heuristic technique, which in its basic form is incomplete, involves maintaining the expressions of the axiom set and those derived as an ordered list, and then only continuing with the first clauses found to be applicable. This is similar to depth-first search, without the backtracking mechanism. A more complicated variant on this method uses an evaluation function to evaluate the potential continuations and selects that expression with the greatest functional value. This technique can be expanded to a branch-and-bound method [8] to delete entire branches of the evaluation tree.

It should be noted that using ordered expressions parallels the development of using ordered productions in production systems, as presented in Chapter 5. In that chapter we saw that ordered productions lead to a particular behavior for the system. Thus we can safely assume that the same is true here: that only a particular set of expressions will be "provable" and that this set constitutes the "behavior" of the DSS. In terms of strict formal logic, this is highly undesirable, since predicate calculus is a general tool for the representation of general information. On the other hand, from an operational point of view, it is sometimes useful to constrain the actions of the DSS by introducing complexity into the PPS rather than the KS itself.

Another kind of heuristic technique uses external information to guide the axiom selection process. This information could be part of the KS, representing a separate set of knowledge about the problem area. Such axioms are called meta-axioms (see Part V). The external information could also be obtained from the user. When several continuations exist with no rationale for selecting any one over the rest, the user would be consulted and asked to select the proper continuation. The first of these techniques requires the formation of meta-axioms or some other form of conveying the appropriate information [6]. The latter assumes that the user is aware of both the available axioms and their meanings, as well as the operation of the PPS and the theorem-proving technique. This is infeasible, not to mention undesirable.

12.12   Collection from the LS

The LS of the DSS delivers the user's request in some appropriate form to the PPS for processing. As noted in the previous chapter, the most appropriate form for the predicate calculus is a predicate calculus expression. Thus we will assume that the language system has taken care of the translation of the original request to some predicate expression.

Once the expression is received, the entire expression must be converted into clause form (i.e., Skolem normal form). However, before this is done, the input expression is negated. The reason for this is that most mechanical theorem provers (PPS) produce a *proof by contradiction*. This proof technique uses the fact that when the axiom set of the KS is extended by the negation of the user's request, the resultant set is inconsistent. The inference rule of contradiction then allows us to conclude that the original request is a valid consequence of the axiom set.

In symbols, suppose that we wish to conclude B from $A_1, \ldots, A_n$. We demonstrate the inconsistency of $A_1 \wedge \ldots \wedge A_n \wedge \sim B$. From this we conclude that $A_1, \ldots, A_n \vdash B$. Model theory can be used to demonstrate the validity of this rule; it is left to the reader as a simple exercise.

Not all theorists and philosophers accept proof by contradiction as a valid technique. These logicians, called intuitionists, do not accept as valid certain expressions of logic that arise in model theory. Consider the expression $\exists x(P(x))$. Taken as a user request, it is negated to produce $\forall x(\sim P(x))$. Should this lead to an inconsistency, the inference rule of contradiction says that $\exists x(P(x))$ is a valid consequence. An intuitionist would claim that all you have demonstrated is $\sim(\sim(\exists x(P(x))))$. In particular this group rejects such tautologies as $P \vee \sim P$ and $P \leftrightarrow \sim \sim P$. The principal argument for this rejection lies with infinite sets; the argument was touched on in the previous chapter: If the domain of discourse is infinite, there is no way to determine directly (i.e., by direct search) the validity of $\forall x(\sim P(x))$.

As a further example, consider the expression $\exists x(T(x)) \vee \sim(\exists x(T(x)))$. If x ranges over a finite domain, then an intuitionist would agree that this expression is true, since it can be ascertained for each particular element c that either $T(c)$ is true or $\sim T(c)$ is true. But for an infinite domain the intuitionist finds no ground for always taking the preceding expression as true, since it can never be directly demonstrated using all the elements of the domain.

Clearly, this is as much a philosophical difference as a mathematical one. Yet is has immediate bearing on the designer of DSS, since the KS can in time grow into such a large collection of information that a direct search to determine the validity of an expression such as $\exists x(T(x)) \vee \sim(\exists x\ T(x))$ becomes infeasible. We have then in this controversy an important limitation of the techniques of formal logic: We assume the correctness of the rule of contradiction as well as the validity of statements such as $P \vee \sim P$. It should be kept in mind that these principles may be difficult to establish directly in an operating environment.

Another problem, mentioned briefly in the previous section, involves the attempt to "prove" a result that is not a valid consequence of the axiom set. For when this expression is negated, the extended set of expressions is consistent. The difficulties of determining the consistency of an axiom set were discussed in the previous chapter. This calculation is extremely resource consuming.

The solution most often accepted to this problem involves the simultaneous calculation of two proofs: one of the negated request and one of the unnegated request. Should the negated request lead to a contradiction, then the user's original query is a valid consequence. If the unnegated request leads to a contradiction, then the user's original query is invalid. If the PPS uses a complete method of theorem proving, one of these two alternatives will occur. If the PPS is incomplete, then it is still possible for the PPS to enter an infinite processing cycle. The only feasible solution for this is to terminate processing after some limit has been reached, measured in either CPU utilization, elapsed real time, or length of proof.

12.20   PROBLEM RECOGNITION

The problem recognition activity of the predicate calculus PPS is the construction of the proof of the user's request. The most common technique used is resolution, which is described briefly below. From the proof, the appropriate response to the user's request can be formulated.

The resolution principle involves matching predicate expressions, or portions of predicate expressions, with one another in order to form a logical continuation of the proof. The matching process is similar to that described in Chapter 5 for production systems. In fact, resolution can be considered as a production system consisting of a single production rule (the resolution principle) and a data base (in the production system sense) consisting of many predicate expressions.

12.21   The Resolution Principle

The inference rules of modus ponens and of contradiction have been previously introduced to explain the mechanisms of logic. The resolution principle is another such inference rule. It is a generalization of the following process: suppose that $A \lor \sim B$ and $B \lor \sim C$ are two clauses derived either from axioms or from some other source. Then these clauses must be true, or we have demonstrated an inconsistency in the clause set. In Fig. 12.2 the model theory analysis of the clauses is performed, along with

A	B	C	$A \lor \sim B$	$B \lor \sim C$	$A \lor \sim C$
t	t	t	t	t	t
t	t	f	t	t	t
t	f	t	t	f	
t	f	f	t	t	t
f	t	t	f		
f	t	f	f		
f	f	t	t	f	
f	f	f	t	t	t

Fig. 12.2.   Model theory analysis.

the analysis of the clause $A \lor {\sim}C$. Note that in each interpretation for which the initial clauses are true, this new clause must also be true. Thus we continue the proof with $A \lor {\sim}C$, since it is a valid consequence of the initial two clauses.

This example demonstrates the *resolution principle:* If two clauses contain the same predicate symbol, which is negated in one and not in the other, then the two clauses can be resolved with each other, creating a new clause called the resolvent. The resolvent is constructed by forming the disjunction of the remainder of each of the original clauses.

Figure 12.3 presents more examples of the resolution process. In Fig. 12.3a the resolution principle is shown to include modus ponens; note that ${\sim}P \lor Q$ is the clause form of $P \Rightarrow Q$. Part (b) demonstrates how longer clauses are handled. Part (c) is particularly important. The clauses R and ${\sim}R$ are resolved, and the result is the null string, denoted by $\square$. The null string is derived in this case because each of the initial clauses is empty once the predicates on which resolution occurs are removed. The null clause represents a contradiction (i.e., the initial clauses are inconsistent). And this is of course true, since the initial clauses are R and ${\sim}R$.

Recall from the previous section that resolution PPS work by negating the user's request and deriving a contradiction, thereby establishing the validity of the original request. The last example indicates that for resolution, deriving a contradiction is the same as deriving the null string. This is the goal of a proof by resolution.

Consider the following argument: $P \Rightarrow Q,\ {\sim}Q \vdash {\sim}P$. The validity of this can be easily established by model theory; however, it is instructive to use resolution on the expressions. The first step (Fig. 12.4) is the translation of the statements into clause form. Note that the conclusion of the argument has been negated, as indicated in the previous section. From clauses (1) and (2) the resolvent clause ${\sim}P$ is obtained. This is the desired contradiction, establishing the validity of the original argument. Note the use of resolvent (4) in the derivation of resolvent (5).

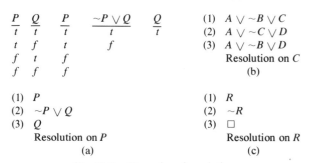

Fig. 12.3. Examples of resolution.

(1) $\sim P \vee Q$ Axiom
(2) $\sim Q$ Axiom
(3) P Negated conclusion
(4) $\sim P$ Resolution on Q, lines (1) and (2)
(5) $\square$ Resolution on P, lines (3) and (4)

Fig. 12.4. A resolution proof.

12.22 Substitution, Unification, and Deletion

When dealing with predicates that take arguments, this situation is more complicated. Recall that in resolution we are dealing with clauses. In particular, all quantifiers have been eliminated, those variables that were existentially quantified have been replaced by constants or Skolem functions, and those variables remaining are by convention universally quantified.

Consider the clauses $P(x) \vee \sim Q(x)$ and $Q(x) \vee \sim R(f(x))$. The common element is $Q(x)$, which appears negated in one clause and not negated in the other. The resolvent of these is then $P(x) \vee \sim R(f(x))$. Now consider this clause in conjunction with $M(y) \vee \sim P(y)$. The terms $P(x)$ and $P(y)$ do not match, since the variable is not the same. However, by definition variables can be renamed without loss of generality. Thus the latter expression can be rewritten as $M(x) \vee \sim P(x)$, and the resolvent becomes $M(x) \vee \sim R(f(x))$. This process is called substitution.

Unification is the process of identifying potential candidates for resolution and noting the differences between them ($P(y)$ and $P(x)$ in the previous example). Substitution replaces one of the variables with some other expression, called the most general unifier. In the example the unifier was a variable, x. The next example shows that the unifier can be more complicated.

Using the clause $M(x) \vee \sim R(f(x))$ from above, suppose that we wish to resolve it with $R(z) \vee \sim S(g(a,z))$, where by our conventions a is a constant and g a Skolem function. The difficulty is that one time R appears with argument $f(x)$, another time with argument z. The solution is to substitute $f(x)$ for z in the second clause. Note that this must occur for every z in the clause, i.e., the clause after substitution reads $R(f(x)) \vee \sim S(g(a,f(x)))$. Now resolution can occur, producing the resolvent $M(x) \vee \sim S(g(a,f(x)))$. In general, the less abstract object is substituted for the more abstract object.

Unification is clearly a complex process. Many times unifiers do not even exist (consider $P(a)$ and $\sim P(b)$, a and b both constants). For the purposes of the present work it is only necessary to be aware of the problems of unification and substitution. For a more complete treatment the reader is referred to Chang and Lee [2]. The significance of unification in the PPS is discussed in Chapter 14.

As mentioned earlier, the process of selecting the next clause to use in the resolution process can be quite complicated. Without some kind of screening strategy, the number of clauses that are potentially available for resolution can grow exponentially fast. The simplest technique is to remove from consideration any resolvents that are tautologies (i.e., always true). It is clear that the removal of true statements will not influence the contradiction in any way. A tautology is recognized by having the same predicate symbol appear both negated and unnegated in a single clause. For example, if we resolve the clauses $A \lor B \lor C$ and $\sim B \lor \sim C$ using the symbol C, the resolvent is $A \lor B \lor \sim B$, which will always be interpreted as true. Thus this resolvent need not be used at any time to further the proof.

Another technique is to remove duplicate expressions from consideration. The generalization of this technique, called subsumption, is to remove clauses whose truth value is duplicated by a clause already on the list. These strategies, which together form what is referred to as the deletion strategy, are not heuristics, i.e., they have been demonstrated to be complete (they do not eliminate any true statements from the provable statements).

12.23   Variants of Resolutions

Even with the use of strategies such as the deletion and subsumption strategies, resolution will often produce many extraneous and irrelevant resolvents in the course of the construction of a proof. A number of different techniques have been devised to reduce the number of clauses generated. Among these are semantic resolution [10], which uses ordered predicates to partition the clauses into classes within which no resolvents are formed; lock resolution [1], which indexes clause elements and only permits resolution on the predicates with the smallest index; input resolution [2], in which for each resolvent one of the parent clauses is an original *axiom or the negated conclusion*. The first two are complete; the latter is not. However, input resolution is efficient and simple to implement.

Another complete variant of resolution is linear resolution [7]. Here the last computed resolvent must be used in forming the next resolvent. Linear resolution is complete, i.e. all "true" statements will be (eventually) proved. It also has a certain intuitive appeal, since there is only a single train of thought running through the proof.

The following example will clarify the technique of linear resolution.

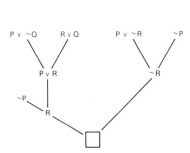

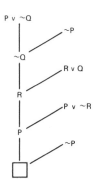

Fig. 12.5.   Resolution proof.

Fig. 12.6.   Linear resolution proof.

Suppose that from the axioms $P \lor \sim Q$, $R \lor Q$, and $P \lor \sim R$ we wish to conclude P. Negating the conclusion gives $\sim P$. Figure 12.5 indicates in graphical form a proof of this argument, using resolution. The branching of the tree indicates the nonlinearity of the proof; that is, there are two separate branches of the proof, one resulting in R, the other in $\sim R$. These resolvents are themselves resolved to produce the null clause.

Figure 12.6 provides a linear proof of the preceding proposition. Notice that there is no real branching in the tree. It simply consists of center clauses (the most recent resolvents) and side clauses. A proof using linear resolution will always have this structurally simple form.

Because of its intuitive appeal, the examples in the remainder of this work will always use a form of linear resolution.

12.30   EXAMPLES OF RESOLUTION

The following examples use resolution logic to solve simple problems. The first example demonstrates how resolution can be used in question-answering systems. The second shows how predicate calculus is used in state space systems (see Chapter 5) to control the use of operators. Other examples are presented in later chapters.

12.31   Question-Answering Systems

Suppose that we have a small warehouse in which three products are stored. The products are simply labeled a, b, and c. We currently have 30 units of product a on hand and 100 units of product b. Moreover, product *a* and product *c* must be used together (i.e., they are both necessary components to some assembly). Therefore company policy dictates that the inventory level of product *c* must always match that of product *a*.

Our sales personnel make frequent inquiries to the warehouse concerning the availability of quantities of products. We allow a sale to be consummated if there are sufficient quantities of the desired product on hand to ship. Inquiries may be formulated in terms of either product *a*, *b*, or *c*, but for those involving *a* or *c* it is assumed that *c* or *a*, respectively, is also desired.

Let us now translate this scenario into a set of predicates. Let $P(x)$ stand for "*x* is a product," $L(x,y)$ for "the inventory level of product *x* is *y* units," and $S(w,z)$ for "a shipment of *z* units of product *w*." Then the following expressions are axioms:

$$\left.\begin{array}{l} P(a) \\ P(b) \\ P(c) \end{array}\right\} \quad \text{product definitions}$$

$$\left.\begin{array}{l} L(a,30) \\ L(b,100) \end{array}\right\} \quad \text{inventory levels}$$

These are already in clause form. The level of product *c* is specified as

$$\forall v \quad L(a,v) \Rightarrow L(c,v) \qquad \text{or} \qquad {\sim}L(a,v) \lor L(c,v)$$

in clause form. Note that we are following the convention of constants coming from the beginning of the alphabet, variables from the end, and predicates capitalized. We relate shipments (or orders) to the inventory by the following statement:

$$\forall x \; \forall y \; \forall z [P(x) \land L(x,y) \land \text{LE}(z,y)] \Rightarrow S(x,z).$$

This states that for each product *x* and its inventory level *y*, if *z* is less or equal to *y*, then *z* is an appropriate shipment quantity. Note the use of the predicate LE to represent "less than or equal to." In using this kind of predicate, we are (in effect) introducing a simple kind of model into the process; one then can evaluate whether (in this case) *z* is in fact less than or equal to *y*. Another way of viewing this is to include implicitly among the axioms all the occurrences of LE, (x,y) which are commonly interpreted as true. Of course, there are an infinite number of these, so that it would be impossible to represent explicitly the predicate occurrences.

Translating this last statement into clause form produces

$$ {\sim}P(x) \lor {\sim}L(x,y) \lor {\sim}\text{LE}(z,y) \lor S(x,z).$$

We shall consider four possible inquiries.

I.   Can 10 units of product *a* be ordered?

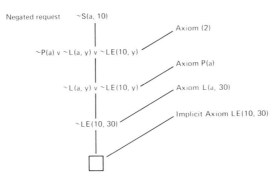

Axioms: P(a)   L(a, 30)   (1) ~L(a, v) v L(c, v)
         P(b)   L(b, 100)   (2) ~P(x) v ~L(x, y) v ~LE(z, y) v S(x, z)
         P(c)

Plus the implicit LE axioms:

Negated request   ~S(a, 10)
                                              Axiom (2)

~P(a) v ~L(a, y) v ~LE(10, y)
                                              Axiom P(a)

      ~L(a, y) v ~LE(10, y)   Axiom L(a, 30)

              ~LE(10, 30)   Implicit Axiom LE(10, 30)

              □

Fig. 12.7. Request I.

Symbolically, the request is to determine if $S(a,10)$ logically follows from the axiom set. The request is negated to give $\sim S(a,10)$. The resolution proof is given in Fig. 12.7. Since the proof succeeds, i.e., the null clause is generated, we conclude that it is all right for the salesperson to take the order for 10 units of product a.

Notice the process of substitution during the course of the proof. In the first step, $S(x,z)$ in axiom (2) is resolved with $\sim S(a,10)$. The substitution replaces *all* occurrences of x with a, and all occurrences of z with 10. In general, the more concrete objects replace the more abstract. Similarly, in the third step, y is everywhere replaced by 30.

II.   Can 150 units of product b be ordered?

The request is again simply $S(b,150)$. This must be negated, and the resulting resolution procedure is diagrammed in Fig. 12.8. The process terminates without generating the null clause. Since the request cannot be proved, the order for 150 units of product b cannot be authorized.

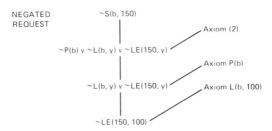

NEGATED   ~S(b, 150)
REQUEST
                                              Axiom (2)

~P(b) v ~L(b, y) v ~LE(150, y)
                                              Axiom P(b)

      ~L(b, y) v ~LE(150, y)   Axiom L(b, 100)

              ~LE(150, 100)

Fig. 12.8. Request II.

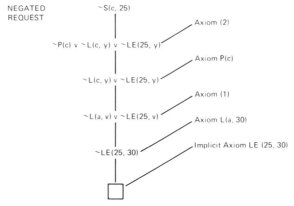

Fig. 12.9.   Request III.

The clause LE(150,100) is not an axiom, since no useful interpretation would have $I(LE(150,100)) = t$. Another way of viewing this is to note that the last resolvent, ~LE(150,100), is a true statement, for which there should be no contradiction.

III.   Can 25 units of product c be ordered?

The procedure is the same for this case. However, since the inventory level of c is not explicitly known, axiom (1) must be used to provide the necessary information. Note also that this is the only clause that could be selected at this point. The proof is given in Fig. 12.9. Again, the substitution process is important to the completion of the proof.

IV.   How many units of product a can be ordered?

This request is of a completely different nature from the previous three. Instead of seeking a "yes/no" answer, an actual data value is desired. Green [5] has developed an ingenious technique for solving this kind of retrieval problem.

Consider the request in depth. Implicit in asking "how many units?" is the question "are there any units?" Thus in symbols the question is $\exists t\ S(a,t)$. If this statement is true, then there will be some value of t that makes it true. And furthermore this value is found in the process of resolution.

As always, the first step is to negate the request: $\forall t\ \sim S(a,t)$, which in clause form is simply $\sim S(a,t)$. The resolution proof of this is shown in Fig. 12.10a. The derivation of the null clause implies that the original request is true. However, the substitutions give the numerical answer. In the fourth step, the constant 30 is substituted for the variable t. And, of course, 30 is

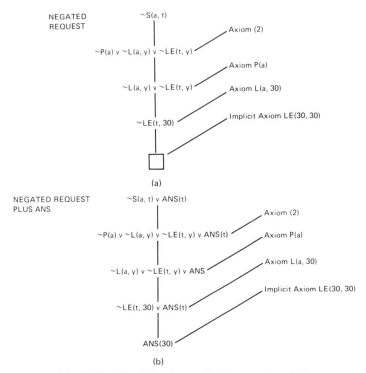

NEGATED
REQUEST   ~S(a, t)

                               Axiom (2)

~P(a) v ~L(a, y) v ~LE(t, y)

                               Axiom P(a)

~L(a, y) v ~LE(t, y)   Axiom L(a, 30)

                               Implicit Axiom LE(30, 30)

~LE(t, 30)

(a)

NEGATED REQUEST   ~S(a, t) v ANS(t)
PLUS ANS

                               Axiom (2)

~P(a) v ~L(a, y) v ~LE(t, y) v ANS(t)   Axiom P(a)

                               Axiom L(a, 30)

~L(a, y) v ~LE(t, y) v ANS

                               Implicit Axiom LE(30, 30)

~LE(t, 30) v ANS(t)

ANS(30)

(b)

Fig. 12.10. First (a) and second (b) steps of resolution.

the correct answer to the question "how many?" Thus by analyzing the substitutions the retrieval can be performed.

Green has automated this process by appending to the negated request an extra predicate called ANS (for ANSWER). Using this addition, the goal is no longer to derive the null clause but a clause consisting solely of the ANS predicate. The proper form to begin with is $\sim S(a,t) \vee \text{ANS}(t)$. Since t appears as the argument of ANS, whenever the substitution is made for t, the proper value will be reflected by ANS. This form of the proof is illustrated in Fig. 12.10b.

The astute reader will already have noticed that a certain amount of hand waving has accompanied this example. In the third step of the proof the implicit axiom LE(7,30) could have been selected, causing the final clause to read ANS (7). The solution to this problem involves a great deal of complication; the (conceptually) simplest solution is to include axioms defining explicitly the notion of "less-than-or-equal-to," as well as "maximum."

The ANS predicate can be used to find more than one value by repeating the proof, each time eliminating the previously returned value. This process continues until the proof can no longer be completed. For example, if the request is "what products do you have?" or in symbols $\exists r\, P(r)$, the first proof would produce ANS(a), the second proof ANS(b), and the third ANS(c). Naturally this process can be automated.

12.32 State Space Systems

In Chapter 4 the STRIPS [3] model was briefly described. The complete description of STRIPS was postponed, since predicate calculus is an integral part of the model. In Chapter 5 the general state space model was conceptually presented. The following is a summary of this particular operationalization of the state space model. The reader should refer to those earlier chapters for the notation and terminology.

In STRIPS a state consists of a list of clauses. These clauses form the current axiom set. In other words, a state is a set of interpretations for which a particular set of clauses is true. The clauses are used to model a "world" situation.

Operators are used to modify the list of axioms. Each operator has associated with it a list of zero, one, or more preconditions. These are clauses that must be logically valid in terms of the current axiom list (i.e., the current state). Resolution is used to prove that the elements of the precondition list are valid. If all preconditions of some operator are valid, then that operator may be applied to the current state.

Also associated with each operator is a deletion list, containing zero, one, or more clauses, which are removed from the axiom list when the operator is applied. Similarly, an addition list contains those clauses that must be added to the axiom list. The actions of deletion and addition produce the new state.

As mentioned in the earlier chapters, most problems addressed by the state space approach are "toy" problems of a very simple nature. Many are unrealistic mental exercises or pertain to such subjects as the control of a robot with a limited capacity of operators. Most of these applications represent closed systems; i.e., systems without external influences. However, most business applications are trivial without the introduction of an operating environment. Rather than present an example of an open system, which must be quite complex, we will also consider a simple closed system, but one in which models provide a form of external influence.

In particular, consider a single server queuing model. We will construct a state space system that operationalizes an event step simulation model [4]. Briefly, customers (or computer programs or assemblies) arrive at a single servicing point in some random fashion. Since the arrivals can occur at any time, it is possible for queues to form while the customers wait for service. Usually the length of time required to serve an individual is also a random value. Time is measured as elapsed time from 0.

Let us define four predicates to represent the single server model. Let $A(x)$ stand for "the next arrival occurs at time x," $D(y)$ for "the next departure occurs at time y," $T(t)$ for "the total elapsed time is t," and $N(z)$ for "there are currently z individuals in the system." Note that z can take on values 0, 1, 2, ... If $N(2)$ is interpreted as true, then the queue length is 1, since the other individual is being served.

There are four basic models that we must include in order to make the simulation work. There must be a function r_a that will produce the interval until the next arrival occurs. This random value is referred to as the interarrival time. On each invocation of r_a, a new interarrival time is computed. Similarly, let r_d represent another random function that computes a (random) service time. These functions are external to the state space process, providing an interface with the real world. Two other functions that this example requires are simple addition and subtraction, for which the customary notations are used.

Normally, the initial state of a simulation would consist of the four axioms: $A(r_a), N(0), T(0), D(0)$. The usage $A(r_a)$ means that the function r_a is evaluated and the numerical value is substituted as argument. It is of course possible to have other initial states. This particular state represents the situation at time 0 when no individual is in the system.

There are three operators defined for this state space system. These operators are PA(x,z,t), process arrival; PD(y,z,t), process departure; and FD(y,x), false departure. The parameters represent predicate calculus variables whose substituted values must be transferred from preconditions to the add and delete lists. The full definition of the operators are given in Fig. 12.11. Preconditions are not in clause form, in order to simplify the definitions. The meanings of PA and PD are clear. False departure is needed to handle the situation when a departure is scheduled to occur, but the system is empty. Note that this case is processed differently in most presentations of event step simulation.

The goal for this kind of state space system can be expressed in a number of ways. Often the goal is to run the simulation for a given length of time, say 480 minutes (8 hours); the goal would be expressed $T(480)$. Another goal may be to process until the queue contains 15 individuals; the goal can be expressed as $N(16)$. Introducing more predicates would allow a wider class of specified goals.

As mentioned earlier, the preconditions listed in Fig. 12.11 must be converted to clause form before any processing can occur. Since these

Process Arrival: PA(x,z,t)
  Preconditions: $\exists x \; \exists y \; A(x) \wedge D(y) \wedge LT(x,y)$
         $\exists z \; N(z)$
         $\exists t \; T(t)$
  Deletions: $N(z)$ Additions: $N(z + 1)$
         $T(t)$ $T(x)$
         $A(x)$ $A(x + r_a)$
Process Departure: PD(y,z,t)
  Preconditions: $\exists y \; \exists x \; D(y) \wedge A(x) \wedge LE(y,x)$
         $\exists z \; N(z) \wedge GT(z,0)$
         $\exists t \; T(t)$
  Deletions: $N(z)$ Additions: $N(z - 1)$
         $T(t)$ $T(y)$
         $D(y)$ $D(y + r_d)$
False Departure: FD(y,x)
  Preconditions: $\exists y \; \exists x \; D(y) \wedge A(x) \wedge LE(y,x)$
         $N(0)$
  Deletions: $D(y)$ Additions: $D(x + r_d)$

Fig. 12.11.   State space operators.

conditions must be proved with respect to the current state (axioms), it makes sense also to negate the preconditions for efficiency. For example, the negated clause form of the preconditions of PA are

$\sim A(x) \vee \sim D(y) \vee \sim LT(x,y)$
$\sim N(z)$
$\sim T(t)$

Initial state:	$A(4), D(0), T(0), N(0)$
Apply operator:	FD(0,4)
New state:	$A(4), D(10), T(0), N(0)$
Apply:	PA(4,0,0)
New state:	$A(9), D(10), T(4), N(1)$
Apply:	PA(9,1,4)
New state:	$A(12), D(10), T(9), N(2)$
Apply:	PD(10,2,9)
New state:	$A(12), D(15), T(10), N(1)$
Apply:	PA(12,1,10)
New state:	$A(19), D(15), T(12), N(2)$
Apply:	PD(15,2,12)
New state:	$A(19), D(16), T(15), N(1)$
Apply:	PD(16,1,15)
New state:	$A(19), D(18), T(16), N(0)$
Apply:	FD(18,19)
New state:	$A(19), D(24), T(16), N(0)$
Apply:	PA(19,0,16)
New state:	$A(22), D(24), T(16), N(1)$

Fig. 12.12.   Application of operators.

Figure 12.12 traces the start of an execution of the state space model. The assumed goal state is $T(480)$. The initial state contains $A(4)$; thus the first value obtained from r_a is 4. The preconditions of the three operators are all checked against the axiom list (initial state). The reader should ascertain that the only operator that can be applied is FD. The operator effects the deletion of $D(0)$ and the addition of $D(10)$; thus the first value obtained for r_d is 6.

The next step is to evaluate the three operators' preconditions with respect to the new state. The appropriate operator is PA and the indicated additions and deletions occur. Figure 12.12 follows the process through four arrivals and three departures.

REFERENCES

1. R. S. Boyer, Locking: A Restriction of Resolution, Ph.D. Thesis, Univ. of Texas, Austin (1971).
2. C. Chang and R. C. Lee, "Symbolic Logic and Mechanical Theorem Proving." Academic Press, New York, 1973.
3. R. E. Fikes and N. J. Nilsson, STRIPS: A new approach to the application of theorem proving to problem solving, *Artificial Intelligence* **2** (1971).
4. G. S. Fishman, "Concepts and Methods in Discrete Event Digital Simulation." Wiley, New York, 1973.
5. C. Green, Application of theorem proving to problem solving, *Proc. Internat. Joint Conf. Artificial Intelligence, 1st* pp. 219–239 (1969).
6. S. C. Kleene, "Mathematical Logic." Wiley, New York, 1967.
7. D. W. Loveland, A linear format for resolution, *Proc. IRIA Symp. Automatic Demonstration*, p. 147–162. Springer-Verlag, Berlin and New York, 1970.
8. N. J. Nilsson, "Problem Solving Methods for Artificial Intelligence." McGraw-Hill, New York, 1971.
9. J. A. Robinson, A machine oriented logic based on the resolution principle, *J. ACM* **12**, 1, 227–234 (1965).
10. J. R. Slagle, Automatic theorem proving with renamable and semantic resolution, *J. ACM* **14**, 4, 687–697 (1967).

Part V

INTEGRATING THE DATA BASE AND FORMAL LOGIC APPROACHES TO DECISION SUPPORT

Part III described a data base approach to DSS development. Part IV discussed decision support systems based on formal logic. The first two chapters of Part V explore the basics of integrating these two approaches. The objective of this integration is to take advantage of the strong points of each approach within a single DSS. Chapter 13 demonstrates correspondences between the two approaches in terms of knowledge representation, problem-processing, and language systems.

In an earlier chapter we saw a data base approach to representing modeling knowledge. Chapter 14 describes how certain modeling knowledge can be represented with formal logic and how such knowledge can be used in a DSS that still employs data base techniques for treating large volumes of empirical, or computed, data. The concluding chapter outlines some paths for future investigation into extending the "intelligence" of decision support systems.

Chapter 13

COMBINING THE DATA BASE AND FORMAL LOGIC APPROACHES

13.00 INTRODUCTION

Several connections between the data base and formal logic approaches are examined in this chapter. Some connections have been alluded to in Chapter 11, where they are examined primarily from the standpoint of "enhancing" a data base-oriented problem processor's capabilities for performing inference. The major aspects of this examination are (1) representing application-specific knowledge needed to perform inference and (2) utilizing that knowledge (within the PPS) in performing inferences to answer problems posed in a stylized language such as that of Chapter 8.

We shall briefly consider the characterization of data base retrieval as an inference process in which axioms are used to control search and retrieval. The bulk of the chapter deals with a mixed system of knowledge representation and its problem processor. Another potential use of axioms in conjunction with a data base is for the specification of data integrity conditions; this is related to the idea of frames [13].

13.10   VIEWING RETRIEVAL AS INFERENCE

The automated retrieval process of category L languages (Chapter 8), in the case of a data base KS, can be thought of as the simplest kind of compaction mapping (Chapter 10). The result is a collection of occurrences of a single record type that are displayed at the user's terminal. This output can be viewed as a virtual file, table, or relation. The output report is virtual in the sense that even though it does not actually exist in the data base, it can be automatically produced.

In Griffeth [7], generation of a virtual table is characterized as an inference process. The knowledge system consists not only of a network data base but also of "inferential rules" that can be expressed as axioms. These axioms are considered to be part of the data base definition, and each is used to specify the inference that can be drawn about some indirect relationship (discussed in Chapter 7). The effect is that indirect relationships are made explicit by giving them names. For example, the indirect relationship giving rise to Fig. 7.2a might have a corresponding (stylized) inference rule such as:

If (CUSTOMER, ORDER) ∈ PLACES and (ORDER, ORDER-LINE) ∈ CONTAINS, then (CUSTOMER, ORDER-LINE) ∈ DETAILS-OF-CUSTOMER-ORDER.

Here DETAILS-OF-CUSTOMER-ORDER is used to describe the indirect (1–N transitive) relationship between a customer and an order line.

In effect, the axioms are paths or path fragments (each consisting of at least two cosets) and they are stored in the KS. These fragments are used by an algorithm (i.e., the PPS) to infer the virtual table desired by a user. See Griffeth [7] and Minker [10] for a discussion of the inference algorithm. Ostensibly, the inferential retrieval and the retrieval based on path finding (Chapter 9) can produce the same collection of virtual tables from a given data base.

In the inferential retrieval, a path (or at least the fragments thereof) to be used for retrieval must be explicitly stated in axiomatic form. The meanings of indirect relationships are specified at the time of data definition. In retrieval that is based on pathfinding (discussed in Chapter 9), a path(s) is constructed at retrieval time. The meanings of the indirect relationships in that path are left for the user to interpret. As pointed out in Griffeth [7], this may be undesirable. A modified approach [1] to retrieval based on pathfinding of Chapter 9 is to give a descriptive name to a sequence of cosets, such that the meaning of the indirect relationships in the path is clear. Such a name can be used to condition a user's retrieval request. This "modified approach" is in the same spirit and appears to have the same net effect as the use of inferential rules, though it may differ in implementation particulars.

13.20   A MIXED SYSTEM OF KNOWLEDGE REPRESENTATION AND ITS PROBLEM PROCESSOR

Section 13.10 briefly suggested a possible use of axioms in conjunction with a data base in order to govern retrieval, such that the resultant tables are unambiguous. We now examine these two forms of knowledge representation from the standpoint of using both of them to capture empirical or computed data. Associated with each method are processes for extracting subsets of the represented knowledge: search and retrieval for the data base and problem resolutions for the axiomatic representation. Our purpose is to examine how the two representation approaches and their associated knowledge extraction processes could be used to complement each other in a single decision support mechanism.

The strength of storing knowledge axiomatically is that it allows the extraction of knowledge not explicitly stated. That is, from explicit axioms inferences can be made, thereby revealing knowledge that is implicit in that axiom set. In contrast, the data base approach requires knowledge to be explicitly stored, although (as indicated earlier) one could argue that search and retrieval involved in generating a virtual table is a simple inference process. Generally, a comparison of the two approaches [15] reveals that data base mechanisms are better suited for situations characterized by large volumes of knowledge that can be organized into comparatively simple logical structures. The inferential approach, on the other hand, is better suited for situations where simple logical structure is unable to represent modest volumes of knowledge.

The bulk of this chapter concerns various aspects of this mixed approach. First we show that a correspondence exists between certain types of predicate clauses and the kinds of information that can be accommodated within a network data base. A procedure for converting a collection of predicate calculus clauses (and an associated set of meta-axioms) into a network data base, plus a residual collection of clauses, is presented. The way the original collection of predicate clauses is stated will influence the resultant network structure.

A discussion follows on the nature of problem processing for retrieval in situations where knowledge about a problem area is organized according to the mixed approach. Additions to the problem processor described in Chapter 9, enabling it to accomplish this sort of processing, are outlined. The query processor of Chapter 9 might be characterized as being a fairly structured question-answering system. This structuredness derives from the limitations inherent in the data base features available for knowledge representation. More flexibility in query processing is permitted when more extensive knowledge representation features are available, as in the mixed approach.

There is some important work related to the topics addressed in this chapter, particularly with respect to the connection between logic and the relational data base notion. Chang [2], Minker [11], and Van Emden [14] among others have examined the use of predicate calculus axioms in conjunction with relations. A comparative study will not be undertaken here, but some of the major results are briefly described. Predicates are viewed as relations that either explicitly exist in a relational data base or can be deduced by applying theorem-proving techniques to general axioms. These researchers present algorithms for the production of virtual relations; that is, relations that are desired by the system users but that are not explicitly stored. Chang proposes a query language in the form of predicate calculus for user specification of the relation to be produced.

13.21   The Predicate Clause—Data Base Correspondence

Data base tools afford an effective mechanism for storing clauses that consist of single predicates having constants as arguments. Suppose there are several such clauses containing the predicate symbol P. Then define a record type P, composed of item types to correspond with the arguments of the predicate P. There is an occurrence of the record type P for each clause whose only predicate symbol is P. Values of the item occurrences of a record occurrence of P are identical to the arguments of the predicate P in the corresponding clause. Thus the set of all occurrences of record type P gives the set of all interpretations of predicate P that have the value true. An example is given in Fig. 13.1.

The same example can be expanded to treat SUPPLIER and PART as predicates, necessitating the clauses shown in Fig. 13.2a. Observe that we are now dealing with three predicates. Adhering to the convention of viewing a record type as a predicate that evaluates to true for all interpretations corresponding to occurrences of the record type, we obtain the data base representation in Fig. 13.2b and 13.2c. In Fig. 13.2b AGENT

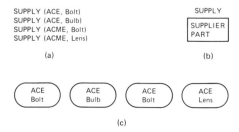

SUPPLY (ACE, Bolt)
SUPPLY (ACE, Bulb)
SUPPLY (ACME, Bolt)
SUPPLY (ACME, Lens)

(a)

SUPPLY

| SUPPLIER |
| PART |

(b)

(ACE / Bolt)   (ACE / Bulb)   (ACE / Bolt)   (ACE / Lens)

(c)

Fig. 13.1.   Representing axioms as record occurrences. (a) Axioms dealing solely with predicate SUPPLY. (b) The record type SUPPLY. (c) Occurrences of record type SUPPLY.

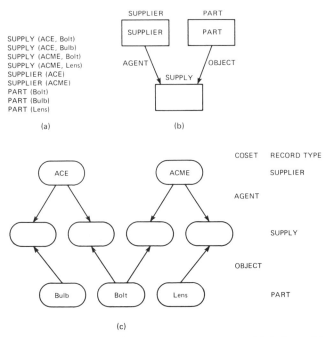

SUPPLY (ACE, Bolt)
SUPPLY (ACE, Bulb)
SUPPLY (ACME, Bolt)
SUPPLY (ACME, Lens)
SUPPLIER (ACE)
SUPPLIER (ACME)
PART (Bolt)
PART (Bulb)
PART (Lens)

(a)

(b)

(c)

Fig. 13.2. Representing axioms in an occurrence structure. (a) Axioms. (b) Data base representation of the three predicates (logical structure). (c) Data base representation of the nine axioms (occurrence structure).

and OBJECT denote cosets. Thus each occurrence of SUPPLY is associated with no more than one occurrence of SUPPLIER and with no more than one occurrence of PART. In our example, each occurrence of SUPPLY is associated with exactly one occurrence of SUPPLIER and exactly one occurrence of PART, because none of the clauses about SUPPLY has an empty argument.

Figure 13.2c displays the nine data base record occurrences that are specified by the nine clauses of Fig. 13.2a. The existence of the two occurrences of the record type SUPPLIER indicates that the predicate SUPPLIER has two true interpretations: ACE and ACME. Similarly, the three record occurrences of the record type PART give the three instances that make the predicate PART true. The record type SUPPLY has four occurrences, which means that there are four instances that make the predicate SUPPLY true. Since each of the four occurrences has exactly one supplier and one part associated with it, the instances that make the SUPPLY predicate true are easily determined. The foregoing examples can, of course, be generalized to predicates of more than two arguments.

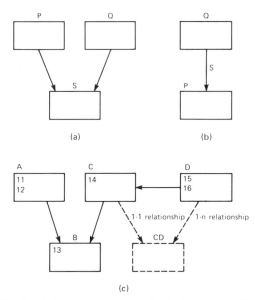

Fig. 13.3. Collapsing logical structures. (a) Logical structure. (b) Collapsed logical structure. (c) Logical structure for query example.

13.22 Expanding the Coset Construct in Predicate Calculus

An important special case of logical structures of the variety shown in Fig. 13.2b must be examined. Referring to Fig. 13.3a, we begin with a data base representation of the three predicates P, Q, and S. Suppose that the predicate S has no argument that does not have the same domain as some argument in the predicate P or in the predicate Q. In data base vernacular the record type S has no data item types. For simplicity of exposition, let us say that the predicate S has two arguments, one for P and one for Q. Thus the predicate S is true for certain pairs of occurrences of P and Q; that is, there is a set of axioms concerning the predicate S that corresponds to the occurrences of the record type S. The predicate S defines a relationship between the predicates P and Q.

Let the predicate S have two arguments, the first of which has the same domain as an argument of P and the second of which has the same domain as one of Q's arguments. A special case of this relationship (which frequently arises) occurs when there are no three clauses of the form: $S(a_1,b_1)$, $S(a_1,b_2)$, $S(a_2,b_2)$, where $a_1 \neq a_2$ and $b_1 \neq b_2$. A condition of this kind provides the basis on which the logical structure of Fig. 13.3a can be collapsed into another logical structure such as the one depicted in Fig. 13.3b.

In the event of no three clauses being interrelated in the form of $S(a_1, b_1)$, $S(a_1,b_2)$, $S(a_2,b_2)$, the relationship between record types P and Q is a coset. This basis for collapsing can be explained as follows. The preceding condition means that clauses consisting of the predicate S may be of any one (and only one) of the following varieties:

1. $\{S(a_1,b_1), S(a_2,b_2), S(a_3,b_3), \ldots\}$
2. $\{S(a_1,b_1), S(a_1,b_2), \ldots, S(a_1, b_m), S(a_2, b_{m+1}), S(a_2, b_{m+2}), \ldots\}$
3. $\{S(a_1,b_1), S(a_2,b_1), \ldots, S(a_n,b_1), S(a_{n+1},b_2), S(a_{n+2},b_2), \ldots\}$.

The first indicates a strictly one-to-one relationship between occurrences of record type P and occurrences of record type Q, allowing us to say that P owns Q or Q owns P in coset terminology. The second indicates a coset relationship in which P owns Q. And the third, which is illustrated in Fig. 13.3b, indicates a coset in which Q owns P. Notice that the collapsed logical data base structure of Fig. 13.3b leads to greater storage efficiencies (fewer pointers to represent the same intrinsic information) than the structure in Fig. 13.3a.

In terms of predicate calculus this type of relationship between P and Q may be stated as

$$(\forall y)P(y) \Rightarrow [[(\forall x)Q(x) \Rightarrow {\sim}S(y,x)] \vee [(\exists w)\{Q(w) \Rightarrow S(y,w) \\ \wedge (\forall z)(Q(z) \wedge S(y,z) \Rightarrow EQ(w,z))\}]].$$

On conversion to clause form, this condition yields the following axioms:

$$\sim P(y) \vee \sim Q(x) \vee \sim S(y,x) \vee Q(f(y)) \tag{1a}$$
$$\sim P(y) \vee \sim Q(x) \vee \sim S(y,x) \vee S(y,f(y)) \tag{1b}$$
$$\sim P(y) \vee \sim Q(z) \vee \sim S(y,z) \vee EQ(f(y),z). \tag{2}$$

The predicate EQ evaluates to true if and only if its two arguments are equal. The result is that we can utilize the structure of Fig. 13.3b instead of that in Fig. 13.3a, only if our set of axioms include (1) and (2). On the other hand, the structure of Fig. 13.3b implies that axioms (1) and (2) are valid.

13.23   A Conversion Procedure

Before we discuss a more formal specification of a procedure for converting axiomatic forms into data base forms of knowledge representation, we introduce the notion of meta-axioms, which are used to indicate the semantics of the clauses to be used. These meta-axioms provide a formal specification of the meaning, or sense, of predicates appearing in the clause list. Meta-axioms are used in the conversion of clauses to data structures. In particular, the meta-axioms describe how predicates are related to each other by having common argument domains. For instance, in order to describe the situation where the first argument of $T(x,y)$ and the argument of $S(z)$ have the same domain (or sample space), the following meta-axioms are stated:

$$\forall x \forall y \; T(x,y) \Rightarrow D_1(x)$$
$$\forall z \; S(z) \Rightarrow D_1(z)$$

These axioms are sufficient for indicating that there is a common domain; the elements of that domain are not of immediate concern. There is a close correspondence between these meta-axioms and principles of multi-sorted logic [4].

To convert a set of clauses, each having one predicate and constants as arguments, into a network data base:

1. Let $\hat{P}$ be the set of all predicates appearing in single predicate clauses that have constants as arguments.

2. For each $P \in \hat{P}$, define a record type P' having one item type for each argument of P.

3. Define a record type D_i' for each domain predicate D_i appearing in the meta-axioms.

4. For each $P \in \hat{P}$, do the following:

let n = number of arguments of P for which domains have been specified;

for $j = 1, n$ define a coset with P' as owner and D_i' as member, where D_i is the domain of the jth argument of P.

5. Collapse the resultant logical structure wherever posssible; that is, wherever a coset is known to exist between predicates (as shown in the previous section). If a collapse results in the deletion of some D_i', then delete, from the resultant member record type(s) P', the item type corresponding to the argument of P with domain D_i'.

6. Delete any D_i' that is not the member of more than one coset relationship.

7. For each clause having a single (constant-valued) predicate, create a record occurrence of the corresponding record type. This proceeds in a top–down fashion according to the logical structure derived in steps 1–6. If the number of a predicate's arguments exceeds the number of item types in the corresponding record type by h, its record occurrence must be made a member in h cosets logically linking it to the owner occurrences specified by the excess arguments. It is possible that an argument may suggest an owner occurrence that does not exist, in which case no coset occurrence is created.

8. For each D_i' remaining in the logical structure do the following:

Let m = number of cosets for which D_i' is a member;
let P_k' $(k = 1, \ldots, m)$ be the owner record types for these m cosets;
let $C = \{p_1', p_2', \ldots, p_m'\}$ be a combination formed by selecting an
    occurrence p_1' of P_1', an occurrence p_2' of P_2', etc.;
let $\hat{C}$ be the set of all combinations C;
for a given $C \in \hat{C}$ and for $k = 1, \ldots, m$, let c_k be the constant value
    of the item type having domain D_i in record occurrence p_k';
if $c_1 = c_2 = \cdots = c_m$, then create an occurrence of D_i' and make it
    the member in m coset occurrences whose owners are the p_k'
    $(k = 1, \ldots, m)$ that constitute C.

Several observations may be made concerning this conversion procedure. First, it is not the only conversion method possible. Second, it is desirable, from the standpoint of efficiency, to collapse the logical structure as much as possible. The degree of collapsing that can occur is a function of available knowledge about the problem area being addressed. A logical structure containing many domain record types is indicative of either a lack of exact knowledge about the nature of interrelationships among predicates or an absence of any relationship among predicates other than common domains. Knowledge of the existence of a coset relationship between two record types (predicates) describes their interrelationship more precisely than if we know only that the predicates have arguments with a common domain. The result of such additional knowledge is a more concise logical structure. In the following examples it is assumed that there is sufficient knowledge to collapse all domain record types out of the logical structures.

The creation of occurrences in step 7 deserves further comment and illustration. Suppose we have the meta-axioms

$$\forall x \, \forall y \, \forall z \; \text{GRADE } (x,y,z) \Rightarrow D_1(x) \wedge D_2(y)$$
$$\forall u \; \text{STUDENT } (u) \Rightarrow D_1(u)$$
$$\forall v \; \text{ASSIGNMENT } (v) \Rightarrow D_2(v)$$

for describing the semantics of the clauses in Fig. 13.4a. The corresponding logical and occurrence structures are given in Figs. 13.4b and 13.4c, respectively. Now suppose that the student ED withdraws but that it is still desirable to maintain the scores of that student for grading purposes. This results in removal of the clause STUDENT (ED) from the clause list (Fig. 13.5a). Correspondingly, the record occurrence of STUDENT for ED must be eliminated. The elimination of ED from the data base necessarily removes all coset occurrences that ED owned (Fig. 13.4b). Thus

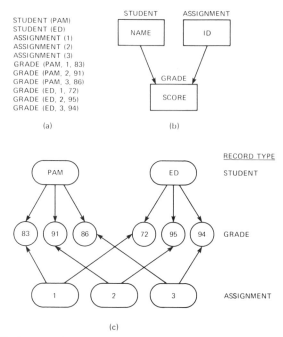

STUDENT (PAM)
STUDENT (ED)
ASSIGNMENT (1)
ASSIGNMENT (2)
ASSIGNMENT (3)
GRADE (PAM, 1, 83)
GRADE (PAM, 2, 91)
GRADE (PAM, 3, 86)
GRADE (ED, 1, 72)
GRADE (ED, 2, 95)
GRADE (ED, 3, 94)

(a)

(b)

(c)

Fig. 13.4.   Student–teacher–grade example. (a) Predicate clauses. (b) Logical structure. (c) Occurrence structure.

queries that refer to ED will give the response that no knowledge is available to satisfy the request. Queries about students cannot return any information about ED. However, information about all grades that have been given for all assignments is still available.

Observe (Fig. 13.5a) that there are some GRADE predicates that still have ED as a first argument. This leads to several anomalies. Using the clause knowledge we can find answers to the queries:

$$\exists x \, \exists y \, \text{GRADE} \, (ED,x,y)$$

and

$$\forall u \, \exists v \, (\text{GRADE} \, (v,u,94) \land \sim\text{STUDENT} \, (v))$$

by determining those arguments that make the queries true. The first finds an assignment and score associated with the placeholder ED; it says nothing about whether ED is or is not a student. With the data base representation of Fig. 13.5b we can still obtain assignment-score pairs, but there is no way to distinguish (in terms of a name) among those pairs that were formerly associated with students. The second query finds all entities that

STUDENT (PAM)
ASSIGNMENT (1)
ASSIGNMENT (2)
ASSIGNMENT (3)
GRADE (PAM, 1, 83)
GRADE (PAM, 2, 91)
GRADE (PAM, 3, 86)
GRADE (ED, 1, 72)
GRADE (ED, 2, 95)
GRADE (ED, 3, 94)

(a)

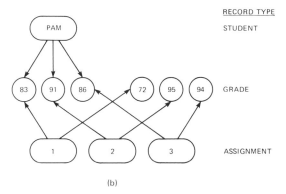

(b)

Fig. 13.5.   Deletion of a student. (a) Predicate clauses. (b) Corresponding occurrence structure.

have a grade but are not students. A semantic issue is raised here; i.e., if an entity is no longer a student, is it desirable to maintain that that entity has a grade? Although this is not done in the network representation of Fig. 13.5b, assignment-score pairs are still maintained. If it is desirable to preserve the fact that ED is a former student, the anomalies can be averted by creating a new predicate FORMER-STUDENT and adding the additional clause FORMER-STUDENT (ED) to the clause list in Fig. 13.5a. This would necessitate a restructuring of the logical structure in Fig. 13.4b, as well as the introduction of additional meta-axioms. (There are other clauses that could convey the same information without requiring a restructuring.)

Suppose one took the approach of representing predicates by Codd relations. Now examine the clauses containing ED in Fig. 13.5a. If we represent these by a relation, there are two approaches for handling the first argument of the GRADE predicate: The corresponding relation field either has semantic information associated with it or it does not. If it does (e.g., the field is called "student"), then an inaccuracy is introduced when ED is removed from the STUDENT relation. This could be averted by eliminating the GRADE clauses containing ED, but the result would be that all assignment-score pairs are no longer available (and the alternative is restructuring of the relational data base). The second approach (fields without direct semantics) would be consistent with the network approach previously described.

In passing we note that the process of splitting item types out of a record type to form sets and new record types is a procedure often employed during the course of network data base design. Moreover, it is directly analogous [8] to normalization procedures applied to relations that are in first normal form.

We conclude that a collection of single-predicate clauses can be converted into a network data base in which each record occurrence specifies one of the clauses. Conversely, a given network data structure can be converted into a collection of clauses. Suppose that we are given a list of clauses akin to those in Fig. 13.2a, except that there are hundreds of suppliers and thousands of parts. Using resolution to answer questions about this list is unwieldy, compared to search and retrieval using the data base representation in Fig. 13.2b. On the other hand, storage of complex axioms is not always easily (i.e., cheaply, in terms of storage) accomplished in a network structure. Several examples follow illustrating the workings of a "mixed" system that concurrently handles knowledge representation of both the axiomatic and data base varieties.

13.24   Retrieval–Resolution Correspondences

An example will illustrate the correspondence between nonprocedural data base queries (in terms of the stylized language from Chapter 8) used to drive a retrieval process and predicate queries used in problem resolution processes. Consider the data structure shown in Fig. 13.3c; data item types are denoted with the prefix I. The dotted lines are not part of the structure per se; however, they suggest how the coset associating C with D could be viewed as the predicate CD, if one were interested in converting occurrences of the logical data structure into a group of predicate clauses.

A sample query is DISPLAY I1, I3, I4 FOR I2 $= a$, I5 $> b$. The data base problem processor constructs an appropriate DML retrieval program to produce a table of occurrences having three columns, for I1, I3, and I4. Entries in this output table are those occurrences that satisfy the stated conditions on I2 and I5. The equivalent query in terms of predicate calculus is

$$\exists w \; \exists x, \; \exists y, \; \exists z \; B(x,a,y,z) \land CD(y,w,v) \land GT(w,b),$$

where GT is a "greater than" predicate. If occurrences organized according to the logical structure of Fig. 13.3c were converted to clause form, these clauses could be used (via an iterative resolution process) to answer the predicate form of the query. The argument-item type correspondence can be established by an appropriate DDL convention, such as the ordering of item type definitions within record types and the ordering of coset definitions. (Once again note that the coset between D and C in the data structure is easily converted to the record type CD, owned by the two indicated cosets.) The result is that the query directing automatic data base retrieval can be expressed as a particular type of predicate calculus query. Moreover, since both queries give the same result, the data base retrieval process must correspond to problem resolution (of a limited sort).

13.25 Mixed System Processing Examples

The knowledge to be represented in the first example deals with the parts that suppliers supply. This could be accomplished axiomatically as in Fig. 13.2a; alternatively, it is accomplished by organizing appropriate occurrences according to the network structure of Fig. 13.2b. The latter course is chosen here. Suppose that we have additional knowledge to the effect that the supplier ROSS always supplies at least the same kinds of parts as some other supplier, say ACE. Using the predicate calculus formulation we have

$$\forall x \; \text{SUPPLY (ACE, } x) \Rightarrow \text{SUPPLY (ROSS, } x)$$

In clause form this gives $\sim$SUPPLY (ACE, x) $\bigvee$ SUPPLY (ROSS, x). Since both ACE and ROSS are suppliers, there is an occurrence of the record type SUPPLIER for each. One method for incorporating this additional knowledge into the data base is to`convert the initial set of clauses:

> SUPPLY (ACE, Bolt)
> SUPPLY (ACE, Bulb)
> $\sim$SUPPLY (ACE, x) $\bigvee$ SUPPLY (ROSS, x)

into

> SUPPLY (ACE, Bolt)
> SUPPLY (ACE, Bulb)
> SUPPLY (ROSS, Bolt)
> SUPPLY (ROSS, Bulb)

The resultant clauses indicate the need for four occurrences of the record type SUPPLY, whereas the initial clauses demand only two such occurrences plus a clause. As the number of parts supplied by ACE becomes large this difference in storage becomes important.

Another disadvantage of this conversion procedure is that it results in a loss of information. On examining the resultant clauses (or their corresponding data base record occurrences) we have no way of ascertaining whether (1) ROSS always supplies the parts supplied by ACE, (2) ACE always supplies the parts supplied by ROSS, (3) ROSS and ACE always supply the same parts, or (4) the appearance of some special relationship between the supply activities of ACE and ROSS is a transitory coincidence. Utilizing a mixed system (having two record occurrences and one clause) there is no such ambiguity.

Clearly, this mixed knowledge representation technique cannot be accessed and maintained by the usual DML (or by query systems based thereon). However, many DML functions can be retained without modification. For instance, in adding a new record occurrence such as SUPPLY (ACE, Casing) the usual DML can be used. Addition of a record occurrence for SUPPLY (ROSS, Widget) also uses the standard DML; the same follows for deletions. Retrieval activities are another matter. To extract a list of all parts supplied by ACE, we simply use standard DML procedures, but to extract a list of all parts supplied by ROSS, additional procedures are needed. Standard DML can be used to extract those parts supplied exclusively by ROSS. Extraction of the remaining parts must make use of the clause $\sim$SUPPLY (ACE, x) $\bigvee$ SUPPLY (ROSS, x). That is, formal resolution procedures must be invoked.

The query in this example can be answered if we can show that the predicate expression $(\exists w)$ SUPPLY (ROSS, w) follows from the clauses inherent in the data base and the additional explicitly stored clauses. Applying resolution with Green's tracing mechanism [6] gives the resolvent shown in Fig. 13.6. The broken line indicates the point where traditional resolution procedures end. At this point there are no further explicitly stored clauses that one can unify with $\sim$SUPPLY (ACE, x).

On reaching such a point, determine whether the variables remaining in the ANS predicate are the same as those left in the remainder of the resolvent. If this is the case, then the remainder is negated to obtain the form of a clause needed for unification. The data base can be searched for occurrences of the variables appearing in this clause form. These occurrences form the answer (i.e., the values that make ANS true). Observe that this negation process yields a conjunctive expression that corresponds (see the previous section) to a query in the existing data base query language. In the preceding example the clause needed for unification is SUPPLY (ACE, ____), where the second argument is a term. This corresponds to the simple query DISPLAY PART FOR

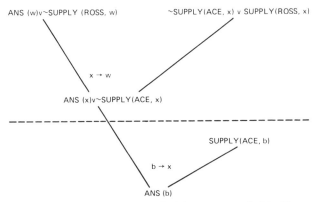

Fig. 13.6.   Using resolution to find the parts supplied by Ross.

SUPPLIER = ACE. The query processor constructs a standard DML program to search the data base for occurrences corresponding to predicates of this kind. For all occurrences of SUPPLY (ACE, b) that are found, b is an entry in the list that forms the answer to the query. Thus some entries are obtained immediately from the data base using DML, whereas others are obtained indirectly by inference.

As a second example, consider a knowledge base consisting of occurrences organized according to the structure of Fig. 13.7a and the two axioms:

$$\forall x \; \forall y \; \{P(x,y) \land P(y,z) \Rightarrow G(x,z)\} \tag{3}$$
$$\forall y \; \exists x \; \{P(x,y)\} \tag{4}$$

These axioms may be rewritten in clause form as

$$\sim P(x,y) \lor \sim P(y,z) \lor G(x,z) \tag{3'}$$
$$P(f(w), w) \tag{4'}$$

The occurrence structure for the logical structure of Fig. 13.7a indicates who is the parent of whom. An occurrence of PERSON, say P2, corresponds to a predicate clause PERSON (P2). An occurrence of P corresponds to a predicate clause having two arguments, each of which is a person's name. If, for instance, P1 is the parent of P2 then there is an occurrence of P whose owner (via the AGENT coset) is P1 and whose owner (via the OBJECT coset) is P2. Correspondingly, $P(P1,P2)$ is true.

Axiom (3) may be viewed as defining a virtual record type G, where x is the grandparent of z. Axiom (4) indicates that every person has at least one parent. In order to have a data occurrence structure consistent with the second axiom, one must create a "null" occurrence of PERSON; this

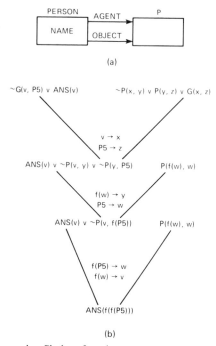

Fig. 13.7.   Interpreting Skolem functions. (a) Logical structure. (b) Resolution.

is due to the finiteness of a data base. A person for whom no parent exists (as an occurrence of PERSON) is associated with the ''null'' occurrence of PERSON, via the AGENT and OBJECT cosets.

To find the grandparents of person P5, the query $\exists x \, G(x, \text{P5})$ must be answered. The resolution process is traced in Fig. 13.7b. Notice that the final resolvent consists solely of an ANS predicate. If this predicate contained no Skolem functions, then the query would be completely answered; in its present form, however, we have only a statement of how to find the answer. More precisely, the Skolem functions specify the path in the data structure of Fig. 13.7a, along which the answer may be found.

In the preceding example (Fig. 13.6) resolution was used to reduce the original query into an expression in the existing query language. The query processor responds to the resultant query by automatically determining the path that allows conditioned retrieval of the requested data item occurrences. In the example of Fig. 13.7, resolution does not give a resolvent that is readily convertible to an expression in the existing query language. Indeed, this step is bypassed in that the Skolem functions indicate the path for conditioned retrieval of the requested data item occurrences.

The meaning of the Skolem function f, in terms of a data base path, can be seen by examining the clause $P(f(w), w)$. It is known (from the previously described DDL ordering convention) that the first argument of the predicate P corresponds to the data item type NAME in the record type PERSON, as it is related to the record type P via the coset AGENT. The second argument also corresponds to the data item type NAME in the record type PERSON. The occurrences of NAME that can appear as constants in the second argument position are those associated with P via the OBJECT coset.

For a given w, say P5, the P5 occurrence of PERSON can own several occurrences of P via the OBJECT coset. This is illustrated in Fig. 13.8, where arcs labeled with A are in AGENT coset occurrences and OBJECT coset occurrences are labeled with O. Each occurrence of record type P has the corresponding predicate form $P(\underline{}, \text{P5})$. The first argument is the name in an occurrence of PERSON that owns the P occurrence via the AGENT coset. Two such occurrences are shown in Fig. 13.8. Labeled α and β, they correspond to predicate clauses $P(\text{P4,P5})$ and $P(\text{P3,P5})$, respectively.

Thus f has a clear meaning from the data base viewpoint. It defines the path from PERSON to P (via OBJECT) and then to PERSON (via AGENT). It follows that $f(w)$ specifies a retrieval procedure, conditioned

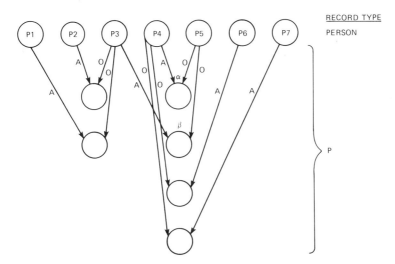

Fig. 13.8. Sample occurrences for the schema of Fig. 13.7a.

on the value of w and using the above path. For instance, $f(P5)$ has the values P3, P4. The answer to $f(f(P5))$ is given by $f(P3) \cup f(P4)$, which is P1, P2, P6, P7.

To summarize, a Skolem function f may be interpreted as a path along which data may be retrieved. Application of f to a constant is analogous to the process of applying the path to data, resulting in some data. The process of applying a path is called retrieval and it is conditioned by the data to which it is applied. Be careful to observe that this is not the only means available for path specification. In the first example, the query obtained from the resolvent implies a path. This implied path is determined by the existing query processor, which proceeds to execute the retrieval.

The point of the grandfather example is to show the close relationship between Skolem functions and cosets. It must be pointed out, however, that this is not a complete method of retrieval in cases of recursively stated axioms. For instance, if we were interested in determining all ancestors of some person, then from the resolution we could generate an infinite number of resolvents. But the data base contains only a finite number of ancestors. This difficulty would entail a modification to the resolution algorithm chosen for inclusion in the extended processor, in order to stop the resolution at an appropriate level of recursion.

The data base problem processor of Chapter 9 must be extended if it is to accommodate a mixed system for knowledge representation. As previously indicated, expressions in the stylized language of Chapter 8 can be translated into equivalent predicate queries. However, not all predicate queries can be conveniently expressed in that stylized language. A revision of the stylized language to provide more expressive power (while maintaining its English-like appearance) would necessitate change in the data base problem processor's linguistic components.

The problem processor must also be extended to include a resolution facility or one of its variants [5, 6] and needs to be interfaced with existing pathfinding and retrieval code. As it is presently visualized, the extended processor first attempts to perform retrieval, on receiving a query. In other words, its first step is to do precisely what the Chapter 9 processor does: Build a table (relation) that answers the query. (The term "retrieval" is used here in the sense of inferential retrieval alluded to in the background section; it does not refer to retrieval of general axioms that are stored explicitly in the data base for use in resolution.)

The result of the initial attempt to answer a query is a table that may be empty or only partial. Thus the system first attempts to answer the query, without resorting to the theorem proving, by using inferential retrieval that builds a virtual relation from a data base. As noted earlier, this kind of inferential retrieval can be characterized as a theorem-proving process, although it need not be implemented by using theorem-proving techniques.

After this initial retrieval is executed (if it is possible to do so), the query is converted to its conjunctive predicate calculus form and subjected to resolution that can involve multistep deductions. If the resolution cannot be performed, or if it does not result in a resolvent that can be converted to a retrievable query, then the results of the initial retrieval (if any) are presented to the user. If the resolution does give a retrievable query, it is executed and its results are appended (with duplicates deleted) to results (if any) of the initial inferential retrieval, giving the final table of data for presentation to the user.

One point that must be emphasized in connection with the system described earlier is that it is not intended to address all the difficulties inherent in resolution procedures. In effect, it utilizes resolution in a different way from its prior use; that is, a resolution algorithm is not used from the beginning to the end of problem solving. It is one step in the problem-solving process. For instance, there are still difficulties of nondeterminism and search techniques that are handled variously, depending on the particular resolution algorithm employed and the kind of axiom set that an algorithm allows. The nature of the particular resolution algorithm chosen for use in the extended query processor determines how these problems are dealt with.

Questions such as whether grandfather can be defined by more than one general axiom or whether axioms can be recursively defined are answered by the resolution algorithm chosen. However, as indicated in the preceding paragraphs, the proposed system would allow an axiom that defines grandfather to coexist in the system with occurrences of a data item type for grandfather.

13.30   KNOWLEDGE REPRESENTATION VIA FRAMES

The case grammar model for knowledge representation [13] can be usefully applied in pointing out the relationships between knowledge representation via predicate calculus and via a network data base. In the case grammar model an event is a predicate and the relationships between a predicate and its arguments are called cases (e.g., agents, objects, etc.). A frame is the graph of an event and its arguments. In the network representation primary consideration is given to binary relationships among concepts [8], i.e., cosets that are used to establish relationships between pairs of record types. An important issue is the extent to which we can represent a more complex relationship that exists among several concepts, such that we can refer to the relationship as a whole. This issue is not addressed in traditional network approaches.

The notion of a frame can provide additional semantics for network data structures. It will also be seen that the predicates corresponding to a group of frame instantiations are constant-valued single-predicate clauses. Regarding the first point, the data structure shown in Fig. 13.9b can be interpreted as the frame in Fig. 13.9a. Suppliers supply parts to customers. An instantiation of the frame corresponds to an occurrence of the record type PART plus an occurrence of CUSTOMER plus an occurrence of SUPPLIER (plus an occurrence of SUPPLY if it has any item types), such that these three are logically associated through a common occurrence of SUPPLY. Finally this "common occurrence" corresponds to a constant-valued single predicate clause. The data structures used in earlier examples can be viewed as frames. The structure of Fig. 13.2b indicates that "SUPPLIERS SUPPLY PARTS." SUPPLIER is the type of agent in the SUPPLY event, and PART is the type of object. Similarly, the

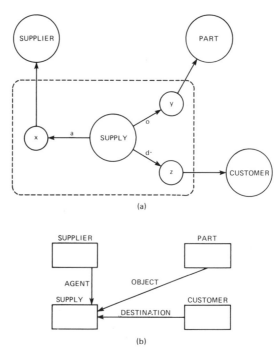

(a)

(b)

Fig. 13.9. The frame–network correspondence. (a) Frame representation. (b) Network representation.

logical structure of Fig. 13.7a is interpreted as "PERSON is parent of PERSON," where *P* is used to denote the event of being a parent. PERSON describes the type of both the agent and the object of this event.

In general, a record type that is "owned" by others may be interpreted as representing an (generic) event that is defined in terms of the "owning" record types (concepts). Each of the owning record types may be viewed as a role that can be filled by any of its occurrences. The coset name indicates the nature of that role with respect to the event.

Just as a frame asserts nothing about actual supply events, the corresponding logical data structure asserts nothing about the actual occurrence structure. For instance, it could be the case that some occurrence of SUPPLY is associated only with a supplier and a part, but with no customer. The corresponding frame instantiation is partial. Roussopoulos [13] indicates how the predicate calculus can be used to specify what might be termed "integrity conditions" with respect to a frame, by drawing such conditions into the pictorial representation.

These integrity conditions are assertions about actual events (e.g., a certain supplier can supply only certain parts and any attempt to alter the data base must not violate this condition). Integrity conditions are conceptually related to feasibility checking [3] that occurs during data base loading and modification.

In this section we have demonstrated the correspondence between frame pictures (without integrity conditions) and network data base structure. Now if integrity conditions are drawn into a frame, is there a correspondence for network data base structure? How can we operationalize these integrity conditions in the context of a network data base system? One solution is to express integrity conditions in terms of axioms that become a part of the data base's logical structure. In earlier sections of this paper we saw how general axioms could be valuable as a part of a data base's contents. It is submitted that they can also be an important part of the logical structure of a data base.

Information is loaded into a data base according to the constraints imposed by its logical structure. Therefore a class of axioms that specify integrity conditions is properly considered as a part of a logical structure. This is an extension to the traditional data base schema definition. Rather than using axioms for question answering, they are here used to govern data base loading and modification. This usage of axioms deserves research to answer the questions of how it can be combined with data definition languages, to what extent resolution techniques can be usefully applied to deduce implied integrity conditions, and how data manipulation language commands must be altered (if at all) to accommodate axiomatic integrity conditions.

13.40   CONCLUSION

We have examined the idea of a mixed system for knowledge representation where some knowledge is stored in a network data base and other knowledge is stored axiomatically. Knowledge stored in a network data base may be viewed as a method for organizing certain kinds of clauses, which allows a rapid resolution (via automatic pathfinding and retrieval procedures) of certain kinds of queries. Axiomatically stored knowledge enables us to represent abstract knowledge without reducing it to more voluminous, concrete facts.

To process a query requiring inference a processor must exist that is capable of transforming strings of the query language into a predicate calculus counterpart. This implies that the language should handle quantification to take advantage of stored predicate calculus clauses. Second, there must be a resolution-performing module capable of resolving the query against the stored predicate calculus clauses down to the point where an automatic pathfinding and retrieval module completes the resolution.

The collection of stored predicate calculus clauses may be divided into three classes. The first contains all information pertaining to data integrity; they give a more sophisticated method for specifying the semantics of a data structure than those facilities traditionally available to data description languages for the network. This is particularly true with respect to quantification [13]. The class of integrity clauses forms an adjunct to the usual DDL description and is used during data loading and modification, assuring that data structure semantics are not violated.

The second class of predicate calculus clauses contains knowledge about the problem area rather than knowledge about organization of such problem area knowledge. These clauses are used only during problem processing (the resolution phase). This second class of axioms served as the focal point of this chapter. The third use of predicate clauses, briefly mentioned in Section 13.10, is for explicitly naming indirect relationships and for controlling which data base path is selected in cases where multiple paths exist for answering a query.

Current research is exploring whether there are demarcation lines between these three uses of axioms. Future research efforts will be directed toward developing the previously mentioned extensions to the extant query language and problem processor. A further interesting question is the relationship between the query processing discussed here and ideas from the field of model theory. The preliminary results presented here, along with other work in a similar vein [7, 9, 12, 14], serve to demonstrate that the mixed approach to knowledge representation and processing deserves further investigation. Another usage of the mixed approach, as a basis for model formulation, is presented in the next chapter.

REFERENCES

1. R. H. Bonczek, C. W. Holsapple, and A. B. Whinston, Design and implementation of an information base for decision makers, *Proc. Nat. Comput. Conf., Dallas, Texas,* (June 1977).
2. C. L. Chang, DEDUCE: A deduction query language for relational data bases, *in* "Pattern Recognition and Artificial Intelligence" (C. G. Chen, ed.). Academic Press, New York, 1976.
3. H. D. Clifton, "Systems Analysis for Business Data Processing." Petrocelli Books, New York, 1974.
4. H. Gallaire, J. Minker, and J. M. Nicolas, An overview and introduction to logic and data bases, *in* "Logic and Data Bases" (H. Gallaire and J. Minker, eds.). Plenum Press, New York, 1978.
5. C. Green, Application of theorem proving to problem solving, *Proc. Internat. Joint Conf. Artificial Intelligence, 1st* (1969).
6. C. Green, Thorem proving by resolution as a basis for question answering systems, *in* "Machine Intelligence" (B. Meltzer and D. Michie, eds.), Vol. 4. American Elsevier, New York, 1969.
7. N. Griffeth, Nonprocedural Query Processing for Data Bases with Access Paths, Discussion Paper No. 313. Graduate School of Management, Northwestern Univ. (December 1977).
8. W. D. Haseman and A. B. Whinston, "Introduction to Data Management." Irwin, Homewood, Illinois, 1977.
9. W. D. Haseman and A. B. Whinston, Problem solving in data management, *Proc. Internat. Conf. Artificial Intelligence, 4th, Tbilisi, Georgia, U.S.S.R.* (September 1975).
10. J. Minker, Performing inferences over relational data bases, *Proc. Internat. Conf. Management Data, San Jose, California* (May 1975).
11. J. Minker, Search strategy and selection function for an inferential relational system, *ACM Trans. Data Base Syst.* **3,** No 1 (1978).
12. J. M. Nicholas and K. Yazdanian, Integrity checking in deductive data bases, *in* "Logic and Data Bases" (H. Galliare and J. Minker, eds.). Plenum Press, New York, 1978.
13. N. Roussopoulos, ADD: Algebraic Data Definition, IBM Research Rep. RJ2060 (August 1977).
14. N. H. Van Emden, Computation and Deductive Information Retrieval, Res. Rep. CS-77-16, Department of Computer Science, Univ. of Waterloo (May 1977).
15. H. K. T. Wong and J. Mylopulos, Two Views of Data Semantics. Department of Computer Science, Univ. of Toronto (December 1976).

Chapter 14

OPERATIONALIZING MODELING KNOWLEDGE IN TERMS OF PREDICATE CALCULUS

14.00 INTRODUCTION

One method for representing modeling knowledge has already been discussed in the last part of Chapter 10. An alternative, or perhaps complementary, approach is the subject of this chapter. The two approaches are similar in that both stem from the framework of organizational roles introduced in Chapter 2. However, the approach presented in this chapter might be described as being more dynamic, in that it involves the construction of an AND/OR graph (a role structure) that is specific to some given problem. This contrasts with the earlier approach of interpreting a data base and its schema as a global role structure, from which a specific role structure(s) can be extracted for a given problem.

The dynamic approach is first described conceptually, as involving the grafting of fragments of modeling knowledge. Each fragment is specified in terms of the AND/OR graph terminology of Chapter 5 and the organizational role framework. Conceptually, this approach has some similarities with aspects of the STRIPS and BDL systems described in Chapter 4. The second part of this chapter shows how the grafting of AND/OR fragments into an AND/OR tree can be operationalized in terms of first-order predicate logic and the resolution principle.

14.10   CONCEPTUAL DESCRIPTION OF THE DYNAMIC APPROACH

Recall that organizational problem solving involves the *selection* and *interaction* of certain information processors (roles) in an organization. In adopting the notation of AND/OR graphs, selection and interaction are represented by OR reductions and AND reductions, respectively. As a brief recapitulation, Fig. 14.1a shows an AND reduction of node X where role X needs information from the leaf nodes below it. Figure 14.1b gives an OR reduction of node Y. This convention for treating reductions is symmetric and assures that no node will have to be viewed as both an AND and OR node.

The AND node α indicates the role whose task it is to coordinate its descendent roles by (1) controlling when (in a relative sense) each of the descendants is to solve its own problem and (2) stating the assumptions under which that subproblem is to be solved. Thus α may be regarded as a synthesizing node that, through its coordination of subproblem processors, furnishes a solution to problem X. The OR node β indicates a role that solves its problem not by interaction, but by selection of one of its descendants. The solution of that subproblem is accepted as the solution of β. The AND and OR nodes clearly reflect the two major kinds cf information-processing roles in an organization.

As a central assumption for this chapter, we assume that modeling knowledge inherent in an organization can be represented as a set of *AND/OR fragments,* where an AND/OR fragment is an AND reduction or an OR reduction. This modeling knowledge is sufficient to determine all possible models that can be formulated in the organization. A problem confronting the organization can be represented as an AND node (i.e., the

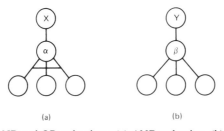

(a)   (b)

Fig. 14.1.   AND and OR reductions. (a) AND reduction. (b) OR reduction.

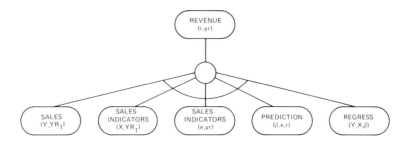

Fig. 14.2.   Reduction of REVENUE.

problem of generating a "report" containing values of some specified data item types). This problem can be used to drive the model formulation process, consisting of a grafting of compatible AND/OR tree fragments.

In order to illustrate these ideas, we use the following example. We first present the modeling knowledge base in terms of AND/OR tree fragments. Consider the modeling fact that the REVENUE problem can be solved if all the following kinds of subproblems can be solved: SALES, SALES-INDICATORS, PREDICTION, and REGRESSION. This is depicted in Fig. 14.2. Note that if there are alternative ways of determining revenue, then the REVENUE node would have additional edges emanating from it for the other AND reductions. The arguments of each problem node are used to indicate the nature of the message passing between roles. This message passing is coordinated through the synthesizing node. A word description of the modeling knowledge in Fig. 14.2 is as follows. To find the revenue r in year yr we must find the sales figures Y for years YR_1, the sales indicators X for years YR_1, the sales indicators x for year yr, the prediction r for sales indicators x and regression coefficients β, and the regression coefficients β for dependent variable observations Y and independent variable observations X.

Clearly, the arguments give several clues as to the appropriate ordering of the subproblem roles. Operationalization of modeling fragments must provide a way for differentiating between those arguments that are inputs to a role and those that are outputs. Note that the arguments can be interpreted not only in the general sense of information passage between roles but also in the more specialized senses of arguments of a subroutine call or arguments of a predicate. The symbols used for arguments are not global, but are significant only within an AND/OR fragment. Role names are global in scope.

Other modeling facts are displayed in Fig. 14.3. Observe that some subproblem roles (e.g., REGRESS) are shared by different problems,

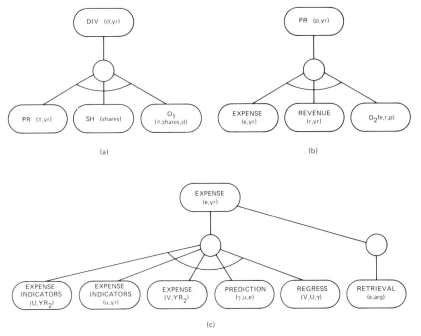

Fig. 14.3.   Reduction of DIV, PR, and EXPENSE.

albeit with different arguments. Notice also the potential for recursion, from Fig. 14.3c. The argument of RETRIEVAL in Fig. 14.3c indicates the *e* is retrieved subject to the values of all arguments theretofore instantiated.

The foregoing are examples of AND reductions. Suppose that we have the OR reductions shown in Fig. 14.4. The IPS role refers to "In Problem Statement". These OR reductions are closely related to the notion of meta-axioms.

Thus we can have a large pool of such fragments of modeling knowledge. Note that we can easily augment this pool. The fragments are independent of one another in the sense that each is a factual statement in and of itself; one fragment could be altered without affecting the other fragments (although such alteration will, of course, mean that there is the possibility of different model formulations). In this respect, the approach to capturing modeling knowledge is akin to that used in MYCIN. Moreover, this approach follows the same philosophy of problem solving as structured programming and BDL. In order to suggest how the knowledge fragments could be grafted to solve a given problem we work through the following examples.

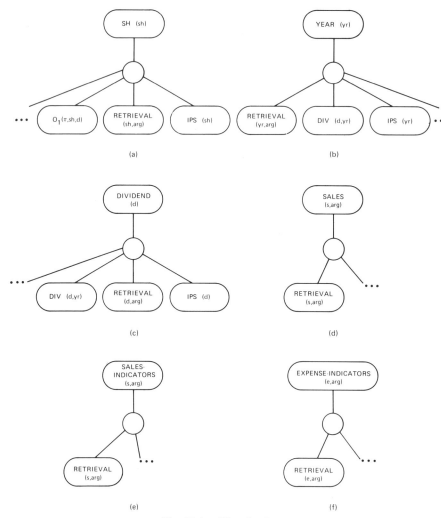

Fig. 14.4.   OR reductions.

Example (1) FIND DIVIDEND FOR YEAR = 1950

In Fig. 14.5 this statement is depicted by node *P*, which is an AND node and therefore what we have referred to as a synthesis node. *P* must "understand" how to coordinate the YEAR and DIVIDEND subproblems (i.e., information processors). For example,

1. Which should be used first, which second?

2. How does the solution of one of these subproblems condition the

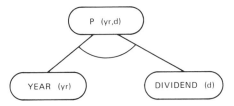

Fig. 14.5.   Problem representation.

subsequent activity of other subproblem solvers (via the information passed by *P*)?

All nine possibly pertinent model formulations based on the modeling fragments presented earlier are seen in the graph of Fig. 14.6.

The model of interest is given in Fig. 14.7. The problem YEAR is solved because it is in the problem statement. This solution of YEAR (i.e., 1950) is passed along by *P* to DIVIDEND. DIVIDEND is not solved by "In Problem Statement," but it is solved by retrieval conditioned by the year 1950.

Thus P coordinates the solutions of YEAR and DIVIDEND. We cannot use retrieval to get just any dividend to go along with the 1950. Nor can we use just any year (via retrieval) and any dividend. Furthermore, *P* influences which of the alternative solution methods is tried first by YEAR, which is tried second, etc. It also determines whether an attempt is made to solve YEAR or DIVIDEND first.

Example (2) FIND DIVIDEND FOR YEAR = 1991 AND SH = 100.

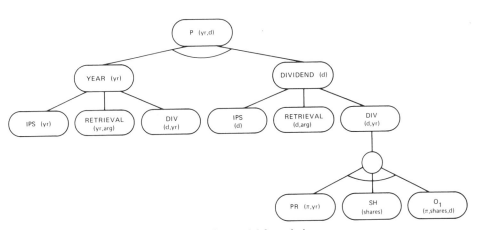

Fig. 14.6.   Nine model formulations.

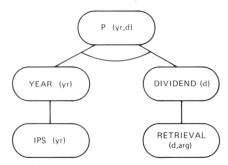

Fig. 14.7. Representation of the model of interest.

In this problem statement the year is once again given. However, historical information as to this dividend for that year cannot be obtained via retrieval, but must be projected. Referring to Fig. 14.8, the reasoning for solving the problem P (share, yr, d) is as follows:

1. SH is given in problem statement.
2. YEAR is given in problem statement. Values of SH and YEAR are passed to DIVIDEND. The descendants of DIVIDEND are grafted on. Consider one of them: DIV and graft on its descendants.
3. SH has already been solved. The problem PR (profit) is not immediately solvable so graft and look at EXPENSE.
4, 4′, 5. These problems are immediately solvable via retrieval. Their values are passed to REGRESSION by EXPENSE.
6. REGRESSION is solved and its results are passed to PREDIC-TION by EXPENSE.

This process continues until 14, when all subproblems beneath DIV are solved. Notice that there is the possibility of recursion (EXPENSE with EXPENSE as a descendant) during the grafting process. Observe also that the specific problem P ultimately controls the role selections (i.e., the model that is formulated). For one P a role may be nonsolvable (a dead end), whereas it is a primitive subproblem for another P. As a case in point, the RETRIEVAL problem under DIVIDEND in Example 2 is not solvable (i.e., assuming our data base is historical), whereas it was solvable in Example 1.

In terms of operationalizing a system for grafting AND/OR fragments, it is important to avoid storing all possible P's (i.e., their synthesizing protocols) in our knowledge system. It is also desirable to avoid (as far as possible) storing the selection or interaction information of any role that can never be a primitive subproblem (e.g., SH, DIVIDEND, EXPENSE, etc.). This is possible to the extent that one can identify the problem

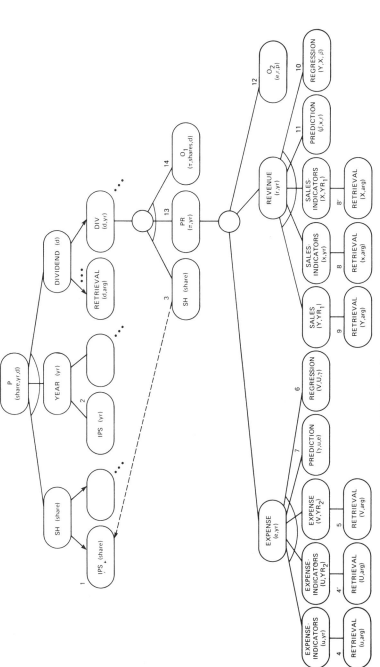

Fig. 14.8. Solution to P (share, yr, d).

recognition and model formulation principles common to all P's and to the roles that are never primitives. These principles can then be incorporated into the design of a problem processor that formulates a model that is appropriate for a given problem, by grafting together tree fragments. There appear to be two basic approaches to this grafting.

The first is to use the grafting process (based on the matching of role names) exhaustively in order to formulate all possibly pertinent models. Then, using values in the problem statement, recognize which of these solves the problem. This was the approach used in the preceding examples, beginning with Figs. 14.6 and 14.8, respectively. It is easy to visualize. In the other approach, the problem recognition ability governs the model formulation, such that model formulation is not necessarily exhaustive. Values in the problem statement are used as the model formulation proceeds. This approach would allow us to obtain Fig. 14.7 for Example 1 without first constructing the graph in Fig. 14.6. In the remainder of this chapter we shall examine one way to operationalize the second approach, through the use of predicate calculus and the mixed method of knowledge representation and processing.

14.20 OPERATIONALIZATION OVERVIEW

We shall show how first-order predicate calculus can be used as a language for formally stating fragments of modeling knowledge. Modeling knowledge fragments stated in this manner can be subjected to the resolution principle in order to "graft" them together into models. Consequently, application-specific modeling knowledge need not be embedded in the problem processor. Rather, it can be stored in a knowledge system and utilized as needed by a problem-processing system employing resolution techniques. Advantages of a decision support system taking this sort of approach are considerable modeling flexibility, capacity for automating the model formulation and execution processes, and compatibility with a high-level user interface language.

Note that the predicate calculus is not the high-level language with which a user states a problem. It is the language for representing fragments of application-specific modeling knowledge, in addition to empirical knowledge as discussed in the previous chapter. We shall refer to the set of all stated axioms having a true interpretation for an application area as the *axiom set* for that application. The axioms within an axiom set must, of course, be consistent with one another. It is assumed that the axiom set is put into clause form prior to resolution, if it is not already in clause form.

An axiom set containing application-specific modeling knowledge is, along with the module pool, in the KS. The axiom set can be stored in a data base by using the schema of Fig. 11.8.

When we speak of predicate calculus as a ''language'' that can be used to express modeling knowledge formally, this does not imply procedurality among axioms in an axiom set. The axioms are used to state facts about how modules may be used in conjunction with each other and with certain data in order to effect certain results. Many such facts, or axioms, are compiled for a particular application area. In essence, these formally stated modeling facts capture the knowledge of an expert (e.g., an operations research practitioner) about a particular application. Different applications (e.g., different businesses) would have different axiom sets and different module pools. But whatever the application, its axiom set is stored in the KS and acted on by the PPS in order to formulate a complete model in response to a user's statement of a problem.

An axiom set can be viewed as a collection of knowledge fragments concerning how to use modules with data in conducting various analyses. Assuming that this knowledge has been elicited from OR experts, it can be used to construct a model(s) automatically that, when executed, gives a desired report. This can be accomplished by implementing the resolution principle as a part of the PPS. How modeling knowledge, stated as axioms, can be used in conjunction with the resolution principle to build a model (out of modules) and determine its data inputs is illustrated in subsequent sections.

14.21   Stating Modeling Knowledge in the Predicate Calculus

Recall that a predicate indicates a particular relationship among its arguments. For our present purposes, it is convenient to introduce the notion of an ''operator'' predicate. Notice that a module formally specifies an operational relationship among its various inputs and its outputs. A predicate that is used to denote a module (i.e., an operational relationship) will be called an *operator predicate*; its arguments are the module inputs and outputs. Operator predicates will be distinguished from other predicates by underlining the operator's predicate symbol.

Another addition to the usual predicate calculus will be the use of *preconditions*. In state space analysis (Chapter 5), preconditions are simply conditions that must be satisfied prior to applying an operator; an operator transforms one state into another state. An analogous situation exists with modules, for a module transforms one ''information state'' into another ''information state.'' Certain preconditions must have been met before a module can be executed to effect the transformation; that is, all inputs must be fully instantiated. Those arguments of an operator predicate, whose instantiations are prerequisites to the execution of the corresponding module, will be called preconditions. They will be underlined in the following examples.

A simple example has been chosen to illustrate the foregoing ideas. Suppose that our module pool contains a regression module, a prediction module, an operator that finds dividends from profit and shares, and an operator that finds profit from revenues and expenses. These four modules are denoted, respectively, by the predicate symbols REGRESS, PREDICT, O_1, and O_2. Facts (in the guise of axioms) concerning their use could be added to the KS while the DSS is being initially readied, or some of it could be added later, as incremental increases to the system's modeling knowledge. Whatever the case, suppose that we (as management scientists, not as users) currently want to add the fact that the regression and prediction modules can be used, together with past sales data and certain sales indicators, to project the revenue in a certain year. This fragmentary modeling fact can be stated as shown in axiom (1) of Fig. 14.9. Although it is not explicitly stated in (1), all variables in the axiom are universally quantified. The same two modules can again be used in tandem, but with different data, in order to project expenses in a certain year. This modeling fact is captured in axiom (3).

A precise word description of modeling knowledge represented in (1) would be fairly lengthy. For instance, *if X* is sales indicators in years YR *and x* is the same type of sales indicators in year yr *and Y* is sales in years YR, *and X,Y* as inputs to a regression module produce the output β, *and* β along with *x* are inputs to a prediction module that gives output *r, then* the

$$\underline{\text{REGRESS}(\underline{Y},\underline{X},\beta)} \land \underline{\text{PREDICT}(\beta,\underline{x},r)} \land \text{SALES}(Y,\text{YR}_1) \land$$
$$\text{SALES-IND}(X,\text{YR}_1) \land \text{SALES-IND}(x,\text{yr}) \Rightarrow \text{REV}(r,\text{yr}) \quad (1)$$

$$\text{PR}(\pi,\text{yr}) \land \text{SH(shares)} \land \underline{O_1}(\pi,\underline{\text{shares}},d) \Rightarrow \text{DIV}(d,\text{yr}) \quad (2)$$

$$\underline{\text{REGRESS}(\underline{V},\underline{U},\gamma)} \land \underline{\text{PREDICT}(\gamma,\underline{u},e)} \land \text{EXP}(V,\text{YR}_2) \land$$
$$\text{EXP-IND}(U,\text{YR}_2) \land \text{EXP-IND}(u,\text{yr}) \Rightarrow \text{EXP}(e,\text{yr}) \quad (3)$$

$$\text{EXP}(e,\text{yr}) \land \text{REV}(r,\text{yr}) \land \underline{O_2}(\underline{e},\underline{r},p) \Rightarrow \text{PR}(p,\text{yr}) \quad (4)$$

$$\sim\underline{\text{REGRESS}(\underline{Y},\underline{X},\beta)} \lor \sim\underline{\text{PREDICT}(\beta,\underline{x},r)} \lor \sim\text{SALES}(Y,\text{YR}_1) \lor$$
$$\sim\text{SALES-IND}(X,\text{YR}_1) \lor \sim\text{SALES-IND}(x,\text{yr}) \lor \text{REV}(r,\text{yr}) \quad (5)$$
$$\sim\text{PR}(\pi,\text{yr}) \lor \sim\text{SH(shares)} \lor \sim\underline{O_1}(\pi,\underline{\text{shares}},d) \lor \text{DIV}(d,\text{yr}) \quad (6)$$

$$\sim\underline{\text{REGRESS}(\underline{V},\underline{U},\gamma)} \lor \sim\underline{\text{PREDICT}(\gamma,\underline{u},e)} \lor \sim\text{EXP}(V,\text{YR}_2) \lor$$
$$\sim\text{EXP-IND}(U,\text{YR}_2) \lor \sim\text{EXP-IND}(u,\text{yr}) \lor \text{EXP}(e,\text{yr}) \quad (7)$$

$$\sim\text{EXP}(e,\text{yr}) \lor \sim\text{REV}(r,\text{yr}) \lor \sim\underline{O_2}(\underline{e},\underline{r},p) \lor \text{PR}(p,\text{yr}) \quad (8)$$

Fig. 14.9. Selected modeling facts.

revenue in year yr is r. Expression (1) is clearly superior to the word description from the standpoints of conciseness, unambiguous documentation, and amenability to computerized processing. Amenability is particularly significant when efforts are made to combine and then utilize fragments of modeling knowledge. In the usual situation, wherein many fragments are available for use, the word form would not be workable for automated formulation. Even if the word form were only to be used during "manual" (i.e., human mental) formulation, the mental processing could become quite cumbersome.

Two additional fragments of modeling knowledge are given in axioms (2) and (4). The former states that if π is profit in yr *and* if "shares" is the assumed number of shares *and* if d is the output of O_1 given the inputs π and "shares," then d is the dividend in yr. The latter states that if e is the expense in yr *and* r is revenue in yr *and* p is the result of operator O_2 where e and r are preconditions, then p is the profit in yr. The clause form for each of these axioms is given in axioms (5) through (8) of Fig. 14.9. These clause forms are what must actually be stored in the KS. The ordering of these four fragments of modeling knowledge is irrelevant here.

Figure 14.10 displays several meta-axioms that we shall be using. All are stated in clause form and make up a portion of the axiom set. Chapter 13 stated that meta-axioms establish the meaning, or sense, of predicates appearing in the axiom set by indicating the relationship between predicate arguments and the data item types that can appear in a user's request for data. For instance, DIVIDEND, YEAR, and SH are all data item types that the user can refer to when making a request using the LS.

To summarize, we have a method for formally representing modeling knowledge. This formal representation can be stored in a computer-based knowledge system. Fragments of modeling knowledge are specified by a modeling expert (e.g., operations researcher), not by the DSS user. Knowledge specified in this manner can readily be added to or deleted from the KS on a continuing basis, utilizing common data base management techniques. The result is a separation of application-specific modeling knowledge from the PPS, thereby allowing PPS generality in terms of the kinds of modeling support. The axiom set serves as a clear documentation of legitimate model building and utilization techniques for a particular application area. For comments on the importance of modeling procedure documentation see Seaberg and Seaberg [8]. Continuing the above

$$\sim\text{DIV}(d,\text{yr}) \vee \text{DIVIDEND}(d) \qquad (9)$$
$$\sim\text{DIV}(d,\text{yr}) \vee \text{YEAR(yr)} \qquad (10)$$
$$\sim O_1(\pi,\underline{\text{sh}},d) \vee \text{SH(sh)} \qquad (11)$$

Fig. 14.10.   Selected meta-axioms (clause form).

example, we shall now see how a PPS with resolution capabilities can formulate a model that, when executed, will provide data requested by a DSS user.

14.22 Model Formulation by Resolution

Resolution makes use of the axiom set plus a predicate calculus expression that states exactly what it is that we are to attempt to infer from the axiom set. This expression is the "theorem" to be proved, a target axiom. The user of a DSS also has a "target" in mind when specifying the data desired in terms of the LS. If the system's user is an upper-level manager, furnishing a LS that is English-like is advantageous. A user should not be required to learn predicate calculus in order to use the DSS. In Chapter 13 it was shown that expressions in an extant, English-like, nonprocedural problem language can be readily converted into clause form expressions in the predicate calculus. Employing the problem language, the user might type FIND DIVIDEND FOR YEAR = 1991 AND SH = 100. The corresponding predicate expression is $\exists z$ DIVIDEND (z) $\wedge$ YEAR (1991) $\wedge$ SH (100) and converting the negation of this expression to clause form gives $\sim$DIVIDEND(z) $\vee$ $\sim$YEAR(1991) $\vee$ $\sim$SH(100).

This negated "theorem" is taken as the initial clause in the first step of resolution. The connection between data item types appearing in the user's request and the modeling knowledge supplied by a modeling expert is established by using meta-axioms during the resolution process. Figure 14.11 traces the application of the resolution principle to the above data request. Observe the last resolvent shown in Fig. 14.11, consisting of (12) and (13). In our use of resolution for model formulation, we do not need to complete the resolution explicitly; however, the procedure undertaken on reaching (12) and (13) is, in effect, a *virtual* completion of the resolution.

Expression (13) consists of those literals in the last resolvent not having operator predicates. As discussed in the previous chapter, these literals correspond to a data retrieval query that can be executed against the KS data base. The correspondence is automatically established with the aid of the meta-axioms. Execution of the resultant retrieval query makes available a list (i.e., 0, 1, or more) of those instantiations of a variable permitting a unification to occur. For example, $\sim$EXP-IND $(u, 1991)$, corresponds to a retrieval query to retrieve expense indicators for the year 1991. If the data base contains such expense indicators (denote them by u_0, where u_0 represents a constant), then the expression EXP-IND $(u_0,$ 1991) is true. The act of retrieving the actual values u_0 may be viewed as a virtual unification $(u_0 \rightarrow u)$ with the last resolvent of Fig. 14.11. Having

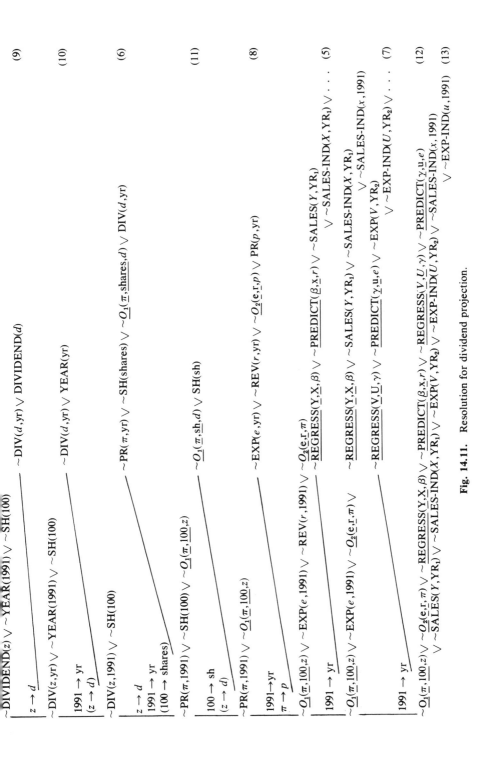

Fig. 14.11. Resolution for dividend projection.

the values u_0 available for use by a module is akin to the substitution of u_0 for u in (12).

In this way all literals in (13) vanish, having been virtually resolved via data retrieval techniques. Now if a data retrieval query gives a null answer, then we cannot proceed; we must attempt some further explicit resolution. We shall return to this issue in Section 14.24. Suppose for the time being that all retrievals are successful. Then (13) is eliminated and we are left with (12) plus the data retrieved for variables Y, X, U, V, x, and u. All literals in (12) involve operator predicates, each having corresponding executable modules. Before a given module can be executed its preconditions must be satisfied; that is, any underlined variable must be instantiated. For instance, before $\underline{O_1}$ can be executed, π must be replaced by some constant.

From the earlier data retrieval, the variables Y, X, U, V, x, and u have been instantiated. If we let X_0 and Y_0 represent the instantiations of X and Y, then in (12) we have the literal $\sim\underline{\text{REGRESS}}\ (\underline{X_0},\ \underline{Y_0},\ \beta)$. If we next execute the regression module, then instantiations β_0 of β are obtained. As a result of this execution, we can assert that $\underline{\text{REGRESS}}\ (\underline{X_0},\ \underline{Y_0},\ \beta_0)$ is true. Note that this unifies with $\sim\underline{\text{REGRESS}}\ (\underline{X_0},\ \underline{Y_0},\ \beta)$ and results in the substitution of β_0 for β. This means that the prediction module can be executed, with β_0 and X_0 as inputs, in order to eliminate $\sim\underline{\text{PREDICT}}\ (\beta_0, \underline{X_0}, r)$ from (12) via a virtual unification. The virtual resolution of $(12')$ to

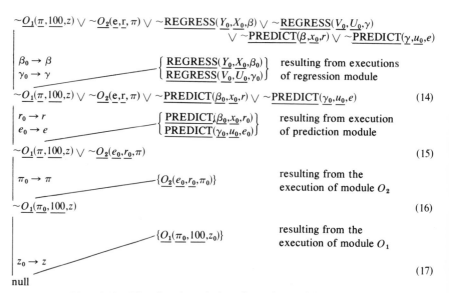

Fig. 14.12.   The virtual resolution of $(12')$ by module execution.

the null resolvent by an ordered succession of module executions is traced in Fig. 14.12. As a starting point for this trace, we take the virtual resolvent (12′) resulting from the application of successful data retrievals. (Symbols with a "0" subscript should be understood to represent constants that result from data retrieval or module execution.)

Figure 14.12 gives an ordering of module executions (14–17) and the substitutions describe the necessary intermodule data linkages. The null resolvent is *virtually* obtained by appropriate module execution. The original user problem was to determine the 1991 dividend if there are 100 shares. Equivalently, the problem was to find an instantiation (i.e., value) of z such that $\exists z$ DIVIDEND $(z) \wedge$ YEAR $(1991) \wedge$ SH (100). Let's review what the PPS has done to solve this problem.

The PPS made use of the K S, which contained modeling knowledge (the axiom set), procedural knowledge (the module pool), and mundane descriptive knowledge (data on past sales, sales indicators, etc.). Explicit resolution was used (Fig. 14.11) until a resolvent was obtained (12,13) that could not be further unified with any axiom in the axiom set. Virtual resolution was performed in the guise of data retrieval (Chapter 13). If all the literals having nonoperator predicates are eliminated by data retrieval, then further virtual resolution in the guise of ordered module execution is attempted. If a null resolvent is *virtually* attained, then the answer to the user's request has been discovered (z_0 in the preceding example). Green's [3] answer-tracing mechanism can be usefully applied, to keep track of where the answer is, in the face of many substitutions.

Thus the PPS has formulated a model consisting of several modules in response to a user-stated problem. The module ordering could be established as shown in Fig. 14.12 or obtained more directly by a matching of preconditions with outputs appearing in (12′). Not only was a model formulated by establishing data relationships among modules, but the PPS automatically handled the data interfaces between modules and the data base as well. The entire process was directed by a user, who does not need any expertise in predicate calculus or data base management techniques.

14.23 Extensions

The previous example was chosen for illustrative purposes. In practice, a much larger module pool, as well as a more extensive axiom set, would be available to the PPS. Thus a particular operator predicate may appear in many axioms and may be a participant in many of the models that the PPS can potentially construct. In practice, some operator predicates may have more detailed, or extensive, argument sets than those in the previous example. We may want to utilize the R^2 output of a regression module, for instance. Then (1) might become

> REGRESS ($\underline{Y},\underline{X},\beta,R^2$) $\wedge$ PREDICT ($\beta,\underline{x},r$) $\wedge$ SALES (Y,YR$_1$)
> $\wedge$ SALES-IND (X,YR$_1$) $\wedge$ SALES-IND (x,yr) $\wedge$ $GT(R^2,.35)$ $\Rightarrow$
> REV(r,yr)

where GT is a "greater than" predicate. This axiom states that if $R^2 > .35$ then r will be considered as revenue in yr; otherwise, it will not be taken as a valid (true) estimation of revenue.

An interesting research issue is how to implement evaluative capabilities into the modeling knowledge. The use of logical comparisons (e.g., GT) is a step in this direction. There are several ostensible ways to treat comparison predicates: treat them as operator predicates, or perhaps treat them as a special class of predicates whose operational details should be incorporated into the PPS, for example. The impact of permitting evaluative capabilities is that they allow branching knowledge to be given in the axiom set. (Of course, branching also exists within modules.) For example,

> REGRESS ($\underline{Y},\underline{X},\beta,R^2$) $\wedge$ $LE(R^2,.36)$ $\wedge$ ECON-DATA (z,yr)
> $\wedge$ SALES-FORECAST (z,k) $\Rightarrow$REV(k,yr)

could be added to the axiom set. If an $R^2 \leq .36$ is obtained, then the model would involve some sort of sales-forecasting module (other than PRE-DICT) with appropriate economic data z from the data base.

14.24 Implementing the Resolution Principle

Earlier, the question was raised as to what happens if we reach a point where a data retrieval implied by some literal in the resolvent is not successful. The resolvent in question here is assumed to be incapable of further explicit resolution. That is, no attempts at virtual resolution via data retrieval are made until a resolvent is attained that cannot be unified with any of the clauses in the axiom set. A similar problem may be encountered even if all data retrievals are successful. It may be impossible to establish an ordering over the remaining operator predicates. Either type of impasse will necessitate some backtracking.

It is in this connection that the selection rule and search strategy used in implementing the resolution principle are important. These involve the two kinds of choices made in resolution implementations: selecting a literal to use as the basis of unification and a search strategy for exploring those members of the axiom set that can be unified on the basis of the selected literal. As the axiom set grows, the search tree for a given "theorem" can become very large. Van Emden [9] comments that the combinatorial problem in implementing the resolution principle has led to criticisms in terms of the practicality of resolution. He emphasizes that nothing in the resolution principle requires an implementation of the "uniform" or "saturation" variety. Several implementations are cited that use various heuristics to guide the inference procedure. In other implementations a foreknowledge of characteristics of an application area are exploited to provide a savings.

Further research aimed at the discovery of heuristics to guide the resolution in the case of model formulation is needed. This research might take several directions. It appears that the meta-axioms can be used to narrow the search tree considerably. The literals within a resolvent can be ordered (based on the degree of instantiation) as candidates for being chosen as a basis for the next unification. Unification on the basis of a literal that contains an operator predicate may be desirable to avoid in the early stages of resolution. It may be useful to base a search strategy on the presence or absence of operator predicates in clauses that can be chosen at a given stage of the resolution.

Finally, we may be able to take advantage of the special form of axioms used to represent modeling knowledge. Each clause in the axiom set given earlier is a special type of predicate calculus expression called a *Horn clause* (see Horn [5]). A Horn clause contains no more than one positive literal. Kowalski [6] has successfully implemented a resolution system for them, and there is a marked correspondence between modeling knowledge stated in Horn clauses and the knowledge representation methods used in production systems, such as MYCIN [1].

14.30   CONCLUSION

The work presented in this chapter is intended as a contribution toward the integration of OR/MS with MIS/DSS as discussed by Edelman [2], Hoffman [4], and Vazsonyi [10]. Predicate calculus was presented as a formal language for capturing and also documenting the modeling knowledge of OR experts. Utilization of the predicate calculus in this manner permits application-specific modeling knowledge to be separated from the PPS code of a decision support system. The predicate calculus expressions can be stored in the KS of a DSS to take advantage of the ease of update afforded by data base management techniques.

The result is a general, flexible DSS that addresses, in part, the corporate modeling shortcomings cited in the survey of Naylor and Schauland

[7]. It reduces modeling inflexibility. Some help is provided in terms of documentation of modeling knowledge. Large data input requirements to modules are handled automatically by the DSS.

The same survey also identified, in a rank order, the desirable features of corporate modeling. Methods introduced in this chapter permit development of a DSS that possesses, to some degree, the most desirable of these features. Sensitivity analysis can be incorporated within modules; one can also compare the results of various modeling techniques (e.g., different forecasting methods can be incorporated into the axiom sets). Data base utilization by modules is accomplished automatically. Flexible report generation can be provided by a "subpool" of report generation modules that is subject to facile updating.

This chapter has presented the skeleton of a methodology for automatic model formulation and utilization. Further DSS research topics are outlined in the final chapter.

REFERENCES

1. R. Davis, B. Buchanan, and E. Shortliffe, Production rules as a representation for a knowledge-based consultation program, *Artificial Intelligence* 8 (1977).
2. F. Edelman, They went thataway, *Interfaces* 7, No. 3 (1977).
3. C. Green, Application of theorem proving to problem solving, *Proc. Internat. Joint Conf. Artificial Intelligence* (1969).
4. G. M. Hoffman, The contribution of management science to management information, *Interfaces* 9, No. 1 (1978).
5. A. Horn, On sentences which are true of direct unions of algebras, *J. Symbolic Logic* 16 (1951).
6. R. A. Kowalski, Predicate logic as a programming language, *Proc. IFIP Conf.* (1974).
7. T. H. Naylor and H. Schauland, A survey of users of corporate planning models, *Management Sci.* 22, No. 9 (1976).
8. R. A. Seaberg and C. Seaberg, Computer based decision systems in Xerox corporate planning, *Management Sci.* 20, No. 4 (1973).
9. M. H. Van Emden, Programming with resolution logic, *in* "Machine Intelligence" (E. W. Elcock and D. Michie, eds.), Vol. 8. Halstead Press, New York, 1977.
10. A. Vazsonyi, Information systems in management science, *Interfaces* 9, No. (1978).

Chapter 15

CONCLUDING REMARKS

15.00 INTRODUCTION

This concluding chapter consists of some philosophical and speculative remarks on the current and future course of development in the DSS field. In our endeavor to develop a perspective for the future, we review the trends in the use of computers in management. However, our interest is in developing a theory of DSS in which the computer is viewed only as a tool for simulating some of the theoretical components in the proposed framework. In this chapter we argue for the importance of developing a view of decision making that explicitly recognizes the vital activities of acquiring, storing, and processing information. We conclude with a brief description of topics that appear interesting for future research.

15.10 BACKGROUND

Computers have been viewed by management primarily as either a computational tool or a storage and retrieval tool. In the 1950s the potential of the computer to store large amounts of data accurately and to permit selective data retrieval was recognized. The computer staffs of many large corporations devised, first in assembly language and later using COBOL, elaborate programs that could store and retrieve financial and accounting data. Instead of focusing on improved decision-making capabilities, the emphasis was on cost savings, achieved by replacement of clerks with more efficient computing machines.

In the late 1940s and in the 1950s the discipline of management science operations research emerged in the form of separate groups (i.e., separate from data storage and retrieval groups) in large corporations. Such groups were charged with the tasks of applying mathematical techniques to rationalize the operation of the company. Linear programming models for representing transportation, storage, and production possibilities were formulated by technical groups in a company, and solution techniques based on various optimization algorithms were applied. However, it was readily apparent that only by using the computational power of the computer could these models and algorithms be effectively utilized to help rationalize company operations.

During the 1960s and 1970s the era of data base management made its appearance. More flexible facilities for data structuring and storage became available, surpassing the capabilities of file systems. Furthermore, there were language enhancements resulting in more powerful and less procedural languages for retrieval. Note that although these retrieval languages often included simple computational capabilities, the major advance provided by data base systems was in the realm of data storage and retrieval.

At the same time advances were being made in the usage of computational tools, such as linear programming. These were expanded into software packages that could manage the large data files needed to support such algorithms. The packages were developed to (1) store files of data that could potentially be used as input to the algorithm, (2) extract data from files and define the linear programming problem, and (3) store solutions in a specified file. What was purely a computational problem slowly evolved into an information system problem involving data storage and retrieval issues.

Both the storage and retrieval approach and the computational approach can be viewed as relevant to a particular decision problem. In the data base–information retrieval context, specific facts are needed from the vast amount of information being stored. To the extent that an individual is able to communicate the requests in an easy-to-use language and have relevant data returned, the information system becomes valuable.

In the computational context, specific facts or expectations are needed from an algorithm. To the extent that the individual is able to communicate the computational requests in an easy-to-use language and have relevant data returned, the package is valuable. The computational problem is one of helping managers analyze and evaluate many different potential alternatives in order to select the subset that would be of interest. Management requirements are stated partially in terms of an objective function, a collection of resource limitations, and possibly other restrictions. The DSS view expounded here is a merging of the two contexts.

As described in Chapter 3, most information systems have been oriented to specific, well-defined problem settings. We have devoted considerable attention to the development of generalized decision support systems. There are various interpretations to the term "generalized," which we shall explore. One interpretation is a system that is able to respond to a wide variety of problems or queries. An example is MYCIN, which, as described earlier, is able to analyze a range of patient illnesses. But with respect to the generic problem of diagnosis and prescriptions, MYCIN software is specific, dealing exclusively with medical diagnoses and prescriptions. Trying to diagnose and prescribe treatments for corporate ills with MYCIN would prove to be futile.

Another view of generalization is in the concepts that underlie the software system. In this sense the computer code allows for many different specific systems to be implemented. Data base management is a prime example of this. The data base software allows for many different information systems to be established. The form of decision support system advocated in the preceding chapters has these generality characteristics.

The main focus of this book is on the construction of generalized software. We have described the various components that make up such a system. Thus we have switched the emphasis away from specific software packages, each of which can be used only for a particular, limited application. The emphasis is instead on generalized software that manages application-specific knowledge.

In the next section we shall explore DSS in the setting of an expanded view of decision making. Certainly DSS should be seen as something other than the computer programs that direct the computer. This is evident from the DSS framework that we have presented, with its major components of a language system, a knowledge system, and a problem-processing system.

15.20   THE SETTING OF DSS WITHIN AN EXPANDED VIEW OF DECISION MAKING

The goal of this chapter is to restate our basic premises, to indicate to what extent we have made progress in developing a theory of decision support, and finally to delve into future research topics. We have attempted to build a bridge between past work (which has been summarized in earlier chapters), the current research (which has been detailed in earlier chapters), and the future, which of course remains uncharted.

The dominant theme of this study has been a model of problem solving. Individuals are constantly faced with an array of decisions ranging from personal to corporate or organizational. In some cases the individual bears the entire responsibility of the final choice, whereas in other cases an individual may be an agent for others. But even in this latter situation good decisions of the agent may be well rewarded, whereas poor decisions may cause termination of the appointment. Thus as individuals we face a series of decision situations where our performance impacts on our well-being.

Historically, the study of decision making focused on the individual, either as a consumer or manager, in his (her) attempt to maximize utility or profits subject to a variety of constraints. The resulting decision is postulated to be rational, and deviations from rationality (utility or profit maximizing) are ascribed to lack of information, changing tastes, or possibly laziness.

From our viewpoint, the important observation is that *no theory of the choice process is presented. No theory is offered that describes how an individual stores and retrieves facts about the world and integrates the relevant facts with mental models and with analysis and evaluation capabilities to reach a decision eventually.*

Aside from the purely intellectual challenge in building a theory of the dynamics of this expanded view of decision making, there is a very practical aspect. With the continued and rapid decline in computing costs, there is the potential of using computers to enhance the decision-making capabilities of individuals. A theory of the entire process of decision making should be the basis for introducing computer technology into decision processes in order to enhance decision-making capabilities. It is from such a theory of decision making that we can build generalized decision support systems.

15.30   AN OUTLINE OF DSS IMPLEMENTATION ISSUES

The implementation issues fall into three categories: those relating to the KS, those relating to the LS, and those relating to the PPS.

A. Knowledge System (KS)

The principal issue here is how to represent needed information using computer technology in such a way that (1) redundancy is controlled (if not minimized), (2) important relationships among data and models are captured, (3) the data and models are sharable, (4) new data are easily absorbed, (5) data exist in a form that is readily usable by the PPS, and (6) data can be quickly accessed (and perhaps modified) by the PPS.

1. Overall strategy:

(a)   use data base techniques for the large volumes of facts describing an organization's environment;

(b)   use a predicate calculus-like technique (couched within a data base structure) for generalizations about the environment;

(c)   use program code (i.e., in some programming language) for the large volumes of detailed procedural knowledge;

(d)   use a Horn-clause (or equivalent) technique for modeling knowledge (i.e., application-specific knowledge about ways to combine the information provided in a–c);

(e)   use schema descriptions, held in a data base structure, for indicating input and output formats of program modules.

2. Specific problems:

(a)   In reference to point (a) above:

(i)   Establish how to structure the data base schema to best support the data requirements of the language system users and the models.

(ii)   Establish the extent of automation of the design process.

(b)   In reference to point (b) above:

(i)   Decide whether to restrict axioms to a limited form such as Horn clauses or single predicates.

(ii)   Design a schema for storing these axioms in such a way that searching them during resolution (or some pseudoresolution) is expedited.

(c)   In reference to point (c) above:

(i)   Decide what modules to use (e.g., should two modules really be separate or should they be combined as one module?). Can a methodology for this be developed?

(ii)   Establish if the modules are devised independently of each other. If not, how can their input and output formats be coordinated? If so, is there some standard form for documenting their I/O structures, so that the syntax and semantics of their inputs and outputs are formally specified in a common manner?

    (iii)   Establish how a module is physically stored and how its documentation is stored. Can multiple modules in the same "family" be easily handled (e.g., multiple "prediction" modules)?

(d)   In reference to point (d) above:

    (i)   Establish schema design for storing these clauses such that accessing them for purposes of resolution (or pseudoresolution) is expedited.

    (ii)   Establish naming conventions to make these axioms consistent with knowledge in (a)–(c).

    (iii)   Establish automation of consistency checking among the Horn-clause set.

    (e)   In reference to point (e) above: design a logical structure to hold this I/O information about each module.

Note: The KS in its broad sense may have human components (that the PPS interrogates) in addition to computer-based components cited earlier.

B. Language System (LS)

    The principal issue here is the identification or creation of a category I language (recall Chapter 3). This language should be general and English-like. By "general" we mean that its vocabulary for one application area is easily replaced by the vocabulary of a different application area. The language must, of course, be readily transformable into an internal form for the PPS.

    Specific problems:

    1.   What degree of ambiguity is permitted?

    2.   How interactive or parametric should the language be?

    3.   Should procedurality be accommodated if a user does not want nonprocedurality?

    4.   What kinds of quantification should be supported?

C. Problem Processing System (PPS)

    There are many implementation issues here, which we partition according to the framework of Chapter 4.

    1.   Information collection from the user:

    (a)   Decision as to the internal form of a compiled problem statement:

    (i)   can this form be used to drive data base retrieval both implicit and explicit (recall Chapter 13)?

(ii)   can this form be used to instigate a resolution-like process (Chapter 14)?

(b)   Decision as to how to gather and store linguistic information specific to a particular application area.

(c)   Implementation of the language compiler or interpreter.

2.   Information collection from the KS:

(a)   generalized implementation of strict retrieval,

(b)   generalized implementation of implicit retrieval,

(c)   generalized retrieval of desired modules from the KS.

3.   Problem recognition:

(a)   Implement the problem recognition process that, given the internal form of a problem statement, recognizes what the problem is by generating a *procedural* specification of the problem. This procedural specification is then executed, thereby solving (i.e., eliminating) the problem. The whole idea here is to automatically generate a procedural problem specification from a less procedural problem specification.

The resultant procedural specification requires some mix of explicit or implicit retrieval from the KS, of data collection from humans, and of a sequence of module executions using retrieved data from a computerized or human KS.

(b)   In response to a user-stated problem, the problem recognizer utilizes (*coordinates*) the PPS information collection ability (from both the user and the KS), the PPS model formulation ability, and the PPS evaluation ability (if any) in order to arrive at a procedural specification. This coordination strategy must be explicitly stated in order to implement the problem recognition ability.

(c)   The implementation must be able to recognize ambiguity in a user's problem statement and eliminate it (e.g., through interaction with the user) and may be able to choose among satisfactorily formulated models.

(d)   Implement a method for allowing the system to learn (to remember past problem recognitions).

4.   Model formulation:

(a)   Model formulation is performed as a service to the problem recognition ability.

(b)   One implementation method is along the lines indicated in Chapter 14. Some specific issues are

(i)   how to take advantage of the Horn-clause form of the

axioms and possibly cast them in the guise of a production system,

(ii) what data structure to use in holding intermediate and final results of the model formulation,

(iii) how to distinguish between single-value, vector, and matrix arguments,

(iv) how to determine the best place to apply meta-axioms,

(v) how to use learned models (e.g., try using learned models prior to attempted model formulation),

(vi) extensions to integrate the model formulation with evaluative abilities (to generate or choose a "best" model),

(vii) how to handle the inability to generate an appropriate model,

(viii) extensions to accommodate intermodule looping and branching (beyond the intramodule looping and branching already permitted).

5. Analysis:

(a) An indication of which modules to interface with which data is included in the explicit problem procedure generated by the problem recognizer.

(b) Analysis ability is implemented by software that performs the actual interfacing of data and modules (drawing on the PPS information collection abilities). This involves

(i) loading needed modules (compiled),

(ii) setting up the mappings of data from the data base to module input, module output to module input, module output to the data base,

(iii) instigating execution,

(iv) treatment of execution errors, if any.

(c) Implementation of this ability will draw, in part, on operating system design principles.

D. Getting Started with the Implementation

1. Select a specific problem solving application area that is rich in modules.

2. As a first approximation, assume coordinated module development.

3. As a pilot, let the PPS output a set of instructions that tells the user which modules to interface and how to interface them (i.e., documentation of their I/O schemata).

15.40   FURTHER RESEARCH TOPICS

Whereas Section 15.30 considered specific implementation issues, this section presents broader, more general research topics. Our framework of analysis focused on three building blocks for DSS development. Each of these elements was analyzed and then developed. Although we have presented the material in some depth, there is naturally further potential for research in this area. We outline in this section our views on the future direction that this research may take.

A. Problem Processor Development

1. *Elaboration of problem processor.* The utilization of the problem processor has been outlined in terms of both the storage of modeling knowledge and dynamics of combining modeling fragments for problem solving. The following are some suggestions for specific research topics:

(a)   For each knowledge fragment there must be *control information.* For an AND reduction, the solving of subproblems must be coordinated; for the OR reduction, some heuristic control could be used—perhaps attempting retrieval—and if retrieval fails, "simple" modules and, finally, "complex" modules could be attempted. Two important questions are the extent to which control procedures can be generalized and embedded in the problem processor and the global coordination of subproblems, so that the same subproblem need not be solved more than once for a user's given problem statement (e.g., the SH subproblem in Fig. 14.8).

(b)   Grammatically, the example's problem-solving dynamics resembled top-down, *generative processing.* How to interpret bottom-up processing of AND/OR fragments is another interesting research topic. The problem processor would observe data generated by an organization and would then attempt to infer what underlying characteristics generated those data. In one approach the user is interested in *data* generated by an intelligent "black box"; in the other, the user is interested in the *causes* that have produced some empirical data.

(c)   *Learned behavior* (i.e., solution method) may be short term or long term; it depends on the extent to which it is reinforced or used. Another research topic is how to handle learned modeling knowledge with respect to its storage and its utilization during the grafting process. Furthermore, we should identify methods whereby the modeling knowledge, learned from our problem-solving experience, can be applied in solving later problems of a similar or analogous nature. One approach could entail the abstraction of results of earlier learning, so that the learning is somewhat general. Another approach could make use of theories of analogical reasoning.

(d)   Assuming that once a problem is stated the problem processor either finds a solution or concludes that a solution cannot be found, we could investigate *utilizing a metric* to measure the distance between the current state of the problem processor and a state that allows the problem to be solved. With such a tool, it should be possible to find the best, or closest, possible solution for a given knowledge base. In the case where the metric value is zero, a solution has been found. Where it is nonzero, a way for evaluating the goodness, or closeness, of the solution has been established. Introducing a metric may also help in processing, by suggesting grafts that reduce the metric.

(e)   The *relationship between the grafting* outlined here *and production systems and resolution* should also be studied.

2.   *Parallel problem solving.* The earlier discussion of a problem-solving theory, while fairly abstract, involves sequential problem processing. A natural extension would permit parallel problem (i.e., subproblem) processing. If the proposed framework is taken as a paradigm of organizational problem solving, then different organizational units (e.g., marketing, production, finance, etc.) would be able to work simultaneously with a given problem. We must formally show, then, how to decompose a problem, how to partition a knowledge base, and how to coordinate parallel processing. Development of practices for parallel problem processing permits decision support systems to be implemented in a distributed processing environment and to be applied to office automation systems.

3.   *Extensions.* There are several ways of developing a formal language to represent modeling knowledge. One possible approach is to use first-order logic, where predicates describe the relationships between input and output variables of a module, and expressions in the language describe preconditions necessary to execute the module. As an operationalization of the grafting process, the resolution principle would then be applied to a knowledge base composed of assertions. The assertions would consist of (a) traditional data base facts (that need not be explicitly expressed in predicate form) and (b) information about model usage (possibly expressed as Horn clauses).

Another approach would be to recognize explicitly the role of models in changing the states of the knowledge base. The concepts of production systems [1] seem applicable to the model formulation issues that interest us. *Primitives* of this approach are transformations that change states of the knowledge base. It should be possible to apply this technique to represent modeling knowledge about combining operators (e.g., DML commands, program modules) in a manner leading to the solution of some stated problem. Some problem-solving algorithm must be developed, which would in effect synthesize the program (i.e., graft the modules) needed for the solution associated with the problem statement.

4. *Comparison of problem processor and knowledge representation between first-order logic and production systems.* At least two issues arise when attempting to compare a problem processor based on first-order logic with a problem processor based on production systems. The major difference is the treatment of program modules, with respect to knowledge representation. In first-order logic a predicate can relate input variables to the assignment of values to output variables. Conditions on program module execution can be expressed as an axiom in first-order logic, whereas in production systems this knowledge would be the precondition concept. Chapters 13 and 14 developed an approach to modeling knowledge representation using first-order logic. With modeling knowledge represented in first-order logic, it is possible to synthesize a model from program modules, using the resolution principle. The model consists of a concatenation of program modules selected by resolution. As noted earlier, one of the research issues is the development of a problem processor based on a production systems approach. The utilization of a production system would permit us to explore program module construction that is not necessarily limited to a single concatenation, but may allow branching and looping structures.

B. Knowledge System Development

The important issues here are methods for acquiring modeling knowledge and techniques for its storage.

(a) Implementation of a computer-based decision support system is based on establishing a connection between the conceptual notion of modeling knowledge and some operational data structures for holding that knowledge. The connection will allow fragments to be operationalized in terms of storage and retrieval in a computer environment.

(b) Modeling knowledge often must be obtained from individuals who have experience with the application for which a knowledge system is being built. Algorithmic knowledge would be available from individuals experienced in such areas as management science. Individuals experienced in model formulation and problem recognition for the application area would provide problem-solving strategies. Obtaining this heuristic knowledge is a complex topic involving issues in the behavioral sciences field. Recent simulation studies founded on extensive psychological research made by Reitman [2] and others allow them to elicit specific strategies from expert human problem solvers. Using this research to acquire modeling knowledge inputs for a decision support system would be an interesting challenge.

C. Language System Development

The approach to problem processor development can come from the angles of first-order logic or production systems. Problem solving in either kind of system is initiated by attempting to prove an expression stated in first-order logic. Thus the problem statement language should be equivalent to first-order logic, viewed as a formal language. From a user interface point of view, however, the first-order logic would not make a suitable language. A more natural, English-like language is desirable. A solution is to find an English-like user language that can be translated automatically into an internal language equivalent to first-order logic.

An English-like, nonprocedural query language for a decision support system, limited to data storage and retrieval (data base management) and based on a transformational grammar, has been developed [3]. Inverse transformations applied to a user's high-level statement are used to generate a string in a deep-structured language. Such a deep-structure string is interpretable as an expression in first-order logic. An interesting research topic, with respect to DSS language system development, is to generalize this transformational approach to the case of a decision support system that performs modeling in addition to retrieval.

REFERENCES

1. N. J. Nilsson, "Principles of Artificial Intelligence." Tioga Publishing Co., California, 1980.
2. W. Reitman, "Cognition and Thought." Wiley, New York, 1965.
3. R. H. Bonczek, J. I. Cash, and A. B. Whinston, A transformational grammar-based query processor for access control in a planning system, *ACM Trans. Database Systems* **2,** No. 4 (1977).

INDEX

A

Abstraction levels, 276–284
Accounting, 45–46
ADABAS, 176
Analysis ability, 36–40, 76, 93, 102–103,
    230–231, 250–251, 313–314, 384
Anthony taxonomy, 16–17
Artificial intelligence, 21–23, 39, 73–74

B

Bachman diagram, 146
Business Definition Language (BDL),
    74–75, 79, 358, 361

C

Compiler, 231–233, 241–242, 254–256
Concept, 128–138, 142–146, 148–150, 153–
    175, 179–181, 276–280
  aggregate, 134–138, 142, 179–181
  associative relationship, 130–131, 134–
    135, 142–143, 179–181
  definitional relationship, 128–133, 276–
    280
  indirect associations, 153–175

indivisible, 128–134, 179–180
M–N associative relationship, 161–163,
    179–181
1–N associative relationship, 143–146,
    151–154, 179–181
CONVERT, 270–272
Corporate modeling, 46, 49–50, 52–54
Coset, 145–148, 340–341
Currency indicators, 193–211
Cyçlic data structures, 172–175

D

Data, 13
Data base, 13, 20
Data base management, 19–23, 125, 176,
    260, 273–274, 378–379
  data base restructuring, 260, 273
  data description, 176, *see also* Data de-
    scription language (DDL)
  data manipulation, 20, *see also* Data ma-
    nipulation language (DML)
  data structure, 125, *see also* Coset; Data
    item type; N : M set; Record type
  distributed, 273–274
  versus file management, 19, 378–379

Data description language (DDL), 176, 347, 356
Data item occurrence, 131–133
Data item type, 131–134
Data manipulation language (DML), 20, 189, 192–218, 223, 226–228, 231–232, 242–247, 260, 273, 348
   for direct *M–N* associations, 209–211
   for file retrieval, 211–218
   loading, 206–208, 260, 273
   macro commands, 204–206
   MDBS commands, 226–228
   retrieval, 192–206, 223, 231–232, 242–247, 348
Decision-making system, 11–12, 14–17, 33–34
   structuredness, 14–17, 33–34
Decision-making abilities, 26–27, 34–41
Decision support system, 12, 17–23, 26–27, 34, 38–41, 45–73, 85, 88, 91, 94, 105, 115, 120, 188, 289, 313, 333, 375–376, 379–388
   classification scheme, 60–67, 188
   generic description, 69–73, 120
Data organization, 125–128
   logical, 125–128, *see also* Schema
   physical, 125–127
Data set, 145
Disjoint data structure, 170, 176
DMS 1100, 176
DSS-Q, 234–242, 252–258

E

Evaluation ability, 36–40, 103

F

File, 131–134, 136–142, 170, 176, 211–218
   manipulation, 138–139, 211–218
Frames, 353–355

G

General Problem Solver (GPS), 77–79
Generality, 6–7, 83–85, 128, 375–376, 379
   computer system, 6–7, 379
   problem processor, 83–85, 128, 375–376
GPLAN, 82–83, 221

Grammar, 112–116, 236
   context-sensitive, 114, 236, 267
   context-free, 113–114, 236–237, 241
   finite state, 112–113
   recursively enumerable, 114, 236
   regular, 112, 115–116
   transformational, *see* Transformational grammar

H

HDBS, 176
Hierarchical data structure, *see* Tree data structure
Host language, 201, 222

I

IDMS, 176
IDS, 145, 176
Implementation ability, 36–40, 77, 233
IMS, 176
Indirect circular *1–N* relationship, 168–169
Indirect reflexive relationship, 166–168
Information, 13
Information collection ability, 35–40, 78, 81, 83, 91–93, 95, 102–103, 108, 230–236, 242–251, 313–319, 356, 382–383
Information processing, 4, 8, 11–16, 26–34
   automation, 4
   framework, 26–34
   human, 8
   procedures, 11–16, *see also* Model
Information revolution, 3–11, 56–57
   human-machine systems, 5–8
   organizational growth, 4–5
   technological innovation, 3–4, 6, 56–57
Integrity conditions, 355

J

Job control language, 250–251

K

Key, 163, 213
Knowledge system, 70–71, 75–77, 79, 81–83, 85, 88–90, 94, 105–109, 128, 149, 176, 188, 211, 218–222, 226, 280, 290–304, 310–311, 313, 336–353, 356, 366–370, 380–382, 387–388

for data base, 128, 149, 176, 188, 211, 218–222, 226, 280
for mixed approach, 336–353, 356, 366–370, 380–382, 387–388
for predicate calculus, 290–304, 310–311, 313
for problem reduction, 94
for productions, 105–109
for state space, 88–90

L

Language, 19, 57–67, 220–222, 336, 338, 344
for computation, 58–65
query, 19, 220–222, 336, 338, 344, *see also* DSS-Q; Mapping language; MDBS.QRS
for retrieval, 57–67, *see also* Data manipulation language (DML)
Language system, 69–70, 75–77, 79, 80–82, 85, 90–93, 95, 107–108, 304–307, 317–318, 344, 346, 352, 356, 367, 382, 388
for data base, 188, 201, 206, 218–226, 236–237
for mixed approach, 344, 346, 352, 356, 367, 382, 388
for predicate calculus, 304–307, 317–318
for problem reduction, 95
for productions, 107–108
for state space, 90–93
Linear data structure, 171
Logic, 21–23, 59, 289–309, 315–318, 337, 341–342, 369–370
axioms, 59, 290–294, 303–304, 336–356
meta-axioms, 337, 341–342, 369–370
model theory, 292–293, 298–301
modus ponens, 293–294
proof by contradiction, 317–318
proof by resolution, *see* Resolution
proof theory, 293–294
searches, 315–317
tautology, 298–299

M

Management information system, 18, 85
Management science, 12–13, 15–16, 19, 45–46, 48
Many-to-many set, 163, 209, *see also* N:M set

Mapping language, 260–270, 272–275
Material requirements planning, 47
MDBS.QRS, 221
Micro Data Base System (MDBS), 56, 163, 176, 186, 209, 226–228, 260
M–N relationship, 158–163
direct, 161–163
indirect, 158–161
Model formulation ability, 35–40, 76–79, 91, 93, 95, 102–105, 128, 230–231, 246–251, 284, 313–314, 366, 369–373, 383–384
Model building blocks, 50–51, 94
Modeling knowledge, 358–370, 373–376, 387
acquisition, 387
operator predicates, 367–368, 373–375
preconditions, 367–368, 373
Model, 12, 35, 40, 45–67, 82–83, 127–128, 222–226, 242–251, 281–284, *see also* Modeling knowledge; Modules
Modules, 55, 79, 248–251, 260–261, 275, 281–284, 359–361, 367–368, 373–374
message passing, 260–261, 275, 284, 360
MYCIN, 80–82, 109, 117–118, 121, 361, 375, 379

N

Network data structure, 175–177
N:M set, 186
Normalization, 142

P

Parsing, 115–117, 231, 241
PLANNER, 75–77, 80, 241
Plex, 209–211
Pointer, 126
Potlatch Forests, Inc., 49–50
Power, 35–38
Predicate calculus, 294–309, 317, 367, 375, 383, 386, *see also* Logic; Resolution
conjunctive normal form, 307, 309
constants, 295
domain of discourse, 295
Horn clause, 375, 383, 386
interpretations, 296–297, 299–304
operators, 295, 297–298
predicates, 294–309, 367
prenex normal form, 307–309
quantification, 295, 301–302

Skolem normal form, 307–309, 317
variables, 295, 300–302
Problem processing system, 71–77, 79–80,
    83–85, 91–93, 95, 108–109, 127–128,
    150, 203, 219, 226, 230–234, 236–238,
    241–258, 273–275, 280, 283–285, 295,
    313–331, 335–337, 346–353, 356, 366–
    367, 370–375, 382, 387
    for data base, 127–128, 150, 203, 219, 226,
        230–234, 236–238, 241–258, 273–275,
        280, 283–285
    for mixed approach, 335–337, 346–353,
        356, 366–367, 370–375, 382–387
    for predicate calculus, 295, 313–331
    for problem reduction, 95
    for productions, 108–109
    for state space, 91–93
Problem recognition ability, 36–41, 78, 81,
    91, 93, 95, 102–105, 108–110, 128, 230–
    234, 237–242, 244–251, 274, 284, 313–
    314, 319–323, 356, 366, 383
Problem reduction, 93–105, 226, 358–361,
    385
    AND reductions, 95–102, 359–360, 385
    AND/OR graph, 95–104, 358–360
    operators, 93, 95
    OR reductions, 97–102, 359, 361, 385
    relationship to information processing
        framework, 103–105
    search procedure, 97–100
Production system, 81, 105–121, 235, 384,
    387
    compared to state space, 120–121
    data base, 106–111, 114–116, 118–119
    generative grammar, 111–114
    for inventory management, 118–120
    parsing, 115–117
    production rules, 105–119, 235
Project management, 46–47
Purposive behavior, 87

R

Record occurrence, 134–137
Record type, 134–137, 220, 276–280, 296,
    338–339, 349
    higher-level, 276–280
    virtual, 220, 349

Relations, 280, 338, 345–346, *see also* File
Remote indirect relationship, 164–166
Report generator, 51, 58, 63–67, 233, 244–
    247
Resolution, 314, 319–331, 347–353, 356,
    370–375, *see also* Predicate calculus
    deletion strategy, 322
    examples, 323–331
    mixed system, 347–353, 356, 370–375
    resolvent, 320
    substitution, 321
    subsumption, 322
    tautology, 322
    unification, 321
    variants, 322–323
    virtual, 370–373
Role, 28–34, 129–130, 149, 281–285, 359–366
    abstract, 29
    associative relationship, 29, 31–32, 130
    concrete, 29
    definitional relationship, 29–30, 129
    group, 31

S

Schema, 147, 170–186, 260–273
    design example, 182–186
    design strategy, 178–182
    mapping, 260–272
    restructuring, 273
    varieties of, 170–177
Semantic integrity, 280
Set type, *see* Coset
Software costs, 8–11
    division of labor, 10–11
    labor–capital substitution, 9–10
    life expectancy, 11
    mass production, 10
SPSS, 48–49, 82
State space analysis, 77–80, 88–93, 226
    goal, 77–80, 88, 90–93
    graph, 92–93
    operator, 77–80, 89–93
    state, 77–80, 88–93
STRIPS, 79, 328, 358
Subschema, 237–242, 254–256
System R, 176
SYSTEM 2000, 176

T

Table, *see* File
Theorem-proving system, 73–75, 79, 314, 317–319, 370
TOTAL, 145, 153, 176
Transformational grammar, 234–242, 244, 254–256, 265–270, 388
  deep structure, 235–238, 241–242, 254–256, 265–270
  inverse transformations, 236–237, 244, 254, 268–270
  phrase structure, 235–236

  surface structure, 236–237, 268–270
  transformational rules, 235–236, 267–268
Transitive 1–*N* relationship, 154–156
Tree data structure, 171–173, 176

W

Weak indirect relationship, 156–158

X

Xerox corporate planning, 52–55, 69